EVIDENCE IN TRAFFIC CRASH INVESTIGATION AND RECONSTRUCTION

ABOUT THE AUTHOR

R. W. (Bob) Rivers is a graduate of Northwestern University Traffic Institute's traffic accident investigation and police management training programs. He completed training with the Canadian Institute of Science and Technology in technical mathematics and areas of physics, studied psychology at the Okanagan Regional College, completed police administration training programs through the Canadian Police College and the University of Minnesota, and patrol management with the IACP. He developed the traffic accident investigation and traffic law enforcement training programs of the Royal Canadian Mounted Police and course training standards for the Canadian Police College, University of Alberta, and the British Columbia Institute of Science and Technology in technical traffic accident investigation. During his 33 years service with the Royal Canadian Mounted Police, Inspector Rivers was employed extensively in general police work, highway patrol, accident investigation, research and planning, and training and development. Since his retirement, Inspector Rivers has authored various internationally-recognized textbooks, acted as a consultant and has assisted in traffic accident investigation training and research studies on an international basis. Since its establishment, he worked for many years as an adjunct faculty member and director of correspondence training with the Institute of Police Technology and Management (IPTM), University of North Florida (<http://members.shaw.ca/mudrivers>).

EVIDENCE IN TRAFFIC CRASH INVESTIGATION AND RECONSTRUCTION

Identification, Interpretation and Analysis of
Evidence, and the Traffic Crash Investigation
and Reconstruction Process

By

R. W. RIVERS

Inspector • Traffic Branch
Royal Canadian Mounted Police (Retired)
Province of British Columbia
Canada

CHARLES C THOMAS • PUBLISHER, LTD.
Springfield • Illinois • U.S.A.

Published and Distributed Throughout the World by

CHARLES C THOMAS • PUBLISHER, LTD.
2600 South First Street
Springfield, Illinois 62704

© 2006 by CHARLES C THOMAS • PUBLISHER, LTD.

ISBN 0-398-07644-8 (hard)
ISBN 0-398-07645-6 (paper)

Library of Congress Catalog Card Number: 2005055967

With THOMAS BOOKS *careful attention is given to all details of manufacturing
and design. It is the Publisher's desire to present books that are satisfactory as to their
physical qualities and artistic possibilities and appropriate for their particular use.*
THOMAS BOOKS *will be true to those laws of quality that assure a good name
and good will.*

Printed in the United States of America
UB-R-3

Library of Congress Cataloging-in-Publication Data
Rivers, R. W. (Robert W.)
    Evidence in traffic crash investigation and reconstruction : identification, in-
terpretation, and analysis of evidence, and the traffic crash investigation and
reconstruction process / by R.W. Rivers.
        p. cm.
    Includes bibliographical references and index.
    ISBN 0-398-07644-8 -- ISBN 0-398-07645-6 (pbk.)
    1. Traffic accident investigation. I. Title.

HV8079.55.R545 2006
363.12'565--dc22   2005055967

CONTRIBUTORS

BERNARD S. ABRAMS, O.D.

Institute of Vehicular Safety
5880 Cleveland Avenue
Columbus, Ohio 43231

ALBERT T. BAXTER

Traffic Crash Reconstructionist
Hudson, Florida

GEORGE M. BONNETT, J.D.

REC-TEC-LLC
Rockledge, Florida

ANNE M. CORBIN, M.A., J.D.

Springfield, Virginia

JAMES A. J. FERRIS, M.D., F.R.C.PATH.

Professor of Forensic Pathology
University of British Columbia
and
National Advisor
New Zealand Ministry of Justice for
National Forensic Pathology Service

MARTIN I. KURKE, PH.D., L.L.B. (DECEASED)

Traffic Safety Consultant
7448 Spring Village Drive
Apt. 118
Springfield, Virginia 22150

L. SATHYAVAGISWARAN, M.D.

Chief Medical Examiner–Coroner
County of Los Angeles
Los Angeles, California

MICHAEL SWEET

Forensics Expert and Consultant
Edmonton, Alberta, Canada

ROBERT WYMAN

Photography Expert
Wyman Enterprises, Inc.
Miami, Florida

To Dr. R. C. (Dick) Hodge
A true friend of the entire traffic crash investigation and
reconstruction profession

FOREWORD

R. W. (Bob) Rivers needs no introduction to those in traffic crash investigation and reconstruction. Since the early 1980s, he has written an impressive number of comprehensive training and reference works in this field as well as a host of shorter manuals on related topics. All have been widely read and many of them used in setting up training programs in the United States and Canada and around the world. Not only has he continued to write, he has also kept abreast of new developments and techniques in the discipline and has earned a reputation for accuracy and dependability from practitioners and technical experts alike.

Bob's latest book, published by Charles C Thomas, is titled *Evidence in Traffic Crash Investigation and Reconstruction* and subtitled *Identification, Interpretation and Analysis of Evidence, and the Traffic Crash Investigation and Reconstruction Process.* It has ten chapters providing detailed information on every aspect of this very important part of working a crash. Many sections draw on specialized expertise of other recognized authorities. This new book also gives the reader a keen sense of why the proper handling and recording of evidence is even more basic to a thorough crash investigation and reconstruction than the ability to apply formulae derived from the principles of physics and requiring the use of math, vital though this ability certainly is.

As Director Emeritus of the Institute of Police Technology and Management, I wish to acknowledge the great contribution Bob has made to IPTM from its founding in 1980 to the present. Traffic crash investigation and reconstruction was one of the first kinds of training this new organization offered and Bob wrote several of the early works that IPTM published in this subject area, including his monumental *Training and Reference Manual for Traffic Accident Investigation.* Over the years, he has not only continued to provide IPTM with relevant manuscripts for publication, but has also designed the array of IPTM plastic traffic templates that have proven so popular. He introduced correspondence training in traffic crash investigation to IPTM and for many years personally conducted this training for our institute. He has represented IPTM at many international conferences and given selflessly of his time to all persons seeking information about traffic crash investigation and reconstruction.

Bob Rivers retired from the RCMP in 1985 as Officer in Charge of Traffic Branch for the Province of British Columbia. During the course of his 33 years of service with the RCMP, Bob performed nearly every phase of police work—highway patrol, traffic accident investigation, general police work, training and development, to name just a few—often in a hands-on but also in a supervisory or managerial capacity. It is noteworthy that even with his breadth of experience in law enforcement, Bob eventually chose traffic as his specialty. Those in traffic crash investigation and reconstruction the world over can be glad that he did.

RUSSELL AREND
Director Emeritus, Institute of Police Technology
and Management, University of North Florida
May 2005

PREFACE

This manual begins with a detailed description of the entire investigation process, outlining the internationally recognized series of events that go into making up the crash investigation process. The material then graduates into the various phases and levels of investigations, showing the levels of training and education normally associated with the levels of investigations and consequently the duties and responsibilities of the investigator and reconstructionist. The manual is intended to place on record the material that will not only lead to good sound investigations and crash reconstruction, but also to outline the evidence expectations of police, lawyers, private investigators, and others who are involved in traffic crash investigation and reconstruction, through proper identification, interpretation, and analysis of evidence that can be encountered in an investigation.

The at-scene area, before vehicles and bodies are removed, holds considerable evidence for crash reconstruction and cause determination. Most importantly are skid marks, other tire marks, and vehicle and roadway damages, all of which can show vehicle placement before and at the time of the crash. For obvious reasons, many persons involved in determining cause or other findings, including attorneys and insurance claims adjusters, must rely on photographs and measurements taken by at-scene investigators, most often the police. This manual covers in detail how to identify, interpret, and analyze such evidence when photographs and measurements are presented.

Using narrative, schematics, and photographs, the mechanical inspection process is described in detail by identifying various vehicle parts, explanations of their functions, and methods of identifying failures.

Human-related factors in traffic crash investigations are discussed at length, including the traffic crash viewed as a systems failure. Looming vulnerability, a recently developed theoretical construct that helps to describe and understand social, cognitive, organizational, and psychological mechanism is described. Errors and tolerances in the investigation process, and how human error may have been made more likely to occur by an error made by the unser/maintainer, trainer, or system designer—or by the negligent action of the victim—are explained. Discussed also is the role of vision in driver performance;

perception as a four-way process; perceptions and reactions; driver's reaction to stress; and the roles of pathologists, medical examiners, and coroners in traffic crash reconstruction.

Who is an expert and expert evidence are described in detail. Errors that can occur in the investigation process and the tolerances that should be considered or allowed are explained.

Often overlooked by the frontline investigator is the importance of calling upon the skills and advice of occupational specialists to assist in the investigation and reconstruction of a crash. The manual covers in detail those professional services. They include senior, experienced, well-trained reconstructionists; lawyers; professional traffic engineers; pathologists; medical examiners and other medical professionals; and bloodstain pattern technologists, who can be called upon at any time during the initial investigation or during the compilation of evidence at or near the end of an investigation, that will ensure that the objectives of a thorough and complete investigation will be satisfied.

The manual explains how an examination of the trafficway, including special photographic techniques and scene measurements, can produce and document considerable evidence on how and why a crash occurred. It is explained how engineering, environmental, and similar other trafficway factors can often explain the action or lack of action by a trafficway user who is either directly or indirectly involved in a crash. Of particular importance are traffic control devices, daytime and nighttime weather and roadway conditions, and their effects and influences on or contribution to crashes. Considerable effort has been made in the manual to explain how to identify, interpret and analyze all forms of highway marks and damages, which can be used in the reconstruction of a vehicle-related crash, very often establishing vehicle placement and the path followed by the vehicle leading up to the crash site, all of which can be related to visibility issues.

Speed analysis is introduced with an explanation of Newton's Three Laws of Motion and terms and definitions, leading into the solving of various acceleration problems; how to calculate drag factors; determine speeds from skid marks, yaw, falls, flips and vaults, and by combining speeds. Many examples are included. As with other published works by this author, all mathematical references are worked out in both the English (U.S.) and SI (metric) measurement systems.

Various appendices covering symbols of interest to the student and investigator, mathematical conversions and speed and velocity problems already calculated to assist the user in his or her work, are included.

Finally, there is a comprehensive quick-find index that takes the reader directly to any topic, formula, or subject matter—or any combination of these.

R.W.R.

ACKNOWLEDGMENTS

I wish to acknowledge my gratitude to Charles C Thomas Publisher and the Institute of Police Technology and Management (IPTM), University of North Florida, for authority to reproduce at my discretion various excerpts from the primary references shown below, authored by myself and published by them, for inclusion in this manual. I wish also to acknowledge with thanks the following traffic crash investigators and reconstructionists for their contributions of photographs, as well as to the following professional, occupational specialists, for their kind contributions to this manual.

Mr. J. R. E. d'Aoust
West-Can VAIR
Sorrento, British Columbia, Canada
(Photographs)

Bryan Lapp
Traffic Crash Reconstructionist
Parksville, British Columbia, Canada
(Photographs)

Charles I. Kirk, CEO
S.T.A.R. Inc.
Specialist Traffic Accident Reconstruction Inc.
Piqua, Ohio
(Photographs)

Francis P. D. Navin, Ph.D., P.Eng.
President
Synetics Road Safety
Research Corporation
Vancouver, British Columbia, Canada

John Ruller
Senior Traffice Crash Reconstructionist and Trainer
Road Accident Investigation Service P/L
Bellbowrie, Qld., Australia

Tim Schewe
Traffic Crash Reconstructionist
Parksville, British Columbia, Canada

Richard C. "Craig" Wilson
Wylie, Texas 75098
Dallas Police Department
Traffic Section
Dallas, Texas
(Photographs)

NOTE

Throughout the manual, various items, components, and situations that should be considered in evidence gathering and in legal presentations are discussed and explained. Many of these are accompanied by conveniently-placed checkboxes that the investigator or attorney can use as prompters or guides in ensuring that various points of topical evidence, which can be considered as the possible or probable collision cause, or as a contributing factor, are covered in a proceeding. These should not, however, be considered restrictive—but to be used only as a guide. While some checkboxes may apply, others may not. Also, in some cases, depending upon the circumstances, additional points should be considered in an examination.

As and where applicable, for each checkbox, questions that should be asked by the investigator, attorney, or the examiner, should be: What about this? Was it examined? What were the results, findings, and/or conclusions of the examination? If it was not examined, why not?

DISCLAIMER

Many published books and technical papers have been studied and participation in many field tests made in the preparation of this manual. The information and practices set out herein are, to the best of the author's knowledge, experience, and belief, the most current and accurate in the traffic crash investigation and reconstruction profession. However, the author, publisher, editors, and contributors expressly disclaim all and any liability to any person, whether the purchaser of this publication or not, as a consequence of anything stated, done or omitted to be done, whether in whole or in part by such person in reliance upon any part of the contents of this publication. Every acceptable procedure may not be presented herein, and some of the circumstances of any given case may require additional or substitute procedures. Also, since statutes, ordinances, and organizational policies and procedures differ widely in various jurisdictions, those of the particular jurisdiction concerned should govern when there is any conflict between them and the contents of this book.

THE METRIC (SI) SYSTEM)

The metric system, **Le Systéme International d´Unités** (International System of Units, abbreviated *SI* in all languages), is used in most countries outside the United States. Because this manual is prepared for international use, all mathematical formulae and problem-solving examples are shown in both the *United States/Imperial or English and Metric (SI)* systems.

In North America, a decimal fraction is generally indicated by means of a (decimal) point on the line (not a dot in the raised or centered position). In this regard, it is important for North Americans and many others to understand that in some countries, it is the dot in the raised position that is used; also, that in some countries, a comma is used. It is the North American practice of using the dot as a decimal point situated on the line that is followed in this manual.

CONTENTS

Page

Foreword–Russell Arend ix
Preface xi

Chapter

1. INTRODUCTION TO TRAFFIC CRASH INVESTIGATION 3
   R. W. Rivers

   Evidence Defined 3
   Traffic Crash Defined 3
   Traffic Crash Investigation Process and Objectives 3
   Traffic Crash Analysis 4
   Series of Events and Human Factors 5
       Definitions 5
       Events and Factors 5
   Crash Analysis Using the Series of Events 8
       Application of the Series of Events 8
   Analyzing the Events in the Series of Events 10
   Crash Cause Analysis 12
       Series of Events Evidence and Investigation Checklist 12
   Phases and Levels of Crash Investigation 12
   Education and Training 13
   Duties and Responsibilities 14
   Safeguarding Evidence 14
   Accuracy, Errors, and Tolerances in Traffic Crash
       Investigation 15
   Significant Digits 18
   Occupational Specialist and Laboratory/Analyst Services 18
   Forensic Specialist Services and Reconstruction 19
       Definitions 19
       Medical Professionals 20
       Pathologist 20

Coroner-Medical Examiners 20
Dentists and Orthodontists 20
Behavioral Science Resources 21
Psychiatrist 21
Medical Laboratories 21
Forensic Laboratories 21
Evidence Technicians 22
Business, Trade, and Industrial Professionals 22
Education Professionals 22
Legal Assistance 22
The Expert and Traffic Crash Reconstruction 22
Definitions 23
Expert Qualifications 23
An Expert's Responsibilities 24
Expert Witness 24
Lay Witness 24
Fact Witness 24
Investigators' Pre-Trial Responsibilities 24
Evidence Evaluator 25
Investigator's Conclusions 25
Information Sources 25
Fraud 26
Documentation 27
Exhibits 27
Ethics 27
Definitions 28
Pre-Trial Consultations and Testimony 28
Pre-Trial Consultations 28
Testimony 29
Inferiority Complex 30
Accreditation Commission for Crash Reconstruction
(ACTAR) 30
The History of ACTAR 30

2. HUMAN ERROR AND TRAFFIC CRASH INVESTIGATION
AND RECONSTRUCTION 32
Martin I. Kurke & Anne M. Corbin

The Traffic Crash Viewed as a System Failure 32
Human Reliability and Human Error 33
Looming Vulnerability and Traffic Crashes 35
Human Error, and Risk-Taking 37
Investigating the Role of Human Error in Traffic Crash
Investigation and Reconstruction 38

3. THE ROLE OF VISION, VISIBILITY, AND DISCERNABILITY IN DRIVER PERFORMANCE AND TRAFFIC ACCIDENT RECONSTRUCTION 42
   Bernard S. Abrams

   Introduction 42
   The Eyes and How They Function 43
      Night and Day = Rods and Cones 44
      The Visual Field 44
   The Brain and Vision 45
   Day Eye vs. Night Eye 45
      Photopic Vision–The Day Eye 46
      Scotopic Vision–The Night Eye 46
   Other Components of Vision 46
      Visual Acuity 46
      Field of Vision 47
      Depth Perception 47
      Contrast Sensitivity 47
      Adaptation 47
   Tests of Visual Performance 47
      Visual Acuity 47
      Contrast Sensitivity 48
   Perception: A Four-Step Reaction Process 48
   Factors That Can Affect Vision 49
      Physiological Factors 49
      External Factors 49
      Environmental Factors 50
   Conclusion 50

4. PATHOLOGY AND ACCIDENT RECONSTRUCTION 51
   James A. Farris

   Part 1

   Introduction 51
   Dynamics of Crash Injury 51
   Location of Victims at Scene 52
   Medical Condition Following the Crash 52
   Prior Medical History 52
   Interpretation of Injuries 53
   Classification of Injuries 53
   Burns 54
   Fractures 55
   Safety Restraint Injuries 55
   The Victim 56
   The Driver 56

The Front-Seat Passenger 56
The Rear-Seat Passenger 56
Infants and Children 57
The Pedestrian 57
Motorcyclists and Cyclists 57
The Post-mortem Examination 58
Conclusion 58

Part 2

THE MEDICAL EXAMINER AND TRAFFIC CRASH
INVESTIGATION 60
L. Sathyavagiswaran

The Expectations of a Medical Examiner in a Traffic Accident
    Investigation 60
General Statement 60
Specific Situations 60
    Pedestrian Victims of Vehicular Crashes 60
    Driver/Passenger Victim of a Vehicular Crash 60
    Motorcycle Accident Victims 60
    The Vehicle Fire Victim 61

5. BLOOD PATTERN ANALYSIS 62
    Michael Sweet

Introduction 62
History 62
Physical Properties of Blood 63
Determining Directionality of Bloodstains 64
Categories of Bloodstains 64
Types of Information Provided by a Bloodstain Pattern Analyst 66
Analyst Assistance in Traffic Collision Investigation 68
At-Scene Bloodstain Photography 70
Blood Sample Collection 70
DNA Exhibit Collection 71
Handling of Bloodstained Exhibits 71

6. FORENSIC PHOTOGRAPHY AND SCENE MEASUREMENTS
    Robert Wyman & R. W. Rivers

Part 1

INTRODUCTION TO PHOTOGRAPHIC APPLICATIONS 73
Testimony 73
Photographic Techniques 76
Policies, Directives and Limitations 77

Traffic Engineering and Photography 78
Photographing the Series of Events 78
    Timelines 79
Personal Injury Documentation 81

Part 2

SCENE MEASUREMENTS AND PLAN DRAWINGS 83

Introduction 83
Scene Evidence 83
Photographs and Measurements 83
Field Sketch 84
Scale Diagrams 84
Instruments 84
Symbols 87
Conventions for Recording Measurements 87
Baselines 89
Reference Points 89
Measuring Methods 90
    Coordinate Method 90
    Triangulation Method 90

7. TRAFFICWAY EVIDENCE 95
   R. W. Rivers

Part 1

ASPECTS OF BASIC ENGINEERING AND DESIGN 95
Traffic Control Devices 95
    Traffic Signs 95
    Sign Descriptions 96
    Traffic Signals 98
    Traffic Control Signal Unit 98
    Detectors 99
    Timing 101
Traffic Engineering Issues 101

Part 2

IDENTIFICATION AND INTERPRETATION OF TRAFFICWAY
OBSTRUCTIONS, DEFECTS, MARKS AND DAMAGE
EVIDENCE 104
    Pavement-Edge Drop-Off 105
    Roadway Damage 105
    Roadway Alignment 105
    Glare 105
    Debris 107

Scrapes and Scratches 107
Groove 107
Chip, Gouge, and Chop 109
Hole 109
Matching Vehicle Damage to Roadside Objects 109
Matching Undercarriage Parts 109
Undercarriage Evidence 110
Tire Marks 112
Tire Shapes and Contours 112
Flat Tire Marks 113
Overloaded or Underinflated (Overdeflected) Tire Mark 113
Shadow Evidence 113
Evidence of Tire Sideslipping 113
Evidence of a Spinning Tire 116
Pavement Grinding 116
Striation Marks 116
Yaw Mark Striations 116
Studded Tire Striation Marks 118
Pass-Over Tire Marks 118
Tire Prints 119
Scuff Mark 119
Acceleration Marks 120
Forward-Reverse Acceleration Mark 120
Furrows and Ruts 121
Skid Marks 122
Skid Mark Defined 122
Weight Shift in Skid Marks 122
Impending Skid Mark 122
Overlapping Skid Marks 123
Offset Tire Marks 124
Braked Wheel Tire Evidence 124
Tire-Roadway Debris Deposit 124
Intermittent Skid Marks 125
Commercial Vehicle Skid Marks 125
Bounce Tire Marks 125
Scrub Mark 128
Detached Utility-Trailer Skid Marks 129
Towed Vehicle Skid Marks 129

8. VEHICLE EXAMINATIONS 131
   R. W. Rivers

Introduction 131
Vehicle Identification Number 131

Automobile Components 133
Commercial Vehicle Components 133
Drive Trains 136
Component Failures 136
Lamps and Reflectors 138
Suspension Systems 139
   Air Suspension 140
   Shock Absorbers 140
Steering Systems 140
   General 140
   Power Assisted Steering Systems 141
Wheel Alignment 142
Wheels and Rims 142
Tires 143
   Types of Tires 143
   DOT/MOT Numbers 144
   Speed Ratings 145
   Load Ratings 145
   Service Description 147
   Tire Marking Standard 147
   Inflation and Tire Failures 147
Brakes 150
   Types of Brake Systems 150
   Brake Inspections 152
Air Brake System 152
Exhaust System 154
Windshield Wipers and Defrosters 155
Mirrors 156
Vehicle Loads 156
Horn, Siren 156
Noise and Other Distractions 156
Door Locks 157
Speed Recording Devices and Methods 157
   Speedometer 157
   Black Boxes 158
   On-Board Computers 158
   Tachographs 158
   Tachograph Charts 158
   Gear Shift Lever/Selector 159
Trailer Breakaway 160
Occupant Restraint Systems 161
Seat Belt Systems 161
Child Restraints 164

Air Bags 165
    How Air Bags Work 165
Vehicle Damages 167
    Principal Direction of Force 168
    Paint Chips and Transfers 170
    Glass Damage and Condition 170
Vehicle Fires 174
Driver and Occupant Seating Positions 178
Recommended References Sites 181

9. SPEED ANALYSIS 183

Part 1

INTRODUCTION: TERMS AND DEFINITIONS 183
Speed and Velocity Defined 183
Physics 183
    Newton's Three Laws of Motion 183
    Force Defined 184
    External Forces 185
    Centripetal and Centrifugal Forces 185
    Curves 185
    Mass and Weight 185
    Motion 186
    Momentum 186
    Work 186
    Kinetic Energy 187
    Gravity 187
    Centers of Mass and Gravity 187
    Vectors 187
    Friction 189
Acceleration 189
    Velocity, Acceleration, and Time 189
    Acceleration, Time, and Distance 190
    Distance and Time 192
Velocity and Speed Change Problem-Solving Formulae 192
Coefficient of Friction and Drag Factor 196
    Coefficient of Friction and Drag Factor Defined 196
    Grade, Slope, and Superelevation 198
Methods of Determining Drag Factor 199
    Test Skids 200
    Shot Marker 200
    Test Skid Procedures 201
    Longest Skid Mark 203

Accelerometer-Electronic Devices 203
Drag Factor Calculation 203
Drag Sleds 204
    Custom-Made Drag Sleds 204
    Drag Sled Operation 205
    Drag Sled Calibration 206
    Drag Factor Adjustments 207
Influences on Braking Distance 211
    Hydroplaning 212
Roadway Coefficient of Friction (Drag Factor) Guide 213

Part 2

SPEED DETERMINATIONS 215
Speed From Skid Marks 215
    Skid Mark Measurements 215
    Slide (Skid)-to-Stop Speed Calculations 217
    Speed Calculation When Skid is on Different Types of
        Roadway Surfaces 218
    Brakeless Utility Trailers 218
    Special Drag Factor Problems 218
Speed from Vehicle Yaw 219
    Yaw Mark Measurements 221
    Speed Calculations Based on Vehicle Yaw 222
Falls, Flips, and Vault Speeds 224
    Falls 225
    Flips and Vaults 226
Combined Speeds 228
Special Speed Problems 229
    Crush Speed Estimates 229
    Commercial Vehicle Crash Investigations 229

10. EVIDENCE MANUAL MOTORCYCLE CRASH
    INVESTIGATION 230
Introduction 230
Types of Motorcycles 230
Controls 231
Basics 233
Dynamics 234
    Rake 234
    Trail 235
    Turning 235
Acceleration 236
Braking 239

Reaction Time 240
Mechanical Considerations 240
Slide-to-Stop Speed 241
Vaults 243

APPENDICES 245
Appendix A: English (U.S.) and Metric (S.I. Measurement Systems
    Conversion Tables 247
Appendix B: English (U.S.) Conversion Tables 255
Appendix C: Metric (S.I.) Conversion Tables 261
Appendix D: Speedometer Accuracy 269
Appendix E: Symbols 271

Recommended Reading 275
Index 277

EVIDENCE IN TRAFFIC CRASH INVESTIGATION AND RECONSTRUCTION

Chapter 1

INTRODUCTION TO TRAFFIC CRASH INVESTIGATION

R. W. RIVERS

EVIDENCE DEFINED

1.001 *Evidence* is defined as *that which tends to prove or disprove something; proof. In law, it is considered to be data presented to a court or jury in proof of the facts in issue and which may include the testimony of witnesses, records, documents, objects.* In traffic crash investigation, this can take many forms, perhaps most important of which are observation, recognition, interpretation, recording, and presentation of items observed or that come to the attention of the investigator whether it be at the scene or during subsequent follow-up investigation. An example of this is the observation, measurement, and documentation (both written and photographic) of a skid mark; and then giving written and/or oral evidence in a court of law of a speed calculation based on the skid mark.

1.002 An often critical problem in traffic crash investigation is the recognition, significance, preservation, and utilization of the physical evidence produced by a collision of a motor vehicle with another vehicle, object, or person, and the events preceding and resulting from an occurrence: physical evidence can either astound and perplex or serve as decisive and valuable evidence in establishing and fixing liability

1.003 Traffic crash investigation involves applying the principles of perception, dynamics, and general physics to the movements of vehicles, bodies and other objects leading up to, during, and after a collision. From a properly done analysis, speeds of vehicles, pedestrian and passenger movements, and driver responses that led to the crash and/or took place at impact and post-impact, can be determined. Additionally, analysis performed from available evidence can be used to determine mechanical failure of critical vehicle components–such as steering, brakes, suspension systems, and tires, which could have been the cause or a contributing factor in the crash.

TRAFFIC CRASH DEFINED

1.004 For the purposes of traffic crash investigation, the term *traffic crash* is defined as:

That occurrence in a series of events which usually produces injury, death or property damage.

For the purposes of this manual, the term *crash* is synonymous with the terms *accident, collision, incident,* or any other applicable, descriptive term used in various jurisdictions and in many published works.

TRAFFIC CRASH INVESTIGATION PROCESS AND OBJECTIVES

1.005 Advanced traffic crash investigation is a process that starts with an investigation and evidence gathering at the scene and continues on until the objectives of advanced traffic crash investigation have been satisfied. This includes the interpretation of evidence, whether gathered by the investigator or another investigator, and arriving at conclusions based on sound, scientific analysis of all available evidence.

1.006 The objectives of traffic crash investigation are to determine:

    a. WHAT happened, i.e., the type of crash
    b. WHERE the crash occurred
    c. WHEN the crash occurred
    d. WHY the crash occurred, e.g., traffic law violation, trafficway engineering defects
    e. WHO was involved

The investigator must also decide upon:

    a. WHAT is the problem
    b. WHAT are the possible solutions
    c. WHICH is the best of all possible solutions
    d. HOW this solution can be implemented

The investigator should also give, but not limit, consideration to:

    a. Identifying high frequency crash sites for further study
    b. Problems in geometric design standards in relation to crashes
    d. The evaluation of safety, enforcement or other programs that are in place
    c. The need for new safety, enforcement or other programs
    d. Obtaining and/or supplying data for the planning of education and/or enforcement programs

1.007 In general terms, an initial at-scene and follow-up advanced traffic crash investigation should gather facts and information that will:

    a. Determine the cause of the crash
    b. Provide information that will assist in crash prevention including engineering, enforcement and education programs
    c. Provide evidence for the prosecution in the event there has been a violation of law
    d. Meet the requirements of traffic crash report completion
    e. Provide sufficient information to meet the requirements of follow-up investigation and reconstruction

1.008 An investigation involves determining how the accident occurred through an analysis based on all available evidence gathered at the scene or during the follow-up advanced traffic crash investigation. There may be a number of hypotheses put forward by police investigators, witnesses, and other persons involved in an investigation. All hypotheses should be considered and evaluated in terms of whether they are credible or ridiculous, given the circumstances and facts at hand, until the reasonable ones have been identified. The most credible of these should then be investigated further, leaving, however, all aspects of the case open for further consideration and investigation as new evidence or information comes to light. Even the apparently non-credible hypotheses may have to be revisited. It is important, however, that the advanced crash investigator appreciates his/her limits in terms of expertise regarding an ability to completely reconstruct a crash. In some cases, it might be advisable or necessary to obtain the services of a properly qualified reconstructionist to interpret evidence gathered and assist in the reconstruction.

TRAFFIC CRASH ANALYSIS

1.009 For the purposes of professional traffic crash investigation, *traffic crash* analysis is defined as:

> *The separation of the whole (the series of events) into its parts or elements, especially to determine the nature, form, etc., of the whole by examination of the parts (events).*

1.010 In order for the investigator to conduct a proper analysis of a traffic crash situation, he/she should be familiar with the various *events* that make up a traffic crash, and then ensure that the investigation covers all aspects of *each* of those events. For the purposes of traffic crash investigation and reconstruction, the *whole* of these various *events* is referred to as the *series of events*, a subject that is introduced in at-scene traffic crash investigation training courses and manuals. Because of the topic's importance to understanding evidence identification, interpretation, and analysis, it is once again reviewed here.

1.011 The following is an outline of events which covers most, if not all, circumstances and/or parameters encountered in traffic crash investigation and reconstruction. There may, however, be other or additional methods that can be used to satisfy analyses of complex reconstruction problems, particularly through the use of modern, sophisticated computer programs.

1.012–1.015 reserved.

SERIES OF EVENTS AND HUMAN FACTORS

Definitions

1.016 For the purposes of traffic *crash analysis*, the *series of events* includes *situations* that are in place or may at any time arise, all of which may be divided into two distinct categories:[1]

a. *Pre-Scene Series of Events.* The events that lead up to the driver's point of possible perception of a hazard.

b. *At-Scene Series of Events.* The events that occur within the on-scene area, including the point of possible perception.

Human factors include, but are not limited to:

a. Perception time
b. Reaction time
c. Driver experience
d. Disabilities

Individual events and factors will be explained and enlarged upon later in this chapter as well as in various other chapters throughout the manual.

Events and Factors

1.017 The *pre-scene series of events* can be further divided into two areas, namely (1) *pre-trip events*, and (2) *trip events:*

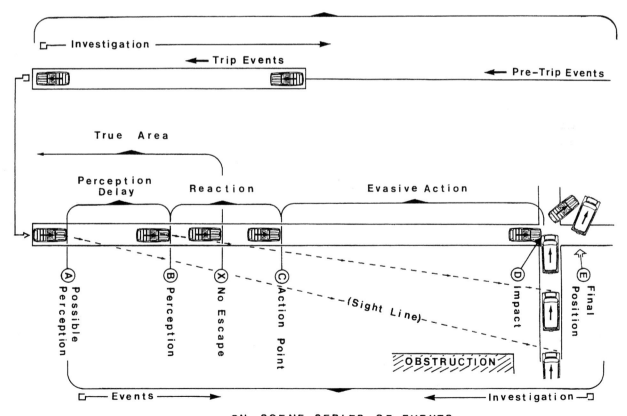

Figure 1–01. An example of the *series of events*.

1. *Pre-trip events.* Generally, those events that occur before and include *situations* that exist *before* the trip is started. They may be considered as backgrounds of the driver and vehicle. Examples of pre-trip events and situations are:

Driver
   a. Driver experience
   b. Driver training
   c. Intelligence
   d. Alertness
   e. Reaction
   f. Habits
   g. General health condition, including age, an illness, and permanent or temporary injury or disability
   h. Fatigue
   i. A happening that caused emotional upset, stress, depression, or preoccupation
   j. Attendance at a party
   k. Limited sleep or no sleep
   l. Consumption of alcohol or drugs

Vehicle
   a. Defective headlights, steering, brakes, windshield, wipers, tires, etc.
   b. Overloaded

As the trip is made, many of these pre-trip *events* or *situations* may carry on into the at-scene series of events, e.g., a situation such as the driver's ability to drive being impaired by alcohol or a drug, or an overloaded vehicle.

2. *Trip events.* Those *events* that occur or *situations* that arise after the trip starts and lead up to the point of possible perception, including factors relative to the driver and vehicle, such as, but not restricted to:

Driver
   a. Stopping for a meal or coffee
   b. Fatigue, illness, or depression
   c. Consumption of alcohol or drugs
   d. Erratic or other unsafe driving (possibly observed by other motorists, pedestrians, businessmen, or other witnesses)
   e. Carbon-monoxide poisoning

Vehicle
   a. Tire blowout
   b. Brake, headlight, or steering failure
   c. Other mechanical failure

   d. View obstructions, e.g., dirty windshield, defective windshield, or load transfer
   e. Load falling off vehicle

Environmental
   a. View obstruction
   b. Weather conditions, e.g., rain, snow, ice

1.018 *At-scene series of events* include:

   a. *Point of Possible Perception.* The place and time at which the hazard could have been perceived by a normal person. It precedes actual perception and is the beginning of perception delay[2] (see also 3.042).
   b. *Point of (Actual) Perception.* The point where a situation is comprehended or perceived as a hazard.
   c. *Perception Delay.* The time involved from the point of possible perception to the point of actual perception.

   Inattention or distractions may cause perception delay. In many instances, actual perception immediately follows the point of possible perception, and there is no actual perception delay. When there is a known perception delay, it may be considered to be 0.75 seconds for investigation purposes. The distance traveled during perception delay is perception distance. The point of possible perception and the point of actual perception may be influenced by many driver and environmental factors, some of which are:

Driver
   i. Experience
   ii. Intelligence
   iii. Judgement
   iv. Alertness
   v. Natural senses (age must be considered)
   vi. Knowledge of area
   vii. Distractions

Environmental
   i. Weather and light conditions
   ii. Load on vehicle and protrusions
   iii. Location of traffic-control devices
   iv. View obstructions

   d. *Perception Distance.* The distance traveled during perception delay. To calculate perception distance, use:

Formula 1–01

U.S.	*SI*
$D = S \times 1.466 \times t$	$D = S \times .277 \times t$

where D = distance
  S = speed in mph (km/h)
  t = time in seconds

e. *Reaction.* The voluntary or involuntary response to a hazard or other situation that has been perceived.[3]

  i. *Simple reaction.* The response to an expected situation, such as responding to a traffic light.
  ii. *Complex reaction.* The reaction involving a decision, such as when the driver has to decide quickly whether to step on the accelerator or the brake pedal.

f. *Reaction Time.* The length of time from when a person perceives a given situation as being a hazard to when he reacts to his perception. If a person's reaction time is unknown, 1.50 seconds may be used for daytime investigation purposes and 2.50 seconds for nighttime.[4]

  Take for example, the task of braking to avoid an unexpected object on the roadway. Once the object in the path becomes visible, the driver must see the object, recognize the hazard, lift his foot from the accelerator, and push the brake pedal.

  The processes involved are (a) seeing the object, (b) processing the initial information, (d) understanding the information or realizing the danger, (e) deciding what to do, and (f) doing it. For such things, the average driver perception-reaction time is 2.5 seconds[5] (see also 3.044).

g. *Simple Reaction Time.* That which involves an non-complex response, such as touching the horn, can be less than a second. Older drivers have longer reaction times than do young drivers. At about 40 years of age, simple reaction times begin to increase to the extent that at about 70 years of age, a driver's reaction time may increase by as much as 50 percent.

h. *Reaction Distance.* The distance traveled during reaction time. (To calculate reaction distance, use Formula 1–01.)

i. *Action Point.* The place where a person takes action, such as braking or steering, based on his perception of a hazard. The action point follows reaction and may be influenced by the driver's:

  i. Operating skills and habits
  ii. Ability to control the vehicle
  iii. Freedom of movement
  iv. Knowledge of vehicle
  v. Reaction time

j. *Evasive Action.* The action or combination of actions taken (e.g., steering, braking) with intention to avoid a collision or other hazardous situation.

k. *Evasive Action Distance.* The distance traveled from the action point to the place where a traffic unit stops by itself or otherwise avoids a collision, or, if a collision is not avoided, to the point of impact.

l. *True (Safe) Area.* The area leading up to the point of no escape in which evasive action could be initiated to avoid a collision.

m. *Point of No Escape.* The place and time beyond or after which the crash cannot be prevented by a particular traffic unit.[6] Because of committed motion and laws of physics, no action will avoid the collision at this point, although action such as braking or steering may reduce the seriousness of injury or damage. The point of no escape may be anywhere along a driver's path before collision depending upon the speeds of vehicles involved, visibility, and so on. This point may be before the point of possible perception, and if so, a crash cannot be avoided.

The point of no escape may be influenced by such factors as:

  i. Visibility of hazard
  ii. Roadway alignment
  iii. Positioning of traffic-control devices
  iv. Driver distractions
  v. Weather and light conditions
  vi. Condition of roadway surface, e.g., ruts, holes, or other roadway damage, slippery conditions or obstructions, etc.
  vii. Type, size, and condition of vehicle being operated
  viii. Cargo being carried

n. *Encroachment.* The entering or intruding into the rightful path or area of another traffic unit.

o. *Point of Impact.* The place, e.g., the point on the roadway, where a traffic unit strikes another traffic unit or some other object, or overturns.

p. *Primary Contact.* The first contact between two traffic units or a traffic unit and another object, or a vehicle's first contact with a highway surface during an overturn.

q. *Engagement.* The initial penetration of one traffic unit into another traffic unit or object during collision.

r. *Maximum Engagement.* The point or time at which there is maximum penetration by one traffic unit into another traffic unit or object during collision.

s. *Disengagement.* The separation of traffic units or a traffic unit and other object after maximum engagement.

t. *Secondary Contact.* A contact occurring when a traffic unit disengages from a primary contact and strikes the opposing traffic unit a second time or strikes another traffic unit or object.

u. *Post-secondary Contact.* A post-secondary contact occurs when a vehicle disengages from a secondary contact and again strikes the same unit or object or has a first or primary contact with a third traffic unit or other object. Under these circumstances, what may be a secondary or post-secondary contact for one unit may be the primary or first contact by another traffic unit.

v. *Final Position.* The location where a traffic unit comes to rest after collision. In determining the final position, it is important to learn whether the unit stopped at the position where it was found or whether it had rolled, been driven, or moved to that position after the collision. For the purposes of this definition, final position does not include a position to which it may have been driven or forcibly moved, such as being towed by a tow vehicle, after it came to rest after disengagement.

w. *At-Rest Position.* A location to which a vehicle rolls, is driven, or moved after disengagement, such as the position at which it stops or rests as the result of being towed by a tow vehicle or forcibly removed from the point of disengagement.

x. *Personal Injury.* For investigation purposes, a personal injury is bodily harm caused to a person during the at-scene series of events.

y. *Fatal Injury.* A fatal injury is an injury that causes death during the at-scene series of events or a personal injury that thereafter results in the death of the injured person as direct result of an injury sustained during the at-scene series of events. (Note: Local legislation generally stipulates a time limit for an initial personal injury classification to be classified as a fatal injury.)

1.019 Drivers and witnesses generally describe pre-scene series of events and at-scene series of events forward and lead up to the result. An investigator, however, must start with the result and investigate back through the events as far as necessary to determine where, when, how, and why the crash occurred. It may not always be necessary for the investigator to extend his investigation into the pre-scene series of events; however, he should extend his investigation as far back as necessary to determine what a driver may or may not have done before the crash that may have contributed to his action or lack of action at the crash scene.

1.020 Each *traffic unit*, i.e., a road vehicle or pedestrian, involved in a crash has its own series of events. Each unit's series of events must be investigated separately. It should be noted, however, that all the events listed in the series of events may not apply to each and every traffic unit in a crash situation. Some events may not be present in the same series for another unit, and vice versa. For example, there may not be a perception delay, personal injury, or secondary contact in the case of a single vehicle crash, or for one particular unit in multiple vehicle collision. Also, even if the events are the same for one or more vehicles involved in a collision, they may not always follow the same sequence.

1.021–1.025 reserved.

CRASH ANALYSIS USING THE SERIES OF EVENTS

Application of the Series of Events

1.026 A *crash analysis* should include the many variables that play a part in the makeup of an crash situation. These include such things as a driver's sight distance to other vehicles or objects, speed, acceleration, deceleration, environmental factors, and the time available for the driver to reach a decision concerning the most appropriate response—all of which should be related to the *series of events*. The following example illustrates how the at-scene series of events may be applied to traffic crashes. This system, in some cases applied in a modified form, is now used internationally. One of the primary purposes of the system is to provide a catalyst to satisfying the objectives of traffic crash investigations. Speed and many other determinations, covered later in the manual, are, of course, also necessary in actual investigations and in the application of the at-scene series of events.

Example

In Figure 1–02, vehicle 1 was traveling east on First Avenue. At point **A**, the point of possible perception, driver 1 saw vehicle 2 approaching an uncontrolled intersection from his right on King Street. Because of a distraction caused by a child playing on the street at point **Y**, driver 1 did not recognize nor perceive vehicle 2 as a hazard.

There was a perception delay of 0.75 seconds, at which time, at point **B**, driver 1 perceived that vehicle 2 was not likely to stop at the intersection. Driver 1 decided to apply his brakes in an attempt to stop his vehicle before the intersection. It took the driver 1.50 seconds to make his decision and to react to that decision. At point **C**, the action point, the driver applied his brakes, but his vehicle skidded (the *evasive action distance*) into the intersection and struck vehicle 2.

In this case, the collision or impact was minor. The vehicles did not move after impact and their final positions were relatively the same as at the point of impact. Had driver 1 perceived the hazard presented by vehicle 2 approaching the intersection at his point of possible perception, he would probably have been able to apply his brakes in sufficient time

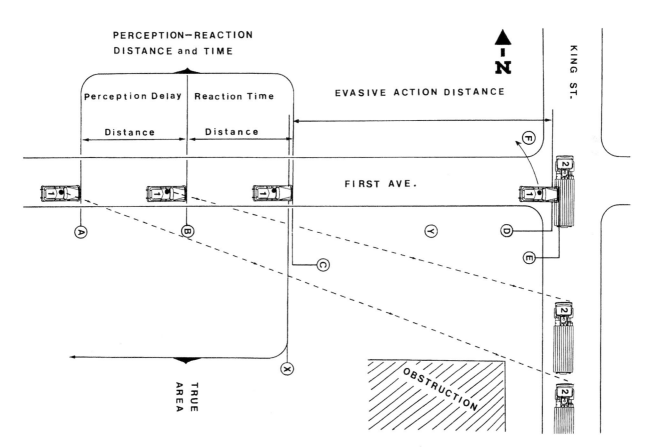

Figure 1–02. Application of the *series of events*.

to stop before the intersection. In this case, the true or safe area for driver 1 extended to just a very short distance before his action point or where he applied his brakes. His action point, however, was past the point of no escape, point **X**, and therefore he could not then avoid the collision.

ANALYZING THE EVENTS IN THE SERIES OF EVENTS

1.027 It is important that the traffic crash investigator analyzes the thoroughness of his or her investigation during and after the completion of the investigation. This can be done by analyzing through the use of *codes* all the events (including *situations*) contained in the *series of events*. By determining each and every event in a particular case (particularly by reviewing an investigator's report that has been prepared of the crash or from a witness' statement), the investigator is able to analyze how and to what extent the investigation has already been applied to each event. Where a lack of information exists for an event, further investigation can subsequently be carried out either at the scene or as a follow-up investigation to satisfy any deficiency.

1.028 A traffic crash investigator will very often analyze a crash situation by reviewing police reports, witnesses' statements, or other written materials, including analytical reports of laboratories and so on. This may be in addition to or in lieu of attending the actual scene. In analyzing a traffic crash situation from written materials, particularly an at-scene investigator's or witness's statement, the investigator

should overline and label recognizable *events* that are contained in the report, statement, or other materials, and select those areas that might need further investigation. Instructions for doing this follow:

1. *Overline* the words in the report or statement which describe the events in a general way.
2. Use the designated series of events *Code letters* shown in Table 1–01 to describe the separate events in the manner outlined in the example that follows.
3. When there is more than one vehicle involved, attach a subscript number to each vehicle's event code letter, e.g., point of possible perception for vehicle 1 would be shown as PP_1. The action point for vehicle 2 would be shown as AP_2, and so on. When one, two or more events occur at the same time or place, they can be identified by one overline, but labeled separately, e.g., **EA** and **AP**.
4. When an event such as road and weather conditions applies equally to all traffic units, a subscript number is not necessary. (Note that road and weather conditions are *situations* that exist or arise and, as such, are included in the definition of *event* for purposes of traffic crash analysis.)
5. Remember that an individual crash may not have all the events listed in the series of events. Remember also that all events do not necessarily fall in the same sequence in all accident situations, nor do they necessarily fall in the same sequence for all vehicles in any one crash situation.

Table 1–01
SERIES OF EVENTS CODES

Codes that can be applied to the analysis of the series of events are:

PTE	Pre-Trip Event	**AP**	Action Point	**MEg**	Maximum Engagement
TE	Trip Event	**EA**	Evasive Action	**D**	Disengagement
PPP	Point of Possible Perception	**EAD**	Evasive Action Distance	**SC**	Secondary Contact
PAP	Point of Actual Perception	**TA**	True (Safe) Area	**PSC**	Post Secondary Contact
PDe	Perception Delay	**PNE**	Point of No Escape	**FP**	Final Position
PD	Perception Distance	**En**	Encroachment	**ARP**	At rest position
R	Reaction	**PI**	Point of Impact	**PI**	Personal Injury
RT	Reaction Time	**PC**	Primary Contact	**FI**	Fatal Injury
RD	Reaction Distance	**Eg**	Engagement		

6. Whenever possible, the investigator should prepare on a separate sheet of paper a sketch of the crash scene showing the location of each event described in a report or statement for ready reference and an understanding of all the events as they become apparent.

Example

See Figure 1–02 and review Figure 1–01 for the purposes of relating *series of events* to the following scenario. In this scenario, it is shown how *events* can be identified in an investigator's report, in the statement of a witness, and/or on a sketch or diagram, and how *codes* for these *events* can be applied. It is in this way that the investigator can identify all of the *events* that are contained in the report, statement, and/or a sketch or diagram and to select those areas that might need further investigation. It should be noted that in this example, a few (not all) of the *events* have been selected simply to illustrate the procedure of identifying events, overlining them and applying appropriate *codes*.

It should be remembered that the term *event*, for the purposes of traffic crash analysis, includes any *situation* that is in place or may at any time arise in the *pre-* or *at-scene series of events*. For examples see Paragraphs 1.016–1.018.

Unit Designations
WHITE–Vehicle 1
ADAMS–Vehicle 2
CHILD–Unit 3

SCENARIO

$\overline{\quad\textbf{PTE}\quad}$ $\overline{\quad\textbf{PTE}\quad}$

WHITE, who had one year's driving experience, attended a party during the evening where he

$\overline{\quad\textbf{PTE}\quad}$

consumed 12 bottles of beer. He stayed at the party until 6:00 a.m. and then decided to leave on

$\overline{\quad\textbf{PTE}\quad}$ $\overline{\quad\textbf{PTE}\quad}$

a fishing trip. He did not take time to sleep. As he drove, he felt dizzy and unsteady because of an

$\overline{\quad\textbf{PPP}\quad}$

overconsumption of alcohol and lack of sleep. As he reached Point A while traveling east on First

Avenue, he saw *ADAMS'* vehicle traveling north on King Street approaching the uncontrolled inter-

$\overline{\quad\textbf{TE}\quad}$

section at King Street and First Avenue. Because he was distracted by a child playing alongside First

Avenue at Point Y, *WHITE* did not recognize or perceive the *ADAMS'* vehicle as being a hazard. After

$\overline{\textbf{PDe}}$ $\overline{\quad\textbf{PD}\quad}$ $\overline{\quad\textbf{PAP}\quad}$

traveling for (x) seconds over a distance of (x) feet [(x) meters], *WHITE* perceived at Point B that

$\overline{\quad\textbf{AP}\quad}$ $\overline{\quad\textbf{EA}\quad}$

ADAMS was not likely to stop at the intersection. At Point C, *WHITE* reacted by applying his brakes,

$\overline{\quad\textbf{EAD}\quad}$ $\overline{\textbf{PC}_{1,2}\ \textbf{Meg}_{1,2}}$

skidded 100 ft (30 m), and came into contact with and penetrated the *ADAMS'* vehicle at Points D and E.

$\overline{\quad\textbf{PI}_{2}\quad}$

ADAMS struck his chest on the steering wheel causing a bruise. The collision or impact was minor

and the positions of both vehicles remained relatively the same as at the point of impact, i.e., at

$\overline{\quad\textbf{FP}_{1,2}\quad}$ $\overline{\textbf{ARP}_{1}}$

Points D and E. Passers-by immediately pushed *WHITE'S* vehicle off the roadway to Point F.

CRASH CAUSE ANALYSIS

1.029 A cause analysis is carried out after the investigation and gathering of evidence is complete by taking into consideration and analyzing all aspects of the crash such as, but not limited to, the drivers, vehicles, roadway, and other environmental factors to determine *why* the crash occurred.

Series of Events Evidence and Investigation Checklist

1.030 The following *Series of Events Evidence and Investigation Checklist* can (a) used by an investigator and reconstructionist to ensure that key items of evidence are considered when an investigation is undertaken; (b) used by an investigation supervisor in assessing the thoroughness/work of the investigator or reconstructionist, and (c) used by an attorney for purposes similar to that of an investigation supervisor, and as a guide in ensuring the various points are covered during prosecution or defense examinations, or in the case of civil proceedings. There are many points in an investigation that are not covered in this checklist, e.g., mechanical inspections, roadway marks, and such; however, these items, as well as additional checklists, can be located by referring to the index at the back of this manual. The *index* may also be referred to for enlargement upon some of the items shown in this checklist.

Review *Series of Events*, 1.016–1.028

☐ Series of events and human factors, see 1.016
☐ Definitions, see 1.016
☐ Events and factors explained, see 1.017
☐ Analyzing the series of events, see 1.026–1.029
☐ Analyzing the series of events *Example*, see 1.027
☐ Pre-scene events, see 1.016, 1.017
☐ Pre-trip events, see 1.017(1)
☐ Pre-scene, see 1.016(a)
☐ At-scene, see 1.016(b), 1.018
☐ Perception explained, see 3.042
☐ depth perception explained, see 3.034
☐ Point of possible perception, see 1.018(a)
☐ Perception delay, see 1.018(c)
☐ Point of actual perception, see 1.018(b). See also 3.042
☐ Perception-reaction time, see 3.044

☐ Reaction, see 1.018(e)
☐ complex, see 1.018(e)(ii)
☐ simple, see 1.018(e)(i)
☐ Reaction distance, see 1.018(h)
☐ Reaction time, see 1.018(f),(g)
☐ Perception distance, 1.018(d)
☐ Safe (true) area, see 1.018(l)
☐ Point of no escape, see 1.018(m)
☐ Action point, see 1.018(I)
☐ Evasive action, see 1.018(j)
☐ Evasive action distance, see 1.018(k)
☐ Point of impact, see 1.018(o)
☐ Primary contact, see 1.018(p)
☐ Maximum engagement, see 1.018()r)
☐ Disengagement, see 1.018(s)
☐ Post-secondary contact, see 1.018(u)
☐ Final position, see 1.018(v)
☐ At-rest position, see 1.018(w)
☐ Personal injury, see 1.018(x)
☐ Fatal injury, see 1.018(y)

1.031–1.035 reserved.

PHASES AND LEVELS OF CRASH INVESTIGATION

1.036 Traffic crash investigation and training are normally carried out in five levels or phases, each of which require a certain caliber of training, experience and/or expertise to meet the objectives of the particular level. The following levels and the criteria for each are those generally accepted by police departments, police training academies and associated college and university training programs based on the need to ensure that a complete and thorough process is in place to meet the objectives of traffic crash investigation and reconstruction. In some cases, non-formal education and training combined with experience can meet the requirements of the levels shown.

These levels and phases include:

1. *At-scene–Phase or Level 1*
   At-scene investigations are conducted at the scene of an crash, either while each traffic unit is still at the crash site or after one or more (or all) traffic units have been removed. This is one of the most important parts of the whole traffic crash investigation process. In

many cases, the success or failure of all other segments of the investigation, including reconstruction, depends almost entirely upon the evidence gathered during the at-scene investigation. After completing an actual at-scene investigation, the investigator must ensure that all points of the investigation are completed by either personally carrying out any follow-up investigations that are required or by coordinating those investigations by others.

2. *Follow-up—Phase or Level 11*
   The at-scene investigation very often has its limits or constraints in terms of gathering evidence such as the taking of statements from witnesses who do not remain at the scene, tracing the pre-scene paths and actions of those involved in the crash (*pre-scene series of events*), and the ability to conduct a thorough mechanical inspection of the vehicles involved. Follow-up investigations are carried out after the at-scene investigation has been completed within the limits or constraints mentioned. Most often, this phase includes, but is not limited to, statement taking, mechanical inspections, preparations for a coroner's inquest or inquiry, and so on. It may also require the investigator to return to the site as part of his investigation, all of which might take place days or months after the time and date of the incident.

3. *Technical or Advanced—Level 111*
   Technical or advanced level investigations include *Levels 1* and *11* responsibilities, but are usually conducted in the more serious or complex cases, such as those where personal injury or death is involved.

4. *Reconstruction—Level 1V*
   At this level, research, data collection, and analysis usually go far beyond that of technical investigations. Experiments are often conducted. The reconstructionist at this level has an above-average knowledge of the problem-solving process, including the knowledge and ability to apply the principles of physics and vehicle dynamics to investigations. He also has the ability to evaluate and apply these principles to evidence gathered during

at-scene and follow-up investigations by other investigators.

5. *Reconstruction—Level V (Advanced Forensics)*
   This level is carried out by *occupational specialists* such as professional traffic crash reconstructionists, and others in specific fields such as medical professionals (e.g., pathologists and medical examiners), biomechanical engineers, mechanical engineers, and civil engineers.

1.037 When engaged at the reconstruction level, the *Level V* professional may not necessarily always attend a crash site, but rather may analyze, interpret, and make decisions or render expert opinions on evidence gathered by another investigator.

1.038–1.039 reserved.

EDUCATION AND TRAINING

1.040 As important as advanced or higher education is to the professional reconstructionist program, education by itself cannot replace the practical experience gained by the many police officers who for many years have been the first investigators to arrive at the scene of a crash, remove bodies, observe vehicles in their immediate crash environment; as well as to gather, photograph, interpret, and document for court and other purposes all forms of evidence including that involving driver injury and behavior, roadway marks, vehicle damages, and so on. Of course, many police officers do not limit their knowledge to such firsthand experience but go on to avail themselves of a mechanical engineering or other related degree, or enter into traffic crash investigation and reconstruction certificate programs offered by recognized training institutions such as the Institute of Police Technology and Management, University of North Florida (IPTM), and Northwestern University Center for Public Safety (formerly the Traffic Institute).

1.041 Training and practical experience have perhaps never been more important than they are in today's professional environment. Investigators and reconstructionists are routinely subjected to rigorous cross-examination by attorneys regarding their conclusions, the procedures they used, and the combination of their training and practical experience that purportedly qualifies them to come to the conclusions they did in their investigation.

DUTIES AND RESPONSIBILITIES

1.042 Sometimes, a major part of traffic crash reconstruction at *Levels 111* and *IV* is devoted to interpreting and evaluating conclusions arrived at or by at-scene and follow-up investigators working at *Levels 1* and *11*. Unless the initial stages of the investigation are thorough, particularly during the at-scene investigation, it can be more difficult for the reconstructionist to arrive at soundly based, conclusive results in the reconstruction of the crash. In such cases, it will often be necessary for him to visit or revisit the scene and initial investigation in order to gather the additional information or evidence needed to meet the requirements of the reconstruction process. In all cases, the reconstructionist must be prepared to solicit whatever additional expert advice might be available or required to supplement or verify his own findings, or to otherwise assist in the reconstruction process. Much of that assistance is available from other professionals, particularly from the *occupational specialists* listed below (see para. 1.071). The conclusions arrived at must be based on proper evaluation of all the evidence. This may require the testing of hypotheses, observing the results, and comparing them to actual results obtained in a practical way and/or through the application of scientific principles. In some cases, a second opinion regarding any conclusion arrived at by an occupational specialist should be obtained.

1.043 In many cases, individual reconstructionists, whether they be police officers, private investigators, mechanical engineers, or other professionals, do not have the facilities, training, practical experience, or special knowledge necessary to carry out a complete and thorough investigation or reconstruction from the time of collision (*at-scene*) to its conclusion in the courts, or otherwise. For example, a police officer-reconstructionist can locate and interpret various aspects of scene evidence, apply the principles of physics to calculate speed as well as satisfy the many other requirements to bring the matter to a satisfactory conclusion. Other professionals may not always attend at-scene, such as a professional engineer or metallurgist, but they can

investigate and make determinations with respect to mechanical failure, metal fatigue or stress, and so on; and a pathologist can determine the cause of death. That is to say, it is of utmost importance that each profession involved in traffic crash reconstruction establish an association with other professionals who have the additional or specific expertise above their own that is necessary to facilitate a proper conclusion of any case under investigation.

1.044 The liaison between the reconstructionist and certain of the occupational specialists is so important that arrangements should be made for the specialists to participate as trainers in programs covering areas in which they have expertise. This participation can include, but should not be limited to:

a. Instruction in the details of injuries typical of traffic crashes, what can be determined from such injuries, and the problems arising from natural disease that can cause or contribute to crashes
b. Instruction in areas where the criminalistic laboratory assists in the handling of evidence of toxins and the interpretation of such findings
c. Instruction in the perception and reactions of drivers and pedestrians
d. Instruction in the advanced application of physics in the reconstruction process

1.045 When there is insufficient data available to properly reconstruct a crash through use of fundamental laws of physics and engineering principles, tables such as a general guide for drag factors (see para. 9.090 and Table 9–02) in calculating speed can very well give reasonable results. Use caution employing such means, however. Evaluation of the final results must take the procedure into consideration. The results and final conclusions of the reconstruction should be able to stand the test of any new evidence discovered or presented by the opposing side in the case at trial or by the trier of evidence.

SAFEGUARDING EVIDENCE

1.046 The reconstructionist should establish a system for the secure and efficient storage, classification, retrieval, and disposition of items of evidentiary or other value that come into his custody. He should maintain at least:

a. A chronological record of each occasion when property is taken into custody by him.

b. A separate itemized list of all items of property that are taken into custody in respect to any part of the investigation.

c. A record that indicates the continuity of the property from its entry into his custody to its final disposition. This record should include the name of each person taking custody.

1.047–1.050 reserved.

ACCURACY, ERRORS, AND TOLERANCES IN TRAFFIC CRASH INVESTIGATION

1.051 This portion of the manual will give the investigator a general idea of the inherent errors that are or might be found in measurements and calculations made in traffic crash investigations, and methods that can be employed to recognize and compensate for them so that the most accurate results will be achieved and reported upon. In most cases, any such error will be associated with the device or with the procedure used to make the measurement. For our purposes, *accuracy* is defined as the difference between the observed value (or mean of the observed values) and the true value. This difference is called *error*, the smaller the error, of course, the greater the accuracy. The *precision* of a stated value refers to the variation implied in the statement of the value. *Error*, defined as the *absolute difference between the true value and the read value*, may be classified as systematic or random. *Systematic* errors are the result of bias in the measuring device or procedure. *Random* measurement errors are the result of a number of random influences which usually follow some statistical distribution.[7]

1.052 In making a determination, e.g., a calculation, if the input data is in error, the result (output) will likewise be in error. The smaller the input error, of course, the greater the accuracy of the output. Accuracy, which must always be strived for, has everything to do with asking the right question and/or having a measuring device that is not biased. An example is when a driver knowingly travels at the posted speed of 60 + 6 = 66 mph (or km/h), and he is checked by the police and given a violation notice for 85 mph (or km/h). The driver knows that there is a bias in his speedometer because it was registering 66 mph (or km/h) and it should have been registering 85 mph (or km/h), *bias* being a *systematic error* in the measuring device or procedure. The circumstances outlined, of course, assume that the police officer was using a *properly calibrated* speed measuring device, *calibration* being a systematic method of comparing the used measuring device to (a) a primary standard, (b) a secondary standard with higher accuracy than the device, or (c) with a known input source. (See Table 1–02 under para. 1.056 and Table 1–03 under para. 1.057.) In this case, the bias or systematic error is 19 mph (or km/h).[8] Also, in the example given, it is quite obvious that the speedometer is measuring the correct variable, so the correct measurement is being made, and the *bias* is in the calibration of the measuring device. Once the driver knows the bias, it is simple for him to correct so that he will drive at the *correct* speed. This is not true for *random errors* which are the result of a number of influences that vary in importance from time to time in ways that are not predictable.

1.053 Traffic crash investigation is undertaken to understand how a crash occurred and, if necessary, to assess blame. The estimate most frequently sought is pre-impact speed, since this can be shown above the legal limit. The methods used to estimate pre-impact speed use a set of field-measured or industrially-accepted values of certain variables that are substituted into the appropriate formula. The values such as skid marks are measured in such a way as to obtain a *conservative* or reasonably low bound on the speed estimate. This particular strategy seems to have proven successful under the pressure of the legal system, but it does not represent the best estimate. The question we should be answering is: *What is the most likely pre-impact speed?* Phrased another way, the question becomes: *What is a reasonable upper and lower value of the estimated speed given the conditions under which the data was collected?*[7] In the absence of any qualification in a case, the precision of a value may be taken to be plus or minus, and many investigators find it to be advisable to use the statement: *Based on my experience, my estimate (or calculation) is correct or reasonable within a range of +/– [e.g., 5 mph (km/h)].* By using a range in this manner, inherent sensitivity issues can very often be avoided.

1.054 *Skid marks and speed calculations.* In cases of skid marks measurements for a crash vehicle and for drag factor tests, the shadow or lead-in mark may disappear or not be evident for a variety of reasons and thereby not form a part of the skid mark measurements for calculation purposes. An extreme decrease in vehicle speed starts immediately after brake application, resulting in lesser wheel revolutions. Therefore, a drag factor that is based on the length of the visible combined shadow or lead-in mark and the true skid mark will, under normal circumstances, result in a drag factor that is lower than the actual drag factor for the roadway surface and consequently, when related to a crash vehicle, a lower speed calculation for that vehicle. Under these circumstances, when measuring and making calculations, there are two uncertainties and/or assumptions:[9]

1. *Actual distance involved in the speed retardation.* *Missing:* Non-visible or obliterated marks to indicate where slowing began.
2. *Actual drag factor for the roadway surface.* *Assumption:* Length of skid being that indicated by shadow or lead-in marks plus true skid mark.

1.055 When a measurement is made, there is sometimes an error associated with the device or in the procedure used. The *uncertainty* associated with a measured value is usually the range of values that is obtained from the true value with a readable instrument. Many such measurements also depend on instrument readability, clearness of the end of the object being measured (especially over long distances), illumination, your eyesight, view angle and other similar factors (see also Para. 1.058). Also, for each instrument, there is a calibration procedure.

1.056 We know from Table 1–02 that an old cloth tape may be considered to be accurate within 1% in a 100 ft (30 m) measurement. It should be noted, however, that the table does not differentiate between an old cloth tape of poor-quality material that might have extended because of age and use, or shrunk because of various conditions under to which it was subjected, e.g., damp, wet weather conditions. Therefore, we should consider that in the case where a 100 ft (30 m) measurement is determined through the use of such a tape, the *actual* distance may be considered accurate within a range of 99–101 ft (29.7–30.3m).

Table 1–02
MEASUREMENT ERRORS BY METHODS AND DEVICES

Method/Device	Distance: 100 ft (30 M)	± % Error
Pacing Method		10.2
Heel-to-toe Method		5.1
Pocket Tape		0.1
Woven Metal Tape (New)		0.2
Woven Metal Tape (Old)		0.5
Cloth Tape (New)		0.3
Cloth Tape (Old)		1.0
Measuring Wheel		0.5

Source: Patterson (1991).[10] Percentage error of measurements taken over a distance of 100 ft (30 m) using various measuring methods and devices. Errors may be classified as systematic or random. The table analysis treats only random error. Systematic errors may be detected by using an acceptable calibration procedure.

1.057 *Speedometer Error.* An inspection of approximately 500 various foreign and domestic vehicles was carried out in Sweden and reported in Nordic Road Transport Research No. 1, 1992 Series VTI Notat T112. The inspection found that on average, 70 percent of the vehicles had a speedometer reading that was too high. The speedometer readings and errors recorded, are shown in Table 1–03.

Table 1–03

Test Speed		Error (High)	
km/h	mph	km/h	mph
30	8.6	3.5	2.2
50	31	4.1	2.5
70	43.5	5.0	3.1
	through to		
90	55.9	5	3.1

The significance of variations between speedometers in different vehicles was found to be great: At a speed of 90 km/h (55.9 mph), 5 percent of the vehicles had a speed difference of 9 km/h (5.6 mph) or more. This points up the necessity of insuring that speedometers used for enforcement purposes, particularly in terms of conducting test skids for purposes of determining drag factor, are calibrated for accuracy.

1.058 *Speed meters and readability.* When dealing with measuring devices, a few of their *scientific* characteristics should be discussed. One is the characteristic of *readability* which refers to the closeness with which the scales of an instrument may be read. In the case of a speedometer, it may have speed graduations marked at 5 mph (or km/h) increments. It is very readable when the needle settles on one of the "5" marks; however, to read speeds between two of the marks it is necessary to make an estimate of the speed. For example, you can correctly read 55 mph (or km/h), but you must estimate a 57 mph (km/h) reading. Many such measurements also depend not only on instrument readability, but also clearness of the end of the object being measured (especially over long distances), your eyesight, view angle, and such other similar factors (see also Paras. 1.055 and 1.063).

1.059 *Tolerance.* Any tolerance must be reasonable under the circumstances, and be able to be explained and justified. Particularly in speed estimate issues, the investigator should, whenever possible, use a range of +/− mph (km/h) in order to avoid sensitivity issues. In all cases, he should be in a position to support the range, based on his personal experience, acceptable published references, or the evidence of an expert in the area at issue. In the case of a speed calculation, the estimated speed should first be made and considered as a middle or probable speed, and then extremes calculated at either end of this middle or probable speed, such as plus or minus 5 percent of that speed. The question we should really be answering is, *what is the most likely pre-impact speed?* Phrased another way, the question becomes, *what is a reasonable upper and lower value of the estimated speed given the conditions under which the data was collected?*

1.060 Procedures where some discrepancy, error, or uncertainty can arise is with measuring devices, as well as the procedures used and calculations made in respect to such things as measuring distances in impending or lead-in skid marks; horizontal and vertical distances in flips, vaults, and falls; chord and middle ordinate in yaw marks; determining drivers' reaction times; and making drag factor, speed, and velocity calculations. It is incumbent upon the investigator to insure that any calculation or conclusion arrived at is as accurate as possible, and that any reasonable discrepancy, error, or uncertainty that is or should be

considered is in fact given due consideration. He may, because of his training and experience, consider it proper to allow a tolerance, but in so doing, he must be able to explain and/or justify such tolerance or uncertainty. In these circumstances, it is advisable to use a range of possibilities (±) in order to avoid any sensitivity issue that might arise. For example, in the case of calculating speed, a calculation can first be made as a middle or *most probable* speed, and then extremes calculated at either end such as, for example, plus or minus 5 percent speeds, which could be considered possibilities within the tolerance range. It can then be said that if a speed is calculated to be 30 mph (50 km/h), that would be the probable speed, but in order to prepare for any sensitivity issue that might later arise, the investigator might feel that, based on his experience and training in the area of that particular calculation, he would give a tolerance of, for example, ± 5 percent. The calculated and most probable speed of 30 mph (50 km/h) could then be said to be within a range of 28.5 mph–31.5 mph (47.5–52.5 km/h).

NOTE: For a detailed analysis of the accuracy and precision of speed determinations, see *The Accuracy and Precision of Speed Estimates from Crash Reconstruction Data*, a paper presented at IPTM's Special Problems Seminar, May, 2000, by Dr. Frank Navin, P. Eng., Professor of Civil Engineering, University of British Columbia, Vancouver, Canada.

1.061 *Additional Measuring Error Possibilities.* Additional possibilities for errors in measuring and recording include:

a. Measuring to one point only on a vehicle or other large object, thereby allowing it to pivot to any one of many positions in repositioning it on a roadway, in preparing a scale diagram, or in giving testimony regarding its precise location on the roadway.

b. Reading the numbers upside-down, e.g., 9 for 6.

c. Reading or recording tenths of a foot as inches.

d. Reading or recording centimeters as meters, or vice versa.

e. Mistaking the apostrophe (') or quote mark (") as *1* or *11*.

f. Losing proper count in such measuring practices as tape lengths or pacing.

g. Failing to reset measuring wheel.

h. Failing to print or draw with a firm hand, thereby allowing the pencil to skip or prepare a number or symbol to be misinterpreted.

SIGNIFICANT DIGITS

1.062 Final answers from computations should be rounded off to the number of decimal places justified by the data. The answer can be no more accurate than the least accurate number in the data. Of course, rounding should be done on final calculations only. It should not be done on interim results. According to Meriam (1975), most engineering-type calculations are considered to have satisfactory accuracy to three significant figures. He goes on to point out that it is often difficult in lengthy calculations to know at the outset the number of significant figures needed to ensure a certain level of accuracy in the answer.

1.063 An original device may only give readings in *integer values*. The lack of decimal places implies that the reader has no knowledge as to the digit that might follow, such as is often found in measuring tapes or speedometers. An example is measuring tape that is divided into one-inch values as its smallest division. In such a case, when the actual distance to be measured falls between 115 and 116 inches (or centimeters), you may easily read a distance of 115 inches from the scale, but the value between 115 and 116 must be estimated and therefore the overall distance must be considered approximate or an estimated distance. Many such measurements also depend on instrument readability, clearness of the end of the object being measured (especially over long distances), your eyesight, view angle, and other similar factors (see also 1.058).

1.064 The numbers of significant figures can influence calculations. In general, the lowest number of significant figures controls the significant figures in resulting values. The simple rules are:

1. When multiplying or dividing two or more numbers, the result has the same number of significant figures as the *least accurate* of the values being used.
2. When adding or subtracting two or more numbers, the number of decimal places in the result is the same as the value with the *fewest* in the

values used. For example, if speed from skid marks is being calculated and it is known with certainty that the distance (D) is 10.06 m and that the drag factor (*f*) is 0.73, then, using *Formula 2–01*, the speed can be calculated as:

U.S.	*SI*
$S = \sqrt{30Df}$	$S = \sqrt{254Df}$

Where S = speed in km/h (or mph)
  D = skid distance
  f = drag factor

$S = \sqrt{30 \times 35.06 \times .73}$	$S = \sqrt{254 \times 10.06 \times .73}$
$S = \sqrt{767.814}$	$S = \sqrt{1865.2151}$
S = 27 mph	*S = 43 km/h*

The drag factor value of 0.73 has two significant figures and determines the number of significant figures in the outcome speed. The fact that we know distance to four significant figures does not change that outcome since the drag factor is the least accurate value in the calculation.

1.065 *Rounding Off to Decimal Places.* It is recommended that when measuring skid distance in skid tests to determine coefficient of friction or drag factor, the results be rounded *up* to the nearest whole foot (or 0.5 meter). Thus, 61.4 feet (or meters) would become 62 feet (or 61.5 meters). When calculating coefficient of friction (μ) or drag factor (*f*), round *down* to the nearest second place in the decimal fraction. Thus 0.753 would become 0.75 and 0.608 would become 0.60. In the case of a final speed calculation, it is recommended that the speed be rounded *down* to the nearest whole number, e.g., 68.8 mph (or km/h), would be considered to be 68 mph (or km/h). These conventions support the practice of using always the minimum speed for the crash vehicle. (For additional human error considerations, see Chapter 2.)

1.066–1.070 reserved.

OCCUPATIONAL SPECIALISTS AND LABORATORY/ANALYST SERVICES

1.071 In many situations, laboratory services personnel, using modern, sophisticated equipment, should be consulted in order to obtain definitive answers regarding specific or technical aspects of vehicle failure. This may include the use of x-ray, stereo-microscope (SM), and the scanning electron microscope (SEM). Examinations can be conducted for various types of failures, including tire and safety restraints. They are also able to provide evidence in terms of very fine measurements that are often required, as well as having a knowledge of the terminology that can be very important to an investigation, and in the presentation of expert evidence in a court of law.

1.072 Each investigation and reconstruction process can be unique in its own right. In the United States, Canada, and indeed most other countries, there are many forensic science service laboratories and/or personnel which are strong in certain scientific disciplines in relation to traffic crash reconstruction matters, including, but not limited to, blood, clothing, fibers, glass, hair, paint, soil, metal damage, fatigue, and stress. It is important, therefore, that the field investigator be aware that almost daily, new methodology and procedures will be presented for the analysis of the physical evidence that he obtains during an investigation, and to learn of the basic scientific services that are available to him that can be used to complement, in a very professional, scientific manner, the rote application of standard, but proper, everyday techniques and formulae to everyday traffic crash situations that some investigators may tend to restrict themselves.

1.073 In this manual, comments are sometimes made regarding probable or possible causes of vehicle defects or failures. These comments are not always intended to be definitive, recognizing that for a proper analysis to be made, the exhibit should be referred to a laboratory setting in order to adequately and properly answer a question of failure. Notwithstanding this, however, in some cases, the advanced traffic crash investigator will be a person possessing the degree of expertise to make a proper analysis.

1.074 Reconstructionists investigate some or all elements of a traffic collision from the initial stages at the scene through to final disposition, which may be in the courts. Applying scientific principles, they also analyze evidence gathered by at-scene and technical level investigators to ensure all aspects of

the investigation have been properly covered. However, very often, in order to reach a conclusion based on scientific principles, the reconstructionist must obtain the assistance and/or advice of *occupational specialists*, such as, but not limited to:

a. Mechanical engineers
b. Metallurgists
c. Design engineers
d. Medical Examiners
e. Coroners
f. Medical professionals, particularly those specializing in:
   i. Pathology
   ii. Psychiatry
   iii. Traumatic injuries
   iv. Medical laboratory technology
   v. Pharmacology
i. Trades persons
j. Vehicle mechanics/repair/diagnostic persons
k. Tire manufacturing engineers and repair persons
l. Educational professionals, particularly those specializing in the physical, natural, and behavioral sciences
m. Behavioral science resource persons specializing in personal problem counseling

FORENSIC SPECIALIST SERVICES AND RECONSTRUCTION

Definitions

1.075 Following are important forensic terms and definitions that should be recognized by the investigator. These terms as well as their applications to various aspects of reconstruction are expanded upon throughout the manual.

- *Forensic. Webster's New Universal Unabridged Dictionary*, 1992, at p.555, defines forensic as: 1. adapted or suited to argumentation. *n.* 2. forensics (construed as singular or plural), the study of argumentation and formal debate.
- *Forensic chemistry. Webster's New Universal Unabridged Dictionary*, 1992, at p.555, defines forensic chemistry as the application of facts concerning chemistry to questions of civil and criminal law.
- *Forensic medicine. Webster's New Universal Unabridged Dictionary*, 1992, at p.555, defines forensic

medicine as the application of medical knowledge to questions of civil and criminal law, especially in court proceedings.

- *Forensic psychiatry.* *Webster's New Universal Unabridged Dictionary*, 1992, at p.555, defines forensic psychiatry as the use of psychiatric knowledge and techniques in questions of law, as in determining legal sanity.
- *Forensic engineer.* It is generally accepted that a forensic engineer is:
  a. A. person having engineering knowledge in fields such as mechanical, civil, or electrical engineering, who applies such knowledge and principles of science to questions of civil and criminal law.
  b. A professionally trained person who applies the principles of science and engineering to traffic crash investigations in such areas as vehicle designs and mechanisms, including braking, hydraulic, suspension and transmissions systems.
- *Forensic mechanics.* It is generally accepted that forensic mechanics is the study of all rectilinear motion, rotational motion and forces generated by bodies in motion. It includes both statics and dynamics. Crashes involving vehicles are subject to investigations by a forensic engineer, sometimes at the scene but more often elsewhere in the course of a follow-up investigation.

Medical Professionals

1.076 The investigator cannot afford to ignore any discipline within the medical field when developing sources from which to obtain the professional expertise in his quest to reach proper conclusions in the reconstruction process. He can approach maximum effectiveness only by considering each discipline and arranging to obtain assistance promptly from each potential source. Medical personnel are able to work up a medical history of a deceased victim, including the details of how and when injuries were sustained, and to chart the course of hospitalization if the victim is not killed outright. Whenever death occurs, whether at the scene or later at some other place, there is the post-mortem examination to be considered along with the necessary microscopic, toxicologic, and other special studies.

Pathologist

1.077 Perhaps the best known and most often used medical professional is the forensic pathologist. It is his or her job to carry out a post-mortem examination in an attempt to solve, in the case of traffic crashes, (a) cause of death, (b) time of death, and in some cases, (c) the identify of the victim. The findings of a pathologist can be varied—including, but not limited to, in the case of traffic crash investigations, tests for body alcohol content and, where considered necessary, for sugar and drugs such as barbiturates. The necessity for determining the alcohol content arises from the fact that the deceased may have contributed to his death by being under the influence of liquor, or being a person who was described as being intoxicated or unsteady by witnesses to the crash.

Coroner-Medical Examiners

1.078 Although the medical examiner's office may conduct its own toxicologic analyses on specimens of various organs and materials obtained, e.g., fingernail scrapings, hair, from autopsies, these specimens are frequently transmitted to a crime laboratory for further examination and return of appropriate feedback to the medical examiner. The medical examiner ultimately reaches a conclusion as to whether the death was a homicide, suicide, or as the result of a crash or natural causes, and prepares a report of his findings and conclusions.

1.079 In many cases, the relationship between the reconstructionist and the pathologist—a relationship that combines the investigative responsibilities of the reconstructionist with the professional expertise of the pathologist—should be such that the pathologist, through the office of either the medical examiner or coroner, is considered an integral part of the reconstruction process.

Dentists and Orthodontists

1.080 In cases involving vehicle fires and burned victims, or bodies submerged in water, such as when a vehicle leaves the highway and falls into a lake, the dental professional can often make positive identification of an otherwise unidentifiable body by comparing the dental work, the arrangement of the teeth in the jaw, the mode of occlusion, or the fissures and grooves in the teeth with data, x-rays, and diagrams from known dental records. Additionally, he (and other face reconstruction specialists) may be able to determine the person's approximate age, the person's general facial characteristics, and whether missing teeth were removed before or after death.

1.081–1.085 reserved.

Behavioral Science Resources

1.086 In contemporary society, citizens are often involved in high stress occupations at their work place. Their work-place stress is then aggravated by the day-to-day maneuvering in and out of traffic when driving is a part of their employment or simply a means of getting to and from work. The result is often that the driver will deliberately cause a collision because he loses patience (*road rage*). Discussions with a behavioral science specialist may in many such situations provide the reconstructionist with a better understanding of why a driver may have acted as he did.

Psychiatrist

1.087 A psychiatrist may be called upon for assessment of a person's sanity. Also, in cases of crashes for which there is no apparent reason, the psychiatrist may assist in determining a motive, thus helping to establish *corpus delicti* (the body as evidence of murder) in vehicular crimes requiring specific intent. Often such assistance will in turn assist the investigator in evaluating a case and determining the course of action to be taken.

Medical Laboratories

1.088 The medical laboratory complements the crime laboratory. Medically related examinations, such as blood-alcohol tests, can most often be performed as satisfactorily by a medical laboratory as by a crime laboratory. There are many involved in criminalistics who advocate maximum use of medical laboratories for all routine medically-related examinations to free the criminalistics laboratory for work pertinent to other than traffic-related investigations.

1.089 The use of legal as well as illegal drugs may be a contributing factor in a collision. The reconstructionist can refer such matters to the laboratory for purposes of drug identification and information as to what reactions might be expected from the use of the identified drugs in relation to driver behavior.

Forensic Laboratories

1.090 Forensic laboratories can be operated and controlled either by the police or by private entities. These laboratories provide advanced forensic science assistance to agencies and individuals utilizing their services, providing timely and efficient processing of physical evidence in many areas of interest to the reconstructionist, including the processing of breath and urine for the presence of narcotics and alcohol.

1.091 DNA or *deoxyribonucleic acid* is the complex genetic material found in the cells of an organism that provides the blue print for its development. As far as science has determined through speculation and observation, no two individuals who are alive or who have ever lived have the same DNA.[11]

When a collision occurs, DNA can be obtained from various items or sources from within, at, or near the vehicle. Of particular importance are the points of contact (see Para. 8.154 and Figs. 8-50–8-53), and in the case of a pedestrian being struck by a car, various outside and undercarriage parts of a vehicle, from which specimens of blood (wet or dried), hair (a single strand will often suffice), dandruff, or skin, can be obtained for DNA analysis relating to the driver or passengers, or struck pedestrian. Other items that may hold DNA evidence are eyeglasses (nose or ear pieces, and lens that may contain sweat or skin); a cigarette butt that may contain saliva; a bottle, can, or glass that may contain saliva or sweat. When related to inside-vehicle contact points, an analysis can often be used to prove or disprove that a certain individual was or was not in the vehicle and, if so, his or her seating position. Similarly, an individual's identification, including that of a pedestrian, can often be established through DNA analysis.

Evidence Technicians

1.092 There are evidence technicians working within and outside (privately) of the police service. In many cases, the laboratory of the coroner or the medical examiner is staffed with evidence technicians who conduct thorough crime scene investigations. The establishment of a working relationship with all such offices may provide the reconstructionist with access to much required evidence information.

Business, Trade, and Industrial Professionals

1.093 Many of the investigator's activities are directly or indirectly affected by his ability or inability to gain information from the diversified industries and businesses in our society. This is particularly true in the case of manufacturers of vehicles and their field representatives or dealerships for passenger cars, trucks, heavy machinery, and various other on- or off-road vehicles and equipment. Of utmost importance are vehicle repair facilities, such as garages and body-repair shops. It is important to maintain close liaison with all the above not only to obtain immediate investigation assistance, but also to keep abreast of on-going research and development in areas of mutual interest.

Education Professionals

1.094 In terms of meeting the objectives of traffic crash analysis and reconstruction, perhaps one of the most important sources of professional assistance is the educational community, particularly at the college and university levels. Assistance can often be obtained in areas such as the behavioral, natural, and physical sciences, all of which can in one form or another be applied to traffic crash investigation, analysis, and reconstruction programs. The reconstructionist can reciprocate by giving assistance in developing school curriculum that incorporates actual experiences of the reconstructionist or case studies into classroom presentations in physics and driver education.

1.095 Police agencies and reconstruction professionals very rarely have the funds available to conduct in-house research. Academic facilities, most often at the university level, are more extensive and more sophisticated than those normally available to the reconstructionist. It will be found advantageous to both the traffic crash reconstruction profession and the educational communities to develop and maintain cooperative research programs.

1.096–1.100 reserved.

Legal Assistance

1.101 Investigators should carry out their responsibilities in compliance with the directives of law. In this regard, attorneys are able to provide legal advice in civil, quasi-criminal, and/or criminal cases, make recommendations on how an investigation should proceed–what is legal and what is not–and make recommendations regarding legal sufficiency in case preparation. Since almost every phase of the investigative role is affected by either substantive or procedural law, the reconstructionist should avail himself of legal advice and information whenever the need or apparent need for it arises. Training bulletins and other reports issued by regulative agencies and law schools are another good source of information concerning recent court decisions that have become part of case law, and of legal information in general.

1.102 For the reconstruction process to meet its objectives, it is essential that close liaison and cooperation be fostered among its various professional components. Members of the legal profession have the credentials and expertise to work out problems and to encourage cooperation among attorneys, police agencies, insurance companies, prosecutors, and defense counsels.

THE EXPERT AND TRAFFIC CRASH RECONSTRUCTION

1.103 Traffic crash investigators should familiarize themselves with the requirements, in jurisdictions of concern, of dealing with the admissibility of traffic crash investigation evidence, qualifications of an expert, basis of expert opinions, permissible scope of cross-examination, demonstrative evidence, ethics and computer graphics, animations and/or simulations, inasmuch as such requirements and admissibility can vary from area to area.

Definitions

1.104 Of importance to the investigator are the following definitions of various terms relating to the word *expert:*

- *Expert. Webster's New Universal Unabridged Dictionary*, 1992, at p.502, defines an expert as: *n.*1. a person who has special skill or knowledge in some particular field; specialist; authority; *-adj.* 2. possessing special skill or knowledge; trained by practice; skillful or skilled; (*often followed by in or at*): an expert witness, expert mechanic, etc., pertaining to, coming from, or characteristic of an expert.
- *Expertise. Webster's New Universal Unabridged Dictionary*, 1992, at p.502, defines expertise as expert skill or knowledge; expertness; know-how.
- *Expert Evidence. Black's Law Dictionary* 1093 (6th ed., 1990), defines expert evidence as evidence of what the expert thinks, believes or infers in regard to facts in dispute as distinguished from his personal knowledge of the facts themselves.
- *Expert Opinion Evidence.* Expert opinion evidence can be defined as an opinion given by an expert on a subject about which he is accepted by the court as being an expert. As with other witnesses, the courts may or not believe the testimony given by the expert.
- *Expert Witness Testimony.* (See *Moore's Federal Practice* 702.1–702.3.) In Rule 702, it is stated that if scientific, technical, or other specialized knowledge will assist the trier of fact to understand the evidence or to determine a fact in issue, a witness qualified as an expert by knowledge, skill, experience, training, or education, may testify thereto in the form of an opinion or otherwise.
- *Consultant. Webster's New Universal Unabridged Dictionary*, 992, at p. 315, defines consultant as one who gives professional or expert advice.

Expert Qualifications

1.105 In terms of crash investigation and reconstruction, and in a legal sense, an expert may be defined as:

A person who can render opinions in specific subject matter based on his or her education, training, knowledge, and practical experience.

To be considered an expert, one must possess above-average or superior skills in the specific area of interest. A qualified expert witness is permitted to render opinions on matters beyond the knowledge of most people.

1.106 Courts most often base the acceptability of an expert's evidence on the following four criteria:

1. *Qualifications.* Do the investigator's qualifications satisfy the requirements, e.g., training, experience?
2. *Relevancy.* Will the testimony be relevant to the case?
3. *Decision making.* Will the testimony assist the court in reaching a properly informed decision?
4. *Exclusionary-type evidence.* Should the testimony be excluded because its probative value is substantially outweighed by its prejudicial effect?

1.107 To qualify as an expert, the investigator must qualify as an expert in the area in which he will be giving expert testimony. Therefore, in addition to whatever details he or she might provide in order to qualify in the eyes of the court, it is very important for the investigator to relate his or her training and experience specifically to the immediate area in which he or he is to give evidence, e.g., speed based on the length of skid marks. Specifically, the investigator must be prepared to:

a. Give evidence only of qualifications that will stand severe scrutiny by opposing attorneys and the courts.
b. State the training and practical experience you have in the traffic crash investigation field, such as the following:

Training
Levels 1 and 11 (basic), 111 (technical), 1V (reconstruction) and V (special, e.g., professional and other specialized courses, certificate programs, degrees, and so on).

Experience
Years involved in *Levels 1 and 11 (basic), 111 (technical), 1V* (reconstruction) and *V* (specialized), including types and numbers of investigations at each level. Include crashes where the reconstruction was based on information, data and/or evidence supplied by other investigators. In the tallying of cases, specific

mention should be made of any limited involvement in the overall investigation or reconstruction process, such as when you only examined the braking system or only calculated speed based on skid marks. Do not, for example, suggest that you reconstructed a crash where your only involvement was the reading of a report and the rendering of an opinion.

Include also authorship of technical papers and professional publications, presentation of lectures, experience as an instructor, participation in technical committees, and other related experiences and activities.

An Expert's Responsibilities

1.108 The responsibility of an expert, including that of a consultant who does research and gives advice, is to determine and establish facts, based on an analysis and evaluation of evidence presented to or gathered by him. The expert then provides such findings in a clear and understandable form either orally or by way of reports to the police or other investigators, as well as to judges and juries or other triers of fact, so that informed decisions can be reached.

1.109 The investigator or reconstructionist may, in addition to reconstructing a crash based on his own personal investigation, be involved in reconstructing a crash based on the information supplied by an investigator who is not necessarily a qualified reconstructionist. In such cases, the reconstructionist must undertake a complete review of the case to ensure that the investigation has been thorough and that all evidence gathered is accurate and complete.

Expert Witness

1.110 When scientific, technical, or other specialized knowledge is helpful to the trier of fact in understanding the evidence, the traditional method of supplying such information is through the opinion of an expert witness. Federal Rule of Evidence 702 allows expert witness testimony if the court determines that the information will assist the trier of fact. As part of its inquiry, the court may be required to determine whether a reliable body of scientific, technical, or specialized knowledge has

been developed in the area of expertise. The court must also determine whether the proffered witness is qualified to give the testimony.

Lay Witness

1.111 A *lay witness* usually may testify only to his or her sensory perceptions, i.e., to what he or she saw, heard, smelled, tasted, or touched. The Federal Rules of Evidence and the evidence codes of most states permit opinion by lay witnesses when the witness cannot readily communicate what he or she has perceived without resorting to opinion, when the witness won't mislead the finder of fact, or when the witness doesn't possess the special knowledge, skill, experience, or training that would allow him to testify as an expert witness. Even lay witness opinions must meet certain predicates before they are admitted.

Fact Witness

1.112 A *fact witness* is someone who has knowledge of information about some matter of relevance to the case and who is called upon to testify regarding this information. In traffic crash reconstruction cases, this person may be a traffic engineer who can testify regarding observations related to such things as the installation and function of traffic-control devices, or an individual who can testify regarding the existence and content of certain records, such as motor vehicle or transportation department records.

INVESTIGATORS' PRE-TRIAL RESPONSIBILITIES

1.113 Before trial, the investigator should communicate with the attorney who will be conducting the side of the case for which the reconstructionist is to appear. Such pre-trial communication can be by way of both verbal and written reports outlining the evidence that is or will be available to present. As an investigator you should:

a. Familiarize the attorney with reconstruction terms, principles, and techniques before the case goes to trial. For example, you might explain how a drag factor differs from a coefficient of friction, and how each is determined and used in the reconstruction process. In this way, you and the attorney will be in a position to familiarize the court with your area of expertise so that the evidence presented can be better understood.

b. Prepare a list of questions with expected answers for the attorney to use in his cross-examination of experts appearing for the opposing side.

c. Advise the attorney of all physical evidence that will be available for presentation, including evidence favorable to the other side. Include in this briefing, information on any examination carried out on an item of evidence, e.g., an examination of a headlamp for *on-off* evidence. The attorney can then make an informed opinion as to whether or not the item should be presented in court.

d. Inform the attorney of your limitations, and whether your responsibilities as a reconstructionist are full- or part-time. Advise him if you are an expert in one area but not in certain other areas that might be the subject of examination in court. You should be prepared to limit yourself to your particular area of expertise. To do otherwise might result in the attorney not being able to give you protection from devastating cross-examination.

e. Advise the attorney of the strong and weak points of the case, and of all facts and assumptions used in arriving at the conclusions presented. Include all other conclusions that could conceivably be reached based on these facts and assumptions.

f. Provide copies of legal documents, investigative reports, statements, photographs, and other materials germane to the case, such as traffic studies carried out in respect to the crash site.

EVIDENCE EVALUATOR

1.114 Experts who have specific areas of expertise are occasionally employed as *evidence evaluators* to assess or evaluate the evidence of an investigator or some other witness, including another expert witness. This evaluation can take place either during the pre-trial stage or during the time when testimony is given. The evaluator will often prepare

questions to be asked of the reconstructionist or other witness, together with expected answers to those questions. As an evaluator, you should be honest and professional. Do not resort to petty criticisms, nor attempt *one-upmanship* or personal attacks on the other side's witness or investigator. Such actions demonstrate a lack of professionalism that can prove extremely embarrassing to you as an expert witness as well as to the party for whom you are appearing or whom you are representing.

INVESTIGATOR'S CONCLUSIONS

1.115 An investigator's conclusions should be based on sound, scientific analysis of all available evidence. In the leading case of Frye v. United States, the court held scientific evidence is admissible if it has gained general acceptance by the scientific community:

> *Just when a scientific principle of discovery crosses the line between the experimental and demonstrable stages is difficult to define. Somewhere in this twilight zone, the evidential force of the principle must be recognized, and while courts will go a long way in admitting expert testimony deduced from a well-recognized scientific principle or discovery, the thing from which the deduction is made must be sufficiently established to have gained general acceptance in the particular field in which it belongs.*

INFORMATION SOURCES

1.116 It is the investigator's responsibility to add as many facts as possible to the *at-scene* and *follow-up* investigation evidence collected by other investigators. Statements from witnesses and interpretations of at-scene evidence and investigation reports should be analyzed for discrepancies and the need for further investigation in particular areas. Most important, the investigator should scrutinize all evidence relating to the *events* that make up the *series of events* in the crash (see Chapter 2). Much of this can be accomplished by reviewing and analyzing the following documents:

a. At-scene and follow-up police crash investigation reports
b. Commercial vehicle driver trip logs
c. Commercial vehicle load documents

d. Driver's licenses and driving records
e. Historical vehicle repair reports
f. *Level V* expert reports, e.g., prepared by occupational specialists
g. Operator's manuals for the vehicles involved
h. Photographs and videos (police, newspaper, personal) relating to the scene and vehicles involved
i. Scale plan drawings and field sketches prepared by investigators and/or a surveyor
j. Statements of drivers, passengers, and witnesses
k. Vehicle damage appraisal reports
l. Vehicle registrations
m. Vehicle examination report
n. Weather and meteorology records for the time and date of the incident. (Various websites can be used to obtain past and present weather information, including at times of day.)

FRAUD

1.117 The investigator must be cautious that the crash was not *staged* with intent to defraud insurance companies or others of money or to cover up some type of crime such as murder. The possibility of a conspiracy to defraud insurance companies of money should be considered particularly when there is a lack of witnesses; there is no reason or reasonable excuse for the crash; a driver or pedestrian states that he or his vehicle suffered injury and the other party involved in the crash freely admits liability; or, in the case of commercial-type passenger vehicles such as vans and buses, persons report that they were passengers injured in the crash when in fact they were not passengers; or when the total number of people reporting themselves as passengers is greater than the number of passengers the vehicle could have accommodated. Other types of crashes such as a vehicle running off the road; driving into bodies of water; striking bridge abutments, utility poles, trees, solid objects, and so on, should always be suspect.

1.118 Driver and occupant insurance coverage is often a reason used to stage a crash.

Suicide
a. A crash may be as the result of a driver's intent to commit suicide. This intent can be

for a variety of reasons, many of which are listed below.
b. Intention to kill himself and his passenger. This may occur when a driver and his passenger, e.g., husband and wife, have an argument and the driver decides to kill both himself and his passenger

Financial
a. Conspiracy between the driver and a passenger to become involved in a collision whereby they both may claim injury compensation. In most cases, the injuries may be relatively minor in nature.
b. Suicide to pay off debts
c. Suicide to provide money to a beneficiary
d. Loss of business or earnings

Workplace problems
a. Employee/employer relationships tied into marital problems
b. Uncertain future employment and earnings
c. School graduate and employment prospects
d. Work-related stress

Alcoholism
Loss of self-esteem
Physical handicap
Death of close friend or relative
Mental illness
Copycat action
a. Recent other suicide

Marital problems
a. Recent divorce
b. Family arguments

Health problems
Depression

1.119 Some indicators of an intentional collision are when:

a. A vehicle strikes a pole, tree, or other substantial object, and the object struck was isolated from other things and an apparent direct line (path) had to be followed in order to strike the object.
b. There is an unexplained loss of control, especially on a straight level roadway when there is no obstruction, light glare, or sun that would give cause for loss of control.

c. Minor injuries are sustained. In these cases, the seating positions in the vehicle, the type of restraint systems in place and/or used, energy absorbing materials present such as that on the dashboard and steering wheel, and air bag deployment should all be examined in relation to the type of injury suffered.

1.120 Local and senior governments and highway and transportation agencies are often the target of lawsuits regarding signing, roadway or highway design, roadway markings, alignment, and various other safety structures, either in terms of their structure and design, or lack of them. Subsequent chapters, particularly those covering the series of events, vehicle inspections, traffic unit placement on the roadway, and speed analysis, outline in detail the various methods of locating, interpreting, and analyzing evidence that will assist the investigator and reconstructionist in relation to investigating all forms of fraudulent acts involving vehicles and pedestrians.

DOCUMENTATION

1.121 The procedures used to document crash investigation evidence are no less important than evidence analysis procedures used in other investigations, including what is often referred to as major criminal investigations. The investigator's documentation effort is very often the first product seen by crash victims, attorneys, opposing experts, judges, and jurors, and can thereby at the outset indicate to them the standard of professionalism carried out in the entire investigation—rather than what could be very professional behind-the-scenes numerical calculations, assumptions, and technical reports.

1.122 Perceptions generated from the documentation effort can steer the case and influence its outcome. A well-designed presentation of evidence will be self-explanatory and easily understood. More importantly, no excuses will be required to minimize the importance of an exhibit that is unsupportive of testimony. Finally, a witness should never be forced to draw upon a juror's imagination in an effort to salvage an inconclusive exhibit.

1.123 Many crash-response caseworkers assign a low priority to the documentation portion of their files. Measurements, photographs, informal sketches.

and even scaled drawings are deemed to be a *supplemental* product of the investigation, not a primary consideration. In some agencies and private companies providing crash investigation services, delegating documentation tasks to low-ranking personnel can often be found to be a common policy. Thus, while a well-trained (and perhaps high-ranking) investigator or reconstructionist observes, tests, calculates, analyzes, and concludes how a crash occurred, his lesser-trained and less competent coworker becomes uniquely responsible for actually illustrating the crash sequence for others to view and understand. A single documentation error or oversight, if related to a critical facet of the case, can quickly confuse or invalidate an otherwise well-executed analysis.

1.124 Prudent crash investigators will recognize that evidence preservation and illustration assignments are of equal value to other tasks such as at-scene observations, mathematical calculations, establishing grounds for a prosecution against a perpetrator, the giving of testimony, and so on.

EXHIBITS

1.125 The investigator will often be required to complete a departmental or other acceptable, similar-type exhibit report. Generally speaking, the retrieving and maintenance of any traffic crash-related exhibit should be handled in a fashion similar to any other exhibit seized for court purposes, and department policy will normally stipulate the procedures to be followed. When a laboratory is involved in an investigation, it is very important that the investigators liaise closely with their personnel regarding any analysis in terms of protocols they may have in place for the handling and submission of evidence.

ETHICS

1.126 High ethical standards are very important to the traffic crash reconstruction profession. The investigator must ensure that at all times he conducts a proper and thorough reconstruction, and that conclusions reached will be based on a sound, scientific analysis of all available factual evidence. He must bear in mind that an objective of the profession is to protect the innocent and to respect the constitutional rights of all members of society. For the good of the profession as a whole, he should set an example and behave in a manner that does not bring discredit himself or to his profession by obeying all the laws, standards, and regulations under which he works and which are expected of him. He must cooperate with all legally authorized agencies and their representatives in the pursuit of fairness and justice. He must never allow personal biases, prejudices, aspirations, or friendships to influence him in his decisions or conclusions.

1.127 Should it occur that an investigator who, after a case has gone to final disposition or judgment, discovers that his testimony was in error and that such testimony was a primary reason for the determination of either guilt or innocence in a criminal matter, or the awarding of monetary damages in a civil matter, he should consider providing such further information to an appropriate authority for any follow-up action that might be appropriate or necessary.

Definitions

1.128 In terms of the traffic crash investigation profession:

Ethics can be said to be:
a. *A system of moral principles;*
b. *The rules of conduct recognized in respect to particular class of human actions;*
c. *Moral principles, as of an individual;*
d. *That branch of philosophy dealing with values relating to human conduct with respect to the rightness and wrongness of certain actions.* (See *Websters New Universal Unabridged Dictionary.* Barnes and Noble Books, New York, and Outlook Book Co., Avenel, New Jersey, 1992, p.489.)

Moral is something that is:
a. *Pertaining to, or concerned with right conduct or the distinction between right and wrong.*
b. *Concerned with the principles or rules of right conduct;*
c. *Founded on the fundamental principles of right conduct rather than on legalities, enactment, or custom.* (See *Websters New Universal Unabridged Dictionary.* Barnes and Noble Books, New

York, and Outlook Book Co., Avenel, New Jersey, 1992, p.930.)

Professional Ethics The American Association for the Advancement of Science (AAAS) defines *professional ethics* as:
> *Those principles that are intended to define the rights and responsibilities of scientists in their relationship with each other and with other parties including employers, research subjects, clients, students, etc.*

The AAAS further states that:
> *The formulation of ethical principles or the adoption of rules of conduct by a professional society can be viewed as a significant indicator of the profession's willingness to accept some responsibility for defining proper professional conduct, sensitizing members to important ethical issues embodies in these standards, and governing member behavior. But the presence of a set of ethical principles or rules of conduct is only part, albeit an important one, for the machinery needed to effect self-regulation. The impact of a profession's ethical principles or rules on its members' behavior may be negligible, however, without appropriate support activities to encourage proper professional conduct, or the means to detect and investigate possible violations, and to impose sanctions on violators. Provisions for actively implementing and enforcing a profession's rules of conduct does not guarantee effective self-regulation; but their presence does make it possible.*

PRE-TRIAL CONSULTATIONS AND TESTIMONY

1.129 The following guidelines may be used for pre-trial consultations and when answering questions at trial. However, in all cases, it is imperative that applicable local jurisdictional policies, procedures, and rules be followed at all times.

Pre-Trial Consultations

Briefly, in a pre-trial consultation, the investigator should be prepared to:

a. Identify and present materials either verbally or by written report, covering the critical issues involve.

b. State the strong and weak points of the case or proposition.

c. Supply copies of reports, legal documents, and statements.

d. Provide, when applicable, the results of traffic studies or research that have been carried out in respect to the location involved.

e. Not rely primarily on computer or scientific simulation reconstruction. Always be in a position to prove the accuracy of such instruments.

Testimony

When giving testimony, the investigator should use the following as a guide:

a. Be forthright. Give testimony in an honest, concise, clear, and objective manner.

b. Provide both oral and written testimony or evidence in a clear, concise, and most importantly, an easily understood manner for those who may not familiar with the mathematically complex issues involved. Speak in a clear and audible voice, loud enough to be heard by all concerned. Do not speak with in an abusive tone. Appear, act, and make your presentation in a professional manner.

c. Provide both accurate and complete testimony. The reconstructionist must be aware of *scientific negligence,* a situation where the reconstruction provides erroneous information without intent to defraud. Ensure you are able to provide an explanation, proof, and/or verification of your testimony, particularly in terms of formulae (derivations) charts, tables, or exhibits. Ensure that your conclusions are founded on proper and training, knowledge, and experience.

d. Give only factual evidence. If you do not know the answer to a question, say so. Do not guess.

e. Do not make pre-drawn conclusions on what happened and then attempt to find evidence to support the conclusion. Conclusions should be based on physical evidence observed at the scene and calculations made must be based on proven scientific principles.

f. Never guess an answer. If you do not know the answer, say so. To do otherwise, can lead to extreme difficulty, particularly during cross-examination.

g. If a question is not understood, request that the question be repeated and, if necessary, some clarification regarding the question.

h. Give consideration to the question asked and be certain of its meaning and intent before providing an answer. A slight pause will also give time for an objection to be raised before the answer is given. Be positive in your answers, and whenever possible, answer with either *yes* or *no.* When giving an answer, be concise; do not equivocate, and do not unnecessarily volunteer unsolicited information.

i. *Technical information.* Provide technical information in a readily understandable manner. Experts must build their credibility before a jury. Do not give evidence beyond your training, experience, and competency. Give explanations in such a way that the answer will be fully understood by those concerned. Do not try to impress with technical jargon. Show that opinions arrived at are based on fact, not mere speculation. In replying to questions, always be courteous and neutral to both sides, as well as to those sitting in judgment or the triers of fact. Even though the attorney appearing for the opposing side will have as one of his objectives to try to make uncertain in the minds of others, your credibility as an expert witness, never lose your temper no matter how rude or contemptuous that he might be.

j. *Be factual.* Do not treat assumptions as fact, particularly those arrived at by others and passed onto you as fact.

k. Do not allow bias based on race, color, sex, or other factors to influence your conclusions.

l. Ensure that your interpretations of data is correct.

m. Always use appropriate values in calculations and base your opinions and conclusions on fact or accepted scientific principles, e.g., do not assume a drag factor or coefficient of friction for use in a speed calculation.

n. *Conclusions.* Ensure that conclusions reached could be duplicated based on the evidence used.

Caution: Never state that you have qualifications that you do not in fact possess. For example, in some jurisdictions, it is a crime to state that you have a degree or title which you do not possess.

INFERIORITY COMPLEX

1.130 An *inferiority complex* often finds its outlet in ridicule, nitpicking, and so on, and is very often directed at and at the expense of others to make oneself look superior. It is of utmost importance that the investigator understands this principle and never allows himself to fall into the trap of ridiculing or degrading the work of others with the sole or primary intent of making himself or his work appear superior. This applies similarly to pre-trial consultations and in the giving of evidence. In the case of investigations, the investigator should consider that an inferiority complex on the part of a driver could be a reason for what is commonly known as road rage. For much more information on this very interesting subject, see works by Adler in many psychology reference materials.

ACCREDITATION COMMISSION FOR TRAFFIC CRASH RECONSTRUCTION (ACTAR)

The History Of A.C.T.A.R.

1.131 In 1985, the National Highway Traffic Safety Administration provided a grant to develop national guidelines for the standardization of training in the field of traffic crash reconstruction. A task force of crash reconstructionists, engineers, police officers, educators, and attorneys met and developed a report entitled *Minimum Training Criteria for Police Traffic Crash Reconstructionists*. In that report, the task force addressed certification of individuals in the field and recommended that "a certification board be formed" to accredit crash investigators and reconstructionists.

Five years later, twelve professional crash reconstruction associations with world-wide representation met to explore the possibility of forming an internationally recognized accreditation program open to both police and civilian crash reconstructionists. The Accreditation Commission for Traffic Crash Reconstruction (ACTAR) was the result of

that coalition. The Governing Board of Directors, comprised of one representative from each participating association, has included police officers, engineers, educators, and private consultants all working in the field of traffic crash investigation and reconstruction within the United States and Canada.

ACTAR was founded by and exists for the benefit of the traffic crash investigation and reconstruction community, as represented by the membership of the participating professional organizations. The Commission has not been obligated to nor controlled by any governmental body or agency. Since its incorporation in 1992, it has been the ongoing goal of ACTAR to promote, within the legal and scientific community, a recognition of the minimum standards established by the NHTSA study, as well as those developed by an ongoing review of the latest technology and trends in the profession.

Minimum standards have been designed to advance the recognition of the ACTAR accreditation program, and in doing so, to encourage the integrity, consistency, and professionalism of those involved in traffic crash investigation and reconstruction; to promote the professional and intellectual development of those individuals, organizations, and institutions involved in traffic crash investigation and reconstruction; to assist the legal and scientific community in weighing the suitability of individuals offering their services as crash reconstructionists and to improve public awareness of the profession as it relates to the legal system.

By way of committee discussions of different aspects of crash investigation and reconstruction training programs, as well as review of other disciplines practicing in the field, the ACTAR Governing Board of Directors developed a formula for minimum training and experience requirements. Applying those minimum standards to a higher level of understanding and knowledge in the collision investigation and analysis field, the Governing Board of Directors created and refined a multi-part accreditation examination. That examination was reviewed by outside independent professionals in the testing field, as well as educators, to ensure an objective, clear, and thorough examination.

Although participation in the accreditation program is voluntary, people who are properly trained and experienced in crash investigation and reconstruction may successfully complete the examination and achieve accreditation. Those accredited must obtain a minimum number of continuing educational units (C.E.U.'s) over a five-year period from completion of the initial examination to maintain their status with ACTAR.

In addition to the many individual, well-defined, and clearly written professional codes of conduct that various investigative departments and reconstructionist organizations and associations have in place, of particular interest to the traffic crash reconstructionist profession is ACTAR. In general, the conduct rules of this organization require that all ACTAR certified traffic crash reconstructionists must be at all times honest, impartial, fair, and ethical in the service they provide. In the practice of this profession, all ACTAR certified traffic crash reconstructionists must conform to a standard of professional behavior which requires adherence to the highest principles on behalf of the public, clients, employers, and the profession. (For more information see http://www.actar.org/history.htm.)

REFERENCES

1. Rivers, R.W.: *Technical Traffic Accident Investigators's Manual.* Charles C Thomas, Publisher, Springfield, Illinois, 1997, pp. 3–17.
2. Baker, J. Stannard: *Traffic Accident Investigation Manual.* Traffic Institute, Northwestern University, Evanston, Illinois, 1975, p. 318.
3. Ibid., p. 319.
4. Abrahams, Bernard S.: Personal Communication (technical report) dated November 1, 1993.
5. Ibid.
6. Baker, J. Stannard: *Traffic Accident Investigation Manual.* Traffic Institute, Northwestern University, Evanston, Illinois, 1975, p. 318.
7. Navin, Francis P.D.: Personal Communication, 1999, and paper: *The Accuracy and Precision of Speed Estimates from Crash Reconstruction Data,* prepared for IPTM's Special Problems Seminar, May, 2000.
8. Navin, Francis P.D.: Personal Communication, 1999, and paper: *The Accuracy and Precision of Speed Estimates from Crash Reconstruction Data,* prepared for IPTM's Special Problems Seminar, May, 2000.
9. Ibid.
10. Patterson, G. (1991). *Significant Figures and Errors for Collision Reconstruction,* cited by Navin, Francis P.D., in: *The Accuracy and Precision of Speed Estimates from Crash Reconstruction Data,* prepared for IPTM's Special Problems Seminar, May, 2000.
11. O'Hara, Charles E. & O'Hara, Gregory L.: *Fundamentals of Criminal Investigation* (7th ed.), Charles C Thomas, Publisher, Springfield, Illinois, 2003, p. 533.
12. Chalk, R., Frankel, M.S. & Chafer, S.B.: *AAAS Professional Ethics Project.* American Association for the Advancement of Science, Washington, D.C., AAAS Publication 80-R-4, 2005.

RECOMMENDED READING

The following are sources referenced in developing this chapter and which are recommended for further reading and study:

Badger, Joseph E.: *Legal and Ethical Responsibilities of the Crash Reconstructionist.* Law and Order Magazine, Skokie, Illinois. October, 1990, Vol. 38, No. 10, pp. 15–16.

Baerwald, John E.C: *Traffic Engineers Handbook* (4th ed.), Part C: Institute of Traffic Transportation Engineers, Prentice Hall, Englewood Cliffs, New Jersey, 1992, pp. 445–447

Branton, J.L. & Lovett, J.D.: *California Depositions, Volume 1A, Trial Lawyers Series.* Knowles Law Book Publishing, Inc., Euless, Texas, 1984–1992.

Brown, J.F. & Obenski, K.S.: *Forensic Engineering Reconstruction of Crashes.* Charles C Thomas, Publisher, Springfield, Illinois, 1990.

Garcia, C.H. & Trucino, C.J.: *Admissibility of Crash Reconstruction Evidence.* Accident Reconstruction Journal, Waldorf, Maryland, Vol.5, No. 5., pp 24–27.

Garcia, C.H. & Trucino, C.J.: *Traffic Crash Reconstruction. Legal Issues in the 1990's.* Institute of Police Technology and Management, University of North Florida, Jacksonville, Florida, 1990.

Meriam, J.L.: *Statistics* (2nd ed.). John Wiley & Sons, New York, New York, 1975.

National Advisory Commission on Criminal Justice Standards and Goals: *Police.* Washington, D.C. January 23, 1973.

Rivers, R.W.: *Technical Traffic Accident Investigators' Handbook.* (2nd ed.), Charles C Thomas, Publisher, Springfield, Illinois, 1997.

Websters New Universal Unabridged Dictionary. Barnes and Noble Books, New York, and Outlook Book Co., Avenel, New Jersey, 1992.

Chapter 2

HUMAN ERROR AND TRAFFIC CRASH INVESTIGATION AND RECONSTRUCTION

MARTIN I. KURKE & ANNE M. CORBIN

THE TRAFFIC CRASH VIEWED AS A SYSTEM FAILURE

2.001 Traffic crash reconstructions are conducted to determine why and how a crash occurred. Results of crash investigations and reconstructions identifying the cause of the crash stimulate designers of vehicle components, the roadway environment, and traffic control devices and regulations to make changes that will improve automotive safety. Crash investigation/reconstruction information is also needed for the assignment of legal liability for any injury or property damage.

2.002 Because the law in many cases regarding traffic crashes demands to know the proximate cause of the crash, it often is convenient to identify the cause of a crash upon the failure of some mechanical or electrical component, poor road conditions, weather, flooding, excessive speed, inattention to road conditions, failure to yield right of way, or some other malfunction of the environment, equipment, or user of the equipment or the victim. In difficult or complex cases, the conclusion of crash investigations often are that the proximate cause of the crash is attributable to *human error*. Proximate cause is:

> . . . *that which in natural and continuous sequence unbroken by any new independent cause, produces an event, and without which, the injury would not have occurred. In criminal and tort law, one's **liability** is generally limited to results "proximately caused" by his conduct of omission.* (Gifis, 1975).

2.003 Too often, however, the inference in the legal doctrine of *proximate cause* is interpreted to mean that there is one critical overwhelming cause that led to a crash and injury. There is increasing recognition, however, that causation refers to a complex interrelationship between a multitude of factors or stimuli, and that reliance upon a single *proximate cause* (usually a recent event) oversimplifies and actually confuses the issue.

2.004 Psychologists and other behavioral scientists look at cause in a somewhat different light. They recognize that when a human being is involved in a crash, there are multiple antecedents. Each antecedent contributes unique quantitatively and qualitatively different influences upon the crash's occurrence and its consequences. They also recognize that virtually all such incidents involve one or more human beings as participants at the scene of the crash, or as a designer or maker of the automotive components, the road, or other operating environment. People operate, maintain, or repair the vehicle in its operational environment. They may also create and comply with or ignore automotive operating and maintenance procedures These procedures may have been dictated by the design of the vehicle or the roadway; or they may have been explicitly established by legal and law enforcement agencies.

Example

A truck driver is driving his rig in a snowstorm at night to make a delivery his employer says must get there by 6:00 a.m. and that his job is on the line if he fails to deliver on time. He has been driving without a break for 12 hours when a sign falls off a building smashing into the truck's windshield and virtually eliminates visibility. The driver tries to slow down, but a front tire blows and the vehicle strays beyond the marked, but now invisible lane markings. The vehicle is nearly brought under control, but driver cannot see the lane markings and the truck drives into a ditch at the side of the road. Despite the best efforts of the driver, the rig jackknifes and overturns, spilling volatile cargo on the road, and the driver suffers a heart attack while trapped in the cab. What is most likely to be designated as the proximate cause of this crash?

In this example, it is not too difficult to identify one or more causes, but naming them will neither identify the relative contribution of the causes, nor will it properly find a single blameworthy person or condition. There was no single component (not even a single human component) to blame. Often the actual cause of the crash was the cumulative effect of two or more minor errors or subsystem failures. Sometimes, that cumulative effect is greater than the simple sum of the consequences of the two or more of the contributing effects. On the other hand, even a critical error or subsystem failure that normally would result in a crash often is compensated for by well-working system elements—both automotive and human—which prevent the crash. Virtually without exception, the introduction of a human element in the design, maintenance operation of management of equipment creates a system with a potential for failure.

2.005 The terms *human error* and *operator error* are used in crash investigation reports as default terms when crash investigators cannot find any reason to point the finger at some demonstrable engineering malfunction such as metal fatigue or power outage in a system managed, operated, or maintained by people. Investigative reports on such incidents often infer that some operator or maintainer was inattentive, had poor training, or was indifferent to or incapable of performing properly. But as Ferguson (1992) pointed out, those terms often are grossly insulting to the person blamed. The human errors that caused the incident may have been caused by

decisions made by the designer of the equipment who, through negligence or ignorance, failed to take into account the inherent limitations of the one component the designer could not control, the people who operate or maintain it. Similarly, the operator or maintainer may not be at fault if that person followed procedures based upon improper training, or if the manager of his/her organization imposes performance requirements that cannot be met without high risk of serious degradation to the cognitive or motor skills and abilities required for safe operation of the equipment.

HUMAN RELIABILITY AND HUMAN ERROR

2.006 Despite its misleading use, the term human error remains useful (and misused) in assigning legal liability for a crash. If the nature of the human error is investigated, it may become possible to determine what should be done to prevent further occurrences of such crashes. There is little doubt that many traffic crashes are due to lapses of attention or other negligent behavior of drivers and other people at the scene of the crash. However, those lapses may very well have had their genesis in a poor match between the engineering design and the capabilities of one or more of the crash participants.

2.007 Some researchers (for example, Moray, 1994) consider crashes as system failures. We concur and agree that any crash must be considered as a system failure if it involves any single or combination of design deficits; operational and/or maintenance dysfunctions or malfunctions involving the interaction of people, equipment, and their social and physical driving environment, the engineering that bands them together; and the administrative (i.e., legal, and management generated), and operational procedures controlling their interactive processes.

2.008 A fruitful approach for crash investigators and reconstructionists is to consider the fact that a crash is the end point of a sequence of events in which selected human characteristics and capabilities are blended with the results of engineering compliance with the system's functional and operational requirements. Those requirements are translated into engineering standards and specifications. In turn, the standards and specifications form the

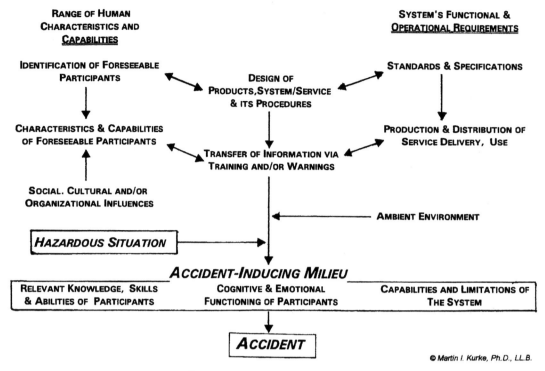

Figure 2–01. Etiology of a crash.

basis of engineering designs. Those designs should take into consideration the capabilities and limitations of the people who will manufacture, operate, and maintain the equipment. Sometimes the user population is definable by the characteristics of people selected to fill a particular job position; sometimes the user is defined by a segment of the general population. In the case of traffic crashes, the personal and demographic characteristics of automobile drivers and mechanics also must be considered.

2.009 Starting at the human capabilities side of the process (see Fig. 2–01), let us consider the particular set of individuals who are involved at the scene of the crash. Except for involuntary participants (often the crash victims), many crash participants (e.g., drivers, service personnel) have been selected or have self-selected themselves to become the users or maintainers of the equipment. Their selection occurred because they have personal characteristics that are compatible with the design, and they are believed to have performance reliability characteristics compatible (or potentially compatible) with

the equipment, its design, or procedures. The gap between the capabilities and other characteristics of people and the product (resulting from specifications and standards which, in turn, are derived from functional and operational requirements) occurs at two levels. The system, its components, and its operating and maintenance procedures are (or should be) designed to be compatible with the characteristics and capabilities of a foreseeable user or maintainer population. To ensure such compatibility, or to bridge lacks of capability, information about the hardware must be communicated to the users/maintainers by training, operational and maintenance manuals, display devices, safety information, and warnings. Many crashes occur because of failure of the information transfer function. Ineffective or deficient communications or failure to respond appropriately to such communications inhibit awareness of hazardous or potentially hazardous situations in time to take measures to avoid the crash or to mitigate its effects.

2.010 An crash-inducing milieu occurs when the engineering and performance development does not blend with the characteristics and capabilities of the people who must be elements of the designed system. In Figure 2–01, we note that both human and non-human components of the system interact to produce an *crash-inducing milieu* when faced with a hazardous situation. This crash-inducing milieu consists of the capabilities and limitations of the entire crash system, including all the participants, the vehicles, and the road; the physical and ambient environment which might include weather, illumination, road conditions–including distracting billboards and advertisements, traffic control signs hidden by foliage, etc. The people in the milieu include the driver, passengers, occupants of other vehicles, eyewitnesses, cyclists, and pedestrians at the scene of the crash. Each such person has an internal environment consisting of, among other things, cognitive and emotional levels of functioning, a set of functioning knowledge, skills and abilities, and an often bewildering array of social, cultural, family, work, and other organizational influences upon what has been perceived and done.

2.011 Thus, the crash which, upon initial investigation, appears to be caused by *human error* may have been made more likely to occur by an error made by the user/maintainer, trainer, or system designer– or by the negligent action of the victim.

LOOMING VULNERABILITY AND TRAFFIC CRASHES

2.012 A recently developed theoretical construct, called *looming vulnerability,* helps us to describe and understand the social, cognitive, organizational, and psychological mechanisms that are brought into play when a person becomes involved in a hazardous situation (Riskind, 1997, in press; Riskind & Williams, 2005). Looming occurs when a situation or object (real or imagined) is perceived as a threat whose dimensions of apparent magnitude, saliency, and intensity are perceived to increase over time. The process of looming is dynamic. It consists of quickly changing concurrent or near simultaneous assessments of the threat and assessment by means of avoiding or diminishing the threat. These processes are filtered through an individual's cognitive, affective, and emotional traits and states. The filtering leads to purposive behavior meant to reduce

the potential for harm to the actor as sensed by a reduction of the threat's apparent magnitude, saliency, and intensity–or its complete elimination. Looming can result in behavior that is a legitimate and appropriate response to the situation with which the person is faced. It also may result in the carrying out of an error laden decision.

2.013 Figure 2–02 presents a useful model of the role of looming in the decision to engage in behaviors that either may lead to or avoid a crash commences with the idea of human reliability (the tendency to avoid counterproductive behavior or error). Kurke (1995) categorizes human reliability into four domains, viz:

1. *Human personal performance ability conditions,* which include factors such as one's physical and mental health states and their dynamics, fatigue, alcoholic or other drug intoxication, ambient physical environment, interpersonal conflicts, personal stress and personal history factors which may include as appropriate to the situation, one's social, cultural, clinical, and legal history.

2. *Knowledge, skills, and abilities* of the parties involved in the crash. Limitations in human performance may result from inadequate knowledge and skills relevant to the tasks facing the individual. Inadequate knowledge and skill may result from: limitations on educability–inadequacy of acquired knowledge– lack of prior use of knowledge–insufficient degree of personal interaction with learning– inadequate compatibility with the organization requiring the knowledge or skill relevant to the job–poor skill potential–low level of prior proficiency–incompatibility with prior habits–infrequent of use of skills–awareness of skill deficiencies.

3. *Affiliative pressures.* Affiliations here refer to relevant work cultures and climates, as well as those arising from other affiliations such as one's family, peer groups, cultural ethos, and norms. Examples of dysfunctional organizational climate and attitudes that influence human reliability include: dysfunctional management and procedures–ignored performance–excellence discouraged or penalized–poor or indifferent performance encouraged–dysfunctional

How Looming Is Involved–The Model

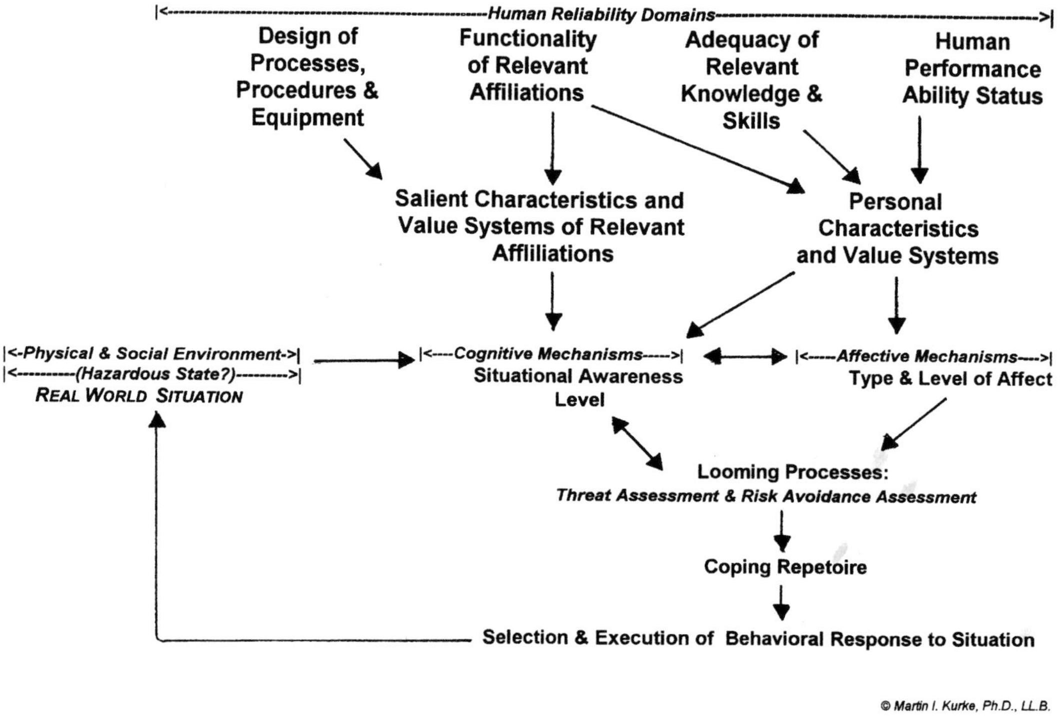

© Martin I. Kurke, Ph.D., LL.B.

Figure 2–02. The role of human reliability, cognition, and affect in coping with hazards.

leaders–goal conflicts–management insistence on maintenance of inefficient or counterproductive procedures. A dysfunctional organizational climate may induce pressure on a driver to make delivery deadlines without regard to safe driving requirements and traffic laws.

4. *Design, development, and implementation of equipment, processes, and procedures* (vehicles and their component parts, traffic control devices, road architecture, traffic flow control systems, traffic law enforcement systems, etc.).

2.014 These four domains shape the characteristics and value systems of individuals and the affiliations that influence their behavior under a variety of situational-specific conditions. They may be understood in terms of (or lack of) functional effectiveness of affective, cognitive, physiological, or social systems and situational factors. Looming, as a time-dynamic expression of affect and cognition peculiar to specific situations, is inherent in each reliability

domain. It then seeks expression in risk detection, assessment, and avoidance.

2.015 The four domains of human reliability and the value systems they engender shape and, in return, are shaped by both the individual and the traffic environment. As shown in Figure 2–02, the value systems and characteristics influence one's cognitive abilities–the ability to become aware of and appreciate hazardous situations while driving. Certain affective traits and states such as anxiety have been demonstrated to sensitize people to danger by enhancing their capability to loom, while other traits, such as depression, appear to be incompatible with looming (Riskind in press, 1997; Riskind & Williams, 2005). When an actual or an imagined threat appears, its perception (the risk the individual attributes to it) is shaped by the value systems generated by the work culture, working conditions, and organizational and other affiliative norms established and maintained by the affiliated organization's leadership in interaction with the threatened individual's traits, states, and value system. As the perceived situation and the anxiety level change in magnitude and intensity over time, the sense of looming vulnerability also changes. The looming process involves concurrent assessment of the changing risk and assessment of risk as they are shaped by cognitive and affective factors, which also shape and are shaped by job- or task-related stressors.

2.016 The risk avoidant options available may range from ignoring the situation when the perceived threat fades away or becomes non-threatening, to non-aggressive displacement behavior, to some form of non-violent aggression (screaming at an offending motorist), to inexcusable aggressive behavior expressed by dangerous driving behaviors, or even by physical assaults directed against another driver.

HUMAN ERROR AND RISK-TAKING

2.017 Some writers (e.g., Norman, 1981; Reason, 1990) have classified human error into the following three categories:

1. *Slip.* A *slip* is an error in carrying out a correct assessment of what needs to be done. Consider the case of a driver who runs a red light and strikes a child who ran into the crosswalk as soon as the lights changed. In this case, the driver had every intention of stopping for the red light, but pressed the accelerator pedal instead of the brake as he approached the intersection, ran the red light, and struck the child. The slip may have occurred as a consequence of insufficient training, failure to maintain skills, fatigue, health deficits, etc.

2. *Mistake.* A mistake is an objectively incorrect act resulting from a failure to form a correct intention. It results from failure of memory, inadequate training, or inadequate, unclear, or conflicting instructions. In this case, the driver saw an amber light, but believing he had plenty of time before it turned to red, did not apply the brake until the red light came on and he first saw the child in the crosswalk. However, it was too late and he struck the child.

3. *Violation.* A *violation* is a deliberate choice to behave in a non-standard or incorrect way, as when violating normal procedures. The violator who ignores both the amber and red lights to cross the intersection usually believes that the non-standard procedure provides a better chance of success (e.g., meeting a delivery schedule, or getting home sooner). Or, the violation may be an example of deliberate malice.

2.018 Because violation errors, and to a lesser extent mistakes, involve the process of looming, it is useful to understand the role of looming in such human error making. In the top tier of Figure 2–03, we posit three underlying conditions for looming during a hazardous situation. The *first* condition consists of the vehicle, roadway, traffic control system, and their procedures. The *second* condition for looming to occur is the participating party's experience under similar conditions. The greater the similarity between past experience and the current hazardous situation, and the greater the frequency of such similar experience, the stronger is its influence. The *third* condition consists of the personality structure of the participating party. Of particular concern are the individual's cognitive process, emotional effect, and history of risk-taking behavior.

2.019 The second tier illustrates the centrality of looming given the products of the first tier elements. Looming is fed by and in turn feeds awareness of hazards and risks. This situational awareness is, in turn, sensitized by the individual's history of similar experiences. The other inputs to situational awareness are cognitive impressions that are shaped by the design of the vehicles, roadway, traffic control system, traffic environment, and how well they are communicated to the individual by system and product design, procedural instructions, and warning displays.

2.020 While situational awareness is stimulated cognitively by and to the looming process, the latter also is influenced by and to the individual's level and type of effect. Looming is increased as anxiety level increases, and is suppressed by depressive states, both of which are, like risk-taking propensities, personal characteristics of the participating party.

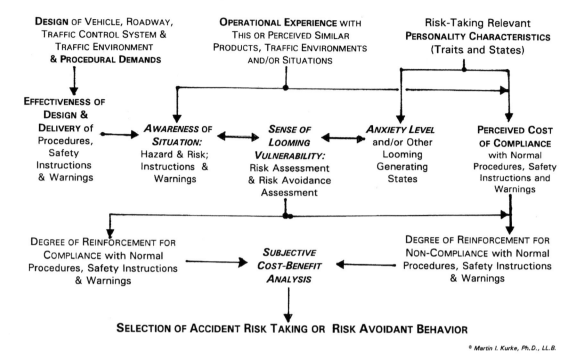

Figure 2–03. The role of looming in crash risk decision making.

2.021 However the sense of looming may be tempered by—or even fully countered by—a sense of perceived cost for not complying with the warnings and normal procedures. Real costs in dollars or in time (supported by impatience) may be a momentary cost that can be avoided by risky driving behaviors. These *costs* and other benefits for non-compliance are balanced by the costs and benefits of complying with normal procedures and safety instructions and warnings. A decision is made then whether or not to behave in a risk-taking or a risk-avoidant mode.

INVESTIGATING THE ROLE OF HUMAN ERROR IN TRAFFIC CRASH INVESTIGATION AND RECONSTRUCTION

2.022 A crash investigator or reconstructionist may have reason to suspect that a particular crash was due in part, or in whole to defective products, defective service delivery, and/or defective human performance and malpractice. The investigator should gather sufficient information to form an expert opinion as to whether the crash environment or the design of the product or procedures was a proximate cause of the crash (Kurke, 2005). The expert opinion may be derived from a forensic task analysis (FTA) that reconstructs the series of events leading up to the crash. The FTA and its follow-up activities seek answers to the following questions:

1. **What did the system, consisting of involved parties (victim, operator, service provider), product/equipment and crash environment, and the procedures to be followed "intend" to do prior to and during the crash?**

Answers to this question provide the baseline for additional questions pertinent to the investigation. A thorough answer to this question will identify each human and equipment and environment element that participated in the crash. Start at the actual time and point of impact, indicate their design objectives (or in the case of the human element, their intended) purpose during the series of events leading to the crash.

This question addresses the preliminary *intention* of each element of the system involved in the crash, i.e., involved humans (operator, victim, service provider, system managers, job supervisors, etc.) the relevant elements of the environment in which the crash occurred, the actual equipment or parts thereof, and the appropriate procedures meant to be followed under situations similar to that of the actual crash. Relevant inquiries might include questions to determine the primary (and secondary or peripheral) functions or purpose of each element of the system. Additional questions would determine the way those functions are performed. Such questions provide the investigator with an initial basis for comparison. If an operator uses a component in a way that does not coincide with its primary or peripheral purpose, such usage may be directly or indirectly responsible for the system's ultimate breakdown resulting in the crash.

2. **What did each element of the system "actually" do that led to the crash and its consequences?**

What deviations from the *intention* occurred? Was there any equipment failure, abnormality in the environment (e.g., unseeable potholes in an unlit road surface, etc.) or human failure to follow appropriate procedures such as excessive speeding, ignoring traffic control devices, failure to yield right of way, etc.

This set of questions regards the specific actions of each element. It is important to determine whether any specific actions directly or indirectly caused the system's ultimate breakdown and the resulting crash. The questions are important in establishing a match or mismatch between actual and intended activities. Comparing the two may reveal possible situations where misuse of one element may have hindered proper use of another. A related line of questions will inquire why the element was misused rather than used properly. The significance of this line of questioning can be understood if proper use of the element is impractical or inconvenient.

3. **Did the design of the equipment, working environment, procedures, training, and/or other safety information transfer procedures facilitate or inhibit the likelihood of the crash or the severity of its consequences? Did the product, procedures, environment,**

etc., **cooperate with the user or the user's personal characteristics to arrive at the crash? Was the crash an expectable consequence of the design?**

This question addresses whether particular elements somehow could have encouraged or discouraged the crash's chance of occurring. The design may have been faulty or inconvenient. The crash environment could have provided distractions or hindrance. The procedures could have been beyond human perceptual or performance capabilities. Training may have been inadequate. The operator, victim, or service provider's performance may have been influenced by alcohol, drugs, fatigue, age, or chronic ill health; or by transient conditions such as a fit of sneezing or a bee in the driver's compartment.

An additional factor that needs to be determined after determining what may have encouraged or discouraged the likelihood of a crash is whether that element is or is not *controllable*. After this has been established, an important issue to be examined is whether the controllable factors could have been manipulated to influence the likelihood of the crash. Alternatively, could the uncontrollable factors have been made more controllable? These questions touch upon the issue of foreseeability. Could (or should) the designer of any element of the vehicle or its operating environment have foreseen any consequence of the design that would have led to the crash? This question is salient to the issue of civil liability for damages resulting from the crash.

4. **What information (training, manuals, labels, warnings, traffic control signs, signals or other devices, etc.) was/was not available to the victim, operator or service provider that could have averted the crash and/or mitigated its consequences? Was there compliance with the training manuals, labels and/or warnings? If not, why?**

This set of questions focuses on potentially preventive information that may or may not have been available to the operator, victim, or service provider. Were they sufficient to create an awareness of hazards? Did the user comply with the available information? The investigator might ask what information was remembered. How was it presented? What remembered information was disregarded or not complied with? What reasons underlie having forgotten or disregarding the information? Answers to such questions are important in demonstrating what points in the information need to be emphasized in the design of warning information meant to increase situation awareness or a sense of looming vulnerability to the level that future crashes are more likely to be avoided under like circumstances.

5. **What did the designer of the product/equipment, crash environment, or procedures do to increase or reduce the likelihood of the crash and/or the severity of its consequences?**

This question centers upon the potential liability of the designer of product, equipment crash environment, or of their related procedures. It helps establish what, if anything, the designer did with those elements that encouraged or discouraged the likelihood of the crash, or of the severity of its consequences. The question focuses on whether the designer overlooked some important factors in regard to those elements that may have been in the chain of events leading to the crash. This is related to the foreseeability issue mentioned in Question 3. The designer may have underestimated or overestimated the severity of the consequences that led to the crash.

6. **When did the vehicle operator and/or the crash victim become aware of the imminence of the crash? What, if anything, did each person do to try to prevent or try to minimize the consequences (personal injury or property damage) of the crash?**

This addresses the temporal issue of the operator's or the victim's awareness of the crash's imminence. Could that person have been made aware of the impending crash any sooner? If so, would it have made a difference? This relates to what elements of the system are involved in relaying that information, and whether those components were intact, damaged, inoperable, or simply inadequate to elevate the operator's or the victim's situational awareness in time to attempt to prevent the crash or to ameliorate its

impact. At issue here is whether these variables are potentially able to be manipulated and, if so, *how* they can be manipulated.

7. **Did the victim, operator, or service provider have (or lack) any personal characteristics that materially increased or reduced the likelihood of the crash or its expected consequences? Should the designer have taken the likelihood of occurrence of such personal characteristics into account when designing the system?**

These questions relate to two of the human reliability domains discussed earlier in this lesson. They include (a) *personal performance conditions*, which include factors such as physical and mental health states and their dynamics, fatigue, ambient environment, interpersonal conflicts, personal stress, and personal history factors which may include as appropriate to the situation, social, cultural, clinical, and legal history; and (b), *knowledge, skills and abilities* of the parties involved in the crash. They relate to human error in both a distal and immediate temporal sense. They are important in establishing the person's background in terms of his/her history of dealing with frustrating or stressful events. When caught in a traffic jam, what kind of a person is more likely to blow the horn, or to nudge a person from behind? Driving and educational histories can serve to provide an idea of the person's cognitive level of functioning and ability. A person's mental or physical state around the time of the crash can help establish whether he/she is directly or indirectly responsible for the crash's occurrence. A drunk driver may have swerved into another lane too quickly to avoid being hit by a careful sober one following the rules of the road. On the other hand, in a similar car on a similar road, a pregnant woman may have felt the baby kick especially hard, or may be experiencing vertigo, and veered a bit.

8. **Did the crash and/or any of its consequences arise from any other deficit in any involved person's human reliability domain characteristics?**

This final question examines human error in a broader sense. Were there any other problems stemming from the humans' involvement in the system? Some car designs are bad fits for people due to faulty design, development, and implementation of equipment, processes, and procedures. Some people are bad fits for good car design. Some people are more aggressive drivers and dangerous to others. Some people have more crashes and in greater frequency than others. Some people habitually drive in such a manner that they cause others to have crashes. They may be nervous drivers who are prone to creating crashes in which they appear to be the victim.

2.023 All eight of the foregoing questions are essential to traffic crash investigation and reconstruction. They each address particular aspects of certain elements of the system that, alone or in concert, are potentially responsible for the crash's occurrence. Given answers to some or all of these questions may enable the investigator to arrive at conclusions as to (a) whether the product or the environment was unreasonably dangerous, (b) whether the crash was an expectable result of a preventable defect in the product, crash environment or vehicle operating procedures; and/or (c), whether either the vehicle operator or the victim was negligent, and whether such negligence was a proximal cause of the crash.

Human Factor Websites of Interest (Source: Rivers Traffic Consultants)

www.shiftlag.com
www.shiftwork.com
www.aaafts.org
www.bettersleep.org
www.sleepfoundation.org

www.circadian.com
www.drowsydriving.org
www.aaafoundation.org/project

REFERENCES

Ferguson, E.S.: How Engineers Lose Touch. *Invention and Technology*, 1992, Vol. 8,(No. 3), pp. 15–24.

Gifis, S.H.: *Law Dictionary*. Woodbury, New York, Barron's Educational Series, Inc., 1975.

Kurke, M.I.: Organizational Management of Stress and Human Reliability. In M.I. Kurke & E.M. Scrivner (Eds.), *Police Psychology into the 21st Century*, Hillsdale, New Jersey, Lawrence Erlbaum, 1995, pp. 391–416.

Kurke, M.I., & Gettys, V.S.: Human Factors Psychology for Law Enforcement. In M.I. Kurke & E.M. Scrivner (Eds.), *Police Psychology into the 21st Century*, Hillsdale, New Jersey, Lawrence Erlbaum, 1995, pp. 467–496.

Kurke, M.I.: A Human Factors View of Product Liability and Malpractice Litigation. In I.A. Noyes & W. Karwowski (Eds.), *Handbook of Human Factors in Litigation*, Boca Raton, Florida, CRC Press, 2005.

Norman, D.A.: Categorization of Action Slips. *Psychological Review*, 1981, Vol. 88, pp. 1–55.

Reason, J.: *Human Error*. Cambridge, UK, Cambridge University Press, 1990.

Riskind, J.H.: *Looming and Loss: Metaphors and Mechanisms in Emotional Dysfunction*, New York, Plenum Press (in press).

Riskind, J.H.: Looming Vulnerability and Threat: A Cognitive Paradigm for Anxiety. *Behaviour Research and Therapy*, 1997, Vol. 35, pp. 685–702.

Riskind, J.H., & Williams, N.L.: A Unique Vulnerability Common to all Anxiety Disorders: The Looming Cognitive Style. In L.B. Alloy & J.H. Riskind (Eds.), *Cognitive Vulnerability to Emotional Disorders*. Hillsdale, New Jersey, Lawrence Erlbaum, 2005.

Chapter 3

THE ROLE OF VISION, VISIBILITY, AND DISCERNIBILITY IN DRIVER PERFORMANCE AND TRAFFIC ACCIDENT RECONSTRUCTION

BERNARD S. ABRAMS, O.D.

INTRODUCTION

3.001 When a crash occurs, fault or cause must be established whether or not litigation results. In the give-and-take of the courtroom, the mind's camera, and its acuity, have been challenged to the point that it is not uncommonly the issue upon which the jury's decision turns.

3.002 What did the driver see? Precisely? And when? These are not easy-to-answer questions. Because much of the visual system functions automatically, without conscious or voluntary control of the brain, vision often is taken very much for granted. Consequently, most people don't think much about how or what they see.

3.003 When investigating a vehicular crash, an understanding of three major factors: (1) *vision,* (2) *visibility,* and (3) *discernibility,* is necessary to understand fully what happened and why. These must be given serious consideration by any investigator who wants to comprehend better what subtleties may well have impaired, impeded, or colored what the driver's mind registered through the eyes.

    a. *Vision,* simply defined, is the faculty of sight.
    b. *Visibility* is the fact, state, degree, or capability of being seen or detected. Visibility of an object depends upon physical factors such as lighting, size, luminance, and contrast.

    c. *Discernibility* results when a visible object is perceived by the driver at the brain level. It is only after what is seen reaches the cognition level that a driver realizes that action may have to be taken to avoid an object.

3.004 Courts have recognized the difference between visibility and discernibility. This can be found in the case of McFadden v. Elmer C. Breuer Transp. Co. (1952), 156 Ohio St. 430, 46 Ohio ops. 354, 103 N.E. 2d 385, where the Ohio Supreme Court cited the Pennsylvania Supreme Court, which had decided a case under Ohio law. There it wrote:

> *The Court stated that none of the cases revealed an intention to ascribe to the word "discernible" a fixed and rigid meaning applicable to every possible situation. The word "discernible" ordinarily implies something more than "visible." "Visible" means perceivable by the* **eye** *whereas "discernible" means* **mentally** *perceptible or distinguishable–capable of being "discerned" by the* **understanding** *and not merely by the senses.*

3.005 Whether it is an automobile on the highway, a motorcycle, or a person, a vehicle operator can only *discern* that there is something (an object) on the highway which requires his/her attention when certain visual and human factors criteria are satisfied by the stimulus given off by that object.

3.006 All *discernibility*–the point where an object can be discriminated and identified–involves human subjective judgement.

3.007 A driver's reaction to a stress situation or a hazard is a four-step process known as the perception-reaction time. It is a process that takes time and requires:

1. Detection
2. Identification
3. Recognition (before it can or cannot be perceived as a danger)
4. A reaction message sent to the muscular skeleton system.

These four steps lead from visibility on the photographic plate of the eye to discernibility at the mentally perceptible brain level, all of which take time. It is only after these four steps have occurred that a maneuver, such as braking, can occur. This process, in turn, can be affected by physiological, external, and environmental factors, as we will discuss later in this part. It also can be affected by a person's emotional state.

3.008 Visual perception, as you can see, is the final outcome of a long chain of events and is directly dependent upon brain activity. To understand vision, visibility, and discernibility, an investigator must first understand how the eye works and how it interacts with the brain.

THE EYES AND HOW THEY FUNCTION

3.009 The eyes, essentially, are image-catching devices, channels of vision that run to the brain. In the end, it is the brain that sees.

3.010 The light entering the eye brings with it crucial image information it has picked up by touching or passing though objects in the field of vision. In a purely mechanical sense, the eye is an instrument that gathers light rays and focuses them into an image registered on its rear surface. The light enters the eye through the *cornea*, a tough, transparent membrane at the front of the eye. Because the convex shape of the cornea is much like that of a camera lens, it tends to bend light rays together. The next tissue structure behind the cornea is the

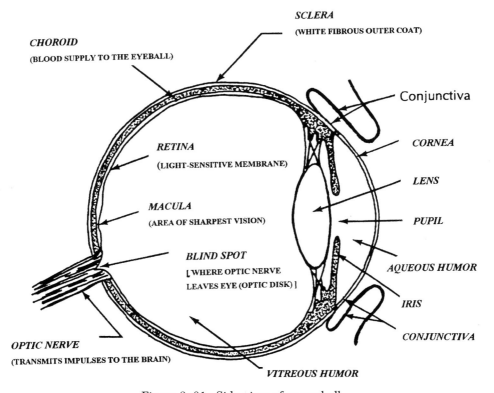

Figure 3–01. Side view of an eyeball.

iris. The iris functions much like a diaphragm in a camera, a spillway in a dam. It regulates the amount of light permitted to enter the eye depending upon how much is needed for visual imprinting. The small circular hole in the middle of the iris is the *pupil.* Turn your eye toward the sun and the iris will constrict to reduce the amount of light entering the eye. Walk from the bright outdoors into a darkened room and it will dilate to gather as much light as possible.

3.011 Light passes through the pupil and into the lens, the purpose of which is to make sure that the light focuses precisely on the *retina.* The retina is the anatomical equivalent of the film in a camera. It is a light-sensitive layer located at the back of the eye. Its photo-sensitive cells translate light energy into images which then become signals carried to the brain by the *optic nerve.*

Night and Day = Rods and Cones

3.012 Of all the elements of visual anatomy thus far discussed, the most crucial in terms of day/night vision are the photo-sensitive cells at the back of the retina. These cells are of two types: *rods* and *cones,* named so because of their respective shapes. The cones require more light to stimulate them; whereas the rods are stimulated in very low light intensity. Cones are used for day or brightly illuminated conditions, and rods are used in low light or night illuminations.

3.013 Both rods and cones contain chemicals which, when excited or stimulated by light, become altered. The alteration of the chemicals marks the transition from light to electrical potentials which traverse the nerves to the brain. The cones have the keenest signal and also possess the light-sensitive pigments that make it possible for us to see things in color. Rod cells are what we use to see at night. Incapable of detecting color, they typically register only black and white, and the images that we form from them tend to be fuzzier and indistinct.

3.014 Then why, you might ask, do we see a well-lit overhead interstate sign at night as both distinct and obviously green if the rods register only black and white? The freeway sign—either through illumination or reflection—imitates daytime conditions and is thus registered by the cones. By contrast, the

dark-clad pedestrian who darts onto an unlit road at night will be seen only in shades of gray, if seen at all. That hazy, ethereal quality of images at twilight occurs because our visual rods are taking over for the cones.

3.015 Some 130 million rods and cones plus their nerve fibers and supporting structures comprise the retina of the eye. The nerve fibers exit the eye collectively, forming a large bundle of nerve fibers (with no rods or cones) as the optic disc. It is more popularly known in lay terminology as our *blind spot.*

The Visual Field

3.016 Additionally, the foveal region of the retina (corresponding to the central 1–2 degree of the visual field) contains exclusively cones; the periphery (corresponding to the remainder of the visual field) contains exclusively rods. The fovea and periphery vary in their capabilities in terms of detection. Those differences depend on light conditions. The foveal region is most efficient for object identification, motion perception, and color discrimination. However, because the fovea is so small, the chances are higher that an object's image will fall on the periphery rather than on the fovea. In general, detection (monitoring) takes place in the periphery due to its size, while identification takes place in the fovea, due to its efficiency. Due to the large size of the periphery, detection can take place in several parts of the periphery simultaneously. Since identification by the brain is a serial process, there is a potential for a bottleneck, with detected objects "competing" for foveal attention in order to be identified.

3.017 There is believed to be a peripheral filter which passes to the fovea only objects of importance for foveal fixation or identification. Studies indicate that peripheral objects that have high information content, high contrast (luminance), flicker, motion, or large size will take priority.

3.018 *Peripheral vision.* For peripheral vision when both eyes are focused forward, the normal driver can see horizontally objects 90 degrees or more to each side and vertically 70 degrees up, 80 degrees down. These objects, however, are without clear detail or color. This peripheral area is sensitive to motion and brightness and serves the driver with a warning capability.

THE BRAIN AND VISION

3.019 Before seeing is possible, a new form of energy, called a nerve impulse, must relay the image message from the eye to the brain along the pathway of the optic nerve. It is with the dark confines of the skull where vision and discernibility are created. As stated earlier, visual perception is the final outcome of a long chain of events and is directly dependent upon the brain activity itself. Eye movements constantly feed bits of information to the brain. When perceptions take on meanings or understanding, cognitive functions of the brain elevate vision to one of the least understood parts of the human mind. The brain handles information very rapidly, but it handles it serially, one thing at a time. In other words, people can typically concentrate on only one thing at a time. However, humans have the ability to rapidly switch from one item of information to another if they wish to do so, and do it quickly.

3.020 Since, as explained earlier, new information is more likely to appear in the periphery, where it is less well seen, it must be strong enough or sufficiently conspicuous enough to capture the attention of a person whose thoughts might quite possibly otherwise be occupied. In motor vehicle operation at night, the time available for this attention-getting process to happen is typically fairly short.

3.021 Fortunately, there is a mechanism, sometimes called the *peripheral filter*, that determines what will come to the attention of the observer. While the way in which the filter works is not understood, the types of stimuli that are likely to pass it on result in a foveal fixation are known. In general, the eye is attracted toward areas that contain a great deal of information, such as:

  a. Concentrations of signs, lights, people, etc.
  b. Objects that differ greatly from their backgrounds in terms of brightness, color, texture, etc.
  c. Objects that are moving.

3.022 *Conspicuity.* Most people would probably agree that the characteristics listed are those that make something *conspicuous. Conspicuity* can be defined as the characteristics of an object that determine the likelihood that it will come to the attention of an observer. The fact that something may be present in the visual field does not necessarily mean that it will be detected, because it may have less conspicuity than other features in the visual field. This is especially true in areas where there is a great deal of information available.

Example

In an urban center, particularly at night, not only is there much to be concerned with (e.g., vehicles and pedestrians, advertising, and various signs and signals), but it would not be unusual for the most conspicuous features of the environment to be something like advertising signs, which are, at best, irrelevant to the driving task.

3.023 Reaction to stress situations, such as a sudden peril, is largely under the control of the brain, yet we do not know what goes on inside the brain when it is responding to stress. Consequently, regardless of time, no one can predict how any individual brain will react to any particular stress situation.

DAY EYE vs. NIGHT EYE

3.024 One of the most fundamental realities of visual anatomy is the fact that the human body has two sets of eyes. This fact often, however, goes unrecognized by traffic engineers, the courts, and crash investigators. The disproportionately greater number of U.S. traffic fatalities and injuries that occur at night is a good indicator of this fact. The death rate per miles driven is at least three times higher at night than in the daytime. Even though there is less traffic on the road at night, one-third of all motor vehicle crashes occurs between midnight and dawn. The toll of night crashes in lives lost, medical expenses, and property damage is staggering.

3.025 An understanding of how vision changes as day moves from light to dusk to dark is an essential element to consider when investigating crashes. Think about the eye's reaction upon moving from a sunlit afternoon into a darkened theater or a highway tunnel. It takes a full 30 minutes of dim light for the eye to reach the peak of its nighttime acuity. Even under the best of circumstances, the eyes require time to adjust. This adjustment is further compounded when the eye must compensate limited vision and sight impairments, along with the effects of drugs or alcohol. Too, simple aging diminishes the ability of the eye to adjust to darkness.

3.026 As you have already learned, day (photopic) vision is distinctly different from night (scotopic) vision. Functionally, we have two sets of eyes–one pair for daytime and quite another for nighttime. By understanding the two types of receptors–cones and rods–and the difference in their abilities to be stimulated by varying light intensities, it is easy to grasp the concept of *day eyes* and *night eyes*. There exists a vast disparity in their acuity and sensitivity, their speed of recognition, and their depth perception. The response characteristics of the rods and cones, and their distribution in the retina have implications for visual performance. The driver who may have 20/40 vision during the day (the minimum legal standard for operating a motor vehicle in most states) will generally have no better than 20/100 vision at night. Depending upon weather conditions and levels of illumination, the 20/40 daytime driver could have his vision reduced by as much as 90 percent at night.

Photopic Vision–The Day Eye

3.027 Daytime vision is mediated essentially or exclusively by cones. It is generally associated with adaptation to a luminance of at least 3.4 candelas per square meter. With our daytime (photopic) vision, we see best near the center or fovea, of that photographic film we call the retina. The quality of vision falls off very rapidly as one moves away from the fovea. For example, in daylight, a person's acuity for objects imaged at just five degrees from the fovea will be about 20/60. Because the fovea is so small relative to the entire visual field, detection typically occurs in the periphery. The eyes may then be shifted to bring the detected object into sharper focus in the fovea as part of the identification process. However, in order to be detected, an object in the periphery must be much more conspicuous than if its image had fallen on the fovea itself.

Scotopic Vision–The Night Eye

3.028 Nighttime vision is mediated essentially by rods. It is generally associated with adaptation to a luminance below 0.034 candelas per square meter. Our night driving is generally done under mesopic conditions, which is vision with fully adapted eyes at luminance conditions between those of photopic and scotopic vision, that is, between about 3.4 and .034 candelas per square meter.

3.029 With our nighttime (scotopic) vision, we see best at the periphery or near the edges of our film. Consequently, if we were standing watch on a ship at night, we could see the threatening periscope of a submarine in the distance better by not looking directly at it, but rather training the eye a little above or below the horizon. To prove this, find a sharply visible star in the sky and look directly at it. You will find that if you shift your vision slightly to either side of it, it will appear brighter.

3.030 One common error investigators make is attempting to estimate nighttime detection distances based on foveal inspection of the scene. *It must be stressed that there are no devices which can objectively measure night visibility with sufficient reliability.*

OTHER COMPONENTS OF VISION

3.031 We have talked about vision generally as a single sensory function. In fact, there are several components of vision that collectively form what we see and how well we see it. These include visual acuity, field of vision, contrast sensitivity, and adaptation. All of the components of vision are subject to performance changes by aging or illness. All of the components of vision are subject to performance changes by external forces such as glare, alcohol, drugs (prescription or illegal), smoking, and youth.

Visual Acuity

3.032 Visual acuity is the most common, quite simply, the clarity and sharpness with which we are able to imprint images on the retina. To use the camera analogy, good visual acuity is a well-focused lens on a very sensitive film.

Field of Vision

3.033 Our field of vision will determine much about our ability to see and react. When we drive, the brain is preoccupied with tracking and object avoidance directly in front of the car, reducing the breadth of our field of vision. The eyes of a driver with a limited field of vision may not register and send information when a child darts onto the road from a space on the periphery of sight.

Depth Perception

3.034 How accurately do we perceive the distance of objects before our visual field? Without strong depth perception, the eye sends faulty information to the brain, and the brain will respond accordingly, sometimes ignoring or misperceiving a true peril.

Contrast Sensitivity

3.035 Our vision is also shaped by our contrast sensitivity. How well do we see dark objects against light backgrounds? How well do we see light against dark? As day becomes night, our contrast sensitivity diminishes accordingly. A vehicle or pedestrian framed against a daytime sky may pose no problem, but at night, it is another matter altogether. Contrast sensitivity refers to how the eye responds to characteristics of an object that cause it to appear different or separate from something else.

3.036 Under daylight levels of illumination, there are a variety of forms or contrast available (color, texture, brightness, etc.). The visual system operates at its highest level of sensitivity during daylight and has the greatest capability of distinguishing differences between objects in the visual field. At night, however, the visual system has a reduced capability for distinguishing differences between objects in the visual field. Brightness contrast is generally the only form of contrast of any consequence. Thus, in order to be seen at night, objects must be sufficiently brighter or darker than their backgrounds.

Adaptation

3.037 Adaptation is one of the most critical components of vision when it comes to night driving.

We have discussed previously the fact that the eye requires time to accommodate itself to the change of moving from light to dark. But with the passage of time, the eye gradually loses its capacity for light transmission. Aging prevents the retina from taking optimum advantage of available light. Pupil size diminishes. Our adaptation speed slows. In some of us, it begins to lose its speed when we are yet in our twenties.

TESTS OF VISUAL PERFORMANCE

Visual Acuity

3.038 The measure of visual performance with which most people are familiar is *static acuity*. Static acuity is a measure of the ability to distinguish fine detail in a stationary target with high luminance contrast. *Visual acuity* is generally measured by *Snellen fractions* and contrast sensitivity. It is expressed by the Snellen fraction, such as 20/15, 20/20, 20/30, etc. The numerator of the fraction tells how far the individual was from the letters which he was able to read. In most examinations, the individual is 20 feet from the letters. Thus, the numerator of the Snellen fraction is usually 20. The denominator tells the distance which the letter must be from the eye in order to produce a visual angle. A visual acuity of 20/40, therefore, means that, while the person was 20 feet from the letter, the letter could produce a visual angle of five minutes when it was 40 feet distant. Thus, the visual acuity of 20/40 is approximately half the normal amount. The usual chart used for measuring visual acuity is called the *Snellen chart*. It consists of a series of letters, with each series of a different size.

3.039 It has been found that the average individual can make out the details of a letter sufficiently to detect what the letter is, when the visual angle produced by the letter is approximately five minutes. Various size letters or objects can be placed at various distances, each of which will produce the same visual angle, and the same size retinal image. The individual who can distinguish the details for the smallest size retinal image has the best acuity. Thus, visual acuity is the inverse of the visual angle size, and if a person needs a visual angle of ten minutes instead of five, his acuity is only half the norm.

3.040 Having 20/20 vision does not mean *perfect vision* as many people often claim. A score of 20/40, which is sometimes set as the lower limit of acuity for a driver's license, means that the person being tested can only resolve fine detail as well at 20 feet as can the standard observer at 40 feet. This means that a person with an acuity of 20/40 can read a highway sign at only half the distance of someone with an acuity of 20/20.

Contrast Sensitivity

3.041 Contrast sensitivity testing uses automated variable-contrast sine waves to evaluate fundamental visual function. A person normally needs relative high contrast to detect low- and high-frequency gratings which correspond to broad shadings and fine detail respectively, whereas relatively low contrast is needed to see medium-frequency gratings. Simply put, the contrast of the sine wave grating is gradually altered so that the operator can find out how much contrast the subject needs to see the bands of the grating.

PERCEPTION: A FOUR-STEP REACTION PROCESS

3.042 As mentioned earlier, a driver's reaction to a stress situation or a hazard is a four-step process and it is a process that takes time. The time which is now accepted in road sight design is 2.5 seconds for the average driver in daytime. The time required for a response equals the time it takes for the driver to recognize the situation, understand the situation, decide to take action, and take action. Or put more simply:

1. *Detection or information*, which is based on *visibility*, is the visual awareness that an object is present in the roadway. At night, it depends entirely on contrast sensitivity.
2. *Identification* is the process of gathering information about the object until enough information is gathered for the driver to make an appropriate decision as to what it is, whether it poses a threat, and whether its existence calls for some responsive action.
3. *Decision* is the next step and this involves the driver making a choice as to the appropriate action to take to avoid the object or condition.

4. *Response* occurs when orders are issued by the driver's brain to the appropriate muscle groups in order to initiate the responsive action decided upon.

3.043 A key point is that these are four different processes and there is no guarantee that correct identification or discernment will automatically follow detection–or that, upon detection, the driver will choose and execute the proper response. A failure in any one of the processes can result in tragedy.

3.044 Existing tables and charts of reaction times based on alerted studies are relevant only as generalities. The brain can be fooled by optical illusions, misinterpretations, and errors in visual performance in non-alerted situations. Every situation must be evaluated on its own characteristics. Take, for example, the task of braking to avoid an unexpected object in the road on a dark night. Once an object in the path becomes apparent or can be seen, the driver must detect and identify the object, discern it as a hazard, lift his foot from the accelerator, and push the brake pedal. Most studies indicate that for the average driver, the minimum perception/reaction time alone is 2.5 seconds. In the real world, however, older drivers operating their vehicles at normal speeds for night driving with low beams cannot effect a controlled safe stop in less than 3.5 seconds. Also, it should be noted that recent research shows advance warning distances may be twice as long as previously determined for the aging driver.

3.045 The study conducted by BioTechnology (an independent human factors research laboratory in Falls Church, Virginia) for the Federal Highway Administration shattered existing concepts about how far in advance a driver needs to recognize a hazard and perform the driving maneuver necessary to avoid the hazard. Traffic experts believed that the stopping distance on dry pavement at 60 mph (96 km/h) was 650 ft (198 m) for a typical automobile and driver. This remains a credible figure–for the vehicle. However, BioTechnology tests illustrated that the decision-sight distance may be closer to 1,275 ft (388 m). This means that the actual total distance from the moment the driver sees a traffic sign or hazard to the completion of the required response maneuver is far greater than was previously indicated. Decision distances go beyond physical reaction times. They are based on the number of seconds it takes the driver to see and recognize a hazard, decide on what action to take, initiate that action, and complete the maneuver. Decision distances and times are affected by many factors–age, eyesight, nighttime vision, type of personality (decisive v. indecisive), blood alcohol level, fatigue, and so on.

3.046 The implications of the study by BioTechnology are clear. In urban areas, where it often is not practical to place a *stop ahead* or other warning sign at a sufficient distance from a hazard or intersection, a high-intensity sign face may be the only way in which to alert drivers early enough to allow for varied decision times. Visibility of road features is important on all roads, but on country roads, 60 to 80 percent of all crashes are single-vehicle crashes. A large share could be avoided by more detailed brightness of their delineations. Failure to give the necessary visual cues by improper, inadequate, or low-performance products is a solvable problem.

FACTORS THAT CAN AFFECT VISION

3.047 Vision and driving are affected in subtle and profound ways by three elements: (1) physiological factors, (2) external factors, and (3) environmental factors.

Physiological Factors

3.048 The eyes are only the peripheral appendages of the visual system. Vision and discernability, as explained above, both depend primarily upon the functioning of the eyes and their interaction with the brain, but these can be affected by such things as age, health, physical condition, emotional status–and even by the time of day. One of the key physiological factors is that the human body has two different pairs of eyes–as explained previously–one for daytime vision and quite a different pair for seeing at night.

3.049 *Color blindness* is a situation where an individual cannot or has difficulty in distinguishing some colors, usually red and green. Color blindness may be a factor in crashes or violations involving traffic-control lights. Eight-nine percent of males show some defect.

3.050 *Age* can be a factor. The youthful driver comprises a disproportionate percentage of nighttime traffic. New to driving, he is still learning about speed, reaction time, and object avoidance. He has more crashes at night than older, more experienced drivers. In states where driver curfews for younger motorists are now the law, traffic fatalities among young drivers have been reduced from 10 to 30 percent. The number of older drivers is increasing. As we age, the risks of being in auto crashes and of serious injuries from them, rise sharply.

3.051 Loss of night vision is common to everyone. No driver can see as well at night as in the day, not even persons with 20/20 vision. One's ability to perceive a pedestrian or a potential road hazard on an unlighted or poorly lighted road may begin to decline when a person is in his/her twenties. As age increases, the speed with which the eye accommodates itself to darkness conditions decreases. By the time one is 50 or so, night vision will be greatly reduced. This makes driving even more difficult where light conditions are changing rapidly.

3.052 *Alcohol* can be a factor. It slows adaptation (a drinking driver takes longer to accommodate glare). It slows the visual imprinting process, the speed with which the optic nerve carries messages to the brain. And, of course, it slows the brain's interpretation and reaction to road hazards. It is conservatively estimated that one driver in six on the road late at night, particularly on the weekend, is alcohol impaired to some extent.

3.053 *Drugs* also impede vision–whether they are prescription or illegal. Consider simply how many prescriptions and over-the-counter medications warn of side effects and caution against operating a motor vehicle.

External Factors

3.054 A *tinted* or *dirty windshield* will dramatically reduce acuity, denying the eye the light it needs to clearly distinguish and interpret objects. *Glare* becomes a serious problem. The vehicle cresting a hill directly in front of us with bright beams on will blind us temporarily and cause us to shift our vision to the berm or center lane to do our visual tracking. *Smoking* affects driving in two ways: First, it creates a film of tar and nicotine on the windshield that reduces the amount of light that can be transmitted through it. Second, the simple act of smoking in a car involves a number of procedures that temporarily distract a driver from the visual tracking of the road in front of him/her.

3.055 *Distractions* also can include such things as using cellular telephones, inserting audio tapes into a tape player, tuning a radio, arguing with a passenger, children acting out, etc.

Environmental Factors

3.056 *Lighting.* How effective are headlights? Most headlights manufactured today begin losing their optimal candle power as soon as we drive that new car off the lot. How clean are they? What was the weather like? How did it affect visibility? How well is the roadway lit? Although there is far more traffic on well-lit interstates, the great majority of night crashes occur on smaller, less-traveled roads, which are typically unlit.

3.057 *Clothing* is a factor, and often a cause, in pedestrian deaths. Despite the fact that retro-reflective items of clothing are available (arm bands, vests, etc.), they are not utilized as much as they could be.

3.058 *Highways.* Poor roads and bridges play a major part in raising death and injury rates on rural roads. By poor roads, I include their physical condition, striping, signs, and signals. Today's high technology automobiles are having to make do with a road system created for earlier means of transportation and generally not intended for use by motor vehicles. The courts of the land are now saying that if the roads are not safe, the government which maintains those roads may be responsible. Thus visibility of road features may become of major importance in crash investigation.

CONCLUSION

3.059 It becomes obvious that "*What did you see?*" does not provide simple solutions to an crash. Any crash investigation should include a comprehensive probing of all the visual elements, especially nighttime crashes, including all of the *physiological, external,* and *environmental* factors that may have been affecting the person(s) involved at the time of the crash. It is essential that the role of *vision, visibility,* and *discernability* in driver performance must be considered and explored during any traffic crash investigation or reconstruction process.

Chapter 4

Part 1

PATHOLOGY AND ACCIDENT RECONSTRUCTION

JAMES A. J. FERRIS

INTRODUCTION

4.001 This chapter will deal with the role of the pathologist in traffic crash investigation and reconstruction and in particular with the nature of the information that the pathologist and the crash investigator require in order to properly interpret the postmortem findings. The type of information that should be made available to the pathologist prior to his postmortem examination can be divided into four broad categories:

1. The dynamics of the crash including the nature and extent of vehicle damage.
2. The location of the victims (if known) before and after the crash sequence.
3. The medical condition of the victims at the scene and on admission to hospital.
4. Any prior medical history and/or drug treatment (see Figs. 4–01 and 4–02).

DYNAMICS OF CRASH INJURY

4.002 In most vehicular crashes there is not only damage to the structure of the vehicles involved, but there will be injuries to the occupants of these vehicles. In the case of pedestrians, injuries may be sustained with little or no evidence of damage to the vehicle involved. Just as the nature and extent of vehicular damage will be determined by the strength and direction of the impact forces, the human body will be directly affected by such dynamic forces and the nature and distribution of injuries sustained can be correlated with the vehicle damage. For the purposes of reconstruction, the human body should be considered as an integral part of the damage sustained in the accident and the injuries interpreted within the context of the entire accident sequence. The pathologist should be provided with the following information:

1. Estimation of speed of impact.
2. Direction of impact forces, ie., head-on collision, side impact, rear-end impact, did the vehicle rotate and in which direction, did the vehicle roll over?
3. Evidence of internal body impact damage, i.e., is there deformity of the steering wheel or dash panel, head strike damage to the windshield, seats displaced from their mounts, blood or hair on interior fabric, which windows are broken, is there impact damage to the controls or instrument switches, is the rear view mirror damaged or displaced?
4. Evidence of impact with some part of the vehicle which could leave an identifiable patterned injury on the body, i.e., the dash grab handle on a Volkswagen Beetle.
5. Were seat belts worn and are they damaged? Were air bags deployed?
6. If a cyclist or motorcyclist, was a helmet worn and what type.

LOCATION OF VICTIMS AT SCENE

4.003 Although by examination of the injuries alone, the pathologist may be able to determine the position of the victims of a crash prior to impact, it is probably much better to indicate to the pathologist the possible positions of the victims and then to rely on the postmortem examination to confirm or refute the evidence. Pathologists will have varying degrees of expertise and experience in crash injury interpretation and performing this element of crash reconstruction as a collaborative effort with the primary investigator will be more rewarding. This means that the person attending the postmortem examination should have firsthand knowledge of the crash and should if possible be able to explain the crash scene by photographs and diagrams. It is inappropriate for the pathologist to be expected to conduct the postmortem without access to this type of firsthand information.

4.004 The location of crash victims can be categorized as follows:

1. The driver
2. Passenger; front-seat, rear-seat (right or left)
3. Occupant but position not determined
4. Known occupant ejected from vehicle
5. Pedestrian
6. Motorcyclist, motorcycle passenger, or cyclist
7. Unknown, body outside vehicle but apparently related to the accident

MEDICAL CONDITION FOLLOWING THE CRASH

4.005 Although this chapter deals primarily with the role of the pathologist in the investigation of victims killed in vehicular crash, vital information can be derived from the analysis of injuries sustained by crash survivors. Proper interpretation of the findings in fatal cases will often require that the postmortem findings be interpreted in conjunction with an analysis of the injuries of the non-fatal cases. When the investigator attends a postmortem examination following a vehicular crash, details of the injuries of the non-fatal cases should be provided to the pathologist. Information concerning the medical condition of all the victims following the crash can be obtained from emergency response personnel including the ambulance and fire crews. The value of the observations of untrained witnesses may be of great value but should be treated with caution.

4.006 The initial assessment of crash victims in the emergency room and their records of treatment in the first 48 hours may also provide valuable information about injuries sustained. Subsequent medical information will be of significance to the pathologist in fatal cases but is unlikely to add greatly to the assessment of the manner and mechanism of injury in non-fatal cases.

4.007 The following injury and medical information should be obtained from witnesses and from the medical records:

1. Speed of loss of consciousness
2. Duration of loss of consciousness
3. Time of death including the time interval between crash and death
4. Description of external injuries
5. Location and site of fractures

PRIOR MEDICAL HISTORY

4.008 The health of an accident victim before, during, and after the crash sequence may have a very significant influence on the results of crash reconstruction. Natural disease or drugs, either prescription or non-prescription, may affect a crash in one of three crash phases:

1. Pre-crash phase
2. Intra-crash phase
3. Post-crash phase

4.009 In the *pre-crash phase*, any disease or drug which is capable of altering the skills and/or the perceptions of the driver may be directly causative. For example, coronary artery disease is not only capable of causing sudden death, but can cause sudden collapse or fainting prior to a crash. Other forms of heart disease such as heart valve disease may also be significant. This means that any history of chest pain, indigestion, pain in the arms, or fainting may be significant indicators of potential crash causing heart disease. The following is a list of some of the diseases which may be of causative significance:

a. Diseases of the heart and blood vessels
b. Abnormalities of heart rhythm including pacemakers
c. Hypertension
d. Heart valve disease
e. Epilepsy
f. Diabetes and/or insulin therapy
g. Mental disorders and severe emotional distress

4.010 Not only alcohol and the common drugs of addiction are important to identify as potential causes of crashes, but many prescription drugs may alter an individual's reflexes, response time, and even level of consciousness.

Drunkenness or intoxication of the passengers may divert the attention of the vehicle operator and an intoxicated passenger may physically interfere with the operation of the vehicle. Many common "over-the-counter" drugs such as cold remedies and cough medicines contain antihistamines and any history which might indicate the use of such substances should be sought. Toxicological analysis is time consuming and very expensive and it is helpful to the toxicologist to be able to target the laboratory analysis at specific drugs or groups of drugs.

4.011 During the *intra-crash phase*, the presence of disease or drugs may render the operator of the vehicle incapable of responding appropriately to a potential crash situation and thus convert a harmless incident into an injury-producing situation. For example, drugs and/or alcohol may prevent a driver taking appropriate avoiding action and the response and reaction time may be sufficiently prolonged to make an avoiding action impossible. A driver who is hypertensive may have his blood pressure suddenly elevated during such a crash phase and as a result may suffer a stroke or cerebral hemorrhage and thus convert a minor incident into a potentially fatal crash. A driver who is physically disabled may not be able to operate the controls with sufficient speed or strength to avoid a crash.

4.012 In the *post-crash phase*, pre-existing medical conditions may result in a change in the nature and effect of injuries and may have serious if not fatal consequences to an individual with heart disease or almost any other significant medical condition. Orthopedic conditions such as cervical disc lesions and previous injuries may be aggravated by the impact forces sustained in a crash. Examples of previous apparently minor spinal injuries which have been aggravated to the point of paralysis and even death have been reported and the aggravation of old injuries is a major medical-legal issue.

INTERPRETATION OF INJURIES

4.013 Since the nature and extent of injuries is an integral part of the crash reconstruction process, it is important for the investigator to know not only the definition of the terms used, but to have a basic understanding of the manner and mechanism by which injuries are produced. All wounds are important, however apparently insignificant. They may demonstrate the nature of the impacting surface, the direction of the impact, and in some instances, the severity of that force. Since immediately prior to impact, the relative position of the victim and the vehicle are for most reconstruction purposes fixed, it is frequently possible to match the nature and location of the injuries with the impact surfaces. The features of injuries that the pathologist will wish to note include:

1. The size, shape, number and location
2. The presence of foreign material such as oil or paint
3. The nature and extent of internal damage
4. Any vital reaction to the injury or other evidence of healing or medical treatment

CLASSIFICATION OF INJURIES

4.014 Injuries associated with vehicular crashes can be classified as follows:

1. Blunt impact injuries (bruises, abrasions, lacerations)
2. Incised wounds
3. Penetrating injuries
4. Burns
5. Fractures
6. Restraint injuries

4.015 *Blunt impact injuries* are caused by blunt non-penetrating force and there are three types which may occur singly or in combination:

1. *Bruises* (contusions) are produced when blood leaks into the subcutaneous or deeper soft

tissues as a result of some blunt impact of sufficient force to rupture blood vessels, usually capillaries. A rapid accumulation of blood is often referred to as a hematoma. Interpretation of bruises requires great caution since the size of a bruise cannot usually be related to either the force or location of the impact.

Since skin bruising is only the external evidence of internal bleeding that has extended to just beneath the skin, a bruise may take several hours to develop and may not appear immediately beneath the actual site of impact. Bruises change color with aging, but such changes may differ from one individual to another and may be subject to many variables. In some instances the bruise may involve only the most superficial layers of the skin and may be made up of tiny ruptured capillaries. This type of bruising is sometimes referred to as petechial bruising and may be significant since these injuries may appear to reproduce specific textured surfaces such as fabric marks.

2. *Abrasions* are superficial blunt impact injuries in which the outer layers of the skin have been compressed and scraped off by movement of the injuring surface across the skin. Unlike bruises abrasions occur at the site of injury. The degree of pressure required to produce an abrasion is determined by the roughness of the impacting surface. The presence of clothing may prevent or modify an abrasion.

A *friction* or *sliding* abrasion is the common graze or scratch. The cuticle layer of skin becomes heaped up by the rough surface and the direction of movement of the skin over the impacting surface may be determined. These types of abrasions are typically seen when a pedestrian accident victim slides along a pavement surface.

Pressure abrasions are associated with much less movement and may reproduce some of the features of the contact surface. A good example of this type of injury are the multiple tiny linear abrasions produced when the skin is impacted by tiny fragments of shattered side-window glass. During life abrasions exude

serum and then form a scab. If the victim dies shortly after injury, then the area of injury dries out and the skin becomes parchmented causing the abrasion to appear much more severe.

3. *Lacerations* are tears or splits of the skid, usually occurring over bony prominences where the skid is less mobile. For example, lacerations of the scalp and face are common; however, lacerations of the abdomen are relatively rare. Lacerations are caused by crushing or shearing forces and the margins are irregular and invariably bruised or abraded. The softer tissues beneath the skin are torn apart and foreign material such as paint fragments, oil, dirt, or gravel are frequently found within the wound depths.

4.016 *Incised wounds* may be found anywhere on the body and have clean-cut margins. They are not usually associated with abraded irregular margins and as their name implies, they occur when the skin and tissues are cut by some sharp edge such as broken glass or torn metal. The deep structures are cleanly divided and fatty tissue often bulges into the wound. They are usually free of foreign material; however, if the wound has been caused by a painted metal surface, then tiny paint chips may be found. It may be important to identify self-inflicted incised wounds if the vehicular accident is suspected as a suicide attempt.

4.017 *Penetrating injuries* are defined as wounds produced by the penetration of some object into the tissues where the depth of penetration is greater than the skin length of the wound. Depending on the sharpness of the penetrating object, the margins will be either clean-cut or abraded and in vehicular accidents, there may be foreign material, often paint, oil, and even pieces of metal or glass, in the depths of the wound. Because of the extreme nature of the impact forces in vehicular accidents, penetrating wounds may be very deep and it is possible for the body to be completely transfixed.

BURNS

4.018 Fire associated with vehicular accidents can be very destructive and the interpretation of the injuries can be masked to a greater or lesser degree by the extent of burns sustained. X-ray examination of the victims may be necessary not only to help with victim identification, but to allow proper injury assessment. In severe cases, the intensity of the heat may produce long splits of the skin which must be distinguished from blunt force lacerations or more rarely incised wounds. Burns can be produced by contact with flame or hot surfaces, by contact with burning fluids, and by scorching associated with a flash fire from exploding gasoline.

4.019 The severity of burn injury depends not only upon the degree of heat applied to the body but also the length of exposure, so that burns may vary from slight reddening of the skin to complete charring with destruction of the tissues. There are several classifications used to describe burn severity, but in medical-legal practice, burn injuries are usually classified as first, second, and third degree. A first degree burn is superficial and will heal with no scar. A second degree burn is more severe and will show evidence of blistering. The tissues immediately beneath the skin are usually permanently damaged. Third degree burns are most severe and may be associated with charring and splitting of the skin. Extensive third degree burns are invariably fatal.

FRACTURES

4.020 The impact forces in vehicular accidents can and often are very great. When these forces are applied to the human skeleton, fractures and joint dislocations can occur. Such injuries are important because they may be taken as an indication of the severity of the forces applied to the body. Fractures, however, do not necessarily occur at the point of impact. Although most bones appear hard and rigid, they are in fact capable of bending and distortion before they fracture. For example, direct impacts to the skull may not only result in a fracture at the site of impact, but bending of the skull can cause a fracture away from this point of impact and fractures can also radiate widely throughout the skull. Impacts to the knees can result in the impact force being transmitted along the length of the femur with resulting fractures or dislocation of the hip joint.

4.021 Fractures can be the result of both direct and indirect force. If the upper tibia and fibula are struck by a car bumper, the fractures may be found at the site of impact. However, because the body as a whole may be projected forward and the body is not a rigid structure but capable of flailing motion, sufficient secondary force may be applied to the bones of the neck to cause fracture-dislocation of the cervical spines in the neck. The nature of the fracture is also affected by the relative elasticity of the bones. For example a twisting force can cause a spiral fracture with longitudinal splitting of the bone. A direct impact will usually result in a local fracture. In some cases the force applied may be so severe that the natural elasticity of the bone will be overcome and the bone will shatter the way a toffee bar will break when it is struck hard and not simply bent.

SAFETY RESTRAINT INJURIES

4.022 Impact against seatbelt restraints and head restraints can produce characteristic injuries. Although these devices are designed to reduce or prevent injuries, there are instances where the accident impact forces are so great that impact with these safety devices will produce injury. The distribution of injuries will depend on the type of device in question. Diagonal belts may cause rib fractures, laceration of the organs in the chest, and laceration of the liver. The lap belt may be associated with laceration of the liver and bruising of the intestines. Skin bruises and abrasions may be found along the line of the seat belts and the buckle mechanisms may cause identifiable injuries at the side of the hips. It must be stressed, however, that seat-belt restraints are not inherently dangerous and that such restraint injuries simply represent another impact surface in a crash vehicle. Seat belt injuries causing death are extremely rare in what would otherwise be considered survivable accidents.

4.023 Incorrectly adjusted head restraints may become a pivot point against which the neck may be hyper-extended. Severe, if not fatal neck dislocations may occur under these circumstances. If there is evidence that head restraints may have played a part in the causation of neck injury the pathologist must be made aware of this concern since a detailed neck dissection may not be a part of the routine postmortem examination.

THE VICTIM

4.024 The role of the pathologist is not only to determine the manner and mechanism of death but to attempt to match the patterns of injury and the location of the victim at the start of the accident sequence. The types of injuries sustained will be determined by the position of the victim relative to the vehicle and the direction and severity of the impact forces. In some crashes, the forces involved are complex and the victim will be subjected to impacts from several different directions. The vehicle may rotate or rollover and the victim may be projected against different surfaces and possibly ejected. The pathologist will attempt to distinguish primary from secondary impacts and in so doing attempt to sequence the injuries to the evolution of the accident. It is important, therefore, for the pathologist to have a good description of the nature of the accident and an indication of the form of the primary impact. Information on the location of the victims both before and after the accident should be available prior to the postmortem examination. Some evidence at the scene will be of great value in relating injuries to impact surfaces:

1. Which windows are broken and is there evidence of head strike on the windshield?
2. Hairs and fibers may be found in areas of impact damage.
3. Blood stains can be related to the location of bleeding injuries.
4. Brake or accelerator pedal imprints on shoe soles.
5. Fingerprints on the steering wheel.
6. Were seatbelts deployed and is there evidence of seatbelt damage?
7. Were airbags deployed?

4.025 Certain patterns of injury will be characteristic of the location of the victim prior to the accident. Injuries to the driver and other occupants can be modified by one individual's body becoming inserted between the victim and the impact surface. Similarly unrestrained occupants may be thrown against each other with injuries produced by these body-to-body collisions. The severity of injury will depend on the parts of the body colliding, but, in general terms, such collisions which produce significant injury to one individual will cause reciprocal injuries to the other person.

THE DRIVER

4.026 Fractures of the ribs and sternum may indicate impact with the steering wheel. Such impacts may be associated with the transfer of severe deceleration forces to the internal chest organs with laceration of the aorta, heart, or lungs. Injuries to the bones of the hand may indicate gripping of the steering wheel at the time of impact. In particular, injury to the joint at the base of the thumb is almost diagnostic of such a *control* injury. Impact forces transferred from the foot pedals to the feet and ankles of the driver may produce typical fractures of the feet and ankles. Such fractures of the hands and feet are not readily visualized at a routine postmortem examination and it may be appropriate, if there is concern at the possible significance of such injuries, to request the pathologist to have x-ray examinations carried out.

THE FRONT-SEAT PASSENGER

4.027 It is most unusual for a restrained front-seat passenger to strike the windshield. Evidence of a windshield strike or significant head injury in the absence of intrusion of the car bodywork into the interior of the vehicle must be considered strong evidence that a seatbelt was not properly deployed. Particular patterns of injury may be associated with impact with the structures in front of this passenger. Imprints of the manufacturer's insignia have left identifiable patterned bruises and abrasions on the forehead of the front-seat passenger.

THE REAR-SEAT PASSENGER

4.028 In general, rear-seat passengers are less severely injured than their counterparts in the front seats. In part, this is due to the fact that in most accidents, the rear compartment is subject to less severe impact forces and is usually less deformed. However, unrestrained rear-seat passengers are projected in all directions and not infrequently are thrown over the front seats and injured against the dash or windshield or even ejected out of the vehicle through the windshield. Because of the instability of rear seat passengers in crash situations, flail injuries of the limbs are common and injuries are often as a result of collision with interior fixtures such as door handles. Location of a body in the front of a crashed vehicle does not exclude the possibility that this person was in the rear seat at the time of initial impact.

INFANTS AND CHILDREN

4.029 The severity of injuries sustained in a vehicle crash is to a large extent a function of the momentum of the body at the time of impact. Momentum is a product of the weight of the individual and their velocity. Since children and infants have relatively low momentum at impact, their injuries tend to be less severe. However, children are often not properly restrained and may fly around inside the vehicle. Consequently, flail injuries are common as are injuries to the neck.

THE PEDESTRIAN

4.030 The patterns of injuries sustained by pedestrians are divided into two groups:

1. Primary impact injuries.
2. Secondary impact injuries.

4.031 *Primary impact injuries* are sustained by the first impact between the victim and the vehicle. These include point of impact injuries such as bumper fractures and lacerations caused by specific parts of the vehicle such as headlamps, radiator grills, and wing mirrors. The height of these primary impact injuries will often indicate the type of vehicle involved. For example, a four-door sedan will usually impact an adult just below the knees causing injuries and fractures to the upper ends of the tibia and/or fibula. Larger vehicles, such as a pick-up truck, will cause impact injuries above the knee. If an even larger vehicle is involved, such as a bus or truck, then the primary injuries may be seen as high as the buttocks, pelvis, or back. Measurement of the height of these impact point injuries above the foot will often indicate the class of vehicle involved. These measurements are subject to a number of variables and it is wrong to assume that the victim was standing upright with both feet on the ground at the time of impact.

4.032 *Secondary impact injuries* are caused by subsequent impacts with other parts of the vehicle or the ground. Depending on the profile of the front of the vehicle, the pedestrian may be knocked down and run over, or dragged under the vehicle. In lower profile vehicles, the victim may be scooped up onto the hood, possibly striking the windshield and thrown onto the ground. A victim dragged under the vehicle will show evidence of abrasions caused by contact with the road surface and/or the undersurface of the vehicle. Contact with the tires can leave patterned bruises and abrasions and if there has been prolonged friction contact with a revolving tire, a characteristic friction burn may be found with black staining of the skin caused by the tire surface.

4.033 The victim thrown onto the upper part of the vehicle may sustain severe secondary head injuries by impact with the windshield pillars and traumatic amputation of the limbs can occur in this type of impact. Flailing of the limbs in a victim who is thrown into the air following the primary impact, can produce serious bone and joint injury without further significant impacts. The final impact with the ground will usually cause additional injuries, but these can often be recognized by the pattern of abrasion produced by the road surface or by staining of the skin or clothing by grass, gravel, or soil.

MOTORCYCLISTS AND CYCLISTS

4.034 Because of the inherent instability of two-wheeled vehicles, the rider and passenger inevitably fall to the ground in a crash. Injuries can occur to any part of the body, but the limbs and head are particularly susceptible to serious injury. Safety helmets are mandatory for motorcyclists in many jurisdictions and they are worn with increasing frequency by cyclists. Nevertheless, impact with the road surface or another vehicle at speed often causes skull fracture, even in the presence of a helmet. A transverse fracture across the floor of the skull, usually called a "hinge fracture," is sometimes referred to as *the motorcyclist's fracture.* The investigator should make the pathologist aware of any significant safety helmet damage. In some cases, the helmet is an unapproved type and may not have afforded adequate protection. Many cyclists and motorcyclists, when thrown from their machines, tumble along the road surface. This type of movement is often associated with compression fractures of the spinal column. Secondary impact injuries are often the most serious injuries in motorcycle crashes.

THE POST-MORTEM EXAMINATION

4.035 Although the post-mortem examination of a road traffic crash fatality will follow the usual procedure, particular attention must be paid to documenting the injuries. Photographs and x-rays may be important methods of keeping a permanent record of the findings. The clothing should be examined prior to its removal from the body and in particular, trace evidence including paint chips and glass fragments should be sought. If at all possible, the clothing should not be cut from the body and should be examined by the pathologist before it is removed. Tire marks may be seen and patterned imprints of license plates, etc. may be identified. If the clothing has been removed as part of emergency medical treatment, this should be retrieved and available for examination.

4.036 There should be a presumption that every case will result in criminal or civil legal proceedings and this will require the pathologist to address not only the issues of manner and mechanism of death, but answers to the following questions should be considered:

1. Who was the driver?
2. What was the position of the victim in the vehicle?
3. Are the injuries consistent with the alleged position?
4. Can specific injuries be matched to vehicle features?
5. Is there evidence of pre-impact incapacitation?
6. Are there injuries not caused in the crash?
7. Does the pattern of injuries fit with the scene?
8. Are drugs or alcohol factors in the crash?
9. Is the death a crash, suicide, or murder?
10. Did death occur prior to the crash?
11. In pedestrian collisions, are the primary impact injuries consistent with the alleged vehicle or is more than one vehicle involved?

4.037 The following samples should be taken and preserved for appropriate forensic examination:

1. For toxicology:
   Blood
   Urine
   Liver
   and, if required:
   Bile
   Stomach contents
   Vitreous Fluid
2. For tissue matching:
   Hair
   Blood for serology and DNA
3. Other trace evidence:
   Paint fragments
   Oil or grease stains
   Glass
4. Clothing and footwear.

4.038 *Toxicology.* It should be a routine part of the postmortem examination of *all* victims of vehicular crashes to have alcohol analysis performed. Prescription and non-prescription drugs may be significant causative factors and can be tested for if required. In some jurisdictions, street drugs like heroin, cocaine, and marijuana are routinely tested. Some prescription drugs such as amphetamines may have been taken inappropriately or illegally. In vehicle fires, carbon monoxide and cyanide should be tested and it should be remembered that carbon monoxide may be inhaled as a result of a leakage of exhaust fumes into the car and can cause inappropriate behavior or even collapse of the driver and occupants.

CONCLUSION

4.039 In the assessment of a motor vehicle crash fatality the analysis must include not only the information about the victim and his or her injuries, but also information on the vehicles involved and the crash circumstances. Only by the integration of all the available information can a better understanding of the reasons for the crash, the mechanism of the crash, and the causation of the injuries be established for later use as evidence in criminal or civil proceedings.

4.040–4.045 reserved.

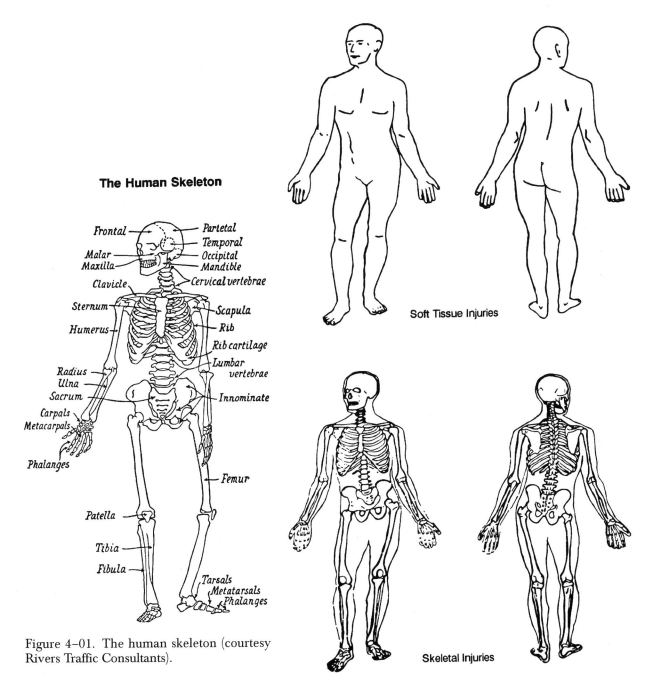

The Human Skeleton

Frontal
Parietal
Temporal
Malar
Occipital
Maxilla
Mandible
Clavicle
Cervical vertebrae
Sternum
Scapula
Humerus
Rib
Rib cartilage
Lumbar vertebrae
Radius
Ulna
Sacrum
Innominate
Carpals
Metacarpals
Phalanges
Femur
Patella
Tibia
Fibula
Tarsals
Metatarsals
Phalanges

Figure 4–01. The human skeleton (courtesy Rivers Traffic Consultants).

Soft Tissue Injuries

Skeletal Injuries

Figure 4–02. Human soft tissue and skeletal injuries (courtesy Rivers Traffic consultants).

Part 2

THE MEDICAL EXAMINER AND TRAFFIC CRASH INVESTIGATION

L. SATHYAVAGISWARAN

THE EXPECTATIONS OF A MEDICAL EXAMINER IN A TRAFFIC ACCIDENT INVESTIGATION

GENERAL STATEMENT

4.046 Police investigators are trained to furnish thorough crash reports which include photographs and diagrams. They are expected to give details of:

a. Environment at the time of the crash, like weather conditions, terrain, and geography.
b. Road factors like location, curves, type of road, posted speed, etc.
c. Vehicle factors like design, functioning equipment, and condition, etc.

4.047 In addition to looking for physical evidence, e.g., hair strands trapped in a glass windshield and blood stains, in cases of suspected suicide, the investigator should look for suicide notes in the glove compartment and collect any medication containers in the vehicle. If these are present and they are the victim's prescription, a medical history from the physician is needed. The telephone number can be requested from the pharmacy listed on the container. In one traffic accident, pills were found in and outside the vehicle—the victim having been ejected. They were steroid tablets and the victim had Crohn's Disease.

4.048 Most importantly, the investigator should attend the postmortem, bringing photographs and diagrams to the autopsy for better analysis of the victim in context of the collision. It is also important to obtain prior driving record and information history of drug/alcohol use, and so on from DMV and from the family.

SPECIFIC SITUATIONS

Pedestrian Victims of Vehicular Crashes

4.049 Any available witness information that a pedestrian was walking, standing, lying or jumped onto the road at the time he was struck by a vehicle will be useful. We had a case where the victim committed suicide by jumping in front of a vehicle. The victim did not have bumper injuries in the leg. All injuries were to the torso/head, consistent with a dive. Medical examiners should look for paint/glass on the victim, especially in the case of a hit and run victim, and the investigator should look for areas of damage on the vehicle. Sometimes patterned injuries are seen on the victim corresponding to the bumper strips or headlights.

4.050 The direction of travel of the vehicle has to be given. Skid marks should be addressed. The average bumper height from ground level is 14 inches (35 cm). Autopsy findings of the severity of fractures in legs can help estimate speed. Generally, 14 mph (22 km/h) can cause bumper fractures.

4.051 Pedestrians are not always hit head-on. They could be side-swiped, in which case, sides of the vehicle may show damage, e.g., side-mounted spare tires, rear view mirrors. They could also leave patterned injuries on the victim. Bumper fractures are the primary impact injury. Secondary impact injury can occur in the head/chest area and a tertiary impact injury can occur when the victim hits the ground and sustains brush burns.

Driver/Passenger Victim of a Vehicular Crash

4.052 Drivers who don't wear seat belts can sustain steering wheel column injury. The investigator should look at the gas/brake pedal to locate footprints by ultraviolet light or shoe sole patterns. The shoes also should be examined. The ankles of the driver are broken and wedged under the front seat in front-end impacts, where the vehicle comes to a sudden halt. A driver can suffer aortic injuries at the level of the aortic ligament. This can also occur in side impact intersection collisions. Pattern of the seat belt on the victim, corroborated with stretched seat belts in the vehicle, may help in driver/passenger seating determinations and whether or not a seat belt was used.

4.053 The investigator should not unbuckle a belt but cut it in order to remove the victim in a manner suitable for later reconstruction. Correlation of dicing injuries by broken glass on the victim and location of broken glass in the vehicle (windshield/door) corroborate passenger/driver locations.

4.054 Death may occur from injuries sustained inside or outside the vehicle, e.g., impact with a protruding part in the car such as a door handle, which can leave a patterned injury. In rollover accidents, a victim can be crushed and the question of whether a victim was ejected through an open door or window or windshield can be answered by finding a patterned injury of the window frame or cuts from broken glass.

Motorcycle Accident Victims

4.055 In the case of injuries sustained by motorcycle operators and passengers, the injuries are severe inasmuch as they are unprotected. The helmet, if dislodged, should be recovered by the investigator for examination by the pathologist. Patterned injuries can occur when the motorcycle falls on the victim. Muffler burns may also be seen. Usually a passenger is ejected over the driver in sudden stops, and is often thrown off before vehicle comes to a sudden stop.

The Vehicle Fire Victim

4.056 Vehicle fires are often experienced in vehicle rollovers and rear impacts. They are primarily fuel fed–though rarely electrical in origin. Autopsy examinations should include an examination of the atlanto-occipital joint as medulla injury can cause sudden death. Tracheas should be vertically incised and inspected in situ for soot. These findings should corroborate with CO in the blood, e.g.; we had a witnessed fiery single vehicular crash where the blood CO was negative, but the victims were exposed to a flash fire with burns. The airway showed some hyperemia/edema.

4.057 When a vehicle fire is not witnessed and there is a victim inside, it is important to establish that the victim was or was not dead before the fire (or a victim of homicide by firearm, blunt/sharp trauma). If the victim died from the fire, it is important to establish the origin of the fire in the vehicle using an arson investigator consultant. For example, we had a case where a girl committed suicide by self-immolation inside a vehicle.

Chapter 5

BLOODSTAIN PATTERN ANALYSIS

MICHAEL SWEET

INTRODUCTION

5.001 Bloodstain Pattern Analysis involves the examination of the sizes, shapes, and distribution of bloodstains at scenes involving bloodshed. This analysis can be of extreme importance in the investigation of vehicle crashes in such things as establishing points of contact and seating positions in vehicles, and can also be particularly helpful in the investigation of pedestrian-vehicle collisions.

5.002 A bloodstain pattern analyst can be a useful member of the team of investigators at traffic accidents. Along with the first police officers at the scene, witnesses, expert traffic investigator, medical examiner, engineers, and lab personnel, the bloodstain analyst can help to reconstruct what has occurred.

5.003 Among the questions an analyst tries to answer are:

1. What was the mechanism responsible for producing the bloodstains?
2. Is this a criminal or accidental death?
3. What was the position of the victim at the time of bloodletting?
4. What was the sequence of events at the scene?

5.004 Bloodstain pattern analysis is an applied science utilizing both mathematics and physics. A bloodstain pattern analyst addresses questions based on what is known about the behavior of blood after it has been shed.

HISTORY

5.005 Research in the bloodstain pattern field goes back almost a century. The earliest study was by Dr. E. Piotrowski, who, after being called to a homicide, attempted to determine how the bloodstains had been produced. He published a book in 1895 outlining his experiments, which included subjecting a rabbit to blunt trauma. In this book, Piotrowski describes bloodstains produced by both ascending and descending droplets.

5.006 Two French researchers, in 1900, were apparently the first to devise a system for classifying bloodstains. By 1939, some important findings had been published in France and Germany that included:

- The relationship between the angle of incidence and the ratio of the major to the minor diameter of the bloodstain;
- The fact that the height of the fall of a blood droplet could not be determined from the diameter of the stain;
- That a demonstration of how geometric principles could be used to determine the location of the blood source.

5.007 Very little research in bloodstain pattern analysis was conducted in the United States until MacDonnell and Bialousz began working in the field in 1970. MacDonnell then started to teach bloodstain pattern interpretation courses in the United States, and published several manuals on the subject. As a result, many qualified analysts are now located throughout the United States and Canada and in various other countries.

PHYSICAL PROPERTIES OF BLOOD

5.008 Blood is a liquid and conforms to the physical properties of fluids. The surface tension of a blood droplet causes it to assume a spherical shape when it leaves the body (a sphere represents the least amount of surface area for a given volume). The surface tension protects the droplet from rupture until it impacts on a surface (see Fig. 5–01).

5.009 The angle at which the blood droplet hits an object and the surface texture of that object determine the final shape of the stain. For example, if a free-falling blood drop strikes a surface at 90°, the resultant bloodstain will be circular. If the surface is smooth, such as glass, the edges of the stain will be smooth. If the surface has a rough texture, the edges of the bloodstain will be jagged.

5.010 When a blood drop hits an angled surface, the resulting stain has a teardrop shape. The stain becomes more elongated and narrow as the angle of impact decreases (see Fig. 5–02).

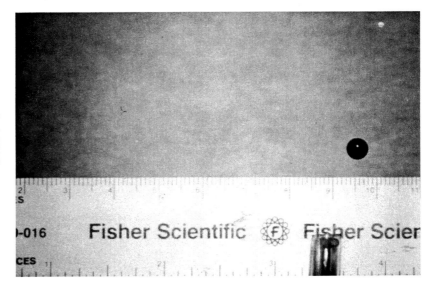

Figure 5–01. An example of the spherical shape a bloodstain assumes after separating from a blood source. The droplet in this case fell 8 in (20 cm).

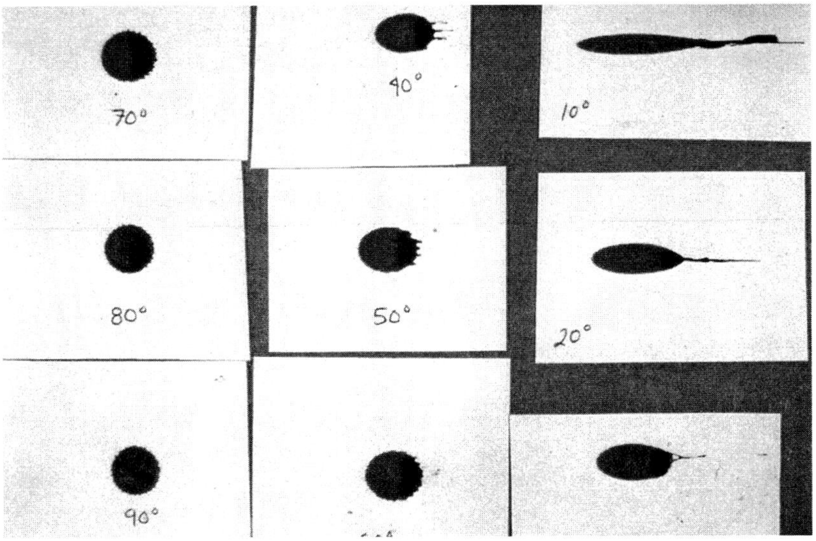

Figure 5–02. Decreasing angles of impact elongate the shape of a bloodstain.

DETERMINING DIRECTIONALITY OF BLOODSTAINS

5.011 The physical law of inertia (the resistance of a moving body to change) enables the analyst to determine the direction of travel of the blood droplet. When the flight path of the droplet is interrupted, the droplet trails off to a pointed end, thereby indicating the direction of travel (see Fig. 5–03). When there are multiple stains, it may be possible to determine points of convergence which indicate the location of the blood source at the time of bloodshed. If there are sufficient bloodstains present, a geometric interpretation may permit a three-dimensional calculation to determine the location of the blood source.

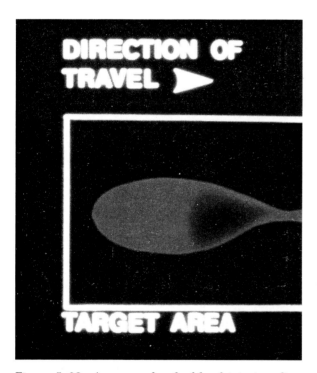

Figure 5–03. An example of a bloodstain traveling from left to right. The tail at the end of the stain indicates the direction of travel.

5.012 Originally, bloodstain pattern analysts used strings to recreate the trajectory of each blood droplet in three dimensions at the crime scene itself. One problem with this method was that strings are thick and can amplify any source of error in the calculations. Although this method is very time consuming,

it is still being used in many countries, and is usually the only method of doing a reconstruction in confined areas such as the interior of a vehicle.

5.013 In Canada, a different method has been in use since 1981. Bloodstain analysts place horizontal and vertical tape measures on each bloodstained surface and photograph the bloodstains. Trigonometric functions are then used to calculate convergence points for the bloodstains.

5.014 The above methods of calculating a convergence point for bloodstains assume that the blood has travelled in a straight line. This is generally true when the blood source is close to the surface struck by the droplets and the droplets are travelling at a high velocity. However, such is not always the case. Droplets travelling further or at a lower velocity will show a parabolic trajectory.

5.015 The motion of a droplet in flight is affected by two forces: (1) gravity and (2) air resistance. Air resistance increases with droplet size, but the greater mass of large droplets may cause them to travel farther than small droplets which have a higher surface area to mass ratio. Air resistance, unlike gravity, is not a constant, but is dependent on the speed of the droplet. Droplet trajectories therefore are not perfect parabolas, and the calculation of flight paths must take into consideration both the speed and size of the droplets.

5.016 The calculation of the effect of air resistance on flight paths has been addressed by Dr. A. L. Carter, Physics Department, Carleton University, in a computer program called *BackTrack* (available from Forensic Computing of Ottawa, Inc., 25 Lakeview Terrace, Ottawa, Ontario, K1 S 3H3). Tests have confirmed that the program will work from photographs as well as at the actual crime scene and that it yields virtually identical results to manual calculations for straight-line, high-speed trajectories. In addition, it is the only practical way now available to deal with curved trajectories caused by air resistance.

CATEGORIES OF BLOODSTAINS

5.017 Bloodstains are divided into three main categories, namely, (1) passive bloodstains, (2) projected bloodstains, and (3) transfer bloodstains.

Passive Bloodstains

These stains are created by free-falling drops affected by gravity. Examples include blood falling from an open wound, cut finger, bleeding nose, etc. On perpendicular surfaces, these stains are usually 1–2 cm in diameter. A collection of passive stains can create a pool of blood, and this can suggest that the blood source was stationary for a time (see Fig. 5-04).

Figure 5–04. Passive droplet about to strike a small pool of blood.

Projected Bloodstains

These stains are created when external force is applied to an exposed blood source. Such bloodstains are subdivided into three groups according to the velocity of the impacting object. They are: (1) low-velocity impact, (2) medium-velocity impact, and (3) high-velocity impact.

Low-Velocity Impact Stains

These stains are generated by the force of an object travelling at a velocity of less than five feet (1.5 m) per second. They are usually larger than 5 mm in diameter. An example of low-velocity impact would be spatter resulting from stepping in a pool of blood.

Medium-Velocity Impact Stains

These stains are generated by the force of an object travelling at 5 to 25 feet (1.5 to 7.5 m) per second. They are between 1 and 4 mm in diameter. An example would be an exposed blood source struck by a baseball bat. This type of stain is usually observed at scenes involving blunt trauma (see Fig. 5–05). It is important to understand that a single blow seldom produces projected bloodstains; an initial blow must break the skin and cause bleeding, while subsequent blows are responsible for the projected bloodstains. The bloodstain analyst can therefore indicate the *minimum* number of blows which have been struck, but not the *maximum*.

Figure 5–05. An example of medium-velocity impact stains traveling diagonally upward from left to right. These stains were generated at a crime scene where the victim was assaulted with a wooden club.

High-Velocity Impact

These stains are generated by the force of an object travelling more than 100 feet (30 m) per second. They are usually less than a millimetre in diameter. Such stains are created by a gun blast, and an aerosol misting is usually observed (see Fig. 5–06). Both forward and backward spatter can result from a high-velocity impact. In general, the smaller the diameter of the bloodstains the greater the force used to generate them.

Figure 5–06. An example of a forward direction, high-velocity impact spatter. These stains were generated experimentally by shooting a 22 calibre bullet into a blood-soaked sponge.

It should be noted that It is important to distinguish between the velocity of the impacting object which is used in the above classification of bloodstains, and the velocity of the blood droplets themselves. Experiments have shown that the velocity of the droplets may be much greater than the velocity of the impacting object.[1]

Projected bloodstains can also be generated by forces within the body. Examples include arterial spurting, sucking chest wounds, coughing, or sneezing (see Fig. 5–07).

A further form of projected bloodstain occurs when blood is cast off from an object during a swinging action, as when repeatedly striking a victim with an object (see Fig. 5–08).

Transfer Stains

This type of stain is created when a wet, bloody surface comes in contact with a secondary surface. Often a recognizable image is seen on the secondary surface. Common examples of transfer bloodstains include handprints, fingerprints, footwear patterns, fabric patterns, hair, etc. (see Fig. 5–09).

TYPES OF INFORMATION PROVIDED BY A BLOODSTAIN PATTERN ANALYST

5.018 At the scene itself, the analyst may be able to determine if the bloodstains were produced by a gun, blunt trauma, or passive bloodletting. The analyst may also be able to offer an immediate investigative tool by suggesting the sort of instrument that may have caused the injuries or a likely chain of events.

5.019 In analyzing photographs of the scene and other evidence, such as clothing, there a number of things the bloodstain specialist may be able to determine. These include but are not restricted to:

- Location of the blood source at time of bloodshed
- Directionality and type of impact that produced the bloodstains
- Position of the blood source and/or objects at the time of bloodshed
- Movement and direction of travel of the blood source during and after bloodshed
- Number of blows or shots, etc.
- Evidence to support or contradict statements given by suspects and witnesses.

Figure 5–07. *Arterial spurting patterns.* These stains can often be recognized as a cluster of large spots with flow patterns adhering to the target surface. This illustration shows the fluctuation in blood pressure as the victim moved along the wall. The victim in this case was slashed across the face, severing a facial artery.

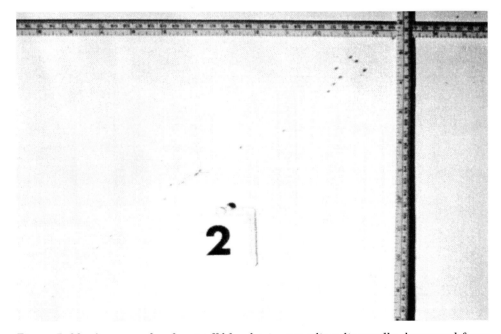

Figure 5–08. An example of cast-off bloodstains traveling diagonally downward from right to left. These stains often appear in a straight line, becoming more elongated the farther they travel from the impact source. These particular stains were generated by a blood stained wooden club impacting the victim's head.

5.020 Bloodstain pattern analysts can provide useful information in hit-and-run pedestrian collisions, other types of vehicle collisions, all types of violent crimes, suicides, and industrial accidents. Essentially, useful information can be provided anywhere and at anytime there has been bloodshed that needs to be explained.

ANALYST ASSISTANCE IN TRAFFIC COLLISION INVESTIGATION

5.021 In a recent case, Edmonton city police were called to what appeared to be a pedestrian-vehicle collision (see Figs. 5–10, 5–11, 5–12). The victim was found lying in a pool of blood beside a vehicle

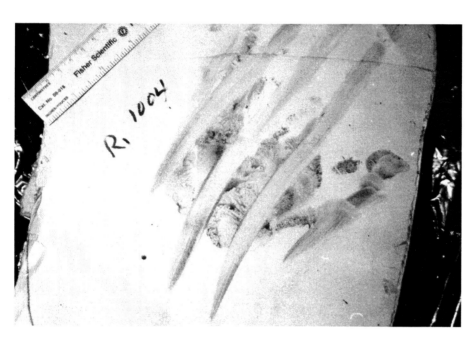

Figure 5–09. Left palm-print transfer and medium velocity impact stains.

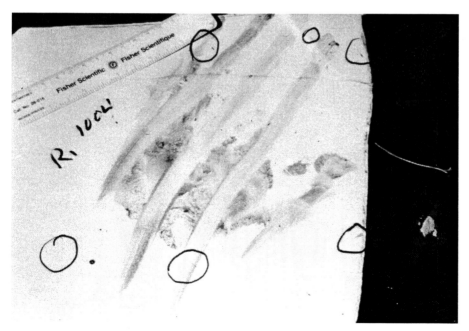

Figure 5–10. Detail of (photograph) Figure 5–09.

Figure 5–11. Victim in position beside the driver's door.

in the parking lot of a local donut shop. The vehicle had run into a window of the store, sustaining extensive damage to the front grill and hood. Collision investigators initially believed that the victim was stuck by the car as he walked in front of the donut shop. It was felt that the force of the collision caused the victim to project diagonally over the hood and land on the ground beside the driver's door. The suspect vehicle was later examined by a bloodstain pattern analyst. Arterial bloodstains were found on the inside lower frame of the driver's door . Transfer stains inside the vehicle indicated that the driver's hands had come in contact with wet blood and that the driver had exited the vehicle while his hands were bloodstained. A bloody right handprint on the driver's lower left pant leg showed that the victim, while lying on the ground, had grabbed the driver's leg as he stepped over him (see Fig. 5–12). After checking the postmortem results, it was clear that the victim had had his throat slit. This was a homicide, not a pedestrian collision. The driver of the vehicle was convicted of murder.

5.022 An analyst may be able to determine the position of a person, either inside or outside a vehicle, at the time of collision. It is possible the analyst may be able to determine the position of a pedestrian at

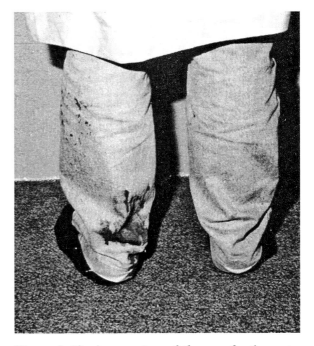

Figure 5–12. A rear view of the assailant's pants, showing projected blood stains on the outside of his left pant leg. This was caused by the victim grabbing the assailant's pants with his right hand, resulting in a transfer pattern on the lower left rear pant leg. This conclusion was also supported by DNA analysis.

the time he was struck by a vehicle by the distribution of bloodstains on the front of a vehicle, such as whether the victim was upright when struck. Such evidence could be used to verify a driver's claim that the victim had already been struck by another vehicle and was lying on the ground when the driver's car collided with the victim. If a driver sustains bloodletting injuries and subsequently flees the scene of a collision, it may be difficult to prove later that his injuries occurred in the collision. Bloodstain evidence inside the vehicle, however, can be correlated with the driver's injuries. If all occupants are thrown from the vehicle, bloodstain evidence, in conjunction with DNA analysis, may be able to establish their positions in the vehicle at the time of the collision.

5.023 *Luminol* can be used to find the presence of blood on the exterior or interior of a vehicle, even if an attempt has been made to clean up the blood. Luminol is a chemiluminescent compound that is used as a presumptive test for blood that may not be visible to the naked eye. Even if a vehicle has been washed, it still may be possible to detect not only the presence of blood but also the type and distribution of the stains. Luminol should, however, be used only by a qualified expert. A more practical field tool for the traffic crash investigator is the *Hemastix®*, a strip of cardboard with a chemical agent on one end. If a stain of indeterminate nature is visible, the Hemastix may be used as a presumptive test for blood. Distilled water is placed on the end of the strip and the strip is then applied to the suspected bloodstain. If blood is present, the end of the strip will turn dark green. Both Luminol and Hemasticks can give false positive readings; therefore, further tests should always be conducted.

5.024 An analyst may be able to obtain bloodstain evidence from a vehicle which has burned or exploded. Although extensive fire damage will destroy bloodstain evidence, lesser degrees of burning may leave some evidence intact. An experiment conducted in 1993 by the RCMP, Edmonton Fire Department, Northwestern Utilities, the Edmonton Police Service, and other agencies showed that a powerful explosion does not necessarily destroy bloodstain evidence. A house filled with gas was blown up. With careful retrieval, bloodstains placed on walls prior to the explosion were still interpretable.

5.025 There are specific limitations to bloodstain pattern analysis, however. It is next to impossible to determine from bloodstain evidence how fast a vehicle was travelling at the time of a collision. Also, it is not possible for the analyst to determine the age of a bloodstain once it has dried.

AT-SCENE BLOODSTAIN PHOTOGRAPHY

5.026 If a bloodstain expert is not readily available at a collision scene, photographs can be taken to record the bloodstains for later analysis. In order for the photographs to be useful, several guidelines must be followed.

1. The bloodstains must be photographed at 90 degrees with a vertical and horizontal scale in place.
2. The photographs should include an overview illustrating the general position of the bloodstains.
3. The photographs must also include close-up views illustrating the bloodstains in position. The scales should remain in view even for the close-up views. Large numbers and/or letters can be attached to the surface to help identify the close-up views.

5.027 There will be times when the bloodstains are situated on a curved surface, such as inside a vehicle. This can pose problems when attempting to photograph the stains at 90 degrees. In such cases, a bloodstain pattern analyst should examine the stains since it will probably be necessary to use strings to manually retrace the flight path of the blood.

BLOOD SAMPLE COLLECTION

5.028 Protective clothing should always be used when dealing with blood. Two of the best field devices for collecting blood samples are the sterile cotton-tip swab and the cotton swatch. It is found that the cotton-tip swab is more useful because it comes in a sterile chamber that can be used to store the blood swab after it dries. The cotton swatch consists of a small sterile section of cloth that is stapled to a stiff piece of cardboard. The cardboard is good for recording information, such as date of seizure and file number. Both devices must be used correctly. A small amount of sterile distilled water should be squirted on the swatch or cotton tip prior to swabbing the stain. Never dip the swab or swatch in the bottle because this will contaminate the distilled water. Only a small amount of water is needed; too much water renders the sample useless for biological testing.

5.029 After taking a sample, air dry the swab or swatch prior to storage. Then store the dry sample in a waterproof container away from heat. Moisture and heat can destroy a DNA sample. Blood samples should always be taken to a laboratory as soon as possible.

DNA EXHIBIT COLLECTION

5.030 Prior to DNA analysis, police agencies relied on standard serology tests to compare bloodstained exhibits. This procedure utilized the ABO blood group system, and could effectively exclude an individual as being the source of a sample. It was much less conclusive in making a positive match, however. Today, crime laboratories use DNA to compare bloodstained exhibits to known samples. In the early stages of DNA, the results were often referred to as a DNA fingerprint.

5.031 The two types of DNA analysis are (1) Restriction Fragment Length Polymorphism (RFLP) and (2) Polymerase Chain Reaction (PCR). RFLP analysis examines DNA sequences in the white blood cells. It is statistically individualizing, but a large bloodstain must be available in order for it to be used. PCR analysis examines DNA sequence that have been copied multiple times. PCR has found usable DNA on older and in much smaller samples than can be used for RFLP; in some cases, it has worked on bloodstains that were less than a *mm* in size and invisible to the naked eye. The most recent methods of PCR are even more statistically individualizing than RFLP.

5.032 DNA results from both types of analysis have been accepted in courts in Canada and the United States. However, in Canada and in some states, crime laboratories have not shifted to PCR analysis exclusively. Court challenges to DNA evidence focus mainly on possible contamination of the sample during collection, handling, or analysis.

It is therefore essential for forensic traffic reconstructionists to follow protocol when bloodstained exhibits are seized at a collision scene.

5.033 Exhibits may include bloodstained clothing, bloodstains on parts of a vehicle, or tissue samples. In order for a bloodstained exhibit to be suitable for DNA analysis, the exhibit must be *kept separate, air dried, individually packaged and kept away from sunlight.* A wet bloodstain can degrade from the formation of microbacterial growth. Wet stains which come into contact with each other can produce cross-contamination. Also, sunlight can bleach the exhibit.

HANDLING OF BLOODSTAINED EXHIBITS

5.034 Frequently, the need will arise to seize bloodied exhibits, such as clothing from a victim at the hospital. All too often, hospital staff place multiple bloodstained garments inside a plastic bag. Sometimes wet bloodied clothing from two different victims is placed in the same bag. Such improper handling presents three very important problems:

1. Cross-contamination will occur when wet, blooded objects come in contact with each other.
2. Plastic bags hold in moisture. The exhibits won't dry and bacteria will grow on them, rendering them useless for DNA or other biological tests.
3. Folding and squashing wet bloodstained garments can alter bloodstains and create new ones, making interpretation difficult.

5.035 Certain precautions should be taken when handling wet, bloodstained exhibits:

- Wear latex gloves
- Keep all exhibits separate
- Air dry all exhibits
- Avoid the use of non-porous containers until the exhibits have dried completely. If you must place the exhibit in a plastic bag for transport, remove it as soon as you can and air dry.
- Keep exhibits away from heat and moisture
- If relevant, have a garment examined by a bloodstain expert prior to using it for a submission to a laboratory.

REFERENCE

1. Sweet, M.J.: Velocity Measurements of Projected Bloodstains from a Medium Velocity Impact Source. *Canadian Society of Forensic Science Journal*, Vol. 26, No.3, 1993.

RECOMMENDED READING

Balthazard, V., Piedlievre, R., & Desoilleh, L.D.: Etude des gouttes de sang projete, Annales. *Med. Legale Criminol.*, Vol. 19, 1939, France.

Bevel, T.: Geometric Bloodstain Interpretation. *FBI Law Enforcement Bulletin*, Office of Congressional and Public Affairs, V. 52, No.5., May 1983, pp. 7–10.

Carter, A.L.: *Physics of Bloodstain Analysis.* Lecture Notes for Bloodstain Pattern Analysis Course, RCMP, Carleton University, Ottawa, May, 1993.

Eckert, W.G. & James, S.H.: *Interpretation of Bloodstain Evidence at Crime Scenes.* Elsevier, 1989.

Hardy, K.: *A Course in Mathematics Relating to Bloodstain Pattern Analysis.* Lecture Notes for Bloodstain Pattern Analysis Course, RCMP, Carleton University, Ottawa, May,1993.

Kirk, P.L.: Affidavit Regarding *State of Ohio vs. Samuel H. Sheppard*, Court of Common Pleas, Criminal Branch, No.64571, 26 April 1955.

Laber, T.L. & Epstein, B.P.: *Bloodstain Pattern Analysis.* Callen Publishing, Inc., Minneapolis, Minnesota, 1983.

Lock, J.A.: The Physics of Air Resistance. *The Physics Teacher*, March 1982, pp. 158–160.

MacDonnell, H.L.: *Bloodstain Pattern Interpretation.* Laboratory of Forensic Science, P.O. Box 1111, Corning, New York 14830.

McDonnell, H.L. & Bialousz, L.F.: *Flight Characteristics and Stain Patterns of Human Blood.* U.S. Department of Justice, Law Enforcement Assistance Administration, Washington, DC, 1971.

Piotrowski, E.: *Ueber Entstehung, Form, Richtung und Ausbreitung der Blutspuren nach Hiebwunden des Kopfes* (Facsimile Edition, Golos Edition), 1992. Introduction by H.L. MacDonnell, Golos, Elmira Heights, New York, (includes English translation).

Pizzola, P.A., Roth, S., & De Forest, P.R.: Blood Droplet Dynamics–1 and 2. *Journal of Forensic Sciences, JFSCA*, V. 31, No.1, Jan., 1986, pp. 36–49, pp. 50–64.

Stephens, B.G. & Allen, T.B.: Back Spatter of Blood from Gunshot Wounds–Observations and Experimental Simulation. *Journal of Forensic Sciences, JFSCA*, V. 28, No.1, April, 1983, pp. 437–439.

Sweet, M.J.: Velocity Measurements of Projected Bloodstains from a Medium Velocity Impact Source. *Canadian Society of Forensic Science Journal*, Vol. 26, No.3, 1993, pp. 103–110.

Chapter 6

FORENSIC PHOTOGRAPHY AND SCENE MEASUREMENTS

Part 1

INTRODUCTION TO PHOTOGRAPHIC APPLICATIONS

ROBERT WYMAN

6.001 Deciding upon the *end-use* of a photograph is actually the *first step* in a successful forensic imaging effort. Without knowing the end-use, a photographer cannot efficiently and competently plan and complete an imaging assignment. That is, a photographic task approached without a plan, and without thought of a desired result, will be an amateur effort at best and a failure at worst. Consider this analogy: a suspect is barricaded and holding hostages. Does the responding agency approach the perpetrator without a plan? Is a course of action implemented without thought of the outcome? A photographic assignment should have a similar level of planning and execution:

1. How will the photographs be used?
2. How will photographs be displayed and viewed?
3. What evidence should be documented first?
4. What evidence can wait until tomorrow, next week, or next month?
5. Is any special equipment needed?

The end-use should always steer the photographer's activities. Furthermore, it is always more professional, useful, and cost-effective to produce a few well-planned photographs instead of dozens or hundreds of random snapshots.

TESTIMONY

6.002 It is sometimes said, "This photograph doesn't show it clearly, but. . . ." When spoken by an investigator, this statement can be an honest one, but one that also can be a terribly damaging testimonial regarding photographic exhibits placed before a client or jury.

6.003 The end-use of a photographic assignment should *begin* a task list that will satisfy the following points:

- What will the photographer need to clearly support any future spoken testimony?
- Can a photographic essay be constructed to illustrate the crash sequence?
- What photographs will a reconstructionist, investigator, engineer, doctor, or other expert ultimately need to highlight their conclusions?

6.004 The following questions are easiest to handle when considered early in a forensic photography case. Other testimony issues, such as camera equipment settings and imaging accuracy, can be anticipated in the same manner:

- What is needed to professionally log or record camera parameters?
- Does a particular wide-angle or telephoto image introduce any optical distortions as a by-product of the camera and lens combination?
- Does an image's *field of vision* reasonably depict what a witness observed?

Predicting such questions requires a healthy dose of common sense, professional experience, and adversarial thinking. What questions would you ask to validate or invalidate a photographic documentation effort?

6.005 To prepare for future testimony, a photographer must simply consider the question: "Does the image fairly and accurately represent the subject?" Any answer to this question other than *yes* is unacceptable.

6.006 The photographer must be able to validate each image being presented to the court. Presentations should clearly state *why* the photograph was completed and *what* the photograph serves to illustrate. Follow-up questions and answers, of course, can further explore the evidence illustrated in the photographs and correlate the image to calculations, occupant kinematic studies, and other points of evidence.

6.007 Regarding the picture's *factual* representation of a subject, it should be remembered that any image-recording device, whether film or digital, will introduce biases into the resulting image. Field-of-vision, depth-of-field, magnification, distortion, and contrast are just some of the variables that are quit certainly altered within the camera as compared to our natural vision. Of importance is the perceptual nature of these variables: although they also manipulate the image in a strictly factual sense, they are more aligned to the viewer's perception of the image, and that issue has been generally accepted by the courts if a proper foundation is established through testimony. For example, it is recommended that a series of questions be asked of the photographer prior to the introduction of any image, including film, digital, sketch, graphic, whatever. The photographer should be asked to:

a. Identify the equipment,
b. Give the length of time in use (including pre-deployment training time),
c. Explain the results of any testing and simulation efforts,
d. Explain how this particular image or photo essay was completed, and
e. Explain whether the images represent the personally-viewed subject *within a reasonable degree of accuracy.*

6.008 The well-prepared photographer will have an equipment list itemized and knowledge of when the equipment was issued and placed into service. Testing and simulation time should always be allocated for new equipment, including a documented comparison to any old equipment that has already been accepted by the local courts. A side-by-side image comparison between old and new equipment, depicting the same subject under the same conditions, can easily be placed into a notebook or made into a handout for use in future court appearances. These tests and comparisons will help validate the equipment (and the photographer's confidence in the images) long before the subject photo is even introduced.

6.009 Cross-examination questions always try to invalidate the image, the photographer, or otherwise introduce doubt as to the accuracy of the exhibit. If all *hardware* issues are volunteered on direct examination, along with testimony concerning the validity and accuracy of *all* images completed with this equipment, perceptual issues are all that remain for discussion. The photographer can then answer cross-exam questions pertaining to accuracy and image-manipulation issues by illustrating that minor camera distortions and, in fact, *all* image-capturing systems do not change the relationship between the physical evidence and the surrounding non-evidential attributes. An image may look brighter or darker, or perhaps more magnified, but if an item like a skid mark is 4'7" from the edgeline in real life, it will still be 4'7" from the edgeline in any image when scaled along proper reference lines.

6.010 The photographer him/herself should have the same validation procedure as the imagining devices: a series of specific questions of the photographer's background, experience, knowledge, testing, and reporting of the subject. All jurors have cameras, so it's just a matter of demonstrating that our camera use is only a little more technical than their camera use. Otherwise, there may be no difference.

6.011 If adversarial questioning seeks to invalidate any image that is not a reasonable depiction of what can be seen with the unaided eye, a carefully crafted answer can both diffuse the premise and promote professionalism.

Example:

In this photograph, we're documenting the existence of damage in a grille. No measurements are being taken from the photographs, and optical distortions do not alter the existence of this evidence.

If necessary, a more elaborate and aggressive answer can be offered:

Optical distortions in this type of image are accepted in the photographic community as an insignificant result of the magnification process. If we are measuring something in the photograph, we can easily quantify the amount of distortion so it doesn't affect the measurement. This image, though, serves to illustrate the existence of minute evidence that cannot be easily seen without magnification. No measurements have been taken from the photographs.

6.012 Items that may raise such questions include magnification, uncontrolled optical distortion, the focal point, and out-of-focus (selective focus) portions of an image. These issues are beyond the scope of this chapter but can be found properly addressed in publications dedicated to photography.

6.013 In addition to validating photographic images, the photographer's own competency may be questioned in some jurisdictions. While personal attacks against the photographer are distasteful (and perhaps unethical), they nevertheless must be anticipated.

6.014 Unfortunately, weak testimony is seen in many investigators and technicians. They are tasked with forensic photography jobs and also have other assignments and disciplines. These employees are essentially part-time or untrained full-time photographers, and their testimony fails to reflect any expertise beyond that of other camera users. Whereas a professional forensic photographer demonstrates his expertise with ease by taking into consideration professional procedures and guidelines:

- Forensic photography requires a planned approach to each photograph subject. No photograph is completed in a random or haphazard manner.
- Forensic photography plays a critical role in evidence documentation, preservation and analysis. Photographs must be technically correct (in terms of camera operation) and functional (in terms of answering a potential question about the case).
- Forensic photography requires knowledge of the best techniques available to properly document

evidence, including camera settings, use of special equipment, and illumination.
- Forensic photography must clearly tell a story with recorded images.

In fact, the best forensic photographs are not used as a supplement to spoken testimony; instead, the spoken word is used to verbally describe what can readily be perceived in the photographs.

6.015 Regarding the archival properties of film and digital prints, properly-stored photographic negatives and photographic (chemical) prints can last for generations. Furthermore, current digital prints made from popular brand-name inkjet prints, ink, and paper are advertised (by brand-name manufacturers) to *last a lifetime* and have been simulation-tested to remain stable for 70 years or more with proper storage. Older inkjet prints, however, and current prints made from lesser-brand inkjet printers, ink, and paper, may experience significantly less desirable results. Fading, sticking, and smearing are the most common problems reported. If poor ink and paper products are used, some prints may never seem to fully dry (always sticking to other sheets), or dry prints may smear at the slightest hint of moisture, even from a fingertip. Agencies and private practitioners using digital cameras have several options for producing archival-quality prints:

a. *Photo-quality Inkjet Printing.* Use of high-quality, brand-name inkjet printer, with ink and paper both approved by the printer manufacturer, will provide excellent results and the greatest range of flexibility. For example, photos can be printed on plain paper for basic, daily reference use and a higher-quality *photo paper* for file and presentation use.

b. *Inkjet Printing Plus Lamination.* An alternative to using costly photo paper (and the additional ink used in photo-quality prints on photo paper) is to print photos on high-quality plain paper and then laminate each page. Special lamination film is produced for this purpose, with UV-resistant film and a low-temperature adhesive that will not alter the ink layer. This solution is most helpful when prints will be handled roughly or used in harsh environments.

c. *Laser Printing.* Color laser printing virtually eliminates all concerns associated with inkjet prints. Economy-grade paper can be used with acceptable results, and the image is just as strong as the paper. That is, color laser prints will not stick, smear, or fade under normal use.

d. *Dye-sublimation.* This is an extremely high-quality technology most often associated with commercial printing facilities. Consumer-grade *desktop photo printers* also use dye-sublimation (sometimes combined with a built-in laminator) to produce lab-quality prints from digital media. These printers only produce photographic prints in this manner and cannot be used for other printing jobs.

e. *Photo-Lab (Chemical) Paper Printing.* The convergence of film and digital photography has allowed most commercial or in-house *one hour* photo labs to accept digital media. Although there are no film negatives to process, the images enter the lab's workflow electronically and are printed using same photographic exposure and printing techniques as film images. The resulting digitally-captured prints are indistinguishable from film-captured prints.

PHOTOGRAPHIC TECHNIQUES

6.016 Special photographic techniques, when utilized, should be explained in a straightforward manner. The photographer must clearly understand why a technique or lens was pressed into service on an assignment and be able to explain such choices without appearing evasive or defensive. Straying from the use of *normal* settings and equipment is not an *abnormality* but instead a professional utilization of photographic resources. In this regard, the investigator should be familiar with the use of macro lenses, which provide close-focusing optics that result in life-sized, or near life-sized, image ratios for small objects. That is, the lens allows an image to be recorded in which the photographic subject is the same size on the image medium as it is in real life; for example, a ¾-inch bolt will be recorded with a ¾-inch dimension (1:1 ratio). Increased image ratios are used for all other lenses, as when an 18-foot vehicle (216 inch) is similarly recorded as a ¾-inch image (288:1 ratio). Macro lenses and resulting life-sized image ratios are useful for recording small, detailed objects. Lamp filaments, component failures, paint transfer marks, roadway gouges, punctures, and detailed injury photos are best imaged in this manner to highlight details and preserve evidence. As an example, Figure 6–01A is a non-macro photograph that shows a damaged vehicle grille. Very little detail is evident. Whereas, Figure 6–02 is a macro view of the grill, being a close-up, magnified image that allows us to observe the subject in greater detail. This view does not, however, change the subject in any way; it just gives us a closer view.

6.017–6.020 reserved.

Figure 6–01A. A nonmacro view of a damaged grille.

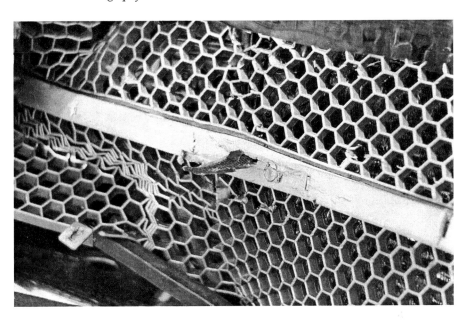

Figure 6–01B. A macro view of the damaged grille shown in Figure 6–01A.

POLICIES, DIRECTIVES, AND LIMITATIONS

6.021 Most professional forensic photographers will use their experience in the field and in court as a guide in their professional undertakings. Simple errors and omissions can be corrected through the use of checklists, forms, and personal protocols that serve as reminders and notes. If a severe procedural deficiency is discovered in a case, such deficiency can usually be remedied for use in all subsequent cases.

6.022 Unfortunately, the professional photographer may be governed by policies and procedures that actually hinder a proper documentation effort. These include, but are not limited to, agency- or company-imposed policies that limit a proper forensic documentation, such as restricting a photographer's time and type of equipment or being under the strict control of a non-photographer supervisor. Counterproductive, restrictive policies often occur in a police agency's Crime Scene Investigation Unit or in a Litigation Support Department of a large insurance organization. In these circumstances, common restrictions include:

- Limitation on the number of images, number of film rolls, or number of digital memory cards allocated for any one case.

- Limitation on the amount of time a photographer is allowed to spend at a crash scene, vehicle inspection, personal injury photography session, or other photography-related task.
- Limitation on the photographic subjects, photography angles, wide-angle images, telephoto images, macro images, or other photographic technique used for the documentation process.

Using an assumption that a professional photographer will not unethically waste time and resources while on assignment, these restrictions are arbitrary and potentially damaging to a case.

6.023 The quantity of images completed for a job, whether using film or digital media, is best governed by the subject at hand. For example, only a few scene and vehicle photographs may be needed for a vehicle that has backed into a parking garage wall, but hundreds of images or more may be warranted at a five-vehicle interstate highway pile-up involving a tire failure, rollover, and fatality.

6.024 Organizations utilizing professional forensic photographers should never place arbitrary restrictions on a documentation effort, especially as a misguided attempt to reduce casework expenses. This also applies to the photographer's time, especially for large traffic crashes where a scene is *held* or closed to the public. Large scenes often require the callout of

Figure 6–02. A view obstruction caused by a tree, limiting sight distance around the curve towards the stop sign and intersection.

a photographer, with dispatch and arrival times taking up to an hour in congested metropolitan areas. These scenes are magnets for news media and citizen requests to open the road as soon as possible, even if it's just one lane or roadside shoulder. Politicians, local government traffic managers and police administrators may contribute to this problem by pressuring at-scene personnel to *complete the job properly, but also get the road open immediately.*

6.025 As a policy, local jurisdictions should simply pick one course of action: Hold all scenes until the work is truly completed, or accept the risk of a scene being compromised and contaminated when attempts are made to balance conflicting needs. Remember, a single image may solve or settle a case, and this image may never be recorded if the photographer is burdened with time or equipment restrictions.

TRAFFIC ENGINEERING AND PHOTOGRAPHY

6.026 To the lay person, the fact that most traffic crash investigators have little knowledge of traffic engineering is a surprising reality. In fact, most crash scene photographs that attempt to document traffic elements are limited to a single photograph of a nearby speed limit sign or other obvious road-side attributes. Such documentation efforts never consider whether a sign is correctly placed or properly maintained. Furthermore, investigators rarely have direct knowledge of sign-installation options or know how these choices ultimately affect motorist behavior and crash avoidance.

6.027 *Traffic engineering* encompasses traffic control devices, which include *signs, signals,* and *roadway pavement markings,* all of which should be considered in at-scene photography. For example, did a view obstruction contribute to the crash? Did a tree branch, advertising sign, or a parked vehicle block the view toward a stop sign? Such circumstances should be photographed immediately lest the evidence be lost. An investigator can sometimes visit or revisit the site at a later time, but often the circumstances as they existed at the time of the crash no longer exist.

PHOTOGRAPHING THE SERIES OF EVENTS

6.028 Detailed views of crash sites and vehicles should be balanced with broader views of the crash event. From a photographic standpoint, this task attempts to establish a chronology of the *Series of Events* (as described in paragraphs 1.016–1.018 and 1.027) and the significant points of view for each driver and witness. To start with, a photograph should show the overall scene from a distance as viewed by the investigator upon his arrival (see Fig. 6–03). Subsequent photographs should then be taken to include the elements listed in Table 6–01.

Table 6–01

Points or events that should be included (as might be applicable) in a photographic chronology of the *series of events*.

- Point of Possible Perception
- Point of Actual Perception
- Action Point
- True (Safe) Area
- Point of No Escape
- Encroachment
- Point of Impact
- Engagement
- Secondary Contact
- Post Secondary Contact
- Final Position
- At-rest Position

Speed calculations are often coordinated with this effort. Crash sequence documentation is similar to Crash Report narratives in which the responding police investigator often records the origin and intended destination points of all parties involved in the crash.

6.029 Photographs can be completed to show origin points (e.g., *pre-scene events*), routing decisions, nearby traffic control devices, traffic congestion and roadway conditions, or any element deemed significant for each driver and witness, all of which can be related to the *series of events*. Such photographs should depict as closely as possible how they would have viewed the scene at the time of the incident. In this regard, it is very important to take photographs as closely as possible from the eye height of the drivers and witnesses involved. In some cases, the route leading up to the crash scene may be significant to the investigation. For this purpose, an aerial view is most helpful (see Figure 6–04).

Timelines

6.030 The photographic chronology should, whenever possible, provide multiple views for each point on the *timeline*. That is, if Vehicle 1 is shown to be at a particular roadway point 4.5 seconds prior to impact, then Vehicle 2 should also be shown at its position 4.5 seconds prior to impact (see Fig. 6–05).

Figure 6–03. An example of an overview or scene orientation of a traffic crash site.

Figure 6–04. An aerial view of a highway, such as can be used to depict the lead-in to an actual crash site area, or to show the various aspects of a trafficway.

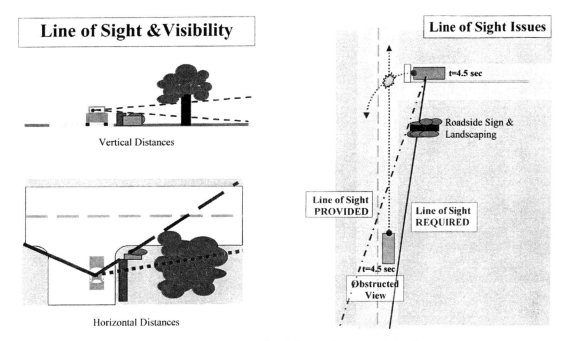

Figure 6–05. An example of the application of timelines.

6.031 Timeline points worthy of being highlighted can be established by several methods:

- Time prior to crash, in which vehicle and witness photographs are solely completed based on the timeline photographs may be completed, for example, starting one minute before impact and continuing in 10-second increments until the point of collision is reached.
- Time prior to crash vs. distance from crash site. This method correlates the timeline to pre-crash distances on the road photographs can begin, for instance, 1,000 ft (300 m) prior to the crash site and progress in 100 ft (30 m) increments until the point of collision is reached.
- Time prior to crash vs. geographic points and roadway attributes leading up to the crash site, such as city blocks, buildings, landmarks, or intersections. This method equates the timeline to readily identifiable landmarks. A resulting photograph, for example, may be identified as "View of Driver No.1 from roadway adjacent to 714 Main Street (approximately 32 seconds prior to impact)."

Timelines can also be reflected in computer-generated graphics, videos, animations, and as a graphical component of Perception-Reaction Time (PRT) calculations.

PERSONAL INJURY DOCUMENTATION

6.032 Photographic documentation of injuries may be one of the most controversial tasks assigned to crash investigators. Just as in domestic violence and assault cases, the timely recording of injury locations and severity may be essential to an investigation. These very same goals, injury locations and severity, constitute the dilemma faced by crash investigators. Of course, first and foremost is the victim's right to privacy, and also the importance of following and adhering to all legitimate regulations or policies that may be in place.

6.033 Traffic crashes sometimes result in extremely graphic and horrific injuries. For fatalities, the medical examiner's office (or coroner in some jurisdictions) can justify full-body, detailed photographs for their casefile, while a public or private crash investigator may not be afforded the same opportunity. Similarly, non-fatal injuries may be documented by medical staff in some trauma centers and hospital emergency rooms but restricted from other interested parties.

6.034 If subsequently confined to a hospital room, the injured victim may then be governed by the health care facility's risk management policies. A total ban upon photography is common, no matter what agency or law firm is being represented by the photographer. Law enforcement officers, of course, may be allowed more freedom in this regard than private investigators, private crash reconstructionists, and consultants.

6.035 Investigators seeking to document injuries, while a patient is in the confines of a health care facility, are advised to meet first with the victim's legal representative (if any) and attending physician(s). When directed by an attorney or doctor, or in response to site policies, the investigator/photographer should meet next with a risk management administrator to determine if photographs will be allowed.

6.036 A photographer's failure to obey the policies of a health care facility may result in legal action against the photographer, regardless of the scientific intent or investigative value of the photographs. Hospitals must follow a wide variety of federal, state, and local regulations that specifically address patients' rights, privacy, and security. Case-specific circumstances will determine whether supervised photos (overseen by hospital staff) or unsupervised photos will be permitted. Also depending upon the circumstance, neither the patient nor his or her legal representative may be able to supersede these directives.

6.037 When photographs are allowed by a health care facility, or completed in a home or other setting, the investigator should again begin with an end-use in mind. Overall, full-body images will help establish the locations of specific injuries, post-surgical scars, and other irregularities.

6.038 Next, section-by-section photographs will illustrate bodily areas most affected by the crash. Typical bodily sections include head and neck, torso, arms, and legs (photographed individually). Care should be taken by the photographer to utilize illumination techniques that best illustrate each injury. Direct, on-camera flash illumination may *wash out* (overexpose) key injury areas, while softer indirect and bounced lighting will provide a more evenly-illuminated image.

6.039 Detailed views of each injury location follow as the next step. Since these close-up (macro) views may be so close as to exclude visual cues regarding their location on the body, careful notes should also be recorded to later identify each image. That is, a close-up photograph may only illustrate an expanse of skin with a laceration or contusion. Where did this occur on the body? Your notes, along with the overall and sectional photographs described above, will serve to fully map each injury point. A small scale may also be placed in the photo to help viewers perceive the actual size of the injured area being photographed.

6.040 Lighting for macro photos is once again critical:

- Soft, even illumination is preferred over harsh, direct illumination in avoidance of overexposed skin surface areas.
- Sunlight or daylight-balanced flash lighting will provide a more realistic skin and injury color than incandescent home lamps or fluorescent office fixtures.
- Lighting angles, between the injury location and source of illumination, should also be adjusted to best highlight scars and other skin surface irregularities.

6.041 As with most subjects in macro photography, the camera system's magnification and depth-of-field parameters will limit the photographer's ability to capture large injury areas or those that follow the curvature of a body. The photographer should choose several representative areas within the injury or around the curved surface, stabilize the camera on a tripod, then focus automatically or manually on the center of the first desired area. This zone will remain in sharp focus, but outlying zones may exhibit a significant fuzziness and loss of detail. Again, this is normal in a macro image.

6.042 Additional portions of the same injured area can then be taken in a similar manner, resulting in an accurate, detailed, close-up sequence of the entire injury. For added precision, the photographer can measure the amount of overlap between each image or place a flexible scale near the injury, with a portion of the scale remaining visible throughout the sequence.

6.043–6.050 reserved.

Part 2

SCENE MEASUREMENTS AND PLAN DRAWINGS

R.W. Rivers

INTRODUCTION

6.051 In all cases of traffic crash investigations, one of the most important evidence-gathering aspects of the entire process is the taking and recording of accurate and adequate measurements. The seriousness of the case will usually dictate the extent to which measurements should be taken, but some measurements should be taken at all crash scenes inasmuch as they can be made quickly and easily; and it is better to have measurements that are not needed later than to need measurements that are not available and can no longer be obtained.

6.052 There are many excellent new and innovative methods available to take measurements and prepare scale diagrams, such as electronic measuring instruments for field measurements, and computer drafting devices for later in-office use. However, many departments and individual investigators cannot afford these items that can be very costly. Additionally, a great number of investigators continue to prefer the usual tape measure and hand methods of making field measurements and then preparing scale diagrams by hand. Accuracy in both approaches depends upon the experience of and the care taken by the individual investigator. Properly done, they can result in an equally accurate product.

6.053 Even though in most cases an investigator is able to adequately measure a crash scene and prepare a scale diagram thereof, in some serious or complicated cases, he should be prepared to obtain the services of a surveyor or engineer to carry out these tasks.

SCENE EVIDENCE

6.054 Evidence at the scene may be divided into one of two categories, depending upon its probable length of existence where it is located (see Fig. 7–11).

1. *Short-lived evidence.* Evidence that should be photographed and measured as soon as possible, such as gasoline spills, water stains, puddles, and spatter.
2. *Long-term evidence.* Evidence that will last for several days, a month, or longer, e.g., chips, gouges, grooves, and other damage or marks to or on the roadway or roadside objects.

Some evidence normally considered *long-term evidence* may become *short-lived evidence*, depending upon the degree of impression or damage caused, and also upon the weather conditions and the amount and kind of traffic at the time.

PHOTOGRAPHS AND MEASUREMENTS

6.055 When circumstances are such that photographs and measurements cannot be taken before an item of evidence such as a motor vehicle is moved or removed from the roadway, its position may be marked on the roadway with tape, crayon, spray paint, or spray chalk for later measurement and recording, or indicated with numbered blocks. In deciding which is to be used, the investigator should take into consideration how permanent or long-lasting the indicator must be. For example, some tape and chalk indicators may soon disappear because of inclement weather conditions, traffic, and so on. There are some spray paints that will last for a considerable period of time, particularly if applied to a dry surface. Whatever is used should be of a contrasting color. Also, whenever possible, photographs should be taken before the position of the item of evidence is marked or is moved from its initial position. This precaution may facilitate acceptance of the photographs in court, as the photographs will then not represent anything other than what was initially found at the scene.

FIELD SKETCH

6.056 A *field sketch* is a rough drawing made quickly, and as soon as possible after the investigator arrives at the crash scene. A prime purpose of a field sketch is to record the positions and measurements of items that will soon be moved, lost, destroyed, altered, or mutilated. Accordingly, the first items to be drawn onto the field sketch in their approximate positions should be those that are classified as short-lived evidence. The sketch need not be made to scale, but all items should be relative in size and distance. Fix items with triangulation and/or coordinates, in the manner explained below. Accurate after-crash measurements taken at the scene may be added to the sketch later.

6.057 In preparing a field sketch, certain items for inclusion, procedures and cautions must be considered by the investigator:

1. Direction of North.
2. Specific locations and/or positions of involved traffic units in respect to each applicable *event* contained in the *series of events* (see Para. 1.018).
3. Specific locations and/or positions of all physical evidence, including such items as roadway outlines, curves, markings, and signs.
4. Baselines and points from which measurements are made, and the measurement method used, e.g., triangulation and/or coordinates.
5. Include only those items that are seen at the time the sketch is made.
6. Do not include things that cannot be explained.
7. Ensure that the person who prepares and records measurements on the sketch is the person who reads the measurements from the measuring device that is used.
8. Do not erase errors; neatly cross out an error and write in the correction. Some jurisdictions may require that the error and correction be initialed in the event a question may be raised in court.
9. Do not include opinions or a witness statement.

SCALE DIAGRAMS

6.058 A scale diagram is a reasonably accurate representation of a crash scene, usually completed to a scale using measurements from a field sketch. The scale used may be 1 inch or any part thereof to represent 1 foot or any greater number of feet. In SI measurements, 1 millimeter or 1 centimeter may be used to represent 1 meter or any greater number of meters. The kind and size of a scale diagram is instrumental in deciding upon the scale to be used in preparing the diagram. If the diagram is to be small, such as a page in a report, the scale may be small, e.g., $\frac{1}{4}$ in = 5 ft (5 mm = 1 m). The basic items that are required to prepare a scale diagram are the following:

1. Sharp-pointed pencil or pen.
   Caution: A dull or broad point may represent several inches (centimeters), particularly when a small scale is being used.
2. Protractor
3. Ruler (Imperial or SI)
4. Compass
5. IPTM's *blueBlitz*© Traffic Template. Available in both Imperial and SI measurement systems (see Fig. 6–06).

INSTRUMENTS

6.059 There are many items of equipment available to the investigator that are useful in making sketches and scale diagrams of crash scenes. These include:

a. IPTM's *blueBlitz*© Traffic Template.
b. Clinometer. An instrument for determining the angular inclination of surfaces.
c. Compass.
d. Flex curve.
e. Traffic templates (*U.S. or SI*), c/w clipboard.
f. IPTM's Grade Gauge©. An excellent, easy-to-use, inexpensive instrument for measuring grades (see Fig. 6–07).
g. IPTM's 360-Degree Protractor© (see Fig. 6–08).
h. Measuring wheel.
i. Ruler.
j. Smart Level®. The Smart Level has several advantages over the standard-type carpenter's level, in that it displays readings in terms of a surface being level or non-level, angle in degrees, percent, or pitch.
k. Tape measures: 100 ft (30 m) and 12 ft (3 m).
l. Transit. A surveying instrument used for measuring horizontal and vertical angles, commonly used to measure crash scenes.

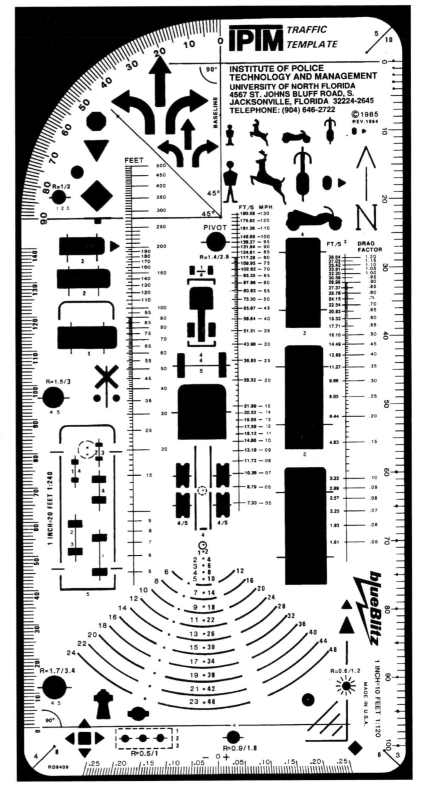

Figure 6–06. IPTM's ***blueBlitz***© Traffic Template. Available in both Imperial and SI measurement systems. Developed by R. W. Rivers for use by law enforcement officers, this template is also ideally suited for use by traffic engineers, attorneys, insurance claims adjustors, and all persons concerned with traffic crash investigation and scale plan drawing. This template contains nomographs for determining speeds and symbols most frequently required for traffic crash diagrams, including motorcycles, pedestrians, automobiles, commercial vehicles, signs, and directional arrows (see www.iptm.org).

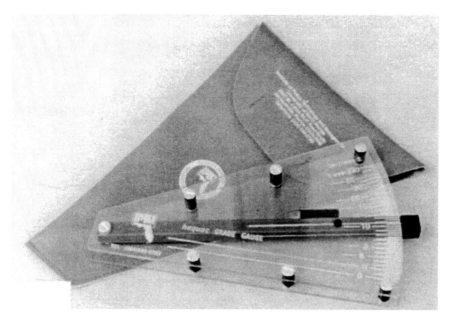

Figure 6–07. IPTM's Grade Gauge©. An instrument that can be used to measure the grade or slope or elevation of any surface.

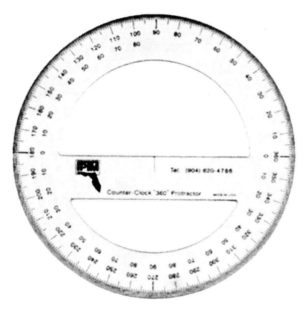

Figure 6–08. IPTM's 360-Degree Counter Clockwise Protractor©. This protractor makes it easy for the investigator to measure angles that are required for applications of linear momentum, as well as in a variety of other applications where angles are a part of the investigation.

(NOTE: For additional measuring methods and inherent errors in methods and in the use of devices, see paragraph 1.055 and Table 1–02.)

6.060 Traditional methods of measuring crash scenes on busy highways, such as in the case of using a measuring tape, involve considerable risk and disruption of traffic flows. However, there are various electronic-type measuring devices that are available that lessen the risks involved which provide easily obtained, accurate, and precise measurements. These include Sonar (Sonic) Measuring Devices (SMD's), Laser Measuring Devices, Electronic Measuring Devices (EMD's), the Accident Investigation Measurement (AIM) System, and the Total Station, which is an instrument that contains many of the attributes of various other measuring devices and one which also stores collected data that can be downloaded to an office computer for the production of maps prepared to scale.

6.061 In all cases, the use of measurement instruments should be carried out in accordance with the manufacturer's instructions and, as required, those of the instructor where instruction in their use is given. Certainly, the total value of many of these instruments can only be realized through proper training and/or extended use or practice. Training that would be necessary for the wide variety of instruments available is beyond the scope of this manual. For specific training information, the investigator should contact the companies/manufacturers direct or schools/police academies that

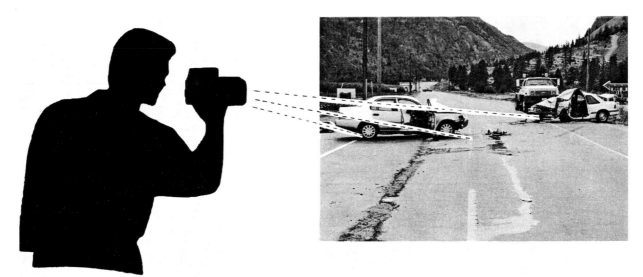

Figure 6–09. An example depicting how an electronic measuring instrument can be used to take a number of measurements from one position.

specialize in traffic crash investigation and reconstruction training.*

SYMBOLS

6.062 Symbols are useful in preparing freehand drawings for field sketches and scale plan drawings. Most symbols can be made with the *blueBlitz©* traffic template (see Fig. 6–06); others can be prepared freehand following the examples shown in Figure 6–10.

CONVENTIONS FOR RECORDING MEASUREMENTS

6.063 When recording measurements, do not use the apostrophe (') and quotation marks (") to indicate

---

*NOTE: There are a number of excellent products available to meet the needs of measuring crash scenes and preparing scale diagrams. To become familiar with these, the investigator may wish to refer to such publications as the *Law and Order* magazine, Buyers Guide, published by Hendon Inc., 130 Waukegan Road, Deerfield, IL, 60015. Tele: (847) 444-3300. Fax: (847) 444-3333. www.hendonpub.com, and the *Accident Reconstruction Journal* and the *Accident Investigation Quarterly*, both of which are published by the *Accident Reconstruction Journal*, P.O. Box 234, Waldorf, MD 20604-0234, Tel/Fax: 301-843-1371, e-mail: accidentrj@aol.com, where many such products are often advertised.

feet and inches because these symbols can be mistaken for the numbers 1 and 11.

6.064 Record feet and inches as illustrated in the following examples:

a. Record thirteen feet and three inches as $13^{\underline{3}}$
b. Record eleven feet as $11^{\underline{0}}$
c. Record ten inches as $0^{\underline{10}}$

When using a measuring device marked in feet and tenths of a foot, place a decimal point in front of the digit indicating tenths of a foot.

a. Record seven feet as 7.0
b. Record seven feet and five tenths as 7.5
c. Record five tenths of one foot as 0.5

6.065 When using the metric system, indicate whether measurements are in centimeters (cm), meters (m), or kilometers (km).

a. Record 7.55 centimeters as 7.55 cm
b. Record 7.55 meters as 7.55 m
c. Record 7.55 kilometers as 7.55 km

6.066 Most measurements using the metric system are in meters or parts of a meter. Therefore, it is acceptable to show all measurements in meters or parts of a meter without their being followed by the meter designation *m*, provided that any measurement in any other unit, such as a centimeter, taken

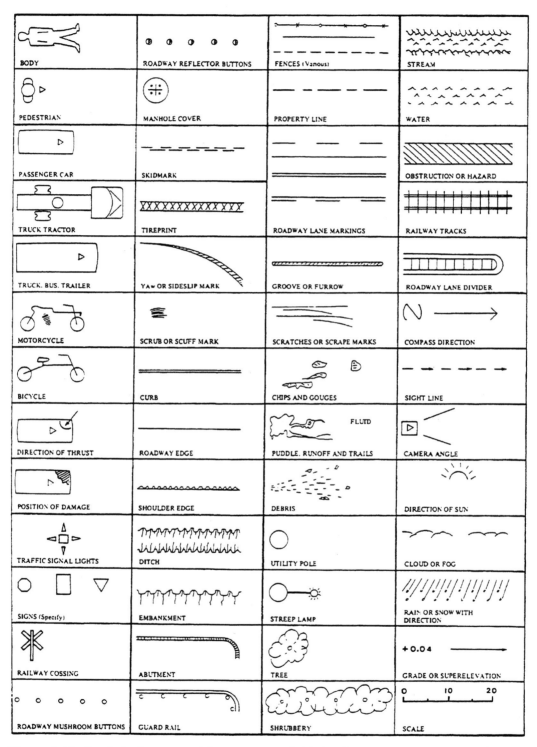

Figure 6–10. Symbols that are useful in preparing field sketches, diagrams and maps. (Reproduced from R. W. Rivers, *Traffic Accident Investigator's Manual. A Level 1 and 2 Reference, Training and Investigation Manual* (2nd ed.), published by Charles C Thomas, Springfield, 1995, p. 127.)

at the scene or otherwise recorded in the investigation, is properly designated.

BASELINES

6.067 One of the very first steps in measuring an accident scene is to decide on the *baseline* (reference line) that will be used. Preferred baselines include such items as a curb, guard rail, fence, roadway edge, center line, or marked center line. Although it is preferred that a baseline be straight, this is not absolutely essential. For example, a roadway edge around a very slight curve can be used.

REFERENCE POINTS

6.068 A *reference point* (RP) is a point *from* which measurements are made to establish or fix points on items of evidence (see Figs. 6–11 and 6–12). Reference points may be *tangible* (permanent) or *intangible* (either temporary or constructed).

1. *Tangible reference points* include such permanent items as posts, buildings, bridges, signs, trees,

fire hydrants, roadway damages, and other permanent objects or conditions. It is common practice when using coordinates, to label as RP only the original or zero point (from which measurements to other points, including other reference points, are made).

2. *Intangible reference points* include such temporary points as crayon, chalk, or spray paint marks placed on the roadway, constructed or temporarily marked curb extension lines, or other temporary identification marked, placed, or indicated on a surface. An intangible reference point should always be related to or in some way identified with a tangible reference point.

6.069 In taking measurements, precise reference points (spots) on objects or baselines should be established and shown, from which or to which the measurements are made. When deemed necessary, these same reference points may also be shown later on diagrams or plans for purposes of explanation. Very often, one point on small items of evidence is sufficient. However, it may be difficult, if not impossible, to later reposition a vehicle on the roadway or place an item of evidence precisely unless

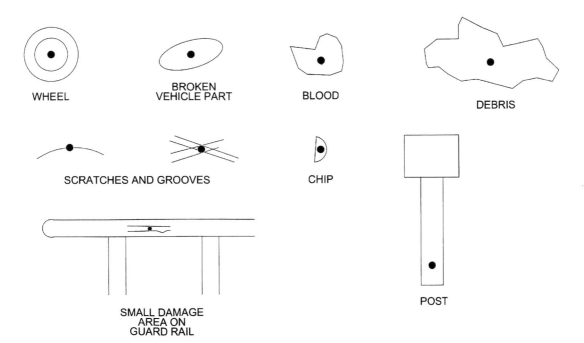

WHEEL

BROKEN
VEHICLE PART

BLOOD

DEBRIS

SCRATCHES AND GROOVES

CHIP

SMALL DAMAGE
AREA ON
GUARD RAIL

POST

Figure 6–11. Examples of single reference points on various smaller items of evidence (prepared with *The Crash Zone*©).

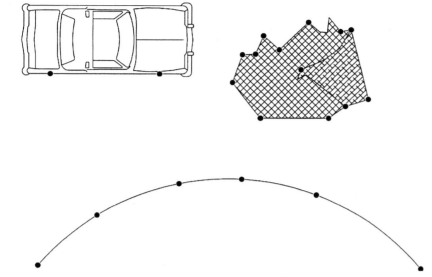

Figure 6–12. Most larger items of evidence required more than one point to fix their positions (prepared with *The Crash Zone©*).

there is more than one reference point established when making field measurements, as well as when positioning the item in the preparation of a scale drawing or plan of the scene. When deciding upon the number of reference points to be used, it should always be remembered that when there is a possibility the item of evidence could rotate around one point, additional points should be used. For example, in measuring the position of a vehicle at rest on the roadway, if one reference point is established on only the vehicle's corner, the vehicle could rotate about that point, thereby possibly giving an incorrect position should it be attempted to reposition the vehicle later, or in the preparation of a scale diagram. This applies to the use of both coordinates and triangulation.

6.070 The difference between a *tangible* or *intangible* reference point (RP) and a *spot* must be well established in the mind of the investigator. The term *spot* is normally considered to be a particular spot on an item of evidence and can be used to identify many things and for many reasons. However, for our purposes, it can be used to identify an intangible reference point, as in the case when a crayon mark is placed on the curb of a roadway.

MEASURING METHODS

6.071 There are two basic methods of measuring the locations or positions of evidence:

1. *Coordinate Method*
   Coordinates are distances measured at right angles from a baseline to an object or point.
2. *Triangulation Method*
   This method uses triangles to connect a moveable object or evidence to reference points.

Coordinate Method

6.072 *Coordinates* are distances measured at right angles from a baseline to an object or point. When the roadway is straight or has only a very slight curve, the edge of the roadway may be used as a baseline. For purposes of location and future reference, the baseline must be related by measurement to a reference point. The reference, or zero, point from which measurements are begun should be a point on the baseline or roadway edge either at or related to a permanent, recognizable landmark, such as a fire hydrant (see Fig. 6–13).

Triangulation Method

6.073 *Triangulation* is a method of locating a *point* or a *spot* on an item of evidence or within an area by measurements taken from two or more reference points (tangible or intangible). The locations and types of reference points used must be identified for future use. (For examples, see Figs. 6–13 and 6–14.)

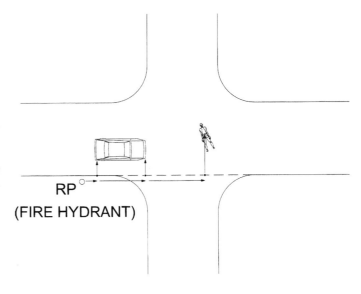

Figure 6–13. An example of how coordinates can be used to fix positions of evidence. In this example, the curb is tied in with the fire hydrant, which is a permanent tangible reference point. Note that the curb forms a baseline, which is extended across the intersection by means of an imaginary line from which measurements are made, using coordinates, to the items of evidence. The positions of all items of evidence can in this way be later established by taking measurements from the permanent tangible reference point, i.e., the fire hydrant (prepared with *The Crash Zone*©).

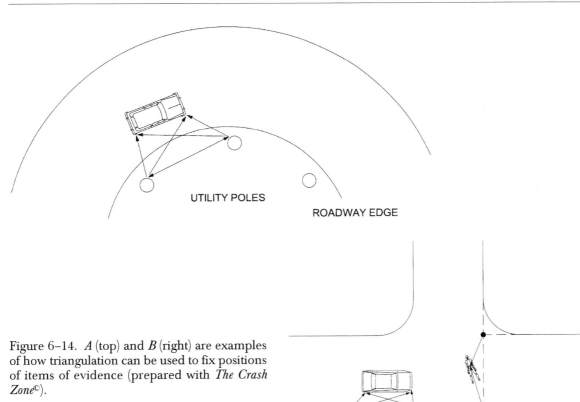

Figure 6–14. *A* (top) and *B* (right) are examples of how triangulation can be used to fix positions of items of evidence (prepared with *The Crash Zone*©).

6.074 When using the triangulation method, the investigator should observe certain rules:

a. Always attempt to select reference points that are a sufficient distance apart to give a reasonably wide triangle base. Do not use long, thin triangles.

b. Fix small objects by measuring to their centers. This procedure is usually satisfactory for small patches of blood or other liquids and small areas of evidence that are not more than 2 feet (0.6 meters) in width.

c. Except for small items of evidence, fix all items with a least two triangles.

d. Use one triangle for each point on an item of evidence to which a measurement is made.

e. Whenever possible, use the same baseline from which to form triangles when fixing points on the same side of an item of evidence.

f. Yaw or other curved tire marks should be fixed by triangles at intervals of 10 to 20 feet (3 to 6 meters), depending on the length and radius of the curve.

g. Irregular angles and marks should be fixed with sufficient numbers of triangles to enable the investigator or some other person to reposition the evidence at its precise location both at the scene and on a scale diagram.

6.075 Triangulation may be a better method of measuring than the coordinate method in areas where it is difficult to locate or establish a good, reasonably straight baseline. Examples of such areas are where a roadway:

a. Does not have an adequate curb line;

b. Has an uneven edge as sometimes found on dirt, snow, or gravel surfaces;

c. Has a sharp curve;

d. Forms a part of and is within a complicated intersection; or

e. Has places to which it is difficult to make measurements from the roadway edge.

6.076 Sometimes it is advisable to use both triangulation and coordinates to fix items of evidence at the scene of an accident. For example, while coordinates may fix the location of a skid mark readily enough, it may be easier to fix the location of a small item of evidence such as a motorcycle helmet by triangulation (see Figs. 6–15 and 6–16).

6.077 The coordinate and triangulation methods satisfy most measurement requirements for measuring a crash scene. However, it is often necessary to take additional measurements in order to satisfy court requirements. These additional measurements most frequently involve the distances between items of evidence, easily done using the *straight line* measuring method (see Fig. 6–16).

6.078 Measurements may be recorded directly on a field sketch or scale diagram (see Fig. 6–17).

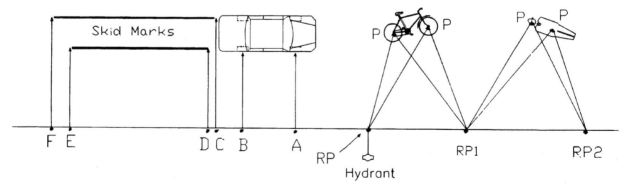

Figure 6–15. An example of how both coordinates and triangulation can be used in combination to fix items of evidence. In this example, a roadway edge has been selected as the baseline. The fire hydrant is a permanent tangible reference point (RP). Crayon marks, shown as A, B, C, D, E, F, and RP1 and RP2, serve as intangible reference points tied to the fire hydrant by measurements. In this example, using the intangible reference points, coordinates (on the left) and triangulation (on the right) fix the positions of the items of evidence (prepared with *The Crash Zone*©).

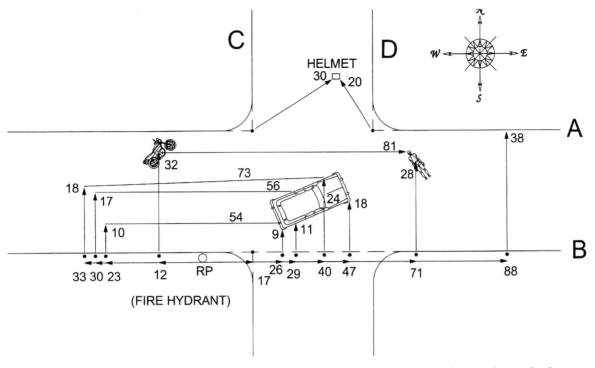

Figure 6–16. Straight line measurements used in combination with coordinates and triangulation. In this example, the distance from the motorcycle to the body is measured by a straight line, a distance of *81*.

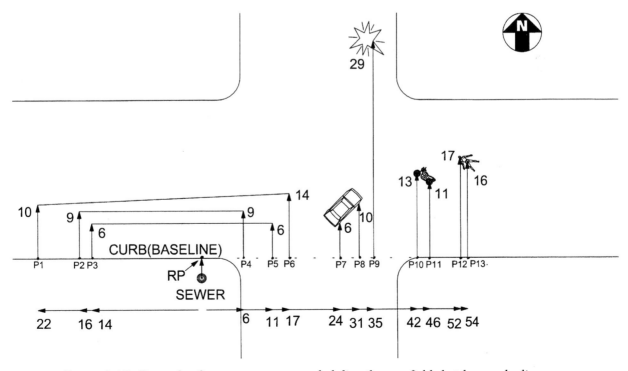

Figure 6–17. Example of measurements recorded directly on a field sketch or scale diagram.

Table 6–02
MEASUREMENT TABLE

From	Dist.E-W	To/from	Dist.N-S	To Comments
RP	W22	P_1	N10	Begin LF skidmark (car)
RP	W16	P_2	N9	Begin LR skidmark (car)
RP	W14	P_3	N6	Begin RR skidmark (car)
RP	E6	P_4	N9	End LR skidmark (car)
RP	E11	P_5	N6	End RR skidmark (car)
RP	E17	P_6	N14	End LF skidmark (car)
RP	E24	P_7	N6	RR wheel, car at final rest
RP	E31	P_8	N10	RF wheel, car at final rest
RP	E35	P_9	N29	Blood spot
RP	E42	P_{10}	N13	Front wheel, MC at final rest
RP	E46	P_{11}	N11	Rear wheel, MC at final rest
RP	E52	P_{12}	N17	Head of MC rider body at final rest
RP	E54	P_{13}	N16	Torso of MC rider body at final rest

Whenever possible, however, the measurements should be recorded as closely as possible to the points being measured to. In Figure 6–17, for example, a measurement is taken from the RP (sewer) 24 ft eastward to the intangible reference point (a crayon mark) P7, and 6 ft northward to the right-rear wheel of the car. Alternatively, a table, such as Table 6–02, can be developed to record these measurements. Additional explanatory detail can also be added to the table at the discretion of the investigator.

REFERENCES

Rivers, R.W.: *Technical Traffic Accident Investigators' Handbook: A Level 111 Reference, Training and Investigation Manual* (2nd ed.). Charles C Thomas, Springfield, Illinois, 1997.

Rivers, R.W.: *Traffic Accident Field Measurements and Scale Diagrams Manual.* Charles C Thomas, Springfield, Illinois, 1997.

Rivers, R.W.: *Training and Reference Manual for Traffic Accident Investigation.* Institute of Police Technology and Management, University of North Florida, Jacksonville, Florida, 1995.

Chapter 7

TRAFFICWAY EVIDENCE

R. W. Rivers

Part 1

ASPECTS OF BASIC ENGINEERING AND DESIGN

7.001 It is important for the investigator to examine the trafficway leading up to and the crash scene itself for environmental and traffic engineering factors that may provide evidence that will be important in the later reconstruction of the crash events. An important element in this is an examination of traffic control devices, e.g., traffic signals, stop-signs, and roadway markings, and as applicable, whether they were properly and effectively maintained, free of malfunctions, kept clean and free from damage, obliteration, or other obstructions that might have interfered with a proper interpretation of the demands of the device.

7.002 Of particular importance in investigating for trafficway evidence is the investigator's ability to:

a. Know the kinds of evidence to look for, and the ability to identify and interpret such evidence during an at-scene or follow-up investigation.
b. Know the effects engineering, environmental, and other trafficway factors have on the action or lack of action by a driver or pedestrian who is either directly or indirectly involved in a traffic crash. These issues include, but are not limited to various traffic control devices, weather and trafficway conditions, and their effects, influences on or contribution to traffic crashes.

c. Identify and interpret highway and roadway marks, and damage to the roadway and other parts of or adjacent to the trafficway, e.g., guard rails, sign posts, utility poles.
d. Document scene evidence as soon as possible, such as by photography, scene measurements and written notes.

TRAFFIC CONTROL DEVICES

7.003 Traffic crash investigators should be familiar with traffic control devices and their intent, namely that devices, such as signs, roadway pavement, curb and other trafficway markings, are the primary means of regulating, warning, or guiding traffic on all streets and highways. Both signs and markings have the function of regulating, warning, guiding and/or channelizing traffic. They are intended to fulfill a need; command attention, covey a clear, simple meaning; command respect of road users, and give adequate time for proper response.

Traffic Signs

7.004 *Traffic sign.* A traffic sign is generally defined as a device mounted on a fixed or portable support, whereby a specific message is conveyed by means of words or symbols placed or erected for the purpose of regulating, warning or guiding traffic. Traffic signs usually fall into one of three categories: (1) Regulatory, (2) warning, or (3) guidance. Regulatory signs represent a mandatory legal requirement established by a statute, ordinance, or some similar legislative act. Warning signs provide an advanced notice of upcoming roadway conditions and offer suggested actions to drivers. Guide signs offer informational and tourist messages that may benefit travelers.

Sign Descriptions

7.005 The standard shapes of signs and their meanings are as follows (see Figs. 7–01 and 7–02):

Diamond: Used for the majority of warning signs

Rectangle: With the longer dimension vertical, is used for majority of regulatory signs and some warning signs

Pentagon: With point up is used only for school and school crossing signs

Pennant: With the longer dimension horizontal, is used only for the No-Passing Zone warning sign

Trapezoid: Used only for recreational use guide signs

Octagan: Used only for the Stop sign

Equilateral Triangle: With one point down is used only for the Yield sign

Circle: Used for railroad crossing advance warning sign and for Civil Defense Evacuation Route Signing

7.006 *Sign Placement.* In countries where driving is done on the right-hand side of the roadway, most signs are normally located on the right-hand side of the roadway facing approaching traffic. Additional signs in other locations, such as overhead and on the left-hand side, may, of course, supplement normally located signs because of information they contain, requiring a specific location. For example, signs on wide streets or on high-speed facilities are frequently mounted overhead.

30"x30"   36"x36"x36"   24"x30"   24"x30"

24"x30"   24"x30"   24"x24"   30"x36"

24"x30"   30"x30"   36"x24"   18"x24"

Figure 7–01. Examples of commonly used regulatory signs.

Figure 7–02. Examples of warning signs used in temporary traffic control zones.

7.007 Sign investigation should look for evidence or take into consideration the following:

a. Specific environmental factors involved in the sign's location, e.g., view obstructions by other signs, trees, tree limbs, the distance of the sign from curb or edge of roadway, and so on (see 6.027 and Fig. 6–02).

b. The angle at which the sign is turned, e.g., is it properly turned toward the roadway and the driver's field of vision, or is it turned at such an angle that it would be difficult for a driver to see the sign's message?

c. Is the sign visible only to the traffic for which it is intended, or could it be visible to other traffic thereby causing confusion on the part of drivers?

d. Are there other signs, each for a different purpose but not properly separated, on the one sign post?

e. When there is more than one sign in the same location, do their placements follow a meaningful sequence in order of priority or importance, e.g., a regulatory sign, followed by a warning and/or guide sign?

Traffic Signals

7.008 A *traffic signal* may be defined as power-operated signal display used to regulate or warn traffic. They are installed to establish right-of-way control at intersecting streets when signs alone are inadequate. While a stop sign also establishes right-of-way control (by identifying a main street versus minor street), a signal adds the element of time. Signals prioritize each movement through the intersection by allowing or inhibiting specific vehicle movements for a specific period of time.

Traffic Control Signal Unit

7.009 The following describe some major parts and functions of a traffic control signal unit (see Fig. 7–03):

• *Signal Section* (1.) The assembly of a signal housing, signal lens, a light source with neces-

Figure 7–03. A traffic control signal unit.

sary components, used for providing one signal indication. (2.) That part of a signal face containing an optical unit.
• *Signal Head* (1.) An assembly of one or more signal sections. (2.) An arrangement of one or more signal lenses in signal faces that may be designated accordingly as one-way, two-way, etc.
• *Signal Face* (1.) Front part of a signal head. (2.) That part of a signal head provided for controlling traffic in a single direction.
• *Signal Indication* (1.) The illumination of a signal lens. (2.) An illumination of a traffic signal lens or combination of lenses at the same time.
• *Signal Backplate.* A thin strip of material that extends outward from the parallel to a signal face on all sides of a signal housing to provide a background for improved visibility of the signal indications.
• *Pedestrian Signal Head.* A signal head that contains the symbols Walking Person (WALK) an Upraised Hand (DON'T WALK), installed to direct pedestrian traffic at a traffic control signal. The head may be separate to or in combination with a traffic control signal unit such as that shown in Figure 7–03.
• *Optical unit.* An assembly of lens, reflectors, lamps, and lamp socket.
• *Cycle (cycle length).* A complete sequence of signal indications.
• *Phase (signal phase).* The portion of a signal cycle allocated to any single combination of one or more traffic movements simultaneously receiving the right-of-way during one or more intervals.
• *Interval.* The part of parts of the signal cycle during which the signal indications do not change. Vehicle signal *change interval* is that period of time in a traffic signal cycle between conflicting green intervals. It is characterized by a yellow warning indication followed by a red clearance indication.
• *Phase Sequence.* A predetermined order in which the phases of a cycle occur.
• *Split.* A percentage of a cycle length allocated to each of the various phases in a signal cycle.
• *Offset.* The time relationship (expressed in seconds of percent of cycle length) determined by the difference between a defined interval portion of the coordinated phase green and a system reference point.

• *Clearance time.* Determine if signal phases are adequate for (i) clearance by vehicles and/or pedestrians, (ii) driver perception/reaction time to stop vehicle when required on the approach to a traffic signal.

NOTE: When investigating matters involving traffic signs and signals, it is recommended that investigators contact local professional traffic engineers for assistance and advice. These professionals can also later become personally involved in trial activity or in public hearings as fact witnesses or as expert witnesses.

Detectors

7.010 Detectors are used to sense the passage or the presence, within a specified zone, of all road users, including motor vehicles of all legal sizes, human-powered vehicles such as bicycles and wheelchairs, and pedestrians[1] (see Figure 7–04).

7.011 Detectors in their transportation application have historically either recognized the presence of a moving or stopped vehicle, recognized passage of a moving vehicle by completing a circuit, or recognized changes in an electrical or magnetic field. Most detectors are comprised of three primary components: the sensor, the lead-in cable, and the interpreter/receiver (usually called an amplifier although it must do much than simple amplification). When coupled with a sophisticated controller unit (see Fig. 7–04C), detector can be used to derive volume, vehicle speed, lane occupancy, queue lengths, and to infer congestion, incidents, stops, and delays.

7.012 *Detector Zones.* Each detector has a zone or area in which it will respond to the arrival, presence, or departure of a road user.[2] Poorly-placed or constructed and inadequately maintained detectors may give improper or misleading responses in the detection of vehicles that are entering in a left-turn lane or departing an intersection.

7.013 *Controller.* A complete electrical mechanism mounted in a cabinet for controlling the operation of a traffic control signal, mounted in the vicinity of the traffic control signal (see Fig. 7–04C).

7.014 There are various types of detectors in use, including:

a. *Inductive Loop Detector.* A wire loop embedded in the pavement carrying a predetermined frequency signal. A vehicle passing over the loop changes the inductance and, hence, the frequency or phasing of the signal. This change is detected and converted to a relay actuation. The detection is maintained as long as the vehicle is over the loop, thereby acting as a presence detector. Because of the reliability and low cost, this detector has become the most commonly used for traffic signal applications.[3]

b. *Pressure-Sensitive Detector.* A detector installed in the surface of the roadway, capable of being actuated by the pressure of a vehicle tire passing over it.

c. *Sonic (Pulsed or Continuous Wave).* 1. Detectors that detect distance to an object. 2. An instrument mounted over or beside the roadway which reflects a beam of ultrahigh frequency sound off the pavement. A vehicle interrupting this beam is detected.[4]

d. *Radar (Pulsed).* Detectors that detect movement.

e. *Magnetic.* Magnetic sensors that detect changes in the earth's magnetic field caused by moving metal. The constant lines of flux from the earth's magnetic field are deflected by the passage of a vehicle causing a voltage to be developed.[5]

f. *Microwave.*

g. *Infrared.*

h. *Pedestrian Detector.* Push buttons mounted on signal poles or on special posts adjacent to the intersection.

i. *Video Detectors.* Detectors that detect movement.

j. *Other Detectors.* Such as those used for special purposes, e.g., light emission to detect priority vehicles or radio-frequency detectors to identify buses.

7.015 *Loop Detectors.* In the case of loop detectors, the detection zone is within the area defined by the loop assembly. An investigation should determine whether or not there was a loop-assembly failure caused by an electrical leakage to the ground and by the loss of conductivity, most often caused by physical damage to the loop assembly either during installation, through pavement movement, or by failure of the embedding or encapsulating sealant.

Figure 7–04A. An example of detectors placed beneath the roadway surface, used to sense the passage or the presence of roadway users within the specified zone shown.

Figure 7–4B. Overhead detector to identify special vehicles such as emergency-type vehicles.

Figure 7–4C. Controller cabinets mounted in the vicinity of the detectors.

Detectors placed within the paved surface, are also subject to the effects of weather, changes in the roadway surface such as erosion, roadway maintenance, frost heaves, lightning, and electrical discharges that may disrupt the detector element or the lead-in cable between the detector element in the road surface and the control cabinet.[6]

7.016 Of all the factors affecting proper operation of detectors, perhaps the most important is proper installation. This particularly true for those detectors with sensors located in the pavement. It isn't necessarily uncommon for loop detectors to cause a signal to become stuck. Problems usually arise because of their being exposed to weather extremes, particularly moisture, and severe roadway loading, shifting, and cracking.

7.017 When traffic signal displays are in dispute, the investigator should check with the local traffic engineer to determine if the detector could have been affected or influenced by lightning, temperature, snow, ice, wind speeds, traffic speeds and densities, and roadway surface type and condition.[7] In incidents involving pedestrians where pedestrian signal lamp tones were relied upon, were they working; were they such as to cause/give misleading information to a pedestrian who had visual disabilities? For example, were the tones affected by extraneous sources of sounds, such as wind, rain, vehicle back-up warnings, or birds.

7.018–7.020 reserved.

Timing

7.021 Timing of signal (light) phases is usually determined by the local traffic authority. It is important to investigate phases, particularly in the case of a rear-end collision. Is the change in phases too short? Should there be more clearance time? Are approach speeds so high that values may place some drivers in a dilemma zone, where they can neither stop safely nor clear the intersection before the cross street green phase commences. Cycle lengths during off-peak periods are usually as short as possible (from 40–60 sec. for two-phase signals). Longer cycles are used during peak periods to provide more green time for the major street. Many factors relate to specific locations and must be considered.

A generalized procedure for timing a pre-timed signal can be found in editions of the Traffic Engineering Handbook. Again, investigators should seek the assistance of a professional highways engineer where light phases might be in question, or might be a factor in a collision.

7.022 Traffic control signals are either pre-timed or traffic-actuated. *Pre-timed control* provides a repetitive controller cycle and controller cycle split timing. *Actuated control* provides variable-length green timing for vehicular phases that are equipped with detectors. For pedestrian movements equipped with detectors, the pedestrian display remains DON'T WALK unless a pedestrian call is registered with the controller.[8] Actuated control assigns the right-of-way on the basis of changing traffic demand.[9]

TRAFFICWAY ENGINEERING ISSUES

7.023 Traffic engineering issues are usually defined by the Manual of Uniform Traffic Control Devices (MUTCD) in the U.S., and by similar local or national manuals in other countries. The MUTCD provides definitions and installation specifications for every nationally-approved sign, signal, and pavement marking. Local jurisdictions may also have additional, special-use traffic devices that do not conflict with national standards. These definitions ensure that traffic control devices convey the same messages and represent the same intentions to all motorists, regardless of location. For example, an *Intersection Ahead* warning sign means the same thing in California as it does in Connecticut. To help convey these messages on a national and global scale, symbolic messages (*symbol signs*) are promoted instead of textual legends (*word signs*) whenever possible.

7.024 Some of the typical evidentiary trafficway engineering questions facing the investigator include:

a. Did the sign(s) and/or pavement marking(s) convey the proper message for prevailing roadway conditions; was the sign or marking misleading, did it lend to confusion on the part of the motorist, and so on? For example, was a No Passing Zone justified? Was a guide sign and directional arrow installed too closely to an exit ramp (thus failing to give motorists enough time and distance to safely decelerate and exit the road in response to seeing the sign)? Was a Stop Bar (pavement marking) placed too far from the intersection to be of value? Was the sign message legible? Were delineation markers suitable for various nighttime or daytime conditions?

b. Did a visual obstruction contribute to the crash? For example, did a tree branch grow out into the road and subsequently block a stop sign from the view of approaching drivers? Did property landscaping or an advertising sign block visibility from a private driveway toward a main road? Did a temporarily-parked delivery van mask a One Way sign at an intersection?

c. What about nearby traffic signals and related electronic devices? Were there any reported signal failures or recent electronic maintenance activities, such as a timing or detector failure, Was the traffic signal connected to an *actuation* system of roadway or roadside sensors? If so, was there a loss of interconnected control? What were the *timing* parameters of the traffic signal displays? Were they adequate for driver response?

d. What about contributing factors from private-property? Did a nearby high-intensity lamp from a private parking lot result in a blinding roadway *glare* for the driver? Did an attractive *roadside nuisance* or special event distract a teenage driver from looking straight ahead?

e. *Environment.* Did a sunrise or sunset cause glare or a significant expanse of shadowing that affected visibility and perception? Did rainwater reflections obscure a roadway centerline pavement marking? Did an apparently-stable roadside shoulder erode into a dangerous roadway edge drop-off condition? Did the roadway have a dry surface as opposed to a wet, snow-covered or oily surface?

7.025 A prudent crash investigator will start the documentation effort for traffic control devices well in advance of the crash scene. Signs, signals, and pavement markings should be photographed and measured (that is, the distance from each traffic control device to the crash scene). Each device should be researched, if necessary, to determine why it was placed and how its message influenced (or failed to influence) the drivers involved in the crash. Alternatives and options should also be researched, since various applications of traffic control devices can sometimes be used to solve the same traffic problem.

7.026 A roadway's design, construction materials, and building techniques are issues of *highway engineering.* A crash-site investigation may sometimes require delving into and comparing the present conditions and features to roadway plans, contract specifications and design standards as an investigative element, especially if one or more parties believe *the road was at fault* in the crash. A problem may be found involving the roadway construction phases, periodic maintenance operations, or normal daily use.

7.027 Important roadway features that must be investigated include the pavement composition, surface friction and condition, guardrail energy-absorption specifications, roadway superelevation designs, and storm-water drainage flow rates–all examples of highway engineering subjects of interest to crash investigators. In the interests of safety and crash causation, the investigator may find it beneficial to review construction plans to determine whether or not roadway was built to specifications. For example, a guard rail placed along a roadway curve immediately beyond the point where a vehicle exited the pavement. Was the guardrail specified for installation in advance of the curve, but actually installed in shorter (and cheaper) segments closer to the point of curvature? An exit warning sign may be too close to the actual exit roadway for a vehicle to safely execute the exit when the speed limit for the area is taken into consideration.

7.028 An investigator's research into highway engineering matters is best directed toward the local government jurisdiction responsible for roadway construction and maintenance. Plans and contracts are generally maintained for many years in paper form, then often archived on microfilm, microfiche, or newer digital imaging (electronic) formats. Roadway contractors (private companies), if known, are supplemental sources of construction plans, work diaries, and contract information. Local highways personnel and roadway construction companies will very often cooperate fully in providing this information.

7.029 Guard rails are a safety feature designed to prevent a vehicle from accidentally straying beyond the roadway edges. Also, in addition to these purposeful roadside features, there are other objects alongside the roadway intentionally placed so as to aid proper traffic flow, such as sign posts and light poles. Other roadside objects are not intended, such as trees. All of which may have been a contributing factor to a crash and its severity.

7.030 Many items of evidence can and should be photographed and measured during the first (emergency) response to a crash site. Otherwise, an investigator may be able to visit (or revisit) the site during similar conditions at a later date or time. Unfortunately, by then many of the initial elements of evidence may have by then been moved, repaired, replaced, or otherwise changed from what was present at the time of the initial crash investigation.

7.031 In summary, it can be said that one of the most important aspects of a trafficway investigation is the examination of traffic-control devices, such as speed-control signs, stop-signs, advisory signs, traffic-control signals, and traffic control roadway markings. This includes evidence of whether or not they were properly placed and adequately maintained, such as being kept clean and free of damage, obliteration, or other obstructions that might have interfered with visibility in terms of the device or marking. Examinations should take place during both daylight and darkness, at other times of the day (as applicable), and under the same or similar light and weather conditions. This should include times when *glare* from headlamps, sun, or other sources of light, e.g., street lamps, illuminated advertising signs, or glare or reflection from windows, rainwater on the pavement, and metal roofs, might have affected the ability of the crash vehicle driver or other trafficway user to see and properly interpret the demands of the device or marking.

7.032–7.036 reserved.

Figures 7–05–7–10 reserved.

Part 2

IDENTIFICATION AND INTERPRETATION OF TRAFFICWAY OBSTRUCTIONS, DEFECTS, MARKS, AND DAMAGE EVIDENCE

7.037 When a vehicle collides with another vehicle or other substantial object, or with a pedestrian, or goes out of control and overturns, the incident will cause various types of damage to and marks on the vehicle and the highway surface or object collided with. It is very important that the at-scene investigator, prosecuting and defense counsels, and others who might later be involved in related proceedings, be able to recognize and interpret all such evidence, and be able to apply meaningful terms and definitions to items included in this evidence.

7.038 The crash scene should be examined for pre-collision, collision point, and post-collision highway marks. The path of travel of a vehicle, possible cause of the crash, and what occurred during the collision may be determined from a proper recognition and analysis of the evidence. Of particular importance is an examination of the underside of an involved vehicle for breakage and abrasions that might be matched up to marks on or along the highway, or objects collided with. Similarly, marks on the highway should be matched up with parts of the vehicle

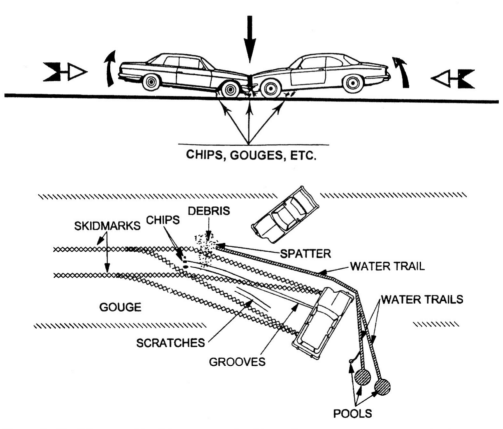

Figure 7–11. Diagram *A* (top) is an example of how chips, gouges, scrapes, and other types of highway damage are caused by vehicles in collision. Diagram *B* (bottom) is an example of postimpact roadway evidence remaining after a vehicle collision.

that caused them. In this way, a determination may be made of the behavior of the vehicle and its placement or position on the highway during the times of pre-collision, collision, and post- collision.

7.039 The investigator should ensure that all applicable items contained in the *series of events* (see Para. 1.016) are covered, many of which may be determined from sources such as:

a. Highway marks (including skid, sideskid, sideslip or yaw tire marks, chips, gouges, scrapes, furrows, and other similar highway marks).
b. Matching damages that indicate direction of thrust or penetration, and vehicle body damages, including evidence from the undercarriage.
c. Final positions of debris and vehicles.

Pavement-Edge Drop-Off

7.040 When a driver fails to maintain his vehicle in the proper lane of travel, resulting in a wheel to drop off the pavement edge, he may be unable to steer the vehicle back onto the roadway in a normal manner. If he oversteers, the vehicle may veer across the road out of control and possibly overturn. Pavement-edge drop-off is considered to most likely occur during poor visibility, such as during rain and darkness, when the driver is impaired, falls asleep, or when entering a curve at an excessive speed.

Roadway Damage

7.041 Roadway damage and defects, such as that shown in Figure 7–13, can cause a vehicle to go out of control. Also, when a driver sees such damage (or a major defect or obstruction in the roadway), his reaction may be to swerve to avoid the damage, resulting in a head-on collision, overturn, or vehicle leaving the roadway.

Roadway Alignment

7.042 Improper roadway alignment may cause a driver to lose control of his vehicle. When examining roadway alignment, many factors should be considered, including vehicle speed, any superelevation or bank, sudden narrowing of the roadway and lack of signs to warn of danger or changes in alignment. A crest in the roadway can be responsible for an unclear view of what lies ahead for the driver, such as a sudden change in roadway alignment.

Glare

7.043 At certain times of the day, sun glare or glare from other sources, such as from windows and artificial light, may obstruct a driver's view of traffic-control devices, such as a stop-sign or a traffic light, making these things and other roadway or roadside objects almost invisible to the driver.

Figure 7–12. An example of pavement-edge drop-off.

Figure 7–13. An example of roadway damage.

Figure 7–14. An example of improper roadway alignment.

Figure 7–15. An example of sun glare.

Debris

7.044 An assortment of debris may be found at a crash scene, including vehicle parts, dirt or load fallen from vehicle, water trails from a burst radiator, and oil from the motor or transmission (see Figs. 7–11 and 7–16). For purposes of explanation, when a collision breaks a radiator, the pressure inside forces the coolant out immediately. Initially the coolant will spatter out onto the roadway as scattered drops (*spatter*). After the pressure has subsided, the coolant will dribble out and, if the vehicle is moving, the dribble will form a fluid *trail* on the roadway. When the vehicle is at rest, the liquid will dribble out to form a *puddle* or *pool*. If the puddle or pool is not absorbed quickly into the surface, there may be runoff in the form of *rills* or small streams. This type of evidence is very helpful in establishing the approximate point of impact and the vehicle's path of travel to its final rest position after impact.

Scrapes and Scratches

7.045 A *scrape* is a wide superficial wound or a wide, clean graze mark caused by a sharp or angular edge being passed over a surface, such as that caused by a vehicle part sliding over a paved roadway. A *scratch* is a long, narrow, superficial wound on a surface, often caused by a sliding vehicle part (other than a tire). Very often, scratches appear as a broad band of rough, parallel striations. Scrapes are often found in combination with scratches.

Groove

7.046 A *groove* is a long, narrow indentation or cut in a surface, such as that which occurs during a collision when a moving vehicle part, such as a bolt or some similar type of protruding part strikes the roadway. A groove may be straight or circular. A straight groove indicates a direct movement; whereas a circular groove indicates that the vehicle

Figure 7–16. An example of scrapes, scratches, and debris.

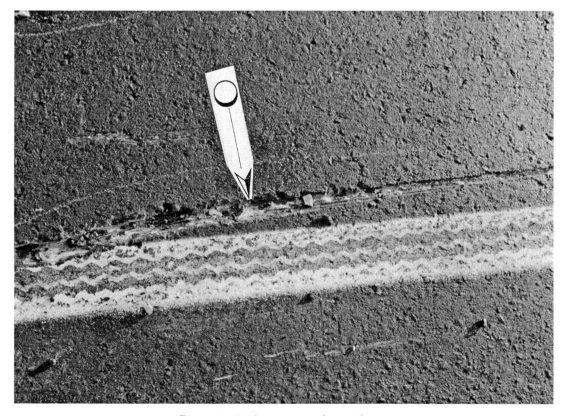

Figure 7–17. A groove in the roadway.

was rotating or spinning. A groove may be deep initially and become shallower toward its end.

Chip, Gouge, and Chop

7.047 A *chip* is a short, small, comparatively thin cavity, approximately 1 in (2.5 cm) in depth, resulting from a piece of material being cut out of the roadway pavement by a sharp, pointed object under considerable pressure, such as a protruding metal part of a vehicle during a crash situation. A *gouge* or *chop* has basically the same elements as a chip except that they are much deeper, i.e., a depth greater than 1 in (2.5 cm). Edges of these cavities may or may not have striations–depending upon the item that caused them. In a practical sense, these three items can be considered to be synonymous.

Figure 7–18. An example of a chip at point *A;* a chop or gouge at point *B.*

Hole

7.048. A *hole* is a round cavity in a surface, very often caused by a protruding bolt, broken rod or a similar round object. Holes will very often have smooth walls when the protruding object stays inserted in the surface or it retracts/ejects in the manner in which it entered, i.e., it does not move laterally. If it does move laterally, the damage will probably appear as a groove.

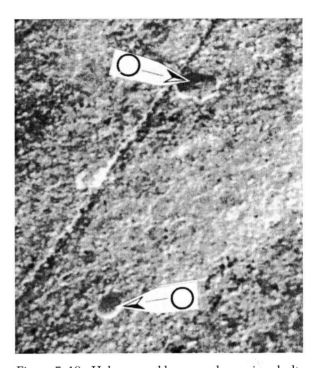

Figure 7–19. Holes caused by an undercarriage bolt.

Matching Vehicle Damage to Roadside Objects

7.049 When a vehicle strikes a roadside object, such as a sign post, utility pole, or some other type of substantial object, an imprint may be left on the object that can be matched to the vehicle part that struck it, or vice versa. This evidence may be found in the form of a hole or scratch from a bolt, imprint from a wheel-rim showing the rim outline, imprints from a door handle or hub cap, as well as many other items that can be directly related to the vehicle or the object.

Matching Undercarriage Parts

7.050 During a collision, many parts of an automobile, such as a cross-member, broken tie rod or bolt, or a disconnected, fallen drive shaft can cause damage to or marks on the roadway. In all examinations, these damages or marks should be related to parts of the vehicle that could have caused them (both of which will show some indication of corresponding damage), and through analysis, a definite determination made. It is very important to take measurements of both the suspect vehicle part and the corresponding roadway mark/damage to assist in the analysis.

Undercarriage Evidence

7.051 In some investigations, such as when a pedestrian is struck and is passed over by the vehicle, evidence of the victim having been under the vehicle can be obtained by examining the vehicle's undercarriage.

7.052 to 7.055 reserved.

Figures 7–23 to 7–26 reserved.

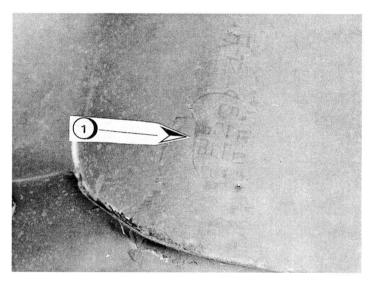

Figure 7–20. An example of a metal vehicle body part (top) that struck a wooden utility pole (bottom). As can be seen, the metal part sustained an imprint of the pole identification markings at point 1. At the same time, the utility pole sustained an imprint of the outline of the metal part (see point 1 in bottom photograph).

Figure 7–21. Photograph *A* (right) shows an example of how measurements can be made of vehicle undercarriage damage. Photograph *B* (bottom) shows evidence of roadway materials adhering to a vehicle undercarriage part, which can then be related to corresponding roadway damage.

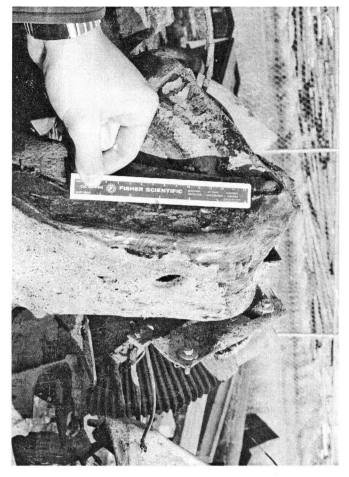

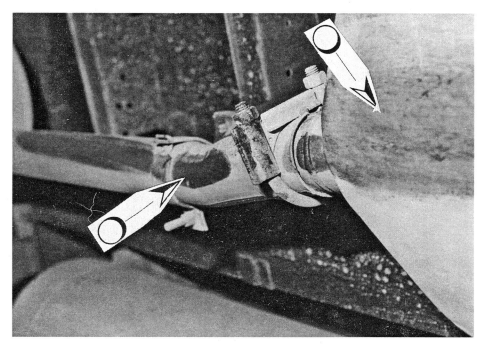

Figure 7–22. An example of undercarriage evidence (blood smear) that can be related to a pedestrian, e.g., in a hit-and-run collision, who was struck and run over by the offending vehicle.

TIRE MARKS

Tire Shapes and Contours

7.056 In order for an investigator to properly recognize, interpret, and analyze tire marks, he/she must first of all understand what the tire configurations are under the variety of circumstances it is operated. This includes operations under normal driving conditions, as well when it is subjected to situations such as when the vehicle undergoes an evasive action maneuver, skids to a stop, is under extreme acceleration, or is out-of-control on the trafficway. In all these circumstances, a tire will experience different shapes or contours and leave individual, distinguishing marks, depending upon its inflation pressure (p.s.i.), whether it is operating with downward pressure or force, or if there is a sideways thrust, and so on.

7.057 Figure 7–27 shows tire parts (Fig. 7–27D), tire pressures, and related tread face contours. Figure 7–27A represents a normally-inflated tire. Note here the full tread-roadway contact. Figure 7–27B represents an underinflated (overdeflected) tire which causes a cupping effect of the tread face, resulting in the outer edges of the tread carrying the greater weight. Figure 7–27C represents an overinflated tire. In this case, the cupping effect is reversed whereby the edges rise and the greater load is carried by the center of the tread. Because of the particular construction of a bias-ply tire, during a cornering maneuver, the inside tire wall tends to lift as indicated in Figure 7–28A; whereas in the case of a radial-ply tire, the tire maintains a primarily full tread contact with the roadway as indicated in 7–28B.

7.058 Each tire mark under investigation should be related to the tire that made it. This can be done in a number of ways, including by counting the number of dark lines in the tire mark and comparing that number to the number of tire ribs of a suspect tire. If the tire is badly worn, such dark lines may not be visible, but then again, this condition can possibly be related to a tire on the vehicle that has little or no tread. When examining the vehicle and its tires, the vehicle that caused the skid marks

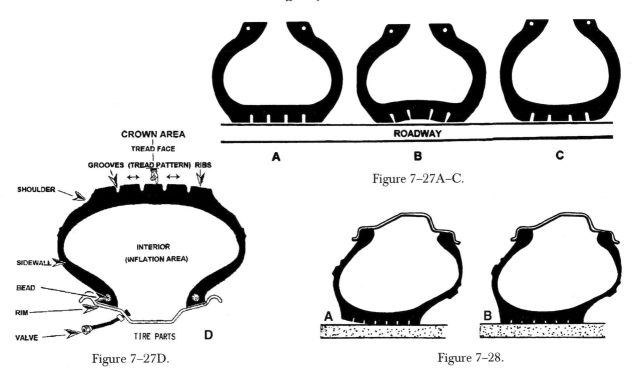

Figure 7–27A–C.

Figure 7–27D.

Figure 7–28.

or tire prints at the actual collision scene may be found at rest a considerable distance from the tire marks. The tire marks left at the scene may be linked to the vehicle in several ways, all of which reinforce each other: matching by the tire prints or tread ribs, by witnesses' and drivers' statements, scrape marks, gouges, and so forth.

Flat Tire Marks

7.059 Deflated or blow-out tire marks should not be confused with underinflated tire marks. A deflated tire mark relates to a tire that has lost all inflation pressure, allowing the tire to literally *flop* on the wheel rim, giving a variety of appearances, such as flopping side-to-side or up-and-down, depending upon the weight carried by the wheel and the angle at which the axle is in relation to the roadway.

Overloaded or Underinflated (Overdeflected) Tire Marks

7.060 A rotating overloaded or underinflated tire will leave a tire mark showing narrow, dark lines at its outer edges. In these cases, the tire tends to *cup*,

as shown in Figure 7–27B. An overloaded tire can be considered to be a tire that has insufficient inflation pressure for the *weight* it is carrying, whether or not the vehicle is actually carrying an auxiliary load. Such marks will most often be seen to cover great distances.

Shadow Evidence

7.061 At certain times of the day, the sun may cause a shadow from an overhead utility wire to fall on a roadway, giving the appearance of a skid mark. When examining photographs of a crash scene, this point should always be borne in mind.

Evidence of Tire Sideslipping

7.062 When a tire sideslips on a roadway that has a rough textured or gritty surface, it may cause sideslip striations across the tread face of the tire, being particularly noticeable on the outside leading rib area (see Fig. 7–32 at point A). The direction or angle of the striations can assist in determining the tire's direction of travel at the time the sideslip took place (see Fig. 7–32 direction arrow).

Figure 7–29. *A, B, C,* and *D* are examples of flat tire marks.

Figure 7–30. An underinflated or overloaded tire mark.

Figure 7–31. Shadows must not be confused for tire marks. In this example, under some circumstances, the shadow (*A*) of the overhead utility wire (*B*) could be misinterpreted as being a tire mark.

Figure 7–32.

Evidence of a Spinning Tire

7.063 When a tire under acceleration from the drive wheels spins on a highway gritty surface, such as in the case of pavement grinding, the tread will show scrapes or striations running along the circumference of the tire tread (see Fig. 7–33 at point A).

Figure 7–33.

Pavement Grinding

7.064 Pavement grinding, which can occur on either wet or dry pavement, results when a collection of fine, hard particles of gritty material that is embedded in or adhering to a tire surface is ground against the roadway surface as the tire slides, as in a skid, sideslips as the result of a collision, sideslips under acceleration, or rotates. Pavement grinding results in various types of scratches or striations on the roadway surface as well as on the surface of the tire. The appearance of the mark on the tire and the roadway depends upon the type of material abrading the surface of each. Pavement grinding most often occurs on a cold or hard pavement surface before the tire has built up enough heat to cause a smear. In the case of a wet roadway surface,

pavement grinding may appear as scratches after the roadway dries.

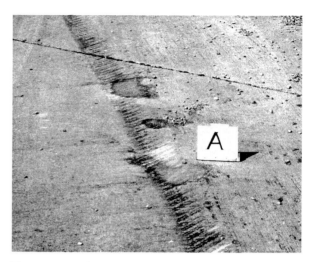

Figure 7–34. Pavement grinding at A, caused by a rotating, sideslipping tire that is under acceleration. Note the striations caused by this tire action.

Striation Marks

7.065 Striation marks are fine, parallel stripes, grooves, or lines that can be caused in a variety of ways. In terms of traffic crash situations, they are commonly caused by (a) tire sideslipping which leaves striations on the roadway from the tire's grooved shoulder pattern; (b) gravel-like particles caught between a spinning, skidding, or sideslipping tire and the roadway; and (c) in damage to the body of a vehicle. In all cases, the direction or angle of the striations on the roadway or other item can assist in determining the direction of travel of the object that made them at the time the incident took place (see the directional arrows in both Figs. 7–32 and 7–35).

Yaw Mark Striations

7.066 *Yaw* is a term applied to a *rotational-sideways movement of a vehicle*–an action of a vehicle in motion *revolving around its center of mass.* Striation marks are very often evident in a mark from a tire that is at the same time rotating and sideslipping, as in the case of a vehicle in yaw.

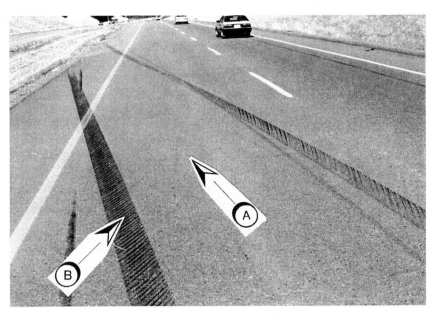

Figure 7–35. An example of striation marks caused by a rotating tire that was sideslipping on the roadway. *A* shows vehicle direction of travel; *B* shows direction of sideslip.

Figure 7–36A (left). *The beginning of a yaw mark*, as shown at arrow *A*, starts as a narrow, dark mark, which widens as the vehicle progresses in yaw, as shown at arrow *B*, traveling in the direction depicted by arrow *C*.

Figure 7–36B (right). A typical yaw mark. Vehicle traveling in the direction shown by the arrow. Note the narrow, dark mark at the leading (outside) edge of the yaw mark.

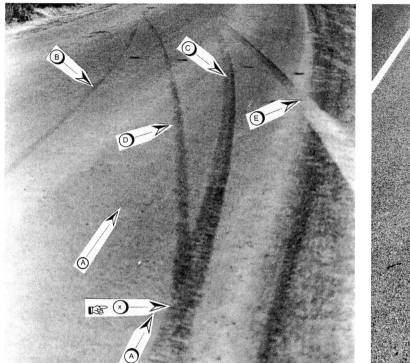

Figure 7–36C (left). *Yaw cross-over marks.* Points *A* show vehicle direction of travel. Tire marks *B* and *C* indicate rear tire paths; front tire paths are *D* and *E*. (Lead-in tire marks, which are not shown, would be at the bottom of the photograph, and would show the rear tire marks tracking inside the front tire marks.) Point *X* indicates where the right-rear tire track (mark), *C*, crosses over the left-front tire mark, *D*. At this point, yaw is considered definite.

Figure 7–36D (right). A *weight shift mark* that gives the appearance of a narrow, dark mark associated with the outside (lead) tire of a vehicle in yaw. These marks do not show the usual forward-sideways sideslip striations that are evident in an actual yaw mark, and they may show travel for a considerable distance of several feet (meters), or even miles (kilometers).

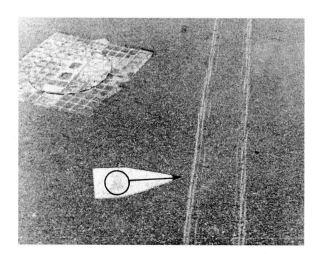

Figure 7–37. Studded tire striation marks.

Studded Tire Striation Marks

7.067 Studded tires on a skidding, sideslipping, or spinning wheel leave thin, parallel scratches or striation marks on a hard surface.

Pass-Over Tire Marks

7.068. Tire marks remaining after a collision can be obliterated or badly obscured by passing traffic that leaves a variety of prints (see Fig. 7–38 at point A) on or over the crash vehicle prints, some of which may be similar (see point B), but some quite different. It is very important to be able to identify the prints left by the crash vehicle to the exclusion of those made by non-related vehicles.

Figure 7–38. Pass-over tire marks.

Tire Prints

7.069 Tire prints are caused by a rotating tire leaving a print of the tire tread pattern on a highway surface. Most noticeable are prints made by a rotating tire that has come into contact with a liquid such as water or oil that dampens the tread and then rolls on a dry surface. Also, if the roadway surface is soft and wet; slightly wet and dusty; or has soft surface materials such as snow, slush, sand, or mud; the tire tread pattern and, depending upon the depth of the soft materials, impressions of the tire tread ridges or rib pattern may be found on the roadway surface as the tire passes over.

Scuff Mark

7.070 A scuff mark is a mark resulting from a tire that is both rotating and sideslipping. Most common scuff marks are flat-tire marks, yaw marks and acceleration marks (see also Figs. 7–29, 7–36, and 7–42).

Figure 7–39. Tire prints.

Figure 7–40. A typical scuff mark.

Acceleration Marks

7.071 An acceleration mark is the result of extreme power being transmitted from the motor to a drive wheel of a motor vehicle causing the tire to spin on the roadway surface. There are a variety of acceleration marks, each having an individual appearance. Under acceleration, the drive wheels experience a weight shift and the tire takes on a contour much the same as a tire that is overloaded. The beginning

of the mark is usually very dark, becoming lighter in appearance near its end. At the beginning of the mark, the spinning tire will often throw roadway surface particles backwards, depositing them on the roadway as debris (see Fig. 7–41A at point 1). Some straight acceleration marks will show the tire groove pattern having a *wavy* appearance as in Figure 7–41B. Invariably, the outer edges of an acceleration mark will have narrow, dark, lines as shown in Figures 7–41B, C, and D. If the wheel that is spinning is lightly loaded, the tire may bounce on the roadway, leaving distinguishable *bounce marks* in the center of the tire mark as in Figure 7–41C. If the tire has low inflation pressure, the center of the tire mark may appear as a cleaning action, but the outer edges of the tire will, however, appear as dark lines as in Figure 7–41D.

Forward-Reverse Acceleration Mark

7.072 Examples of forward-reverse acceleration marks are shown in Figure 7–42A and B. In Figure 7–42A, note evidence of an acceleration mark at point 1; immediate reversal in the mark at point 2, with evidence of tire-roadway debris thrown back at this point–lying on the roadway at the end of the acceleration mark. Note in the reverse acceleration mark, evidence of narrow, dark lines at the outer edges of the mark (point 3) because of a weight shift onto the drive wheels, resulting from extreme acceleration; and a dark scuff mark in the center of the

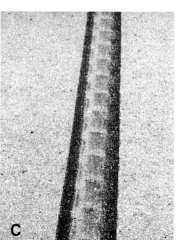

Figure 41. *A*, *B*, *C*, and *D* are examples of acceleration tire marks.

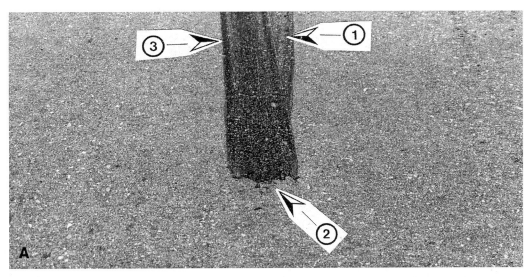

Figure 7–42. Forward-reverse marks.

tire mark, having parallel striations caused by the spinning wheel.

Furrows and Ruts

7.073 A *furrow* is a channel or deep depression made in soft material by the skidding or rotating tire of a vehicle, most often occurring off the traveled portion of a highway, such as on a soft shoulder or in the boulevard area (see Figs. 7–43A and B at points 1). Very often the soft material will be pushed ahead of the tire and deposited as a lump or small mound at the end of the furrow (see Fig. 7–43A at point 2). To be considered a furrow, it is

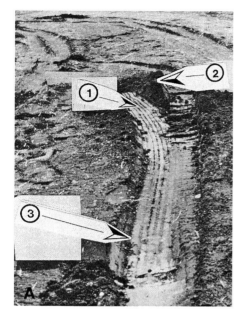

Figure 7–43. Furrows and ruts.

suggested that the depth should be in excess of 4 in (10 cm). A *rut* is similarly a depression left in soft material by a skidding or rotating tire, except that it is most often a comparatively superficial depression of 4 in (10 cm) or less, such as shown in Figure 7–43A at point 3. Whether a tire skids or rotates, tread grooves may be visible as shown in Figure 7–43A at point 1. However, if the tire is rotating a tread pattern will very often also be visible.

7.074–7.083 reserved.

Figures 7–44–7–50 reserved.

SKID MARKS

Skid Mark Defined

7.084 A *skid mark* is a tire mark caused by a locked wheel sliding on a hard surface. A skid mark is most often caused by a wheel that is braked, or locked by vehicle body or part damage as the result of collision; and, although rarely, for other reasons such as a mechanical deficiency or breakdown, e.g., seized wheel bearing. In some circumstances, a skid-type mark caused by a locked wheel can be referenced by other names such as *scrub mark.*

Weight Shift in Skid Marks

7.085 When a vehicle brakes into a skid, there is a forward shift of weight from the rear tires of the vehicle to the front tires. This shift in weight causes the front tires to *cup* in much the same manner as an overloaded tire or an underinflated tire with the greatest weight being carried on the outer edges of the tire, resulting in the front tire marks having dark, parallel lines as in Figure 7–51 at points A and B (see also Fig. 7–27B). At the same time, the rear tires lift taking the shape of an overinflated tire with only the center of the tread touching the roadway surface as in Figure 7–51 at point C (see also Fig. 7–27C). In straight, overlapping skid marks, the rear tire skid mark will track inside the front tire skid marks as indicated by Figure 7–51 at point C.

Impending Skid Mark

7.086 During pre-wheel lock-up stages, when brakes are applied in an attempt to stop a vehicle, there are considerable retarding forces at work. Once a tire starts to skid or slide on an asphalt surface, the heat build-up is gradual and the tire will slide for some distance before the temperature is great enough to draw the tar to the surface to leave

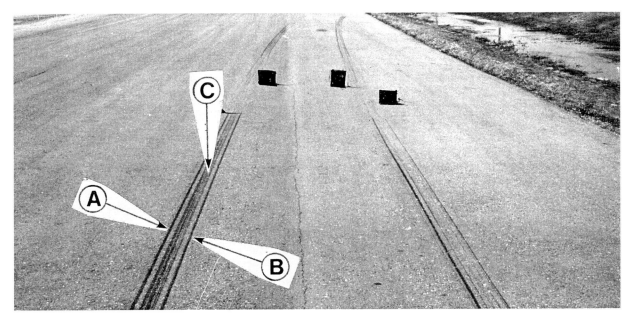

Figure 7–51. Weight shift indicators.

a visible skid mark. During this distance of travel, the tire mark may appear as a cleaning or erasing action, often referred to as a lead-in, impending, shadow, or incipient skid mark (see Fig. 7–52, points A to B). This type of mark is particularly true on very hard surfaces, such as cement or concrete.

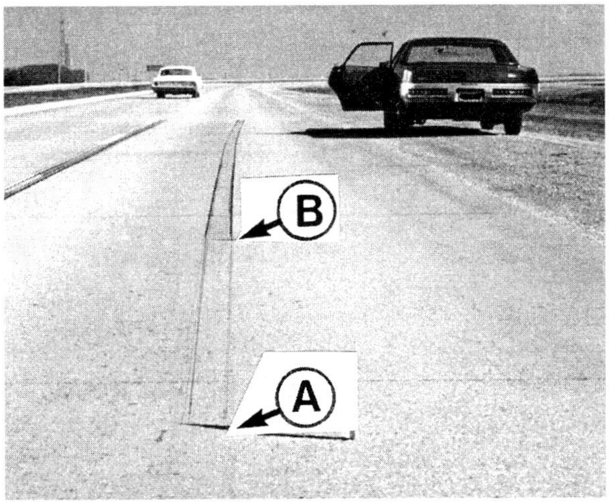

Overlapping Skid Marks

7.087 In a straight skid, when a rear tire leaves an overlapping skid mark that tracks totally within or somewhat to the side off the front tire skid mark, the rear tire skid mark will appear as a slightly narrower

Figure 52. Impending skid mark. In this example, the pre-lock up area that shows pavement erasing, also known as an impending skid mark, starts at point *A* and ends at point *B*.

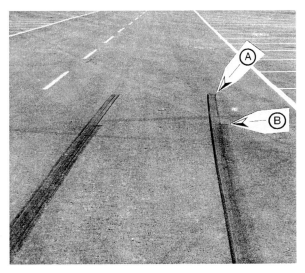

Figure 7–53. Overlapping skid marks. *A* indicates the end of the front tire skid mark; *B* the end of the rear tire skid mark.

mark similar to the skid mark of an overinflated tire (see also Figs. 7–27C and 7–51 at point C). For skid mark measurement purposes, it is important to examine marks for their ends. A most distinguishing feature of a front tire mark will be a dark, narrow line at the outer edges of the mark caused by a weight shift onto the front tires (see also Fig. 7–51 at points A and B).

Offset Tire Marks

7.088 When a vehicle skids or travels to a point of impact with another vehicle, it will very often abruptly change its direction of travel at the point of collision, particularly when the other vehicle is crossing its path applying force that changes the direction of the vehicle. An offset, most often appearing as a scrub mark, will provide evidence of the location of the tire at the point or time of collision.

Figure 7–54. Offset skid marks at *A* that often appear as scrub marks (see Fig. 7–60).

Braked Wheel Tire Evidence

7.089 When a tire skids, including sideways, on a roadway, the portion of the tire that is in contact with the roadway will appear to be cleaned or scraped. If the roadway is hard and gritty, it may cause the tire to have rough abrasions. The tire should be examined for striations which will establish the direction

of tire movement at the time the cleaning/skidding action took place (see also Fig. 7–32).

Figure 7–55. Evidence of a braked wheel. Note evidence of tire cleaning action at *A*, indicating that the wheel was locked and skidding.

Tire-Roadway Debris Deposit

7.090 When a tire skids on a roadway, roadway surface materials may accumulate in the tread grooves (see points in Fig. 7–56A). When movement ceases, i.e., when the vehicle comes to a stop, the dirt may be deposited and be quite visible on the roadway, particularly in the case of a hard surface (see point 1 in Fig. 7–56B). On some hard roadway surfaces, the tire may burn off particles from the roadway or collect grit and push and deposit them on the roadway at the end of the skid mark where the tire comes to a stop (see point 1 in Fig. 7–56C). Such evidence, however, is very often short-lived inasmuch as it may be obliterated by passing vehicles or destroyed by weather conditions, e.g., rain, wind. In all cases, the deposit is good evidence as to where the vehicle came to a stop (see also Fig. 7–43A). It should be noted that point 1 in Figure 56B is a deposit left by the rear tire. Point 2 of this figure shows the customary narrow, dark lines at the outside of the tire mark caused by a weight shift onto the front tires during the skid (see also points A and B in Fig. 7–51).

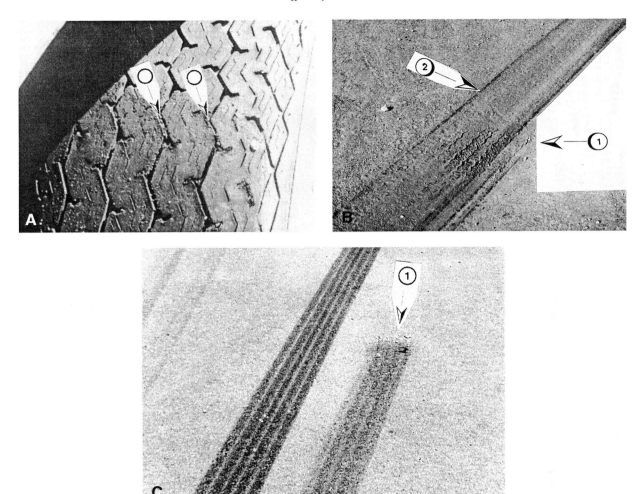

Figure 7–56.

Intermittent Skid Marks

7.091 Intermittent skid marks are caused by *pumping* the brakes on-and-off so that there is full brake application resulting in complete wheel lock-up, and then releasing the brakes so that there is free wheeling. Blank spaces between the skid marks are usually about 15–20 ft (4–6 m), depending upon the speed of the vehicle at the time of brake applications.

Commercial Vehicle Skid Marks

7.092 Commercial vehicle skid marks are usually of two kinds: (1) dual-wheel skid marks, and (2) skip skid marks.

Bounce Tire Marks

7.093 A bounce tire mark can occur when the tire strikes an uneven portion of roadway, e.g., pothole, and becomes somewhat airborne, or when there is a weight shift off a wheel, such as often occurs when a vehicle is in collision with another vehicle and continues to travel along the roadway, typically appearing as in Figure 7–59A. A bounce tire mark can be caused by both a skidding tire as well as rotating tire. If the wheel is locked at the time, much of the mark will appear as a regular skid mark. However, a rotating tire may leave the appearance of a scuff mark. When a bounce occurs, the tire rises and may take on the shape of an overinflated tire (see Fig.

Figure 7–57. Intermittent skid marks.

Figure 7–58A. *Dual-wheel skid marks.* Two tires on one wheel (a dual wheel) leave two side-by-side skid marks. Unless circumstances dictated otherwise, they are to be counted as one skid mark.

Figure 7–58B. *Skip skid marks.* Skip skid marks occur most often when an unloaded or lightly loaded trailer has its brakes applied, particularly in the case of large, commercial semi-trailers being towed by a vehicle equipped with a braking system that locks rear wheels before the front wheels so as to prevent jackknifing. The length between skip skid marks is usually about 3 ft (1 m).

7–27C), whereby the center of the tire tread may be the only portion of the tire that leaves a mark, as shown in Figure 7–59A at point 1. Bounce tire marks are very short skid-type marks, usually about one foot (.3 m) in length. These marks should not be confused with skip skid marks (see Fig. 7–58).

Figure 59A. An example of a bounce skid mark in which the tire is in a raised position at point 1, giving the shape of an overinflated tire, allowing only the center of the tire tread to touch the roadway. At point 2, full weight is restored on the tire allowing for full tread contact. As is the case with other skid marks, the outer edges of the mark will show a dark, narrow line as the result of the cupping action of the tire, as indicated at point 3.

Figure 59B. An example of a combination of bounce and scrub marks as the result of a vehicle passing over the body of an animal.

Scrub Mark

7.094 A scrub mark is a tire mark resulting from a wheel that is locked or jammed during collision so that the tire then slides along the roadway, very often in a sideways movement. Striation marks may be left on the roadway by the ribs of the tire face, not the grooves between them; and striations from the tire tread edge (shoulder area) may also be left–all depending upon the direction the tire slides. The beginning of a scrub mark can often assist in determining the point of impact between two vehicles.

Figure 7–60. Scrub marks.

Detached Utility-Trailer Skid Marks

7.095 When a utility trailer coupling detaches from the towing vehicle, leaving only a safety chain hookup, the trailer will swing freely as the towing vehicle proceeds along the highway. If the trailer is equipped with automatic break-away brakes, the skid marks will appear to be very erratic as shown in Figure 7–61.

Towed Vehicle Skid Marks

7.096 When a damaged vehicle is towed or moved from the actual crash site, one or all of its wheels may be in a locked position thereby causing skid marks as it is towed. The investigator must be able to interpret and explain these and all other marks found at an crash scene or appearing later in photographs.

Figure 7–61.

Figure 7–62. Skid marks left by vehicle that is towed.

Particular attention should be made to ensure that marks caused by the vehicle being towed are not confused with pre- or post-collision skid marks that are actually associated with the cause of the collision.

REFERENCES

1. Traffic Detector Handbook, Publication No. LP-124A (2nd ed.). Washington, DC: ITE, 1991. Cited in *Traffic Engineering Handbook* (5th ed.), Institute of Transportation Engineers, Washington, DC, 1999, p. 509.
2. *Traffic Engineering Handbook* (5th ed.). Institute of Transportation Engineers, Washington, DC, 1999, p. 510.
3. Homburger, Wolfgang S. & Kell, James H.: *Fundamentals of Traffic Engineering* (11th ed.). University of California, Institute of transportation Studies, 1984, p. 17–18.
4. Homburger, Wolfgang S. & Kell, James H.: *Fundamentals of Traffic Engineering* (11th ed.). University of California, Institute of transportation Studies, 1984, p. 17-8.
5. Homburger, Wolfgang S. & Kell, James H.: *Fundamentals of Traffic Engineering* (11th ed.). University of California, Institute of transportation Studies, 1984, p. 178.
6. *Traffic Engineering Handbook* (5th ed.). Institute of Transportation Engineers, Washington, DC, 1999, p. 511.
7. *Traffic Engineering Handbook* (5th ed.), Institute of Transportation Engineers, Washington, DC, 1999, p. 510.
8. *Traffic Engineering Handbook* (5th ed.). Institute of Transportation Engineers, Washington, DC, 1999, p. 510.
9. Homburger, Wolfgang S. & Kell, James H.: *Fundamentals of Traffic Engineering* (11th ed.). University of California, Institute of Transportation Studies, 1984, p. 17-4.

RECOMMENDED READING

Vehicle Traffic Control Signal Head, Standing of the Institute of Transportation Engineers, Publication No. ST-008B, Washington, DC, 1985 [Cited by Royal L. Wilshire, P.E., *Traffic Engineers Handbook* (4th ed.) (Traffic Signals)], Institute of Transportation Engineers, Prentice Hall, Englewood Cliffs, NJ, 1992, pp. 288, 291, and *Traffic Engineering Handbook* (5th ed.).

Homburger, Wolfgang S. & Kell, James H.: *Fundamentals of Traffic Engineering* (11th ed.). University of California, Institute of transportation Studies, 1984.

Traffic Engineering Handbook (5th ed.), Washington, DC, 1999. New editions of this handbook are published periodically by the Institute of Transportation Engineers, 1099 - 14th Street, NW, Suite 300 West, Washington, DC, 20005-3438 USA, Telephone +1 (202) 289-0222, Fax: +1 (202) 289-7722. ITE on the web: http://www.ite.org.

Manual on Uniform Traffic Control Devices: Part VI. U.S. Government Printing Office, Superintendent of Documents, Washington, DC, 1993.

Rivers, R.W.: *Tire Failures and Evidence Manual for Traffic Accident Investigation.* Charles C Thomas, Springfield, Illinois, 2001.

Chapter 8

VEHICLE EXAMINATIONS

R. W. RIVERS

INTRODUCTION

8.001 As stated by Dr. L. Sathyavagiswaran, M.D., Chief Medical Examiner-Coroner, County of Los Angels, because of the possible ramifications in both criminal and civil court proceedings, the importance of thorough vehicle inspections cannot be overemphasized:[1]

The vehicle should be thoroughly examined for brake malfunction, cruise control defects, seat belt operations, etc. I have testified on a case where a car manufacturer was sued over a malfunctioning cruise control that resulted in the death of a solo driver who went off the road due to automatic acceleration of the vehicle. I testified on another case where a rental truck company and a truck refurbishing company were sued due to their not having replaced the driver's seat belt when they refurbished the vehicle where the renter died as the result of being ejected when the truck overturned–even though he had caused the accident by speeding and committing a sharp turn.

8.002 When in-depth inspections or examinations of such items as braking systems or headlight filaments are required, they should normally be carried out by persons having the expertise necessary to qualify them to testify as expert witnesses. These generally include qualified traffic crash reconstructionists, mechanical engineers, laboratory technicians, and others who through training and experience are so qualified. For example, a metallurgist or materials engineer is the professional who can be called upon to determine if such failure is due to inappropriate materials or was caused by undue stress. If a weld is involved, such as is often the case with industrial equipment and heavy commercial-type trailers, the metallurgist can determine whether the weld was improperly done, or if the break is outside the weld, if the break failure was as the result of an unsatisfactory heat-affected zone (see also Para. 8.006 and Figs. 8–05 and 8–06).

VEHICLE IDENTIFICATION NUMBER

8.003 When built, vehicles are assigned a *vehicle identification number (VIN)* by the manufacturer. This number comprises of 17 digits and characters specific to that vehicle, stamped in a plate which is usually located in the upper left-hand side of the instrument panel and visible from outside the vehicle. The number is also stamped on various original components of the vehicle, such as the frame.

VEHICLE IDENTIFICATION NUMBER (VIN)_

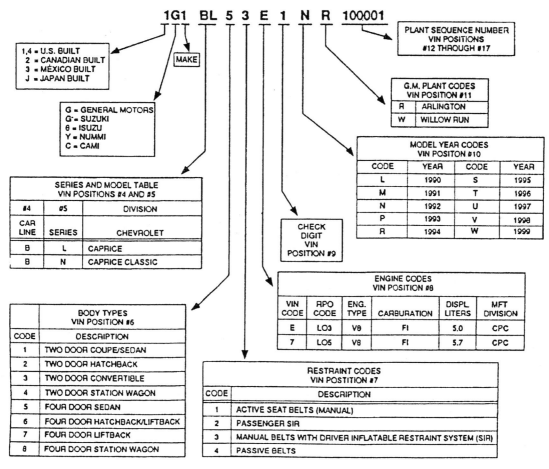

Figure 8–01. An example of a vehicle identification number.

Table 8–01
OVERVIEW OF VEHICLE INVESTIGATION ITEMS

☐ Vehicle Description
  ☐ Passenger
  ☐ Commercial
  ☐ Other
  ☐ License plate no.
  ☐ State or province
  ☐ Make
  ☐ Year
  ☐ Model/Type
  ☐ Color
  ☐ Registration no.
  ☐ Serial no. (VIN)
  ☐ Odometer mileage

☐ Accelerator
☐ Air Conditioning Unit
☐ Brakes
☐ Doors
☐ Electronics, e.g., radio/cassette player
☐ Exhaust System
☐ Frame
☐ Gadgets, window or windshield stickers, ornaments, etc., both inside and outside of vehicle
☐ Gear selector, type, position
☐ Horn

☐ Lights (lamps), e.g., headlights, taillights, signal lights, reflectors
☐ Loads and binders
☐ Locks, door
☐ Mirrors
☐ Mobile telephone
☐ Parking brake
☐ Power Train
☐ Reflectors
☐ Safety Equipment, e.g., seat belts, air bags

☐ Speedometer
☐ Steering
☐ Suspension system
☐ Tires
☐ Vehicle
☐ Vision Obstructions
☐ Wheels
☐ Windshield and Windows
☐ Windshield Wipers
☐ Windshield and Window Defrosters

AUTOMOBILE COMPONENTS

Figure 8–02. An example of an automobile frame and some common components:

1. Tie rod end
2. Rack and pinion
3. CV (constant velocity joint
4. Steering column
5. Transmission coil spring
6. Universal joint
7. Drive shaft
8. Coil spring
9. Shock
10. Frame
11. Rear drive differential

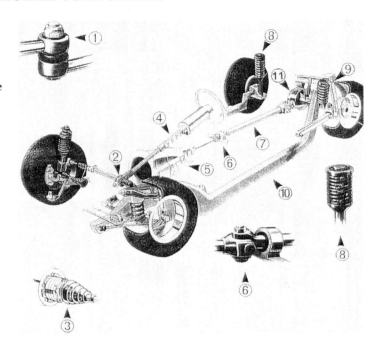

COMMERCIAL VEHICLE COMPONENTS

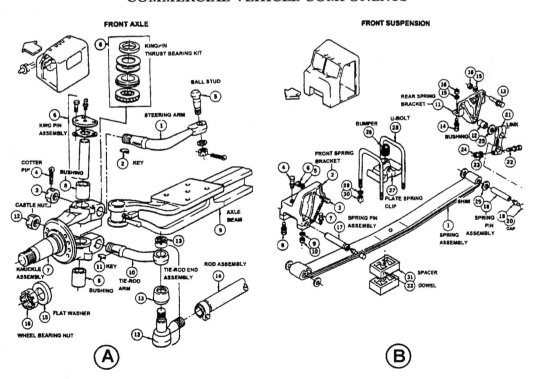

Figure 8–03. Commercial vehicle wheel, brake, suspension and steering assemblies: *A*–front axle; *B*–front suspension.

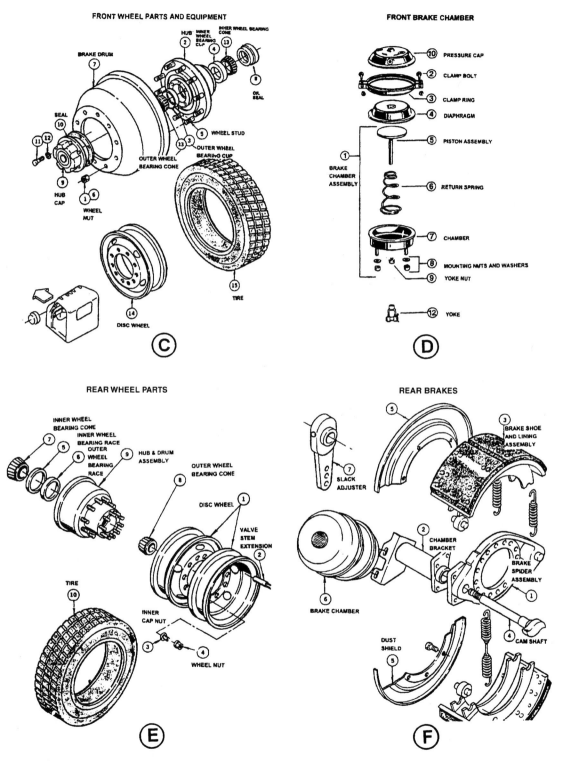

Figure 8–03 (*Continued*). Commercial vehicle wheel, brake, suspension and steering assemblies: *C*–front wheel parts and equipment; *D*–front brake chamber; *E*–rear wheel parts; *F*–rear brakes.

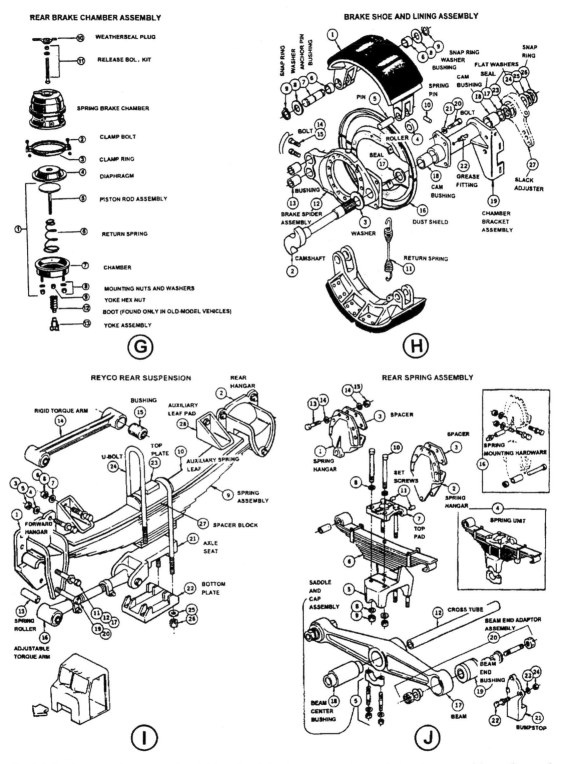

Figure 8–03 (*Continued*). Commercial vehicle wheel, brake, suspension and steering assemblies: *G*–rear brake chamber assembly; *H*–brake shoe and lining assembly; *I*–Reyco® rear suspension; *J*–rear spring assembly.

GENERAL LAYOUT OF POWER STEERING SYSTEM

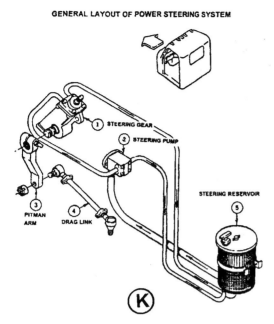

Figure 8–03 (*Continued*). Commercial vehicle wheel, brake, suspension and steering assemblies: *K*–general layout of power steering system (courtesy of Western Star Trucks).

DRIVE TRAINS

8.004 There are two basic drive train systems:

1. Rear-wheel drive (RWD)
   A system in which the vehicle has the engine mounted longitudinally and power is delivered to the rear wheels by way of a drive shaft that connects the engine and transmission to a rear differential and rear axles (see Fig. 8–02).
2. Front wheel drive (FWD)
   A system in which the engine is mounted transversely or sideways. The transmission and drive axle are combined into a single unit called a transaxle, connected to the front wheels, thereby eliminating the need for a drive shaft (see Fig. 8–04). In this system, the front or steering-axle wheels, rather than the rear wheels, provide power to move the vehicle.

8.005 A 4-wheel or all-wheel drive (AWD) vehicle combines front- and rear-wheel drives so that power can be supplied to all wheels at the same time. Many such models, however, permit the front

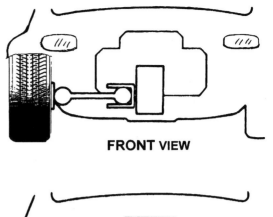

FRONT VIEW

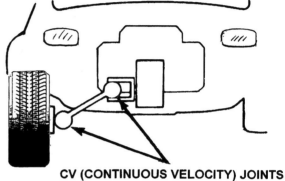

CV (CONTINUOUS VELOCITY) JOINTS

Figure 8–04. An example of a front-wheel drive, transaxle configuration.

wheels to be disengaged when they are not needed for traction.

☐ Drive system: ☐ RWD ☐ FWD ☐ AWD

☐ AWD: ☐ Engaged ☐ Disengaged

COMPONENT FAILURES

8.006 A vehicle inspection, and any subsequent proceeding, should consider the following points for relevancy, i.e., in what way they may have contributed to a vehicle crash, and what good evidence is available. A broken metal part will most often display a gritty or rough surface. Old breaks or cracks such as those that often occur as the result of metal fatigue are discolored. New breaks give a shiny appearance. A combination of discoloration and shiny metal in a break usually indicates an old crack and a fresh or recent break. If a part is broken as the result of impact, the part normally shows damage where it was struck (see Figs. 8–05 and 8–06).

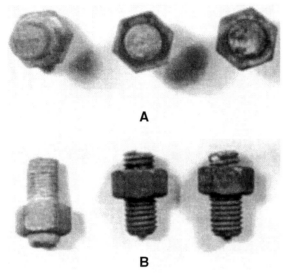

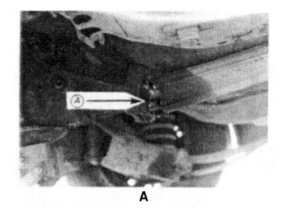

A

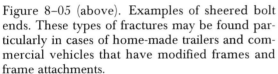

B

Figure 8–05 (above). Examples of sheered bolt ends. These types of fractures may be found particularly in cases of home-made trailers and commercial vehicles that have modified frames and frame attachments.

Figure 8–06 (right). Fractured vehicle components. Photograph *A* is a drive shaft that became fractured under stress as the result of a collision. Photograph *B* is a broken pipe such as is found with brake-fluid lines. Note the shiny, gritty appearance of the new breaks indicated by arrows *A*. In the case of Photograph *B*, there is also an older, particular break (darker/discolored portion) indicated by arrow *B*.

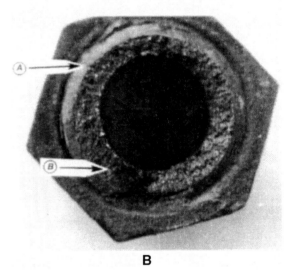

B

Table 8–02
COMMON COMPONENTS AND FAILURE INDICATORS

☐ *A lack of lubrication*
  ☐ Wheel bearings
  ☐ Evidence of melted or burned steel that appears indigo blue, indicating that the item was operated at a much higher temperature than what would be considered a normal operating temperature. Such high temperatures may also melt some metals and will almost always melt or decompose plastics.

☐ *Altered part or component*

☐ *Component substitution*
  ☐ Substituted by a low-cost, discount inferior but similar product.
  ☐ Replaced with an oversized or undersized unit causing stress and eventual failure.
  ☐ Evidence of odd-size, worn and/or broken bolts, often found with home-made trailers and commercial vehicle frame attachments (see Fig. 8–05).

☐ *Wheel-bearing failures.* Particularly in out-of-control recreational trailer crashes, where cheaply manufactured, improper size or inadequate replacement bearings might have been used.

(*continued*)

Table 8–02
COMMON COMPONENTS AND FAILURE INDICATORS (*Continued*)

☐ *Broken or weakened metal part.* Steering and suspension system components, drive shaft, braking and wheel assemblies and any other metal part such as the windshield wiper assembly that might have malfunctioned because of breakage or weakness.

☐ *Accelerator.* An examination should be done both visually and manually.
    ☐ Evidence of binding or sticking, and return action after the accelerator pedal has been depressed–several times.
    ☐ Bent linkage rods, worn connections, defective retrieval spring, or evidence of binding that could have caused the accelerator to malfunction.

LAMPS AND REFLECTORS

8.007 As applicable, all lamps, e.g., headlamps, clearance lamps, signal lamps, dash lights, and so on, should be examined to see if they are in working condition, and if they were in operation at the time of the collision. The headlamp high-beam indicator is important in accidents involving oncoming vehicles being forced off the roadway because of *bright* lights; accidents involving pedestrians; and accidents attributable to a driver overdriving his headlights or driving too fast for conditions, e.g., darkness, fog, slick pavement.

8.008 Some push-pull type headlamp switches will change positions (in or out) as the result of forces exerted on it during rear-end or front-end collisions, and in the case of a variety of switches, whether their position had been changed as the result of being impacted dead-on or sideswiped by the driver's body or some other article within the vehicle.

8.009 If the headlamp switch is in the *off* position and there is a suggestion, e.g., a driver's or witness's statement that the lights were on, it is recommended that the switch not be turned to the *on* position because in doing so, the filaments may be damaged thereby destroying the only physical evidence available that, through expert examination and analysis, will determine whether a lamp was displaying a light at the time of collision.

8.010 It is important that a complete examination of bulb *filaments* be made in instances where there might be some doubt as to whether a lamp was in fact on at the time of collision or when there must otherwise be evidence of the bulb's (light) status at that time, such as in the case of a rear-end collision when the status of the brake lights and taillights would be important evidence. Lamp analyses performed by experts in this field, generally in a laboratory setting, can determine whether a bulb was lighted at the time of collision, and/or which filament was lighted. In addition to headlamps, such examinations can be extended to include all other vehicle lamps, such as taillamps, licence-plate lamps, and clearance lamps, as well as damaged traffic-control signal lights where the light phase can also be established. Such an examinations should be carried out by someone who can qualify himself as an expert in lamp examination.

8.011 Bulb filaments are very fragile. Extreme care must be taken in their removal, handling, and storage. Non-damaged bulbs or lamps may be removed at the scene and transported elsewhere for examination. Where such removal might present a problem, a *qualified examiner* should be requested to attend the scene and remove the bulbs and/or carry out the examination. The investigator should make careful notes of the lamp analysis process, including exhibit appearance at the scene, method of removal, and the continuity of possession of the exhibit.

8.012 Commercial and oversize vehicles generally require clearance lights and reflectors at their outer extremities. Additionally, large commercial-type trailers must display reflective sheeting or tape on the rear and sides. When involved in a collision, particularly sideswipe, underride, and intersection collisions, these types of vehicles should be checked for the presence and serviceability of such equipment and markings. In all cases, investigations into lighting and reflector requirements should take into consideration the requirements of the local jurisdiction as well as any applicable federal, state, and/or provincial legislation that may be in place.

- ☐ Lights, general (type, color, number, location, condition)
  - ☐ Headlamps
  - ☐ Tail-lamps
  - ☐ Signal lamps
  - ☐ Brake-lamps
  - ☐ Clearance
  - ☐ Fog lamps
  - ☐ Back-up lamps
- ☐ Type of switch
  - ☐ Lever
  - ☐ Push-pull
  - ☐ Other
- ☐ Switch position
  - ☐ On
  - ☐ Off
- ☐ High-low beam switch position
- ☐ High-beam indicator light
- ☐ Reflectors, general (type, color, number, location, condition)

NOTE: For complete procedures in the handling and analysis of lamp exhibits, see: *Traffic Accident Investigators' Lamp Analysis Manual* by R.W. Rivers and Fredereick G. Hochgraf, published by Charles C Thomas, Publisher, Ltd., Springfield, Illinois, 2001.

8.013–8.015 reserved.

SUSPENSION SYSTEMS

8.016 *Suspension system* is a term that applies to a vehicle's spring arrangement, plus a damping arrangement, such as a shock absorber and snubber, along with their support elements.

8.017 There are a variety of spring systems used in vehicles. They include (a) leaf springs, (b) coil springs, (c) torsion bars, and (d) a combination of coil springs in front and leaf springs in back or coil springs in front and back. Most commercial vehicles are equipped with semi-elliptical leaf springs all around. A vehicle may be equipped with either a non-independent or an independent suspension system. The difference between the two is that an *independent system* allows one of the wheels on an axle to move vertically without imposing any corresponding movement on the other wheel (see Figs. 8–02, 8–03, 8–07 and 8–08).

8.018 Unsafe vehicle stability can be result from a variety of suspension deficiencies, including (a) broken or missing leaves; defective spring shackles, U-bolt clamps, and spring clips on a leaf spring; (b) loose attaching bolts, weak shock absorbers, broken or weak coil springs; and (c) misaligned wheels.

8.019 *Modifications.* Alterations to a vehicle's suspension system, such as raising or lowering a vehicle from its designed height can adversely affect the

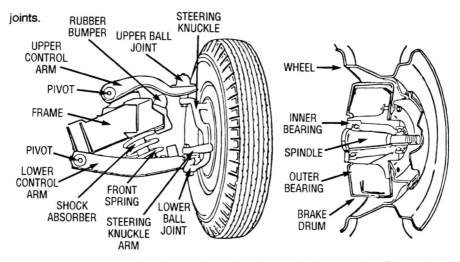

Figure 8–07. An example of an independent front wheel suspension (front wheel mounting).

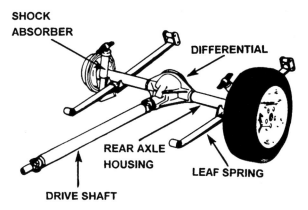

Figure 8–08. An example of a solid axle, rear suspension system.

stability and handling characteristics of the vehicle. For example, when a vehicle is raised from its designed height, the center of mass becomes higher with greater potential for rollover.

- ☐ Modified suspension
  - ☐ Raised or lowered
  - ☐ Improper or non-factory-approved replacement parts
- ☐ Loose or broken spring leaf
- ☐ Loose or broken coil spring
- ☐ Broken, loose, or missing U-bolts, spring shackles, or spring clips

Air Suspension

8.020 In an *air suspension system*, columns of air support the vehicle in rubber and nylon-diaphragm air springs, replacing metal coil or leaf springs. Using a compressor, air reservoir, leveling valves, and regulators requiring assorted plumbing connections, air springs overcome certain shortcomings of the metal springs. The objective is a level, stabilized ride with proper road clearance under all road conditions.

Shock Absorbers

8.021 A *shock absorber* is a generic term which is commonly applied to a hydraulic mechanism in the suspension system that produces a damping effect on the system, installed on each front and rear wheel to prevent excessive spring rebound. A

shock absorber operates very much like the hydraulic check installed on doors to prevent slamming. It contains a piston or fan, which moves in a hydraulic fluid.

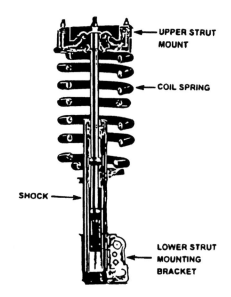

Figure 8–09. A shock and strut combination. (Source: Monroe Shocks and Struts®.)

STEERING SYSTEMS

General

8.022 An initial examination of the condition of the steering assembly should be made by turning the steering wheel as fully as possible in each direction. Conduct quick, short turns on the steering wheel which will often provide evidence of there being loose or worn parts in the system. Steering wheel free play in excess of one inch (2.54 cm) is a possible indication of a worn or defective steering linkage or steering box and a further more in-depth examination would be warranted. Examine all steering system parts for continuity, and the steering column for loose mountings. An examination may often be made most effectively when a tow truck lifts the vehicle in removing it from the accident scene.

8.023 An on-the-spot examination can be carried out by raising and rotating each wheel separately to check for *binding*. Check each for evidence of *wheel-bearing play* by grasping either side of the tire of a

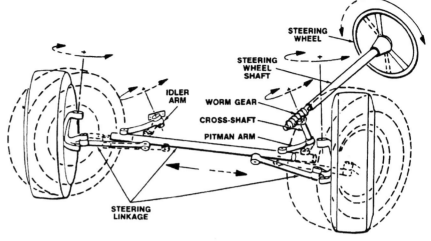

Figure 8–10. An example of a typical steering system structure. (Source: National Automobile Manufacturers Association.) (See Figs. 8–02 and 8–03A.)

raised wheel with both hands (one on each side) and attempting to move the wheel in and out. Worn or loose bearings can cause steering difficulty, particularly at high speeds. Evidence of looseness or play during this process would be grounds to have a more thorough examination carried out in a proper inspection facility.

- ☐ Type
  - ☐ Power
  - ☐ Manual
- ☐ Linkage, general
- ☐ Tie-rods
- ☐ Idler arm
- ☐ Drag links

Power-Assisted Steering Systems

8.024 The most common power-assisted steering system failures can be traced to steering pump fluid levels and drive belts. If the drive belt is missing, the engine compartment as well as the roadway leading up to the point of collision should be examined for evidence of the belt or its remnants. Belt deficiencies, such as poor tension, can cause slippage which in turn can result in loss of steering control and braking deficiencies.

- ☐ Fluid level in pump reservoir
- ☐ Broken, disconnected, or leaking hoses
- ☐ Presence of drive belt
- ☐ Drive belt tension for slippage
- ☐ Drive belt damage or breakage

Table 8–03
STEERING EVIDENCE

Evidence or Complaint of	Possible Cause (Examine for)
☐ General steering problems	☐ Improper or non-factory-approved replacement parts and amateur modifications to system
☐ Pulling to side	☐ Air pressures (low or flat tire) ☐ Wheel alignment ☐ Weak or broken suspension spring; loose or worn ball joints or attaching bolts ☐ Worn control arm shaft bushings ☐ Weak front springs; incorrect wheel alignment ☐ Bent control arm or steering knuckle
☐ Pull to one side while braking	☐ Loose or worn ball joints or attaching bolts ☐ Bent control arm or steering knuckle ☐ Weak front springs or weak shock absorbers
☐ Unable to steer	☐ No power available in the case of power steering, e.g., a broken hose ☐ Binding in the system ☐ Looseness in steering system ☐ Disconnected linkage

(continued)

Table 8–03
STEERING EVIDENCE (*Continued*)

Evidence or Complaint of	Possible Cause (Examine for)
☐ Hard steering	☐ Ball joints galled or in need of lubrication ☐ Incorrect front-end alignment ☐ Bent control arm or steering knuckle
☐ Wanders or shimmies	☐ Loose or worn ball joints or bushings ☐ Loose suspension attaching bolts ☐ Weak shock absorbers or front springs ☐ Incorrect front-end alignment
☐ Excessive steering play	☐ Loose or worn ball joints or attaching bolts ☐ Loose or worn ball joints or a attaching bolts ☐ Worn control arm shaft bushings ☐ Weak front springs
☐ Floating, wallowing, and poor recovery from roadway bumps	☐ Weak shock absorber; weak springs

WHEEL ALIGNMENT

8.025 Improper wheel alignment can be caused for a variety of reasons. The result is that a vehicle can be found to be hard to steer, may pull to one side or the other, and may wander on the roadway. Worn tires (see Fig. 8–11 and Table 8–03) is an indication of improper wheel alignment and other possible front suspension problems. When improper wheel alignment is evident or suspected, examine the steering system for evidence of bad design, accidental damage, worn or non-approved replacement components, amateur modifications, or fitting of larger diameter tires than proper for the vehicle. Any of these conditions may affect the self-centering action of the front wheels.

☐ Evidence of worn tires
☐ Suspension damage, e.g., from a collision
☐ Unsafe, inadequate or improper design, e.g., by manufacturer

☐ Worn suspension parts
☐ Improper or non-factory-approved replacement parts
☐ Amateur modifications
☐ Improper size tires and/or wheels

Figure 8–11. An example of tire wear caused by incorrect wheel alignment.

WHEELS AND RIMS

8.026 When there is evidence of an apparent tire and/or rim failure, an examination should be made to determine whether or not the tire and rim are compatible, i.e., do they meet the manufacturers' mounting standards or specifications. Many tires will fit more than one rim width. Mismatching tire and rim diameters is dangerous and can result in a tire-rim failure. This examination can be done by checking the P-metric, European Metric, or Millimetric measurements shown with the unit and check these against the compatibility charts that are available at tire or motor vehicle service centers.

8.027 A wheel and rim examination should include looking for cracks; unseated locking rings; broken, loose, or missing lugs and lug nuts, studs, or clamps; bent or cracked rims; *bleeding* rust stains; and impact and other damaged areas. The examination should also include a search for overtightened or loose lug nuts (torque) which can damage the brake disc or drum. Loose wheel lug nuts, for example, allow the rim to move back and forth and cause lug nut holes to become elliptical. Lugs can then eventually wear through and break off. When any one or a combination of these abnormalities occur, a tire-wheel unit may fail and the vehicle may go out of control.

im compatibility
- [ ] Lug and lug nuts (e.g., missing, broken, torque)
- [ ] Damage to wheel or rim
- [ ] Weakness from age, wear, and tear

TIRES

Types of Tires

8.028 There are basically two types of tire construction:

1. Bias-ply construction
2. Radial-ply construction

Three basic types of tires are manufactured using these two types of construction:

1. Bias-ply tires
2. Bias-belted tires
3. Radial tires

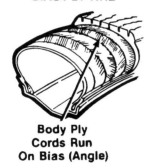

BIAS-PLY TIRE

Body Ply
Cords Run
On Bias (Angle)

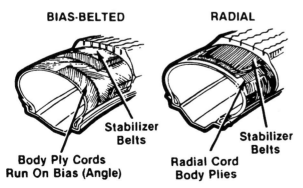

BIAS-BELTED   **RADIAL**

Stabilizer
Belts

Body Ply Cords
Run On Bias (Angle)

Stabilizer
Belts

Radial Cord
Body Plies

Figure 8–12. Tire types and construction.

A *bias-ply tire* is a pneumatic tire in which the ply cords that extend to the beads are laid at alternate angles substantially less than 90 degrees to the centerline of the tread (sometimes called a cross-ply tire). A *bias-belted tire* is basically constructed like a bias-ply tire, but a reinforcing belt of fiberglass, rayon, or steel is wrapped around the circumference of the tire just beneath the tread.

A *radial tire* is a pneumatic tire in which the ply cords that extend to the beads are laid at approximately 90 degrees to the centerline of the tread. The design allows it to function as two completely independent working parts:

1. The casing (for cushioning power)
2. The tread (for adequate contact area)

Radial tires should not be mixed with other types of tires. To do so can cause vehicle directional instability.

8.029 The investigator should record the descriptive data for any tire that will be used as an item of evidence. This information, found on the sidewall of the tire, is shown in Figure 8–13:

8.030 The words *tubeless* or *tube type* will appear on at least one of the sidewalls. If the tire is a radial-type tire, the word *radial* will appear on at least one of the sidewalls. Tire type applications are classified into the following categories:

- [ ] P – passenger car applications
- [ ] LT – light truck
- [ ] T – temporary spare
- [ ] TR – Trucks, buses, and other vehicles with rims having bead seat diameters of nominal + .156" or + .250"
- [ ] ML – Mining and logging tires used in intermittent highway service
- [ ] MH – Tires for mobile homes
- [ ] NHS – Not for highway service
- [ ] ST – Special tires for trailers in highway service
- [ ] HC – Tires for heavy trucks having 15° tapered bead seat rims of 17.5" diameter designated HC. The HC suffix differentiates these tires from light truck tires of 17.5" bead diameter.

Sources: GM Service Technology Group, US Rubber Manufacturing Association, Washington, and Rivers Traffic Consultants Ltd.

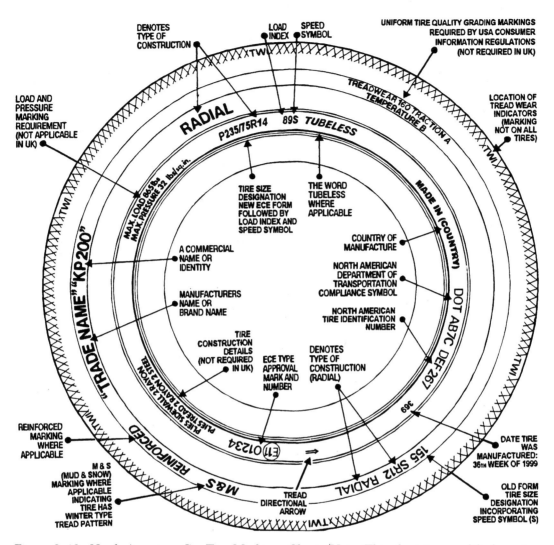

Figure 8–13. North American Car Tire Markings Chart. (Note: This chart is a modified version of the original chart, as amended by Rivers Traffic Consultants Ltd. to meet North American standards/requirements.)[2] (Original source: British Rubber Manufacturers Association Ltd., London, supplied in the interests of traffic safety.

DOT/MOT Numbers

8.031 The *DOT* designation signifies that the tire complies with the U.S. Department of Transportation (or *MOT*, Canada Ministry of Transportation) tire safety standards, and provides manufacturing information.

Example

DOT MA L9 XXXX 0301
DOT = Department of Transportation approved tire

MA = Manufacturer and plant
L9 = Tire size and code number
ABCD = Manufacturers' symbols used to Identify the brand or other aspects of the tire
0301 = Indicates that the tire was manufactured in the 3rd week of 2001. (Note: In July, 2000, the 4-digit week and year code replaced a 3-digit code. Previously, in this example, the code would have been shown as: 031.)

Speed Ratings

8.032 Tire manufacturers specify the maximum speeds at which their product should be operated. A maximum speed rating does not indicate how well a tire will handle or corner at various speeds. Rather, it indicates what maximum speed the tire is designed to tolerate. In general, a Z-rated tire is a better handling tire than a less-rated unit. High-speed rotation of a tire can cause extreme tire distortion, thus the flexing of the tire components will cause heat build-up, and can result in tire failure in a very short period of time. This type of tire failure is normally identified as a ply and/or tread separation, due to excessive heat, melting of the inner components, and can result in a complete tire failure in the form of a blow out. A flat tire at high speeds does not dictate that the vehicle will necessarily experience a loss of control, but the surprise factor on the part of the inexperienced driver, coupled with the sudden change in vehicle stability often contributes to a loss of control. If such a failure occurs within a curve in the roadway, a loss of control is often experienced.[3]

A speed symbol is used to identify the speed rating of passenger car tires. Ratings are based on applicable laboratory road-type tests conducted in accordance with SAE J1561 and ECE Regulation 30. The ratings are not applicable if the tires are underinflated, overloaded, worn out, damaged or altered. Symbols and maximum ratings are shown in Table 8–04.

Load Ratings

8.033 *Load rating* can be defined as the carrying capacity of the tire at a specific air inflation pressure (Source: Kelly-Springfield Tire Company). The load range usually appears on at least one of the sidewalls in the form of a single designation letter. Factory-installed tires and wheels are designed to operate satisfactorily with loads up and including the full rated load capacity when inflated to the recommended inflation pressures. A vehicle's specific load rating can be found on the tire loading information label located in a vehicle, most often on the rear edge of the driver's door.[4]

Table 8–04
SPEED RATING CHART

Speed Symbol		Maximum Speed
W		* 169 mph (270 km/h)
Z		** Above 149 mph (240 km/h)
V	(No service description)	** Above 130 mph (210 km/h)
V		149 mph (240 km/h)
H		130 mph (210 km/h)
U		124 mph (200 km/h)
T		118 mph (190 km/h)
S		112 mph (180 km/h)
R		105 mph (170 km/h)
Q		100 mph (160 km/h)
P		95 mph (150 km/h)
N		87 mph (140 km/h)
M		81 mph (130 km/h)
L		75 mph (120 km/h)
K		68 mph (110 km/h)
J		62 mph (100 km/h)

* Source: British Rubber Manufacturer's Association Ltd.
** Consult tire manufacturer for maximum speed.

TABLE 8–05
TIRE LOAD INDICES CHART

Li	kg	lbs	Li	kg	lbs	Li	kg	lbs
40	140	309	67	307	677	94	670	1477
41	145	320	68	315	694	95	690	1521
42	150	331	69	325	716	96	710	1565
43	155	342	70	335	739	97	730	1609
44	160	353	71	345	761	98	750	1653
45	165	364	72	355	783	99	775	1709
46	170	375	73	365	805	100	800	1764
47	175	386	74	375	827	101	825	1819
48	180	397	75	387	853	102	850	1874
49	185	408	76	400	882	103	875	1929
50	190	419	77	412	908	104	900	1984
51	195	430	78	425	937	105	925	2039
52	200	441	79	437	963	106	950	2094
53	206	454	80	450	992	107	975	2149
54	212	467	81	462	1019	108	1000	2205
55	218	481	82	475	1047	109	1030	2271
56	224	494	83	487	1074	110	1060	2337
57	230	507	84	500	1102	111	1090	2403
58	236	520	85	515	1135	112	1120	2469
59	243	536	86	530	1168	113	1150	2535
60	250	551	87	545	1201	114	1180	2601
61	257	567	88	560	1235	115	1215	2679
62	265	584	89	580	1279	116	1250	2756
63	272	600	90	600	1323	117	1285	2833
64	280	617	91	615	1356	118	1320	2910
65	290	639	92	630	1389	119	1360	2998
66	300	661	93	650	1433	120	1400	3086

Source: Rivers Traffic Consultants Ltd.

Service Description

8.034 *Service Description.* A typical service description is:

90 H
/ \
Load Index **Speed Symbol**

The *Load Index* is a numerical code (90 in this example) associated with the maximum load a tire can carry at the speed indicated by its *Speed Symbol* under specific service conditions. (See *Speed Ratings Chart, Table 8–04,* and *Load Rating Chart, Table 8–05.*) The maximum tire load capacity will be found stamped in pounds and/or kilograms on the lower sidewall of the tire. In this example, the speed symbol *H* in the service description means a maximum speed rating of 130 mph (210 km/h) (Source: *RMA Bulletin,* '89).

Tire Marking Standard

8.035 After 1990, the international standard for marking tires is, for example:

P205/60R15 90H

In this case, the tire size *P205/60R15* has the following meaning:

P = Passenger car tire
205 = Nominal section width in millimeters
60 = Nominal aspect ratio (section height-to-width ratio), i.e., in this example, the tire is 60 percent as high as it is wide.
R = Radial tire construction
15 = Nominal rim diameter in inches

As shown in this example, the load index and speed rating symbols are included as an adjunct to the tire size designation:

90 = Load index: 1323 lbs (600 kg)
H = H speed rated tire [130 mph (210 km/h) maximum]

Inflation and Tire Failures

8.036 Tire tread wear can indicate whether a tire has been operated *underinflated* or *overinflated.* In collisions where tire failure appears to be a contributing factor, examine the air pressure of all remaining tires to determine whether the driver habitually operated the vehicle on underinflated or overinflated tires.

8.037 Improper inflation and incorrect wheel alignment (toe-in and camber) can be the cause uneven tire wear. (See also incorrect alignment, Figure 8–11; and Tire Shapes and Contours, Paragraph 7.057, Figure 7–27A, B and C.)

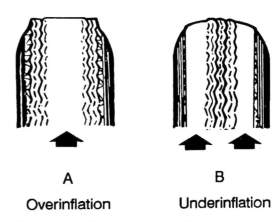

A
Overinflation

B
Underinflation

Figure 8–14. Tire pressure, tread-wear patterns.

8.038 On wet roadway surfaces, tread *grooves* channel water off to the rear and out to both sides of the tire. When the tread is worn to the extent the tread bars (built-in wear indicators) are worn down, the grooves become too shallow to disperse surface moisture effectively, and in the case of water lying on the roadway, the tire may lift from the road and ride on a film of water–*hydroplaning.* When *hydroplaning* takes place, a vehicle's steering control can diminish or be virtually eliminated.

8.039 Poor quality *recaps* on tires may become loose and fail or tear away from the casing, or the tire may fail for a variety of other reasons. Such failures may cause difficulty in vehicle control. When a tire indicates a failure and a collision is involved, the highway should be examined for tire fragments leading up to the point of collision to determine whether the tire damage or failure occurred before or resulted from the collision (see Fig. 8–17).

8.040 When there is evidence of tire air-pressure loss, examine the tire inside and out for the reason for the loss, such as evidence of a puncture, cut or tear, or a broken body part that punctured the tire.

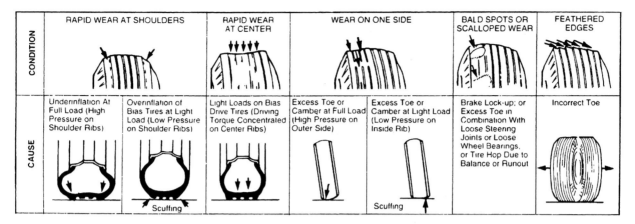

	RAPID WEAR AT SHOULDERS		RAPID WEAR AT CENTER	WEAR ON ONE SIDE		BALD SPOTS OR SCALLOPED WEAR	FEATHERED EDGES
CONDITION							
CAUSE	Underinflation At Full Load (High Pressure on Shoulder Ribs)	Overinflation of Bias Tires at Light Load (Low Pressure on Shoulder Ribs)	Light Loads on Bias Drive Tires (Driving Torque Concentrated on Center Ribs)	Excess Toe or Camber at Full Load (High Pressure on Outer Side)	Excess Toe or Camber at Light Load (Low Pressure on Inside Rib)	Brake Lock-up; or Excess Toe in Combination With Loose Steering Joints or Loose Wheel Bearings, or Tire Hop Due to Balance or Runout	Incorrect Toe

Figure 8–15. Diagnostic chart for tread-wear patterns.

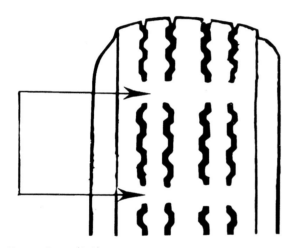

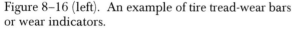

Figure 8–16 (left). An example of tire tread-wear bars or wear indicators.

Figure 8–17 (right). Example of tire remnants leading up to the point where tire suffered complete failure. (Reproduced from: Rivers R.W.: *Tire Failures and Evidence Manual for Traffic Accident Investigation*. Charles C Thomas, Publisher, Springfield, Illinois, 2001, p. 41. Reproduced with permission.)

The roadway up to the point of tire failure may provide evidence of a foreign object that was struck by the tire, and so on. In all cases of tire pressure loss, the cause should be determined and any tire damage should be matched to the item that caused it. Also, when being slammed into a pothole or driven at excessive speed around a curve, an underinflated tire may momentarily pull loose from the wheel rim along part of the rim's circumference, causing air loss and consequent loss of vehicle control.

8.041 When a driver claims that his vehicle suffered a *blowout*, examine the tire and vehicles closely to determine if the tire had been struck and damaged by some vehicle part that caused the loss of air pressure. Examine also the roadway leading up to the point of collision for evidence of a flat tire mark prior to the collision point. That is to say, look for evidence (visible at the scene) that will determine whether or not the tire went flat as the result of the collision rather than at some point prior to the collision. Prior air loss can, of course, be a contributing factor in a vehicle's going out of control, but the roadway will usually show evidence of such loss either by debris or flat-tire marks (see Fig. 7–29).

8.042 It is often necessary to remove a tire from its wheel rim in order to conduct a more thorough analysis than can be carried out at the scene. In such cases, the tire and rim should have corresponding marks made on each before the tire is removed so that the tire, rim, and any evidence of damage can later be related to each other (see Fig. 8–18).

Figure 8–18. An example of tire damage at A and rim damage at B. C shows a method of marking the position of the tire on the wheel rim before it is removed from the rim so that the damages can later be related as to location or position. (Reproduced from Rivers, R.W.: *Tire Failures and Evidence Manual for Traffic Accident Investigation.* Charles C Thomas, Publisher, Springfield, Illinois, 2001, p. 28.)

8.043 *Warning: Mounting and de-mounting dangers. Multiple-piece wheels (rims) and single-piece rims.* The National Highway Administration (NHTSA) has cautioned truck owners, operators, and service personnel about the dangers of improper servicing or repair of *multi-piece wheels*, and announced the availability of informational material through the agency's toll-free hotline. Such wheels (sometimes called rims) consist of two or three pieces: a rim base, a side ring, and in some designs, a lock ring. When the wheel is assembled, the side or lock rings hold the bead of the inflated tire on the rim base. The wheels are commonly found on medium to large size trucks, buses, and trailers. NHTSA cautioned that if the side ring is not properly seated on the rim base before the tire is inflated, the ring can fly off with explosive force. This may occur during tire mounting or de-mounting. There is no warning, and the result can be serious injury or death. It is emphasized that no one should attempt service on multi-piece rims without adequate training and knowledge. NHTSA also warned that *single-piece rims* used with tubeless tires can also be hazardous if handled and serviced improperly.[6]

8.044 In summary, a tire can fail for a number of reasons, including a manufacturing or repair deficiency, usual wear-and-tear, damage from roadway hazards, e.g., glass, nails, sharp rocks, and so on. The majority of tire failures, however, can usually be traced to operator neglect, such as failure to maintain proper air pressure.

- ☐ Tire construction
- ☐ Inflation
- ☐ Tread type (e.g., summer, winter, studded)
- ☐ Tread wear (e.g., sides, center, uneven)
- ☐ Tread depth (new, % worn)
- ☐ Tread wear bar or indicator
- ☐ Valve stem breakage
- ☐ Casing break or damage
- ☐ Tread separation
- ☐ Fabric or rubber deterioration
- ☐ Bead failure
- ☐ General condition (e.g., cuts, abrasions)
- ☐ Maximum speed tire is designed to tolerate
- ☐ Maximum load capacity tire is designed to handle
- ☐ Tire-wheel-rim compatibility

☐ Nails, glass, or other foreign objects embedded in the tire tread or walls
    ☐ Outside   ☐ Inside
☐ Tire remnants, debris, flat tire marks on roadway leading up to point of collision.
☐ Identification points related to location on tire and rim when tire is removed from rim.

Since statutes, ordinances and organizational policies and procedures differ widely in various jurisdictions, those of the particular jurisdiction should govern when there is any conflict between them and the contents of this manual.

Tire specifications can be found in the following U.S. Code of Federal Regulations:

49CFR393.75 Subpart G-Miscellaneous Parts and Accessories and Appendix G Minimum Periodic Inspection Standards

49CFR569 Regrooved Tires

49CFR570.9 Vehicle in Use Inspection Standards, Tires

49CFR571.119 New pneumatic tires for vehicles other than passenger cars

Many of these documents can be purchased in book format from U.S. Government Printing Offices. Further information is available by searching: <http://www.access.gpo.gov/>.

8.045–8.050 reserved.

BRAKES

Types of Brake Systems

8.051 There are two types of brake systems in modern vehicles:

1. *Drum brake*–A brake unit that uses a circular rim or support that is attached to the wheel, on the inside of which brake shoes expand and press against the rim to stop the wheel's rotation (see Fig. 8–19).
2. *Disc brake*–A brake unit that uses a disc which rotates with the wheel and against which brake pads held in a vise-like caliper are pressed to stop its rotation (see Fig. 8–20).

Some vehicles may be equipped with either drum brakes or disc brakes. Others may be equipped with a combination of these (see Fig. 8–21). Both systems use hydraulic fluid to active the brakes. Some large commercial vehicles are equipped with *air brakes*. While air is used to activate their brakes, these vehicle still use drum or disc wheels systems.

8.052 A parking brake, operated by a lever, handle, or small foot pedal, is designed to lock the rear wheels or drive shaft of a vehicle. The operational efficiency of this brake is very important in the investigation of *parked-vehicle-run-away* crashes.

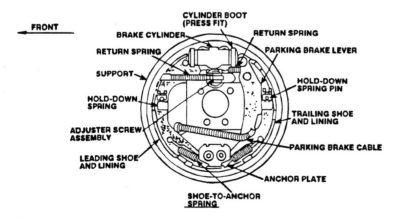

Figure 8–19. An example of a typical drum brake unit. (Source: Brake Service Manual supplied in the interests of traffic safety by Allied Automotive–Bendix Aftermarket Brake Division.)

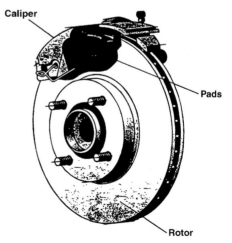

Figure 8–20. Typical disc brake.

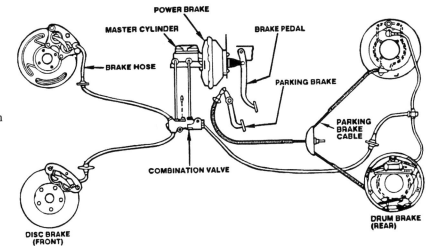

Figure 8–21. An example of a drum and disc brake combination.

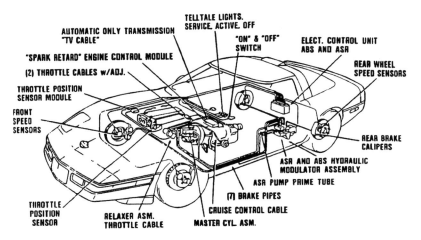

Figure 8–22. Controls, sensors, cables, and assemblies utilized in acceleration slip regulation (ASR) and an antilock braking system (ABS).

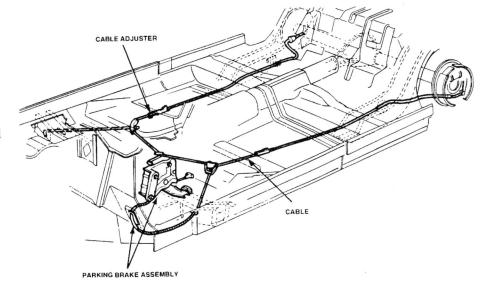

Figure 8–23. A typical parking brake system.

Brake Inspections

8.053 *Brakes and skidmarks.* When the driver states that he applied the brakes, but there are no signs of braking on the roadway, i.e., no skid marks leading up to the collision point, it may point to evidence of a brake failure; whereas a skid mark is good evidence that there was braking capability on the wheel that left the mark. By itself, however, such a skid mark does not prove that the braking efficiency or capability of the entire braking system was either adequate or inadequate. A wheel(s) that does not leave a skid mark may have had either defective braking or proper braking. A wheel that does not leave a skid mark may, in fact, have good braking efficiency and put forth extreme retarding forces in an effort to bring the vehicle to a stop. For example, if a wheel (or wheels) of the vehicle was loaded beyond its safe carrying capacity, the wheel(s) may have had good braking efficiency but not have been able to lock up because of the vehicle's momentum. In such cases, a single wheel that was not overloaded may lock up and leave a skid mark, thereby resulting in only one skid mark that is visible; thus, a good reason to carry out a mechanical inspection of all wheel brakes when there is any doubt about the braking capability or efficiency on any one or all wheels of the system.

8.054 *Brake-fluid loss.* Brake failure often occurs as the result of brake-fluid loss. Brake fluid lines may crack through normal wear and tear, be broken by outside forces, as from rocks or collision, or be worn by rubbing against a wheel or other vehicle part. If brake-line failure is evident, check the roadway leading up to the point of collision for evidence of fluid loss caused through the application of brakes. Conversely, examine the collision point for fluid loss indicating that fluid lines were broken and fluid lost as a direct result of the collision.

8.055 As brake linings wear, it may be necessary for the operator to depress the brake pedal farther in order to activate the brake. When there is evidence of this, the investigation should examine for evidence of improperly-working automatic brake adjusters which normally will take up this slack and maintain proper or adequate brake pedal travel.

8.056 When one or more wheels causes the vehicle to pull to the right or left, or there is brake fading, it can be because the brakes are poorly adjusted, linings are wet or damp from water, or the linings are contaminated by grease or oil. In these cases, the investigator should examine the roadway leading up to the collision point for evidence of water or other contaminants that might have affected braking efficiency.

8.057 *Low pedal reserve.* Examine precisely how far the brake pedal can be depressed. If there is low pedal reserve, determine whether full brake-pedal reserve can be restored by *pumping* and, if so, how many strokes are required to restore it to normal. The time necessary to restore braking efficiency by pumping the brake pedal could very well have a bearing on why the brakes were not activated. When there is apparent brake-pedal deficiency (low brake pedal):

- ☐ Check the fluid level in the master cylinder.
- ☐ Inspect the fluid lines from the master cylinder to all wheels.
- ☐ Check inner-side of the wheels for fluid stains and fresh fluid. If stains are evident, the wheel cylinder has been defective or leaking for a longer period of time. Fresh fluid on the inside of a wheel indicates a recent break in the wheel cylinder or at least that the brakes were recently applied.

8.058 *Hills.* When brakes are applied constantly over extended periods of time–such as on steep hills–the brake linings become hot, causing a possible *fading* or loss of full braking efficiency without the usual evidence of brake failure being available to the investigator. This is more common with commercial transport than with passenger vehicles.

8.059 reserved.

AIR BRAKE SYSTEM

8.060 An air-brake system consists of five main components:

1. Compressor
2. Reservoir
3. Foot valve (brake pedal)
4. Brake chambers (and slack adjusters)
5. Brake shoes and drums

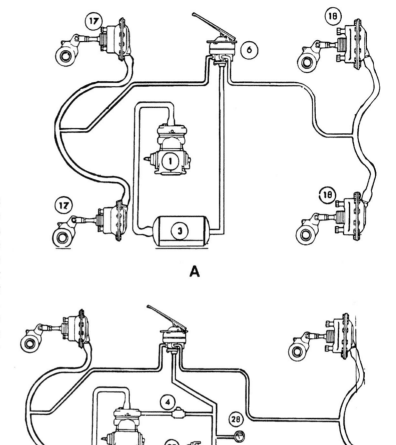

Figure 8–24. (*A*) System summary. In this part of the figure, air is pumped by the compressor (1) to the reservoir (3). Air is made available from the reservoir to the bottom of the foot valve (6). When the driver pushes down on the foot valve, air under pressure flows to the front and rear brake chambers (17 and 18). (See Fig. 8–25.) (*B*) In this part of the figure, the system contains a safety valve (5) in the service (dry tank) reservoir, and has an additional second (wet tank) reservoir.

8.061 An air-brake system generally operates as follows (see Fig. 8–24):

a. A compressor pumps air into the reservoir, where it is stored under pressure.

b. An air-pressure gauge, usually mounted on the dashboard of the vehicle cab, indicates the air pressure in the main reservoir system. (Federal and state legislation usually govern the minimum and maximum amounts of air pressure required for vehicle operation.)

c. The foot valve draws the compressed air from the reservoir when the brake is applied.

d. Upon brake application, the compressed air is directed through a series of lines and valves to the brake chambers, transferring the force exerted by the compressed air to mechanical linkages and the brake shoes and drums.

e. Slack adjusters take up the slack in the brake linkages. Important Evidence: If slack adjusters are not properly adjusted, braking efficiency can be substantially reduced or be totally destroyed (see Fig. 8–25).

8.062 *Brake chamber and push rod.* A brake chamber is usually mounted on an axle near the wheel that is

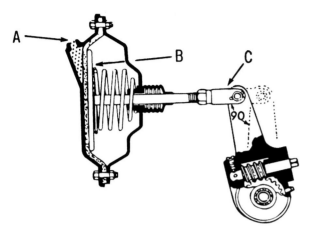

Figure 8–25. A typical brake chamber. *A* indicates the port, *B* the diaphragm, and *C* the slack adjuster.

equipped for braking (see Fig. 8–25). Air pressure is fed though an inlet port. In braking, the air pushes against the diaphragm and the push rod. The push rod is connected to a crank arm lever called a *slack adjuster*, which is linked to the brake shoes. As indicated by its name, the slack adjuster is also the means of adjusting the *slack* or free play in the linkage. When the slack adjuster is not properly adjusted, effective braking is reduced and brake lag time is increased. If too much slack is present, the diaphragm may bottom out in the brake chamber and the braking efficiency will be negligible.

8.063 Trucks generally have two or more air tank reservoirs for storage of compressed air. The tank connected to the compressor discharge hose is called the wet or supply tank. The name wet was earned because, as warm air from the compressor enters the tank, any moisture in the air condenses on its cold walls and collects in the bottom. A drain cock is provided to allow the collected moisture to be expelled. It is recommended (by industry) that all air tanks, both supply and reserve, be drained of water and other contaminants daily. Neglect of tank draining can cause early valve failure, reduced air volume (and possible brake failure) and make the system freeze up during cold weather.[7]

8.064 When possible, a basic air-brake system examination should include:

☐ Compressor efficiency
☐ Air gauge reading

☐ Reservoir pressure
☐ Foot valve operation
☐ Brake chamber condition
☐ Condition of slack adjuster linkages
☐ Push rod travel on all chambers
☐ Audible air leaks throughout the entire system
☐ Damaged or broken lines and connections
☐ Moisture in reservoirs
☐ Evidence of required reservoir tank draining

CAUTION TO INVESTIGATORS: Although much of an air-brake inspection can be done visually, it is cautioned that an in-depth should be conducted only by those fully qualified to do so. When conducting in-depth inspections, some of the safety precautions to follow include: (1) block vehicle wheels; (2) drain system pressure before removing hoses, plugs, or components; (3) never go beneath a vehicle with the engine running; and (4) wear safety glasses.[8]

☐ Drum brake
☐ Disc brake
☐ Combination: Drum-Disc
☐ Hydraulic system
☐ Air system
☐ Fluid level (master cylinder)
☐ Fluid leaks
    ☐ In lines
    ☐ At wheels
☐ Power-assisted brakes
☐ Anti-skid brake system
☐ Pedal reserve
☐ Brake pedal tread (good, worn, slippery)
☐ Brake fading, e.g., on hills
☐ Brake adjustment (pull to side)
☐ Parking brake
    ☐ Foot pedal
    ☐ Lever
    ☐ Handle
    ☐ Transmission lock
☐ Braking evidence
    ☐ Skid mark(s)

EXHAUST SYSTEM

8.065 An exhaust system consists of a series of pipes and chambers intended to ensure that the exhaust

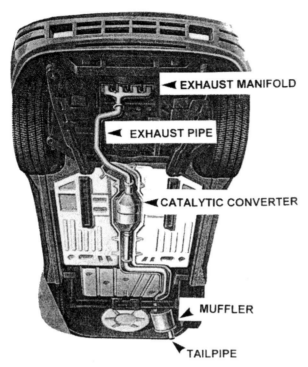

◄ EXHAUST MANIFOLD

◄ EXHAUST PIPE

◄ CATALYTIC CONVERTER

▲ MUFFLER

▼ TAILPIPE

Figure 8–26. A typical exhaust system.

gases from the engine are carried safely and without leakage from the exhaust manifold to the tailpipe, thence expelling the gases to outside of the vehicle (see Fig. 8–26). A typical exhaust system includes:

    a. Exhaust manifold(s)
    b. Front exhaust pipe (engine pipe)
    c. Catalytic converter (modern vehicle)
    d. Rear exhaust pipe (with catalytic converter) (*Catalytic Converter*. A device intended to remove much of the pollution from the exhaust gases before they leave the vehicle.)
    e. Muffler(s)
    f. Tailpipe

8.066 *Carbon monoxide*, which is an odorless, colorless, poisonous gas, is contained in motor vehicle exhaust. A defective exhaust system, such as damaged or improperly fitting parts, or corrosion of any of its main parts, may allow carbon-monoxide to filter its way to the passenger compartment through improper body fittings and corroded or damaged areas of the vehicle, such as in the floor boards, or holes in the trunk compartment. When these deficiencies are present, rather than drawing in clean,

fresh outside air, some air-conditioners recirculate inside air within the vehicle and at the same time suck in carbon-monoxide gas through openings in the vehicle body. When there is an indication that a driver or passenger has suffered the effects of carbon-monoxide poisoning, a thorough follow-up examination of the air conditioning unit should be made.

8.067 An exhaust system examination should include:

    ☐ Manifold connection
    ☐ Exhaust pipe
    ☐ Muffler
    ☐ Catalytic converter
    ☐ Tailpipe
    ☐ Connections

Air Conditioning Unit
    ☐ On
    ☐ Off
    ☐ Defects (drawing in exhaust fumes, etc.)

WINDSHIELD WIPERS AND DEFROSTERS

8.068 During inclement weather conditions, windshield wipers and defrosters that are either inadequate or not working that would cause inadequate wiper-blade-windshield contact thereby not clearing the windshield as required can be a contributing factor in many accidents, particularly during rain, snow, or other inclement weather conditions when the windshield must be kept clean in order for the driver to have adequate visibility. During inclement weather, visibility problems become especially acute on secondary and dirt roads. Darkness further complicates visibility on any class of road. Additionally, the windshield-wiper, defroster, and air-conditioner control switches should be checked for working order, general condition, and *on* or *off* position, all of which could have a bearing on windshield and window visibility (see also Paras. 8.147–8.149).

8.069 A driver's compartment glass examination should include:

    ☐ Type and condition of windshield and windows (e.g., clear, tinted, view obstructions, damage, visibility, general condition)

☐ Wiper-blade system (e.g., electrical, vacuum, mechanical)
☐ Wiper-blades
☐ Blade arms
☐ Wiper-blade damage, deterioration, or improper adjustment
☐ Defroster
☐ Air-conditioner (see also Para. 8.066)
☐ Switches (e.g., type, location, on or off)
☐ Controls (e.g., high, low, off)

MIRRORS

8.070 Improper inside or outside mirror positioning or adjustment may result in a view obstruction during certain vehicle maneuvers, particularly in collisions involving:

☐ Pullout and sideswipe
☐ Back-up
☐ A parked vehicle while backing up
☐ An overtaking vehicle when attempting to change lanes

Related to:

☐ The location, position and type of mirror
☐ Driver's seated height
☐ A vehicle part, e.g., pillar or headrest, the position of which might have obstructed the driver's view
☐ An inside or outside load on the vehicle, including seated positions of passengers

8.071–8.075 reserved.

VEHICLE LOADS

8.076 The manner in which the load is placed and secured in or upon a vehicle can cause a hazard to the driver, other trafficway users, and the ability of the driver to control the vehicle from overturn, or in the maneuverability of the vehicle itself. The manner in which a load is carried and/or secured can contribute to a collision, including the following:

☐ Load or part of the load that falls from the vehicle.
☐ Inadequate binders or other restraining devices.
☐ Load shift causing the vehicle to go out of control, and/or overturn.

☐ Driver's view or movements being obstructed by the manner in which the load is placed in or upon the vehicle.
☐ Load that extends too far at the sides, top, or rear of the vehicle, striking bridges, utility poles, utility wires, etc., or other highway users.
☐ Load that is so high that it throws the vehicle off balance, causing it to tip over.
☐ *Interior load, luggage, passengers, etc.* An overload of passengers as well as any object being carried obstructing the driver's view or interferes with the driver's ability to steer or control his vehicle, or strikes the operator during a maneuver.

HORN, SIREN

8.077 A horn or siren warning can influence crash avoidance or the outcome of a crash, such as in cases involving pedestrians, pullout and sideswipes and intersection collisions.

Examinations

☐ Type (e.g., electrical, vacuum, air)
☐ Siren
☐ Switch (e.g., ring, button, shroud, spoke)
☐ Was the horn used?
☐ Was the siren used?
☐ Was the horn/siren functioning properly?
☐ Audibility (see also Para. 8.148)
☐ Windows
  ☐ open
  ☐ closed

NOISE AND OTHER DISTRACTIONS

8.078 Excessive noise or sound within a vehicle, that may come from a number of sources, as well as the driver's preoccupation with controlling electronic instruments, e.g., turning a radio dial or dialing a telephone number, can interfere with his ability to adequately perceive a real or potential hazard and consequently to take appropriate evasive action, e.g., as in cases of a driver's failure to hear or perceive the importance of a siren or horn. In cases where noise within (or from outside the vehicle) is a possibility, the investigation should cover the various possible sources of the noise and its extent (volume), which should include:

- ☐ Car radio
  - ☐ On ☐ Off ☐ Volume   Station____
- ☐ Cassette player
  - ☐ On ☐ Off ☐ Volume
- ☐ CD player
  - ☐ On ☐ Off ☐ Volume
- ☐ Car telephone/CB radio
  - ☐ Hand-held ☐ Other
  - ☐ Punching in a number at time of crash
  - ☐ Used at time of crash
  - ☐ Volume
- ☐ CB equipped
  - ☐ Hand-held ☐ Other
  - ☐ Used at time of crash
  - ☐ Volume
  - ☐ Punching in a number at time of crash
- ☐ Inadequate muffler
- ☐ Vibration noise from some part of the vehicle or load
- ☐ Loud voices of passengers, including children
- ☐ Windows
  - ☐ open
  - ☐ closed

(See also Para. 8.148.)

When a car radio was on, the driver or a passenger may be able to recall what was being broadcast when the crash occurred. This information can be useful, through further investigation with the station, in determining the exact time of the crash if the *time* is essential and is not otherwise available.

DOOR LOCKS

8.079 Inadequate or improperly adjusted door locks and latches may allow a passenger to be ejected from the vehicle or may have prevented him from leaving the vehicle in a time of an emergency. Evidence should be obtained by checking both visually and manually for that which would suggest a reason for a door or door lock malfunction, including:

- ☐ Handles
- ☐ Latches
- ☐ Safety catches
- ☐ Door lock adjustment

- ☐ Binding or looseness
- ☐ Dents or bends of sufficient dimension to permit a door to unlatch, or to prevent the door from opening.

SPEED RECORDING DEVICES AND METHODS

Speedometer

8.080 The speedometer location or position in the driver's compartment, type, readings in mph or km/h, visibility to the driver while he is seated in the vehicle, and speed registered or showing at the time of on-scene investigation should be noted and recorded. Generally, the reading will be zero. Occasionally, however, the needle will stick at the speed being registered at the time of collision because of impact damage, which can be used as corroborative evidence of speed. Speedometers may be mechanically- or electronically-driven. In the case of an electronically-driven speedometer, an after-collision reading may, however, be as the result of a variation in voltage or a short-circuit. In either case, a stuck speedometer needle reading should be used with caution unless it can be established that the needle did not *bounce* and stick at that position at the time of collision. In all cases involving a speedometer head-on, after-collision examination, it can be helpful to the investigation to have a simple laboratory examination carried out using an ultraviolet light to determine whether there are traces of luminous paint which could have been transferred from the needle to the faceplate or dial during impact, which might show the needle position at the time of impact (see Fig. 8–27).

- ☐ Location (where the speedometer is positioned in the vehicle)
- ☐ Visibility from driver's seated position
- ☐ Increments: 1, 2, 5, 10 ___
  - ☐ mph ☐ km/h
- ☐ Reading: _____ mph (km/h)
- ☐ Color of face plate
- ☐ Color of numerals
- ☐ Method of drive:
  - ☐ Cable
  - ☐ Electronic
- ☐ Damage to speedometer
- ☐ Illumination

Figure 8–27. An example of a damaged speedometer reading at time of investigator's arrival. (Courtesy of Thomas Watters, Pres., IMPACT, Forensic Analysis Inc., Saint John, New Brunswick, Canada.)

Black Boxes

8.081 Since the early 1990s, some cars have been equipped with *black boxes* that record pre-crash data that include air bag operations, seat belt status, vehicle speed, velocity change in milliseconds, engine rpm, percent throttle, brake switch circuit status, and signal light status, all of which can be downloaded to a laptop computer. In many cases, however, manufacturers consider it to be proprietary information and it will not be released. When this information is not otherwise readily available or where it would be of assistance as supporting evidence, the vehicle dealership and/or manufacturer may be contacted to determine the status of obtaining this information. *In many jurisdictions, there may be legal and privacy constraints or implications in place regarding the retrieval and use of this information that should be fully recognized and adhered to.*

8.082 When black box information can be retrieved and used, some of the evidence that may be available is:

☐ Air bag operation
☐ Seat belt use
☐ Vehicle speed
☐ Acceleration/deceleration (change in velocity)
☐ Engine rpm
☐ Percent throttle
☐ Brake switch circuit status
☐ Signal light status

On-Board Computers

8.083 Some on-board recorders combine the functions of a speedometer, odometer, and employee time clock–all wrapped up in a dashboard instrument about the size of a tape deck. On-board recorders keep track of vehicle speed, mileage, duration of travel, and number and duration of stops as well as time and day. They typically track who's driving via smart cards or other driver inputs. Information on driving hours is accessible by motor carrier or enforcement personnel. These are the basic requirements for on-board recorders in the Federal Motor Carrier Safety Administration's hours of service proposal. It is important to distinguish on-board recorders in trucks from so-called *black boxes* also known as event records. The latter are used specifically for crash analysis and accident reconstruction, while the recorders proposed by the Federal Motor Carrier Safety Administration would be primarily to track truck drivers' hours. Some on-board recorders do keep event data, and some work with global positioning systems to help motor carriers pinpoint the locations of their truck rigs. Other recorders include engine monitoring systems to improve maintenance. Some are linked with wireless routing and navigation systems.

Tachographs

8.084 Commercial vehicle tachometers allow users to record vehicle activity modes, such as driving or being at rest. Tachographs can be either (1) *mechanical*, i.e., driven by a cable attachment to the speedometer or gear box, or (2) one that operates on electrical impulses sent from the gearbox through an electrical cable.

8.085 The investigation and examination of a Tachograph–all of which are dependent upon the type and condition of the tachometer, and any permissible tolerances and references as to time and distances that might be inherent in the device, usually spelled-out in applicable tachograph literature, e.g., instruction and maintenance manual–should generally include:

☐ Time, with visible evidence that the clock is working
☐ Distance in mph (km/h) traveled by vehicle
☐ Speed in mph or km/h
☐ Driving time

☐ Other periods of work or of availability
☐ Breaks from work and rest periods
☐ Disruption in the power supply of the recording equipment
☐ For a vehicle operated by two drivers, simultaneously but distinctly activities of each driver.
☐ Engine rpm
☐ Gear used
☐ When engine left running, but vehicle in stopped position
☐ When the instrument case containing the record sheet is opened

Further, a microscopic analysis can be made for evidence of:

☐ Speed peaks
☐ Speed reductions
☐ Accelerations and decelerations, with time intervals
☐ Major braking, distance, and time measurements
☐ Precise time of stops, such as at the time of collision
☐ Road speeds

Tachograph Charts

8.086 Recordings are made on a chart by a recording stylus when the vehicle accelerates or brakes, or when any other recording criteria are met. It is important that it be determined whether or not the chart is an approved type for the tachograph. Approval designations will be found on the chart. If the chart is not an approved type for that tachograph, the readings may not be correct. Most charts are designed to cover a 24-hour period represented over the whole 350 degrees of the chart, divided into five minute intervals. However, some charts cover 12 hours to seven days, or as high as 31 days, depending upon the kind of instrument and chart involved. Once inserted, the chart is accessible only by opening an access door. Opening the door will cause a mark to be made on the chart.

8.087 A tachograph analysis can be carried out to determine if the device, including the chart, has been tampered with for fraudulent purposes, or has suffered any form of abuse or damage that might affect its evidence.

☐ Chart
   ☐ Approved type
   ☐ 24-hr period   ☐ 12 hrs,   ☐ 31 days
   ☐ Other _____
☐ Security examination

Gear Shift Lever/Selector

8.088 The position of the gear shift/selector may indicate the possible speed that could have been attained in that position, thereby corroborating other evidence such as statements of witnesses

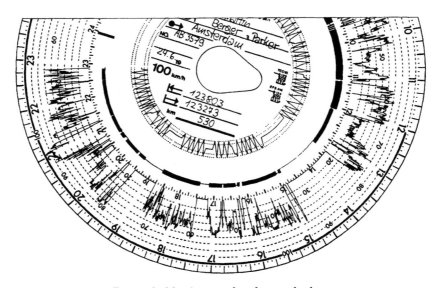

Figure 8–28. A typical tachograph chart.

and/or the driver, or a stuck speedometer needle, bearing in mind that the lever might have moved from its pre-impact position to another position as a result of the collision. For example, a low-gear range would indicate the possibility of a slower speed than that which could be attained in a higher-range gear. If the investigator is not totally familiar with the shifting mechanism in certain manual-shift vehicles (for example, large commercial trucks or farm tractors), he should have the gearshift lever position explained to him by a competent operator.

TRAILER BREAKAWAY

8.089 When a trailer-breakaway collision occurs, a thorough investigation must be made of the circumstances under which the towing vehicle and the trailer were operated, including how the trailer was equipped to facilitate safe towing, braking capability and efficiency, and the options available to the operator to control the breakaway once it occurred.

8.090 A trailer-breakaway examination should include:

- ☐ Method of control by the vehicle operator
- ☐ Type of coupler and/or hitch
- ☐ Auxiliary breakaway connections (such as *safety chains*, used to back up couplings and couplers and hitches)
- ☐ Fifth-wheel connection (used primarily by tractor and semi-trailer units)
- ☐ Damage or malfunction of the electric, air, and/or hydraulic lines
- ☐ Apparent *direction of immediate travel* at the time of and after breakaway which can be related to brake function (uneven braking)
- ☐ Parts: Sheared bolts, bent parts, abrasions, worn or rubbed parts
- ☐ Brakes

For an example of out-of-control trailer skid marks caused by a failed trailer hitch, see Figure 7–61.

8.091–8.095 reserved.

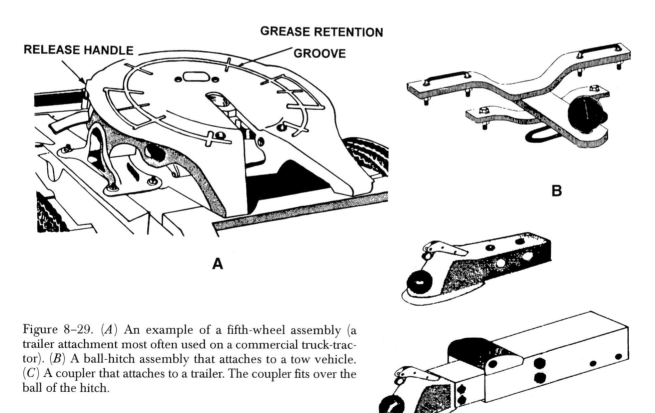

Figure 8–29. (*A*) An example of a fifth-wheel assembly (a trailer attachment most often used on a commercial truck-tractor). (*B*) A ball-hitch assembly that attaches to a tow vehicle. (*C*) A coupler that attaches to a trailer. The coupler fits over the ball of the hitch.

OCCUPANT SAFETY RESTRAINT SYSTEMS

8.096 The primary purposes of a occupant restraint systems is to control occupant movement within a vehicle, to prevent or lessen the extent of injury, and to prevent an occupant's ejection from the vehicle during a collision. These safety restraint systems fall under two major categories:

1. Seat belts
2. Air bags

SEAT BELT SYSTEMS

8.097 In general, seat-belt restraint systems fall under the following three categories:

1. *Active*
   A system that requires the occupant to manually engage the system by fastening a buckling device.
2. *Passive*
   A passive restraint system that generally operates automatically without passenger interaction. It is designed to protect the occupants in conjunction with manual lap or manual lap and shoulder harnesses.
3. *Passive/active*
   A system that employs a manual lap belt and an automatic shoulder belt. One type of 3-point system is a type that automatically secures the occupant as the door is closed. With other types, some manual operation is also required.

8.098 A seat belt assembly consists of the following hardware items:

a. Floor anchor–see Figure 8–32
b. Retractor–see Figure 8–33
c. D-ring–see Figure 8–34
d. Latch plate or tongue–Figure 8–35

8.099 A typical seat belt is made of polyester or nylon. Manufacturers and government agencies regularly check materials for compliance. The regulated belt breaking strength will be found in FMVSS 209 (or CMVSS 209). For standards, see the Code of Federal Regulations, Transportation, Parts 571.208 and 209, revised October 1, 1998. For Canadian standards see CMVSS 209. See also Safety Performance of Seat Belt Retractors in SAE paper 79080, authored by Murray Dance. There is also computer

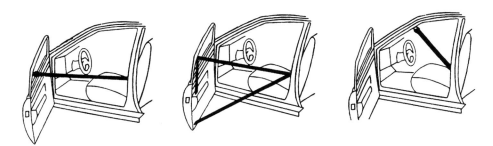

Figure 8–30. Seat belt configurations.

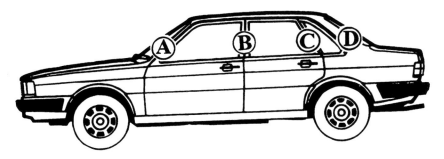

Figure 8–31. Vehicle pillars.

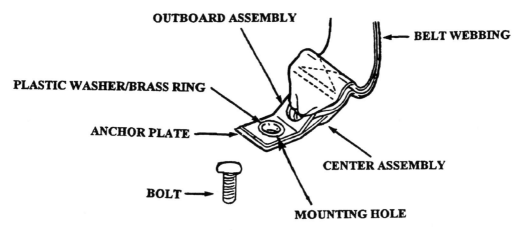

Figure 8–32. A retractor (exposed, showing internal workings.

Figure 8–33. A retractor (exposed, showing internal workings.

Figure 8–34. D-ring.

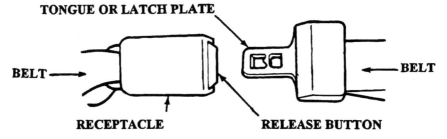

Figure 8–35. Latch plate and receptacle (buckle unit).

software available that is useful in estimating such forces based on the CRASH or SMAC programs.

8.100 A seat belt examination should follow the seat belt path, starting at one end of the assembly, going through to the other end, and including each item of hardware involved. An explanation of the location and function of each hardware item follows:

Seat Belt Path

The outboard end of a seat belt assembly belt is attached to an integral part of the vehicle body by an anchor (see Fig. 8–32), usually located on the outboard side of the vehicle body sill for a front seat and to the lower quarter panel for a rear seat. For center seats (and central attachments), the belt is usually anchored to the floor pan. In the case of lap/shoulder safety belts, the front seat safety belt extends from its anchor to a retractor (see Fig. 8–33) mounted on the adjacent lower *B*-pillar (see Fig. 8–31) or other part of the lower vehicle structure, and up to a *D*-ring (see Fig. 8–34) that is mounted on the *B*-pillar post. The webbing then extends from the *D*-ring above and behind the occupant's shoulder, and from there is directed downward at the proper angle over the occupant's shoulder and chest to the lap belt buckle (see Fig. 8–35). The belt has a slip tongue on it which latches to the lap belt buckle. The belt then continues through the tongue to a floor anchor. The front and rear seat shoulder safety belt retractors are designed to let the webbing move in or out freely except during vehicle deceleration, when it is automatically locked by a mechanically actuated inertia sensor.*

8.101 *Retractor function examination.* Examine the function of a retractor by gently pulling on the webbing to determine whether or not it is locked up in some way. In some cases, a belt will become folded at or near the retractor or *D*-ring which prevents it from retracting fully. When this occurs, the occupant will experience a related amount of slack. Before conducting any function tests, make sure any physical evidence is properly documented and

*Sources: Ford Motor Company and Rivers, R.W.: *Seat Belt and Air Bag Systems Manual for Traffic Crash Investigation and Reconstruction.* Institute of Police Technology and Management, University of North Florida, 2001, pp. 41–42.

that it will not be destroyed or damaged in any way by the testing.[9]

8.102 *Belt-sensitive retractor tests.* The vehicle's owner's manual will usually identify which type of retractor the vehicle is equipped with and give instructions on how to check its operation. Most modern cars, however, use a vehicle-sensitive retractor, which locks when it senses any quick movement of the shoulder belt. There are several ways to test a belt-sensitive retractor. These include:

a. Hold the shoulder part of the belt and give it a very sharp pull. The belt should lock before it is pulled out more than a couple of inches. If it does not lock, it may mean that it is not functioning properly or that it is a vehicle-sensitive retractor which will lock only when it notices a quick change in the motion of the vehicle.

b. While pulling on the webbing, strike the vehicle in the immediate structure near the retractor (slap test) with either a fist or a hard object.[10]

8.103 When investigation reveals that belt is cut, attempt to determine who cut the belt and the reason for cutting it. In many cases, ambulance attendants or other persons present at the scene cut a belt to release an occupant.

8.104 Check the injury diagnosis. People wearing lap and shoulder belts show a decreased likelihood of head injury. Belt-associated injuries from shoulder restraints are rib fractures, sternal fracture, and clavicle fracture. Occupant restraints may result in such injuries as bruises on the chest and abdomen. When the torso is restrained, limbs are still mobile and shins may be bruised from striking the steering column or underneath the dashboard.

8.105 The interior of the vehicle should be examined for any mark or damage indicating that an occupant struck a certain point during impact. This type of evidence will often help ascertain whether a seat belt was used as well as the seated positions of occupants at the time of the collision. The mark or damage should be matched to any injuries suffered by the occupants, e.g., teeth marks on the dash matched to mouth injuries. You should look at all possibilities when attempting a match, even the possibility that a rear-seated passenger might have been thrown to the front[11] (see also Para. 8.153 and Fig. 8–50).

8.106–8.109 reserved.

8.110 There are many points that should be investigated which will provide evidence as to whether or not a seat belt was used by an occupant at the time of a collision, or was a belt that experienced frequent use. Many of these points are listed in the following summaries:

SEAT BELT INSPECTION SUMMARY

IMMEDIATE ON-SCENE INVESTIGATION EVIDENCE OVERVIEW

- ☐ Occupant still restrained
- ☐ Position of lap and shoulder belts on body
- ☐ Belt(s) tight/snug or slack
- ☐ Evidence of body tissue and/or blood adhering to belt(s) or some part of the vehicle
- ☐ Evidence of damage to clothing, e.g., tears, or traces of blood, in the vicinity of the areas that were contacted by belts.
- ☐ Condition of belts, e.g., cuts, fraying
- ☐ Seat belts:
    - ☐ Retracted ☐ Stowed
    - ☐ If not retracted, inches (cm's) extended
- ☐ Marks, abrasions, blood, skin, clothing fibers, and plastic transfer on webbing (both sides)
- ☐ Fore/aft recline position of the vehicle seat
- ☐ Deformation of occupant's seat
- ☐ Intrusion of damaged vehicle part into occupant area
- ☐ Damage or deformation to occupant's compartment
- ☐ Cut or released belt(s) by others, e.g., emergency rescue personnel or tow-truck operator

IMPORTANT: Relate physical evidence to statements of occupants. If victims are removed before investigator's arrival, obtain statements of those who removed them in terms of the foregoing.

EVIDENCE OF USE AND NON-USE

Non-Use

Evidence that the belts were probably not used includes:

- ☐ Belts not accessible, e.g., pushed down behind seat

- ☐ Shoulder belt stowed away
- ☐ Belts buckled together in front of, behind, or under the seat
- ☐ Vehicle deformation caused by impact which intrudes, compressing the belt anchorage against the seat. (If the belt was worn, could it have retracted? If not and if the belt is not visible, it was probably not worn.)
- ☐ Windshield impact damage, such as a spider-web pattern and bulge toward the outside of the vehicle. (The damage was probably caused by incorrect or non-use of a seat belt.)
- ☐ Damaged steering wheel caused by driver impact
- ☐ Occupant ejected from the vehicle
- ☐ Damaged upper dashboard (instrument panel) caused by occupant
- ☐ Occupant injuries which are not compatible with seat-belt use

Use

Evidence that belts were probably used includes:

- ☐ Stripped threads of floor anchor bolt and/or its receptacle
- ☐ Floor anchor bolt is deformed, its stem is bent, and/or the bored hole in the anchor is deformed, appearing oblong in shape
- ☐ Stretching or *loading* of the belt fabric
- ☐ Marks on latching mechanisms
- ☐ Transfer on clothing or belts
- ☐ Compatible injury patterns to occupants
- ☐ Belts jammed in the *out* position due to side intrusion preventing belt retraction
- ☐ Belt webbing cut to release an occupant
- ☐ Occupant remains in an original seating position and his injuries are less than what would be expected from the severity of the accident
- ☐ No head injuries but presence of belt injuries
- ☐ Belt stretch detected through a laboratory examination–might indicate seat belt use.
- ☐ Marks on the buckle possibly showing the belt was used on a regular basis.

CHILD RESTRAINTS

8.111 In all cases, the investigation should determine if the child restraint meets the requirements of the local jurisdiction, and if the installation of the seats and anchor points are strictly in accordance with the manufacturer's instructions. In some cars, station wagons, and pick-up trucks, installation of the top anchor strap may be difficult or impossible. When this is the case, an approved seat that does not require a top anchor strap might have been available and perhaps should have been used. All states (and Provinces) have primary laws requiring the use of restraints that meet federally set standards (FMVSS 213); and also set their own additional requirements, penalties, and fines.

8.112 There are many different types of child restraints; many look alike but may be equipped differently, and instructions for use from one model to another may differ substantially.

ON-SCENE INVESTIGATION-EXAMINATION CHILD STILL IN CAR SEAT

- ☐ Position of child
- ☐ Fitting of harness straps on child
- ☐ Position of harness retainer clip, if used
- ☐ Direction seat is facing:
  - ☐ Rear
  - ☐ Forward
- ☐ Seat
  - ☐ Tight
  - ☐ Loose
- ☐ Length of the securing seat belt from latch plate to lap belt anchor
  - ☐ Proper
  - ☐ Improper

CHILD CAR SEAT INVESTIGATION/EXAMINATION

- ☐ Make and model of the child car seat
- ☐ Installed according to regulations and/or manufacturer's instructions
- ☐ Car passenger seat on which child car seat is installed
- ☐ Auxiliary equipment:
  - ☐ Locking clip
  - ☐ Belt shortening clip
  - ☐ Other

- ☐ Lap belt retractor (type):
  - ☐ Emergency locking retractors (ELR)
  - ☐ Automatic locking retractor (ALR)
  - ☐ Switchable retractor (ALR/ELR)
  - ☐ Mode: ☐ ALR ☐ ELR ☐ NA
- ☐ Marks, abrasions, plastic transfer, etc., on the seat belt
- ☐ Length of the harness straps on the car seat
- ☐ Harness slots used
- ☐ Recline position of the car seat
- ☐ Marks and abrasions on the car seat, particularly the areas loaded by the seat belt and harness straps.
- ☐ Damage to car seat

AIR BAGS

8.113 An air bag system is an automotive vehicle passenger safety device consisting of a passive restraint in the form of a bag which is automatically inflated with gas to provide cushion protection against the impact of a collision (Source: *McGraw-Hill Dictionary of Scientific and Technical Terms*, 1994).

How Air Bags Work

8.114 An air bag is connected to sensor(s) mounted in the vehicle. The sensor is activated when the vehicle experiences a sudden deceleration such as that which occurs at the time of a collision. When activated, the sensor sends an electrical signal that ignites a chemical propellant within the bag. This propellant then produces nitrogen gas, which inflates the air bag. The process occurs very quickly—in less than one-twentieth of a second or faster than the blink of an eye. Most air bags have internal tether straps that shape the fabric and limit the movement of the bag. Vents in the rear allow the bag to deflate slowly to cushion the head as it moves forward into the deploying air bag (see Figs. 8–36 and 8–37). (Source: *Transport Canada Information Bulletin*).

8.115 Air bags are controlled by *sensors* mounted in the vehicle. Each air-bag manufacturer uses a slightly different system of sensors. If an air bag fails to deploy in a collision, the investigator should consult with an expert in air-bag technology before conducting an inspection (see Fig. 8–38.)

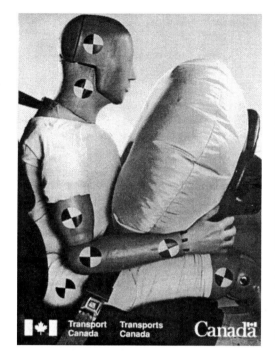

Figure 8–36 (left). An example of inflated driver's side air bag which is mounted in the steering wheel. (Courtesy of Transport Canada, Ottawa.)

Figure 8–37 (right). Deflated-deployed driver and passenger air bags. (Courtesy of Barry Walker, West Chester, Ohio.)

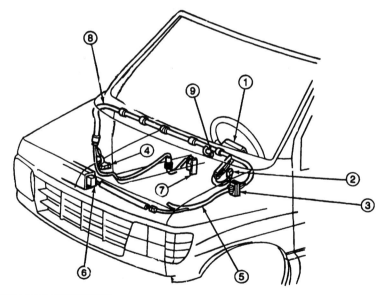

Item	Description
1	Air Bag
2	Diagnostic Monitor
3	Connector at Safety Wall
4	Safing Sensor

Item	Description
5	Engine Compartment Harness
6	Crash Sensor
7	Crash Sensor
8	Instrument Panel Harness
9	Readiness Indicator (Light)

Figure 8–38. Supplemental restraint system component locations. It should be noted that some vehicles are equipped with sensors at three different locations: (a) primary sensor at the center of the radiator, (b) a primary crash sensor on the right frame rail, and (c) a primary safing sensor at the right-side cowl kick panel. (Source: Force Motor Company.)

8.116 Ziernicki et al. (1997) state that in order for an air bag to be fully deployed before any significant forward excursion of the driver's body occurs, the air bag must be fully inflated in 40–50 ms. These high inflation rates can result in air-bag initial fabric velocities of 200 mph (320 km/h) or more. Vents on the back side of the air bag allow the gasses to flow out, making it possible for the air bag to deflate completely in approximately 2 seconds. The pressure inside the air bag returns to atmospheric pressure within about 0.2 second after deployment.[12]

8.117 Side air bags are designed to deploy from either the doors or the outboard side of the seat. Some new vehicles feature rear-seat side air bags. Due to the close proximity of the occupant to the door, side air bag sensors have less time to sense impact; four to five milliseconds instead of the 15 to 20 milliseconds in frontal crashes; furthermore, side bags also must inflate faster, within 20 milliseconds after initial impact, compared with 40 to 50 milliseconds for frontal air bags.[12,13]

8.118 Air bag systems are various and complex. **Except for visual inspections, an inspection of an air bag system in place should be carried out only by fully qualified personnel.** At all times, position yourself so as to avoid injury in the event the air bag deploys accidentally.

CAUTION: Different safety procedures may be required for the variety of air bag systems that now are or in the future may be in use. In all cases, the manufacturer's recommended safety procedures and instructions should be followed. Failure to do so may result in personal injury.*

8.119 *On-off switch.* Only people who are considered high-risk and who fit into one of four risk profiles, or who transport someone in one of these profiles, may obtain an on-off switch. The four profiles include the following persons, respectively:[14]

1. Those who cannot adjust their driver's position to keep back 10 inches (25 cm) from the steering wheel. This is perhaps the most-common use of air bag on-off switches.
2. Those who cannot avoid placing rear-facing infant seats in the front passenger seat.
3. Those who have a medical condition that places them at specific risk.
4. Those who cannot avoid situations–such as a car pool–that require a child 12 or under to ride in the front seat (Source: NHTSA Safety Fact Sheet).

8.120 In a NHTSA *Executive Summary* (reported in DOT HS 809 689, NHTSA Technical Report, November 2003, Results of the Survey on the Use of Passenger Air Bag On-Off Switches), it is stated that the benefits of the switches are contingent on how they are used: the air bag should be turned off when a high-risk individual is seated behind it, and it should be turned on at other times. The passenger air bag should be deactivated when there is a child or infant seated in the right and/or center front seat and activated when there is an adult seated in the right front seat and there is no child or infant in the front center seat. (It should be noted that it is a requirement of NHTSA that when an on-off switch is installed, it must have a telltale light that indicates when the switch has been activated.)

AIR BAG INSPECTION SUMMARY

☐ Deployed: Yes   No
☐ On-off switch: ☐ On   ☐ Off
☐ Telltale light
☐ Sensors
☐ Speed of vehicle
☐ Item impacted by vehicle
☐ Impact location on vehicle
☐ Marks on air bag, , e.g., cosmetics, blood, body tissue
☐ Occupant ejected

8.121 8.125 reserved.

VEHICLE DAMAGES

8.126 *Major and superficial damages.* Damage can be either major, such as that which occurs during a

---

*Source: Rivers, R.W., *Technical Traffic Accident Investigators' Handbook* (2nd ed.). Charles C Thomas, Publisher, Springfield, 1997, pp. 58–59. Also, when a vehicle has been involved in an collision and deployment has not taken place, the deployment mechanism becomes very sensitive. A jar may activate a sensor in such a way as to cause deployment—depending, of course, upon the seriousness of the related impact damage done to the vehicle.

head-on collision, or superficial, such as a scratch or an abrasion, usually appearing with striations. Superficial damage does not usually penetrate the body part, often appearing as *ruboff.* Superficial damages can be caused by a side-swipe collision, but can also be present with major damage. A close examination of these two types of damage is very important in determining how vehicles came together and how they separated.

Principal Direction of Force (PDOF)

8.127 The principal direction of force, sometimes referred to as the direction of thrust, is usually best determined by considering the direction of movement of some specific part of the vehicle, as indicated by collapse. A study of damage will indicate the direction of force at maximum engagement, when collapse and the forces producing it are at their greatest. Caution, however, must be exercised in evaluating damage evidence when determining the direction of force, because after initial contact the direction can be altered as a vehicle rotates, especially before maximum engagement has been reached.

8.128 *Superimposed damage.* Superimposed damage is damage that is caused by a secondary impact, i.e., damage upon damage. Such damage can occur, for example, when the vehicle was in a previous collision, or when a vehicle is struck by an opposing vehicle and then spins out of control and strikes a utility pole–suffering damage at the same point on the vehicle. Another example is in the case of a rollover where the same parts of the vehicle come into contact with the ground perhaps several times, suffering some damage each time on or over the previous damage.

Figure 8–39. An overhead view showing the angle at which two vehicles collided while they remain in the impact position. Arrow indicates the principal direction of force (thrust). (Courtesy of Brian Lapp, Senior Traffic Collision Reconstructionist, Parksville, B.C., Canada.)

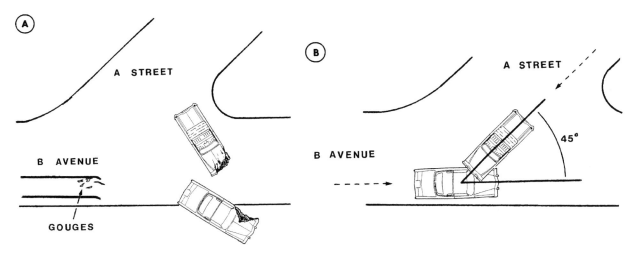

Figure 8–40. *A.* An after collision scene when vehicles have been moved from their point of impact, showing a method of determining vehicle pre-collision path of travel, placement on the roadway at the time of collision, and direction of thrust or principal direction of force. This is accomplished by taking careful measurements and a sketch of damages and roadway marks making it possible to place vehicles in their positions at time of impact, *B.* (Reproduced from: Rivers, R.W.: *Technical Traffic Accident Investigator's Handbook.* Charles C Thomas, Publisher, Springfield, Illinois, 1997, p. 127.)

8.129 *Induced damage*, also known as *incidental damage*, is damage of a vehicle part resulting from pressure or force exerted by a primary engagement elsewhere on the vehicle. For example, the trunk lid might be forced open when a vehicle is struck in the side and toward the rear, or the roof might buckle during either a rear-end or front-end collision. Induced damages are generally indicated by folds, creases, or wrinkles rather than by scratches or crumbling. Damage to the differential or to the universal joints is almost always induced damage, because these parts are seldom in contact with another object during collision. To mistake induced damage for direct contact damage could very well lead to an incorrect interpretation of the vehicle's direction of travel and its position on the roadway at the time of initial contact.

8.130 *Imprints.* An imprint can be left when two objects come together. Although imprints can vary greatly, each will have some form of pattern, whether it be similar to a tire tread pattern, shoe sole, or from a hard piece of metal such as that caused by a car bumper; or the hand or palm print of a pedestrian (see Fig. 8–41). In the case of a tire print, if a distinct tread pattern is evident, it is an indication that the tire was not rotating; however, if it is a smear-type imprint, it could indicate that the tire was rotating or that the imprint was left as a side-swipe.

8.131 Measure the width and length of any major or superficial damage, as well as any imprint. Include the distances from other major, identifiable vehicle

Figure 8–41. An example of hand and palm prints left on a vehicle when the vehicle collided with a pedestrian.

parts, and the height from the roadway. For matching purposes, the same type of measurements should be taken of the part that caused the damage or imprint. This information, together with roadway tire marks and damage, is very important in terms of determining a vehicle's pre-impact direction of travel, approach angle at the time of impact, principal direction of thrust, and the departure angle and post-impact direction of travel.

8.132. When examining damage to vehicle(s) involved in a crash, examine for:

- ☐ The relationship of one vehicle to another (or in relation to another object collided with). For example, where on each vehicle the damage is concentrated.
- ☐ The relationship of vehicles to the roadway.
- ☐ Skid marks leading up the point of impact [evidence that will assist in determining the principal direction of force (PDOF)], and any post-impact rotation.
- ☐ PDOF evidence that can be used to align the vehicle(s) so that angle at which they came together (and their pre-impact direction of travel) can be established.
- ☐ Damage to vehicle exterior showing evidence that a pedestrian was struck.
- ☐ Evidence of induced damage.
- ☐ Evidence as to who was driving , e.g., body contact with steering wheel.
- ☐ Evidence of body contact inside vehicle for seating determinations.
- ☐ Width and length measurements of any major or superficial damage on vehicle.
- ☐ Width and length measurements of the part that caused the damage or imprint to/on vehicle (or matching purposes).
- ☐ Approach angle at the time of impact, and principal direction of thrust.
- ☐ Departure angle and post-impact direction of travel.

Paint Chips and Transfers

8.133 Paint manufacturing involves the use of a very wide variety of liquids, oils, resins, solvents, organic polymers, fillers, binders, and other substances. As a paint, it is applied to a vehicle body in layers of various composition and thickness, adding to the variability (and uniqueness) from one year, manufacturer, and model to the next. Paint chips or paint residue can be very useful evidence in identifying a vehicle involved in a collision, such as in the case of a hit-and-run. Such evidence may be found adhering to an opposing vehicle or embedded in the clothing of a pedestrian. In terms of vehicle identification, a laboratory analysis can yield such information as physical and microscopic features, gross color, surface characteristics, and the number, thickness, type and composition by layer of paint which can be matched against a suspect vehicle, proving or disproving its possible involvement.

8.134 Layers of paint on motor vehicles, because they are so strictly controlled and monitored, provide excellent material for comparison, the layer pattern of paint often being confined to very few models produced between verifiable dates. Most motor vehicle manufacturers keep extensive records and sample lists of all paints used in production. Comparison of samples can normally be carried out under a microscope, but if identification is difficult or inconclusive, paint is suitable for analysis by chromatography and spectrometry (in particular, emission spectrometry).[15]

8.135 The National Bureau of Standards maintains a color reference guide of automobile finishes (primers and outer coats) used by manufacturers. The guide, first published in 1974, is updated annually. If a paint sample can be matched to a reference sample, the year and manufacture of the unknown vehicle can be determined. The investigator should not overlook the possibility that local vehicle dealerships and body repairs facilities will have similar information for purposes of vehicle identification.

8.136–8.140 reserved.

Glass Damage and Condition

8.141 Technically, glass is defined as:

A hard, amorphous, brittle, transparent substance made by fusing one or more of the oxides of silicon, boron, or phosphorus with certain basic oxides, followed by rapid cooling to prevent crystallization.

Of particular interest to crash investigations are two specific types of glass:

1. *Tempered Glass*

   This is the glass-type that is normally used for side and rear windows. When overstressed or impacted, it breaks into pea-size pieces. Because of the nature of disintegration, it is virtually impossible to determine whether the breakage occurred as the result of a direct impact or as the result of induced stress on the glass.

2. *Laminated Safety Glass*

   This type of glass consists of two layers of glass held together by a clear plastic, adhesive-type material. It is the type of glass usually used for windshields. Whereas tempered glass breaks into literally thousands of small pieces, laminated glass tends to stay in one piece when impacted. As explained later, impact damage usually results in fracture lines radiating from the contact point, with circular (concentric) fracture lines starting very close together at the contact point and increasing in space as the distance from the contact point becomes greater.

8.142 *Glass fragments.* It is also important for the investigator to be able to identify glass fragments that may have come from a source other than a window or a windshield. Such fragments may be found on the roadway, inside the vehicle, or in the case of a hit-and-run, embedded in clothing or a body.

- *Headlamps*–The lens is clear, relatively thick, breaks into irregular fragments, and may have an identifiable pattern. Fragments of reflectors are curved and mirrored on one side.
- *Directional Signals*–The lens may be clear or colored (yellow-orange), and may be glass or plastic.
- *Taillights*–The lens may be clear (back-up lamps), red (brake lamps), or yellow-orange (directional), and may be glass or plastic.
- *Bulbs*–The glass is clear, relatively thin and brittle, can break into irregular fragments, and may have an identifiable shape.

8.143 Glass can be damaged or fractured directly or indirectly by:

a. A passenger's or driver's head, or some object carried inside the vehicle, striking the inside of the windshield or window during a collision (see Fig. 8–42).

Figure 8–42. Contact damages with *outward* bulges caused by the driver's and passenger's heads striking the windshield from within the vehicle, providing evidence that they were not wearing seat belts at the time of the collision. Note the radial and concentric damage cracks appearing in a spider-web pattern, radiating from the actual contact points.

b. A person's body, an opposing vehicle or some other object outside the vehicle, striking the exterior of a windshield or window, as in a pedestrian- or cyclist-vehicle collision (See fig. 8–43).

c. A bolt, rock or other article lying loose on the roadway or that drops off another vehicle, that is flipped up and catapulted through the air, or an item thrown by a person, which strikes the window or windshield (see Fig. 8–44).

Figure 8–43. Contact damage with *inward* bulge caused when the vehicle struck a pedestrian who was thrown into the windshield. Note the major, concave indentation from head impact. Except for the direction of the bulge, the appearance of the damage is similar to that shown in Figure 8–42.

Figure 8–44. Rock impact fracture.

d. Stress resulting from an impact on a nearby, separate part of the vehicle resulting in induced or incidental damage (see Fig. 8–45).

e. Being struck by an air bag cover during deployment (see Fig. 8–46).

8.144 *Contact damage.* Contact damage is damage caused by a force, such as when a passenger's head impacts the inside of a windshield during a head-on collision. In this type of impact, if the force generated is great enough, the glass will experience

Figure 8–45. Induced damage to glass caused by an indirect force or pressure being applied on the windshield from another part of the vehicle; in this case, as the result of pressure exerted on it by a crushed roof and bent A-pillar. Induced damage generally makes at least two sets of parallel cracks crossing each other in a checkerboard fashion.

Figure 8–46. Windshield damage indicative of it being struck by an airbag cover during deployment. These damages are similar in appearance to that caused by an occupant striking the windshield.

both radial and concentric fractures that appear in a *spider-web* pattern extending outward from the impact point, and depending upon the amount and direction of the force may also experience an outward or inward bulge (see Figs. 8–42 and 8–43). However, in the case of an impact by a relatively small object such as a small pebble, radial fractures without concentric fractures will often occur (see Fig. 8–44).

8.145 *Induced damage.* Induced damage is damage other than contact damage. It is often indicated by coupling, distortion, bending, and breaking. Induced glass damage is damage caused by another part of the same vehicle (e.g., pressure exerted on a windshield) or by the shock of collision[16] (see Fig. 8–45).

8.146 *Impact and damage sequence.* If a windshield experiences two or more impacts and/or damages, it is frequently possible to determine the sequence in which they occurred. When the first impact occurs, radial, and perhaps concentric, fractures will result. When the second impact occurs, radial fractures will radiate from the point of impact but will not extend beyond the fractures caused by the first impact. The same effect will be experienced by a third impact and so on. This rationale can be applied to both impact and induced damages.

8.147 The windshield and windows of a vehicle involved in a crash should be examined to determine whether or not their condition contributed or could have contributed to the crash. Dust, dirt, mud, ice, snow, drops of water, or fog on the outside surfaces of windshields or windows can obstruct the driver's view as can stickers, mist, condensation, or a heavy smoke film on the inside surfaces. The cause of chips, gouges, or cracks in a windshield should also be determined. A damaged windshield or window can block the driver's view of other traffic on the highway and cause glare from sunlight, headlights or other bright lights to also obstruct his view. When the existence of glass damage prior to the collision is suspected, a driver's seated height should be established and his sight line related to the windshield and/or window damage.[17]

8.148 The positions of all windows, including any air-vent windows, should always be examined. This is particularly important when there is inside *mist* or *condensation* on the windshield or windows.

When windows are closed, condensation is not allowed to dissipate as readily as it would with fresh air. This inspection should also include checking the adequacy of the defrosters when inside mist or condensation is a factor. It is also important to determine whether windows were or were not open or partially open as it might be claimed that an insect or some other object entered the vehicle, striking or distracting the driver, or that a siren or horn of another vehicle was not heard.

8.149 Glass examination can assist in determining the possible cause and/or contributing factors in a collision, and provide a better understanding of the results and consequences of the crash. A driver's compartment glass examination should include (see also Para. 8.068):

☐ Type and condition of windshield and windows (e.g., clear, tinted, view obstructions, damage, visibility, general condition)
☐ Type of glass

VEHICLE FIRES

8.150 The objectives of a vehicle fire investigation and examination are to determine:

1. How the fire started
2. Where the fire started
3. Who was responsible

8.151 In cases of single car accidents, such as rollovers or running off the roadway or into some substantial object, the investigator should consider the possibility that the driver or owner deliberately set the fire. The motives for doing so are many, including:

☐ Obtaining money through a false insurance claim.
☐ To forego a loan on the vehicle.
☐ Avoiding a costly vehicle repair bill, particularly when there is a large deductible clause in the insurance policy.
☐ Being involved in a crash where the vehicle would provide evidence of a driver/owner at-fault situation.
☐ To cover up a criminal offense in which the vehicle was used.
☐ The vehicle was stolen.

☐ Depending upon the circumstances, a possible attempt at suicide.

☐ An act of revenge.

☐ A psychotic need, such as the gratification gained or excitement experienced from the act–pyromaniac.[18]

8.152 In vehicle fires, it is important that the advanced crash investigator gathers and documents as much evidence as possible, including the taking of color photographs. To assist him, the following *Vehicle Fire Examination Guide* is provided, covering in a general way the points necessary to satisfy investigation and examination objectives. However, when arson is suspected, the investigator should, unless he has reasonable experience in these investigations, also seek the advice and/or assistance of a fire forensic specialist in completing the investigation. In many cases, laboratory services personnel can provide essential input, such as determining the type of accelerant that was used, soil or fabric samples that can be analyzed for accelerant contaminants, as well as many other very important analyses.

Caution: Industry warns that *Freon*, used in automobile air-conditioning systems, should, in an airborne state, be considered a poisonous gas, and should not be inhaled. Another source of danger for the investigator is an acid that can form when gaskets in the engine compartment melt during fire. If this acid happens to get onto the skin, it can result in severe injury. When carrying out the investigation, the investigator should wear protective clothing, including safety glasses, and he should not touch the engine unless he is wearing proper protective gloves. Also, he should be careful to not come into contact with any contaminated water that may be left after a fire department might have hosed down the engine area.

VEHICLE FIRE EXAMINATION GUIDE

Environmental

Check the vehicle and immediate area for fire starters, containers and supplies, and other evidence indicating that the fire was intentionally started, including the following:

☐ Evidence of suspicious footprints that could be associated or related to the position the culprit would have had to stand in igniting the fire, e.g., at the gas tank.

☐ Electrical wire lying on the ground, pieces of which might have been used to connect an electrical ignition source.

☐ Match packages or spent matches.

☐ Syphon hose.

☐ Evidence of vandalism, e.g., damage that cannot associated with a collision or the result of fire damage.

☐ Evidence that all usual automobile parts and articles, such as radio, aerial, mirrors, spare wheel, tape deck, and so on, were removed before the fire started. (Or if they are they still in the vehicle, were they, damaged, destroyed, or obviously protected in some way from damage?)

☐ Ashes of rolled-up or formed paper or cloth, outside or inside the vehicle, that may have been used as a wick. These items will very often retain their original shape and retain the odor of an accelerant.

☐ Places near the vehicle where an accelerant may have been spilled onto the ground, saturating the soil. In these cases, an odor may linger in the area of the spill.

☐ Lack of personal belongings in vehicle.

Accelerants and Containers

☐ Gasoline or other accelerant containers in the vicinity should be checked to determine whether they were in any way associated with the fire under investigation. Were they empty, were caps or covers on, or were they missing? Was the size of the orifice consistent with the evident size/spread of the fire trails? Were ashes from rolls of paper or cloth, used as a wick, evident in the vehicle or outside the vehicle? If so, was there any evidence of their having been saturated with an accelerant, such as the odor of gasoline or other accelerant liquid?

☐ Were there any damp spots on the ground or in some part of the vehicle that were caused by an accelerant liquid–places where an accelerant may have been spilled saturating the area but did not readily burn? This can very often be determined from the odor of the accelerant, particularly in soil and fabric that is not totally destroyed.

☐ Was there evidence of an accelerant having been spread around inside the vehicle? This evidence may be in the form of ash trails caused by fast burning and intense heat.

Gas Tank and Cap

☐ Is the gas tank cap missing? Is there any evidence that gas might have been drawn from the gas tank? For example, if the cap had been removed before the fire, so that gas could be siphoned, and not replaced until after the fire, there would likely not be any sign of scorching on the cap

Fuel Lines

☐ Is there evidence that would indicate that a gas line failed from normal wear and tear, such as rusting out or rubbing against some other vehicle part? Or is there any indication that the fuel lines from the gas tank through to the engine had been tampered with, such as signs of breakage or being purposely disconnected that would prove to be good evidence that the fire was deliberately set?

Oil Lines

☐ Is there evidence of oil leakage, e.g., from transmission, onto muffler system that could have caused the fire?

Electrical Sources

☐ Was there an electrical defect that would give reason to believe it was the fire ignition source, e.g., engine harness, lighting system, under dash electrical systems?

Engine Compartment

☐ Did the engine compartment burn to the degree that it should be considered the probable source of the fire? If evidence points to the fire starting at a place on or about the engine that cannot be connected with the usual sources of accidental fires under the hood, such as the fuel pump, carburetor, and electrical wiring, it is a good indication that an accelerant was used. It should be noted that a carburetor backfire, cracked manifold, or blown gasket may allow flame to escape, which can ignite a fuel source. And while gasoline will normally evaporate quickly, its vapors can ignite by an ignition source that may be in the area of the flame (see Fig. 8–47).

Figure 8–47. A fire that started in the engine compartment.

Trunk

- ☐ Were trunk items and the trunk itself damaged to the extent it was probably the fire source?

Windows

- ☐ Were windows partially or fully open? Fire requires oxygen to burn. If windows were open, particularly during adverse weather conditions, the possibility exists that they were opened to facilitate burning.

Body Damage

- ☐ Was there noticeable sagging of the roof, trunk lid, and hood, and of the seat and axle springs that would indicate extreme heat?
- ☐ Was the destruction consistent with fire, or was there damage other than what would be expected to be caused by the fire?
- ☐ What was the fire pattern? Was there evidence of a point where the fire appeared to have started, such as where a heavy saturation of accelerant was poured or sprayed; and then, what path was followed, as evidenced by fire paths or trails?

- ☐ Was there evidence of a collision point-of-impact that could be directly related to an electrical short-circuit or a vehicle part that could in turn be considered an ignition point?

Non-Metallic Vehicle Part Damage

- ☐ Did the tile glass and soft materials such as those found in radiators, fuel pumps, and carburetors, and the lead used in body repairs melt, and what was the pattern of melting—did they lose their original shape? It should be noted that when an accelerant is used, these materials usually suffer considerable damage because of the intense heat.
- ☐ Did evidence show that the fire could have started as the result of a smoldering cigarette, such as a lighted cigarette being left on the car seat (see Fig. 8–48).

Fire Intensity

- ☐ Did evidence indicate a hot fire or a smoldering fire? If an accelerant was used, there should be evidence of a hot fire in at least the area where the accelerant was used. Evidence of a slow-burning or a smoldering fire could be the result of a non-accelerant method of

Figure 8–48.

starting the fire, such as simply setting alight the vehicle fabrics with a match. Slow-burning and smoldering fires very often leave evidence of soot build-up on railings and pillars.

Mechanical Defect, Tires and Wheels

☐ Was there any evidence of a mechanical defect that could have caused the fire? An overheated wheel bearing or the continued operation of a locked wheel can cause oil or grease to burn. Also, the continued operation of an underinflated or deflated tire, particularly those found on a commercial vehicle dual-wheel system, can cause the tire to erupt into flames (see also Fig. 8–49).

Figure 8–49. An example of an overheated tire that experienced severe melting of rubber. Possible causes include (a) overheated brake drum, and (b) high speed with wheel lock-up on a roadway having a high coefficient of friction. A vehicle fire in the vicinity of the tire may also cause the tire to have a similar appearance. (Reproduced from: Rivers R.W.: Tire Failures and *Evidence Manual for Traffic Accident Investigation.* Charles C Thomas, Publisher, Springfield, Illinois, 2001.)

DRIVER AND OCCUPANT SEATING POSITIONS

8.153 During a collision, the driver and other vehicle occupants may be thrown around within the driver-passenger compartment, including those who may be seated in a rear seat. Occasionally, a rear-seat passenger may be catapulted over the back of the front seat and strike the windshield or dash.

8.154 There are many possible contact points that a person may strike, such as the dash, pillar, windshield, and window (see Figs. 8–50 and 8–51). When there is an indication that an occupant did in fact impact some part of the vehicle, e.g., evidence of injury or torn clothing, the vehicle should be examined for any blood, skin, marks, imprints, or damage that can be directly related to that evidence. Marks, injuries, and damages that can often be matched are teeth marks on the dash that can then be matched to mouth injuries. This type of evidence can serve many purposes, including whether a seat belt was or was not used by the person, as well as the seated positions of occupants at the time of the collision. An examination should consider all possibilities when attempting a match, even the possibility that a rear-seated passenger might have been thrown to the front (see also Paras. 8.105–8.112, and DNA analysis, Para. 1.091).

POINTS	CONTACT POINT
1, 2	Sunvisor
3, 5	Windshield
4	Rear-view mirror
6, 10	Side windows
8	Steering wheel
7, 9	A-pillars
11, 18	B-pillars
12, 17	Door handles
13, 14	Driver knee contact points
15	Console
16	Dashboard

8.155 *Driver identification.* When the driver's identity is in question, examine the accelerator pedal for shoe sole imprints which might then be matched to the shoe soles of the suspect driver. Similarly, examine the shoe sole for brake pedal (or other pedal) imprints which may also be matched up (see Fig. 8–53A and B).

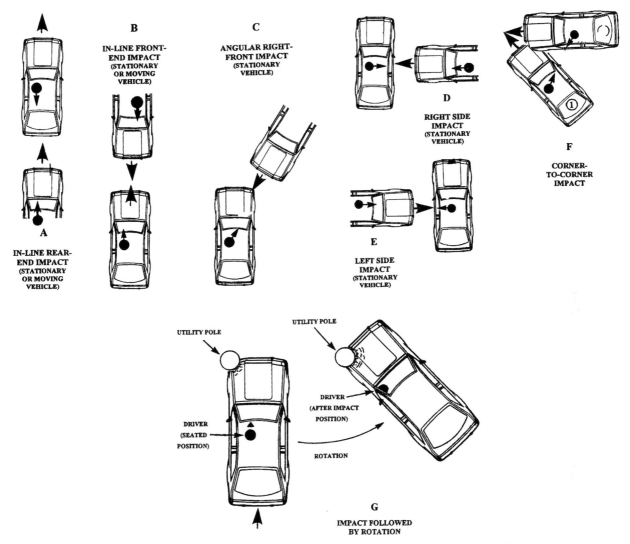

Figure 8–50 A, B, C. Predictable occupant movements within a vehicle in collision.

Figure 8–51 (right). An example of some of the various contact points within a vehicle, particularly in relation to driver and front seat occupants. (Source: Rivers, R.W.: *Seat Belt and Air Bag Systems Manual for Traffic Crash Investigation and Reconstruction.* Institute of Police Technology and Management, University of North Florida, 2001, p. 18. Reproduced with permission.)

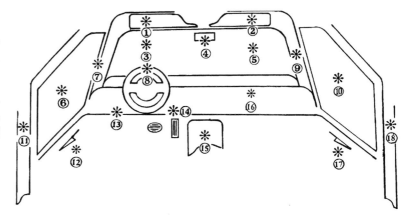

Figure 8–52. An example of a face impact with a side window. Note facial features in the imprint, and blood and hair adhering to the glass; all of which can be related to injuries suffered by the person. This type of evidence may be found both inside and outside of a vehicle that is impacted by a person.

Figure 8–53A and B.

RECOMMENDED REFERENCE SITES

For further information about a specific vehicle, contact the vehicle manufacturer. For general information about air bag systems, contact the NHTSA Office of Traffic Injury Control Programs, Occupant Protection Division (NTS–12), 400 Seventh St., S.W., Washington, D.C. 20590, or the USFA Office of Firefighters Health and Safety, NETC, Emmitsburg, MD 21727.

WEBSITES OF INTERESTS

United States Government

http://www.nhtsa.dot.gov/
http://www.hhtsa.dot.gov/index.html
http://www.nhtsa.dot.gov/airbag.html
http://www.access.gpo.gov/nara/cfr/cfr-table-search.html
http://www.nhtsa.dot.gov/people/injury/ems/airbag/index.html

Insurance Institute for Traffic Safety Status Reports

http://www.highwaysafety.org

Canadian and Other Sites

http://www.tcgc.ca/actsregs/mvsa/tocmvsrg.htm
http:www.tc.gc.ca/securiteroutiere/absg/airboce.htm
http://www.access.gpo.gov/nara/cfr/index
http://www.sanjuan.edu/schools/arcade/AirbagBC.html
http://.ibc.ca/english/airbags.htm

COMMERCIAL VEHICLE WEBSITES

Federal Motor Carrier Websites

FMCSA Official Website
www.fmcsa.dot.gov
Federal Safety Regulations and Interpretations
http://www.fmcsa.dot.gov/rulesregs/fmcsrhome.htm
Descriptive Statistics and Analysis
http://ai.volpe.dot.gov/
Motor Carrier, Broker, or Freight Forwarder's Application, Insurance and Process Agent
http://fhwa-li.volpe.dot.gov/

Motor Carrier's Profile
http://www.safersys.org/snpquery.asp
Motor Carrier's Safety Performance
http://ai.volpe.dot.gov/
Safety Ratings, Inspections and Accident Data Summary
http://www.safersys.org/snpquery.asp
Safety Programs
http://www.fmcsa.dot.gov/safetyprogs/saftprogs.htm
Hazardous Materials
http://hazmat.dot.gov.
Analysis on Truck and Bus Safety
www.fmcsa.dot.gov and http://ai.volpe.dot.gov/
Tire Tire Information–U.S. Code of Federal Regulations
49CFR393.75 Subpart G-Miscellaneous Parts and Accessories and Appendix G Minimum Periodic Inspection Standards
49CFR569 Regrooved Tires
49CFR570.9 Vehicle in Use Inspection Standards, Tires
49CFR571.119 New Pneumatic Tires for Vehicles Other than Passenger Cars

Note: Many of these documents (in book format) may be purchased from some regional U.S. Government Printing Offices. Check telephone books for locations. Further information may also be found by searching: <http://www.access.gpo.gov/>.

REFERENCES

1. Personal correspondence from L. Sathyavagiswaran, M.D., Chief Medical Examiner-Coroner, County of Los Angeles, Department of Coroner. (See also Chapter 4, Part 2.)
2. Rivers, R.W.: *Tire Failures and Evidence Manual for Traffic Accident Investigation.* Charles C Thomas, Springfield, Illinois, 2001, p. 17.
3. Rivers, R.W.: *Tire Failures and Evidence Manual for Traffic Accident Investigation.* Charles C Thomas, Springfield, Illinois, 2001, p. 20.
4. Rivers, R.W.: *Tire Failures and Evidence Manual for Traffic Accident Investigation.* Charles C Thomas, Springfield, Illinois, 2001, p. 22.
5. Rivers, R.W.: *Tire Failures and Evidence Manual for Traffic Accident Investigation.* Charles C Thomas, Springfield, Illinois, 2001, p. 23.
6. Rivers, R.W.: *Tire Failures and Evidence Manual for Traffic Accident Investigation.* Charles C Thomas, Springfield, Illinois, 2001, pp. 28, 29.

7. Wright, Allan C.: *Air Brakes from the Driver's Seat.* Allan C. Wright, Burnaby, B.C., Canada, 1984, pp. 3, 4.

8. Wright, Allan C.: *The Air Brake Connection.* Allan C. Wright, c/o Presto Print Ltd., Richmond, B.C., Canada, 1991, 128 pp.

9. Rivers, R.W.: *Seat Belt and Air Bag Systems Manual for Traffic Crash Investigation and Reconstruction.* Institute of Police Technology and Management, University of North Florida, Jacksonville, Florida, 2001, p. 47.

10. Rivers, R.W.: *Seat Belt and Air Bag Systems Manual for Traffic Crash Investigation and Reconstruction.* Institute of Police Technology and Management, University of North Florida, Jacksonville, Florida, 2001, p. 47.

11. Rivers, R.W.: *Training and Reference Manual for Traffic Accident Investigation.* Institute of Police Technology and Management, University of North Florida, Jacksonville, Florida, 1995, p. 296.

12. Ziernicki, Richard, Finocchiaro, Carl, Hamernik, Jubal, & Fenton, Stephen: Automotive Airbags. *Accident Investigation Quarterly* (Victor Craig, editor), Waldorf, MD: Fall Issue, 1997, p. 28.

13. Huelke, D., Gilbert, R., & Schneider, L.: *Upper Extremity Injuries from Steering Wheel Air Bag Deployment.* SAE Paper 970493, Air Bag Design and Pereformance TOPTEC, August, 1997.

14. Rivers, R.W.: *Seat Belt and Air Bag Systems Manual for Traffic Crash Investigation and Reconstruction.* Institute of

Police Technology and Management, University of North Florida, Jacksonville, Florida, 2001, pp. 81, 82.

15. Lane, Brian: *The Encyclopedia of Forensic Science.* Headline Book Publishing, London NW1 3BH 1992, pp. 449, 450.

16. Baxter, Albert T.: *Accident Investigation and Reconstruction Terminology.* Albert T. Baxter, Suncoast Collision, Analysis, 14840 Atlantic Avenue, Hudson, Florida 34667–1006, 1998, p. 98.

17. Rivers, R.W.: *Training and Reference Manual for Traffic Accident Investigation.* Institute of Police Technology and Management, University of North Florida, Jacksonville, Florida, 1995, pp. 283, 284.

18. Lane, Brian: *The Encyclopedia of Forensic Science.* Headline Book Publishing, London NW1 3BH, 1992, p. 63.

RECOMMENDED READING

DuBois, Robert A.: *Insurance Fraud and Motor Vehicle Collisions.* Northeast Collision Analysis, Inc. Rochester, New Hampshire, 1992.

IIHS Status Report. *Accident Reconstruction Journal,* Vol. 11, Jan/Feb, 2000.

Rivers, R.W.: *Seat Belt and Air Bag Systems Manual for Traffic Crash Investigation and Reconstruction.* Institute of Police Technology and Management, University of North Florida, Jacksonville, Florida, 2001.

Chapter 9

SPEED ANALYSIS

R. W. RIVERS

Part 1

INTRODUCTION: TERMS, AND DEFINITIONS

SPEED AND VELOCITY DEFINED

9.001 *Definitions.* In this manual, except when the context dictates otherwise, a reference to *speed*, designated by the upper case letter **S**, means a measurement in mph (km/h). A reference to *velocity*, designated by the upper case **V**, means a measurement in ft/s (m/s).

PHYSICS

9.002 The term *physics* is derived from a Greek word meaning nature. It explains and quantifies the physical world around us. Physics, as an exact science, deals with matter and energy in terms of motion, and is knowledge possessed as the result of study and practice, which is classified and accumulated.

Newton's Three Laws of Motion

9.003 The principles contained in Newton's Three Laws of Motion form the basis of the whole subject of speed analysis in the field of traffic crash investigation and reconstruction, and should be thoroughly understood by the student, investigator and examiner. The three laws are:

First Law

Law 1 is defined as:

Everything remains at rest or moves with constant velocity (in a straight line) unless acted upon by an external unbalanced (not counteracted) force.

Or, stated another way:

A body at rest remains at rest, and a body in motion remains in motion with constant velocity, unless acted upon by some external force.

This First Law is commonly called the Law of Inertia.

9.004 *Inertia,* from a Latin word meaning idleness or laziness, relates to the force necessary to change an object's motion and is defined as:

The property of matter which requires that a force be exerted on a body to accelerate it.

It is the tendency for any object to resist change in velocity, magnitude, or direction. That is to say that if the object is at rest, it tends to stay at rest, and if the object is in motion, it tends to maintain the same speed and direction. If it is in motion, inertia is that property of matter by which it maintains a constant velocity in the absence of an unbalanced external force, and continues in motion in a straight line with constant velocity until some external force changes its state of motion. It is the mass of the object that determines the quantity of inertia that is possessed by a body.

Second Law

Law 2 is defined as:

A free body acted upon by a constant force moves with constant acceleration in the direction of the force. The amount of acceleration experienced by a body is directly proportional to the acting force and inversely proportional to the mass of the body.

Or, stated another way:

The time rate of change of the momentum of a body is proportional to the net external force acting upon the body and is in the direction of this force.

Newton's 2nd Law proves to be a powerful tool for understanding natural phenomena. For any body, it relates the external force acting on the body, its mass, and its acceleration. If any two are known, the third can be found; thus:

a. If we know the resultant of all the forces acting on a body as well as the body's mass, we can deduce its acceleration and predict its motion.
b. If we know the forces acting on a body and can measure the body's acceleration, we can calculate its mass.
c. If we know the mass of a body and can find the body's acceleration by observing its motion, we can determine what net force is acting on the body. Even if we do not know the mass, from our knowledge of the motion, we can infer the ratio of force to mass.

Third Law

Law 3 is defined as: *To every action there is an equal and opposite reaction.*

Or, stated in other ways:

Whenever one body exerts force upon a second body, the second body exerts an equal and opposite force on the first.

To every action there is an equal and contrary reaction. (Here the term action is used to imply force.)

It should be noted that action combines force and time. The force exerted by one body on the other is equal and opposite to the force exerted by the other body on the first body. And, of course, when the first body is in contact with the second, the second must be in contact with the first. The force × time concept is important when dealing with collisions, and is known as Impulse.

9.005 Examples of the Third Law are:

a. The wheels of a vehicle traveling along a roadway push backward on the roadway surface, but at the same time, the roadway surface pushes forward on the wheels with an equal force.
b. The weight of a vehicle causes the tires to push downward on the roadway surface with a force equal to that which the surface exerts upward on the tires.
c. When tires are skidding on a roadway surface, they exert a force on the roadway surface. At the same time, the roadway surface exerts a force on the tires that is equal in magnitude but opposite in direction.
d. A semitrailer pulls back on a truck tractor with exactly the same force as the truck tractor pulls forward on the semitrailer.
e. When two vehicles collide with each other, the force of vehicle 1 against vehicle 2 is equal and opposite to the force of vehicle 2 against vehicle 1, even if one is stationary and massive and the other is light and moving quickly.
f. When a vehicle collides with a utility pole, the forces sustained by both objects are equal and opposite, though the effects on each may be quite different.

Force Defined

9.006 *Force* is that which can impose a change of velocity on a material body, its direction of motion, or both as explained by Newton's Second Law of Motion, often referred to as the principle of inertia (meaning idleness or laziness). The principle of inertia requires that in the absence of a force, an object will remain at rest if at rest, or at a constant velocity if it begins in motion. We use the term mass to quantify a body's resistance to having its velocity, direction, or magnitude changed. Force is expressed algebraically as:

Formula 9–01

$$F = Ma$$

where F = the net external force acting on the body
  a = acceleration
  M = mass

External Forces

9.007 When two bodies collide, each body exerts an external force on the other, thereby causing a change of velocity in each body.

a. All objects, or bodies, consist of a collection of atoms. Every atom has a very small amount of mass. It is this collection of atoms that constitutes the mass of the object. The greater the number and size of the atoms, the greater is the mass. From Newton's Second Law, as the mass is increased, the greater will be the force necessary to generate a unit value of acceleration.

b. Inertia is a term that means that a body is reluctant to change its state, i.e., to change its velocity. It is identical to the mass of the body when dealing with translational (straight line as distinct from rotational) motion. Inertia and mass can be used interchangeably for translational motion. It has the units of pounds mass in the English system and kilograms in SI.

Centripetal and Centrifugal Forces

9.008 *Centripetal Force* is defined as (a) center-seeking; (b) directed, tending, or drawing toward a center; (c) pointing to the center of a circle. A force attracting a body toward a center around which it revolves; (b) a force that is required to hold a moving object in a circular path, such as a curve in a highway.

9.009 *Centrifugal Force* is defined as (a) the inertial reaction by which a body tends to move away from the center of rotation; (b) force that is the reaction to, or equal and opposite to centripetal; (c) an object's inertial resistance to being caused to move in a curved path. In purely scientific terms, centrifugal force is an imaginary or apparent force, best explained by the term *inertia*: An object's inertia causes it to *want* to go straight by being pulled inward and forced to travel in a circular path–the inertia *feels* like it is pulling the object away from the center of travel.

If a body is moving at a constant speed in a constant direction, a force is necessary to change either its speed or direction. When a vehicle is traveling at a constant speed around a curve, however, its direction is changing all the time. In such a situation, centrifugal force (inertial force) acts on the vehicle, tending to maintain its direction along a tangent (straight line) to the curve at each successive point. Centrifugal force may be thought of as an object's inertial resistance to being caused to move in a curved path. If it were not for centripetal force counteracting centrifugal force, the vehicle would not be able to travel around the curve.

Curves

9.010 When a vehicle is in motion, there is the tendency for it to remain in motion and to continue in a straight line. In the case of traveling at an excessive speed in a curve, the result could be that the vehicle would sideslip and leave the highway tangent to the curve (in a straight line). In the case of a vehicle traveling in a curve, an occupant tends to be pushed towards the outer side of the vehicle, or perpendicular to the direction the vehicle would have traveled in a straight line if it had not followed the curve (see also Speed from Vehicle Yaw, Para. 9.106).

Mass and Weight

9.011 *Mass* is the amount of matter in a body and is constant everywhere in the known universe. The difference in mass between substances having the same volume relates to the composition of the molecules and atoms of the substances. On Earth, the mass of an object is its weight divided by the gravitational pull (acceleration) of the Earth. *Weight* is the force with which an object is attracted to the Earth by the gravitational pull of the Earth, i.e., it is the force of gravity acting on the mass of an object that gives the object weight. It is a force like any other force, vertical and unavoidable, and has the units of a force:

Formula 9–02

$$M = \frac{W}{g}$$

where M = Mass
W = weight
g = acceleration of gravity

9.012 Formulae 9–02 and 9–03 can be used to show the relationship between mass and weight. It should be noted, however, that in SI, weight shown in kg is in reality the mass of the vehicle; therefore, in the following SI examples, there is no need to divide or multiply (as the case may be) the weight by the acceleration due to gravity. Further, it should be noted that in those countries where the use of SI units is relatively new, an object's weight is often expressed in kg. For example apples may be sold by the kilogram and thought of as the weight of the apples. In fact, the purchase is apples having a mass of 1 kilogram. Another example is when a vehicle's weight is described as 1250 kg it is in fact the vehicle's mass that is being described. In Australia and many other countries there is no room for confusion inasmuch as a vehicle's specifications will read, for example, 1250 kg mass.

Example 1

A vehicle weighs 2,000 lb (907 kg). Its mass would be:

Formula 9–02

$$M = \frac{W}{g}$$

English   *SI*

$$M = \frac{2000}{32.2}$$ M = 907 kg

M = 62.11 slugs (lb mass)

Example 2

A vehicle has a mass of 62.11 slugs (907 kg). Its weight would be:

Formula 9–03

$$W = Mg$$

where W = weight in pounds (newtons)
M = mass in slugs (kilograms)
g = acceleration due to gravity

English   *SI*

W = 62.11 × 32.2   W = (907 × 9.81) 8897.67 N
W = 2000 lb

Note: Because of the confusion that sometimes exists between the terms *mass* and *weight*, one solution is to refer to *mass* as a measure of the amount of material in the object upon which no force is acting, when mass is intended, and to *force of gravity* as the *weight* when gravitational pull is intended. A force of gravity, pulling downwards, acts on each mass on the earth. Thus mass and force of gravity, while entirely different characteristics, are linked. Perhaps unfortunately, in everyday usage, weight is ambiguous in that it sometimes means mass and sometimes force of gravity, depending on the context, or the country in which one lives. It is very important for the investigator and the trainer in physics therefore to understand the difference between the uses of kg and mass when using formulae that require weight to be divided by gravity, in particular energy equations. If SI units are used, the information available may already, in fact, be described in mass units.

Motion

9.013 Newton's 1st Law of Motion states: *Everything remains at rest or moves with constant velocity (in a straight line) unless acted upon by an external force.* Motion can therefore be defined as being a change of place or position.

Momentum

9.014 *Momentum* is a term describing the inertial qualities of an object and is defined as the mass of an object multiplied by its velocity. It follows, therefore, that heavier vehicles have more momentum than lighter vehicles traveling at the same speed and that faster vehicles have more momentum than slower vehicles of the same mass.

Work

9.015 In traffic crash matters, *work* can be defined as the deformation experienced by an object when acted upon by a *force*. Thus, in vehicle crashes, work is done in the bending and crushing of the metal. In a technical sense, work is defined as the force multiplied by the distance through which the force is applied.

Kinetic Energy

9.016 When a body is in motion, it is said to possess kinetic energy. Kinetic energy is defined as one-half the mass of a body multiplied by the square of its velocity:

Formula 9–04

$$KE = \frac{1}{2}MV^2$$

where KE = kinetic energy
M = mass
V = velocity

9.017 The expression *kinetic energy* represents the average distance through which force acts in any given time period. Thus kinetic energy is equivalent to work. *Work*, as used in physics, involves a unit of force multiplied by a unit of length, and is defined as:

A transference of energy from one body to another resulting in the motion or displacement of the body acted upon, expressed as the product of the force and the amount of displacement in the line of its action.

If the force does not produce a displacement, no work is done in the sense in which work is used in physics. In application to car crashes, this means that a heavy vehicle at high speed does a great deal of work on–damage to–an object with which it collides. Since an object possessing kinetic energy is able to do work, it is possible to determine the traveling speed of a vehicle from a skilled examination and analysis of the damage caused (work done) by the vehicle in a crash. However, such speed determination is usually beyond the scope of many investigators in the field and is done rather by professional engineers or professional reconstructionists.

Gravity

9.018 Gravity is a given value, derived from one pound (one kilogram) of force acting for one second upon a mass of one pound (one kilogram), imparting to this mass a velocity at sea level of 32.174 ft/s² (9.806 m/s²); rounded off to 32.2 ft/s² (9.81 m/s²). In terms of acceleration due to gravity, all objects fall at the same rate if air friction is neglected.

Centers of Mass and Gravity

9.019 The generally accepted definitions for the center of mass and the center of gravity are:

a. *The point where a vehicle or other object would be in equilibrium or perfectly balanced if suspended by or at that point.*
b. *The point where the mass and the pull of gravity can be treated as being concentrated.*

In this manual, center of gravity (CG) and center of mass (CM) are considered identical and will be treated as one and the same unless the example or problem requires otherwise, at which time the difference will be indicated. Technically, however, the lower portion of a vehicle is a mite closer to the center of the earth than its upper portion, so the lower portion is more strongly under gravitational influence. The center of gravity is therefore consequently located very slightly below the center of mass. While there is a difference, under ordinary conditions on earth, and for the purposes of traffic crash investigation and reconstruction, the difference in location is so ridiculously small that the two terms can be considered synonymous.

9.020 It is necessary and convenient to consider all the weight or all the mass of a body (including a vehicle) as acting through one particular point called the *center of mass*. If a force is applied to such an object with its direction aimed exactly through the center of mass, then the object will move in the direction of the force without other effects. If the force does not quite act through the center of mass, some kind of rotation or spin will occur (see Figs. 9–01A and B).

9.021 For practical investigation purposes, one can consider a vehicle's center of mass to be located at some point on the central axis, usually halfway between the front and rear axles (see Fig. 9–30). Generally, this point is at approximately one-third of the height of the vehicle measured from the ground level.

Vectors

9.022 A *vector* is a quantity that has both magnitude and direction. Velocity is defined as the speed of an object in a given direction. Speed is velocity's magnitude property, and the direction in which the speed occurs is velocity's directional property. In

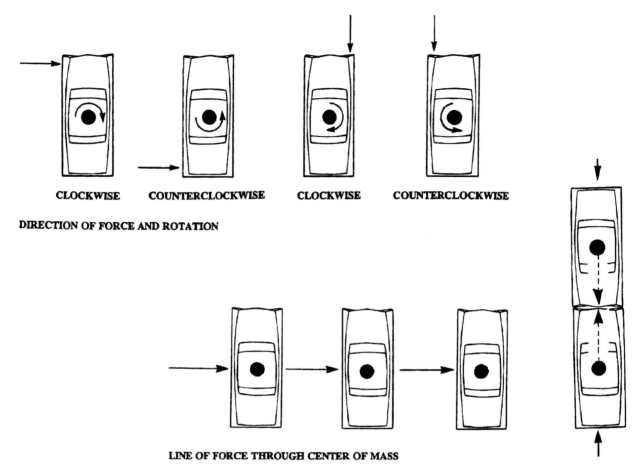

DIRECTION OF FORCE AND ROTATION

LINE OF FORCE THROUGH CENTER OF MASS

Figure 9–01. Vehicles (*A*, top left)) acted upon by an external, off-center (eccentric) force with subsequent rotation. `Line of force through a vehicle's center of mass (*B*, bottom right) causes a translational movement, i.e., the vehicle does not rotate, but rather moves along the line of force (see Paras. 8.153 and 8.154, and Fig. 8–50).

order for speed to become velocity, direction must also be known. Vector quantities (units) as a group include displacement, velocity, force, acceleration, momentum, force moment, and angular velocity.

9.023 A vector may be represented by an arrow drawn to a convenient scale. The length of the arrow corresponds to the magnitude component. The arrow itself points in the direction line which the magnitude component acts. Once all of the relevant vectors are represented in the diagram, we can find their resultant or net effect by simple measurement or by applying the *Pythagorean Theorem*, which states that the square of the longest side *(c)* of a right triangle is equal to the sum of the squares of the other two sides *(a)* and *(b)* (see Fig. 9–02).

Formula 9–05

$$c = \sqrt{a^2 + b^2}$$

where c = longest side of triangle
    a = one other side
    b = other side

Example

$$c = \sqrt{4^2 + 3^2}$$

$$c = \sqrt{16 + 9}$$

$$c = \sqrt{25}$$

c = 5 units [ft (m), in (cm), mi (km) and so on], 37% east of north.

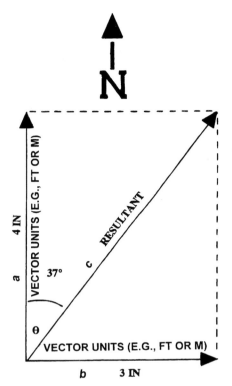

Figure 9–02. When vectors act at an angle to each other, their net effect or resultant is their geometric sum.

Friction

9.024 *Friction* is defined as *a force tending to prevent motion between two surfaces that are in contact.* In the case of a resilient tire sliding over a roadway surface, it is known as *mechanical interlocking.* Resistance is greatest just prior to actual sliding, e.g., immediately before wheel lock-up.

9.025 Friction can be divided into two categories:

1. *Static friction*–The friction between two surfaces in contact that are not moving relative to one another.
2. *Dynamic or kinetic friction*–The friction that is developed as a result of two surfaces that are in contact and sliding over each other.

ACCELERATION

9.026 The immediate following is intended to provide an understanding of acceleration (which is in addition to the material covered under Newton's Laws of Motion reviewed earlier in this chapter) and its application to crash investigation and reconstruction. Following this, will be found a number of examples of such applications.

9.027 *Acceleration* and *deceleration* are rates of speed or velocity change per unit of time, usually measured in feet per second per second (ft/s/s or ft/s^2) or meters per second per second (m/s/s or m/s^2). In a scientific sense, acceleration can be said to be either positive (+) or negative (–). However, when operating a motor vehicle, it is commonly understood that to accelerate causes an increase (+) and to decelerate causes a decrease (–) in speed or velocity, and contemporary usage of the terms in traffic crash investigation is simply acceleration for positive acceleration and deceleration for negative acceleration.

Constant acceleration is a term for uniform rate of acceleration (or deceleration) of a vehicle or other object.

9.028 In reconstructing and giving evidence in relation to a properly investigated vehicle crash, the investigator should be able to explain and/or show the relative positions of vehicles and/or traffic units as they were throughout the entire at-scene series of events. In the presentation of evidence, it reasonable to expect that acceleration and/or deceleration at or between various points can be clearly explained. One recommended method of doing this is with a scale diagram. Acceleration and/or deceleration issues related to applicable events found in the *at-scene series of events* (see Para. 1.018) should include, but not necessarily be limited to, evidence of:

a. The relative positions of vehicles, pedestrians, and other objects throughout the series of events.
b. The driver's *point of possible perception* of another traffic unit or object, e.g., a pedestrian.
c. Point of *actual perception.*
d. Where any *evasive action* took place.
e. Skid distance.

Velocity, Acceleration, and Time

9.029 Experiments have shown that if a free-wheeling vehicle is on a roadway that is inclined at a particular angle, the distance it will travel (roll) over time, due to gravity, will be:

> 1 ft (m) in 1 sec
> 4 ft (m) in 2 sec
> 9 ft (m) in 3 sec
> 16 ft (m) in 4 sec
> 25 ft (m) in 5 sec

Thus, we can see that the distance that the vehicle travels is directly proportional to the square of the number of seconds. From this, we may say that the vehicle traveled (rolled):

> 1 ft (m) in the 1st sec
> 3 ft (m) in the 2nd sec
> 5 ft (m) in the 3rd sec
> 7 ft (m) in the 4th sec
> 9 ft (m) in the 5th sec

The numbers 1–3–5–7–9 show that the motion was uniformly accelerated at a rate of 2 ft/sec (2 m/sec) for each second the gravitational force was applied. Since velocity is the rate of change in distance at a given period of time, and since acceleration is the rate of change in velocity at a given time, the term *acceleration* is expressed in ft/s^2 (m/s^2). Also, if the acceleration is uniform, the velocity at the end of any second is proportional to the time.

Example

A vehicle at rest (zero velocity) is accelerated uniformly, increasing its velocity at a constant rate of 10 ft/s^2 (3 m/s^2). In 2.5 sec after starting from the point of rest, the velocity will be 25 ft/s (7.5 m/s), and so on. That is to say, the velocity change is in proportion to the time of the acceleration involved. Further, it can be said that when the acceleration ends, the final velocity of the vehicle at that time is equal to the product of the acceleration multiplied by the time: $V = at$ (Formula 9–06). In these cases, a is a constant that holds true for any size of object under acceleration. Applicable formulae are:

Formula 9–06

$$V = at$$

Formula 9–07

$$t = \frac{V}{a}$$

Formula 9–08

$$a = \frac{V}{t}$$

where a = acceleration
     V = velocity
     t = time

As can be seen from the above, to solve velocity, acceleration and time problems, use Formulae 9–06, 9–07 or 9–08 to find an unknown value of either *V*, *a*, or *t*, if any two of the other values are known. See also Newton's 2nd Law, Paragraph 9.003

The following represents a velocity-time graph for motion with *constant* or *uniform* acceleration. When velocity is plotted as function of time, motion with constant acceleration, starting from rest, is represented by a straight line coming out of the original *0*. The slope of the line depends on the numerical value of the rate of acceleration. In the form of such graph, the results appear similar to Figure 9–03.

Acceleration, Time, and Distance

9.030 When a vehicle travels at constant speed of 50 mph (80 km/h) for 30 minutes, the distance traveled will be 25 miles (40 km) [(50 (80)/2)]. However, if the vehicle constantly changes its speed (±) during this time, the subsequent distance traveled will be different.

Example (see Fig. 9–04)

A vehicle accelerates from a starting velocity of *0* at a constant velocity of 4 ft/s^2 (1.2 m/s^2). Applying Formula 9–06 ($V = at$), the velocity at the end of a 12 second interval is 4 ft/s^2 (1.2 m/s^2) × 12 = 48 ft/s (14.4 m/s). Inasmuch as the vehicle traveled at a constant acceleration, the distance covered is the same as if it had moved all the while at a *constant* velocity equal to the *average* velocity of 24 ft/s (7.2 m/s) over the interval of 12 sec, expressed algebraically:

Formula 9–09

$$\bar{V} = \frac{V_o + V}{2}$$

Since $V_o = 0$, we have:

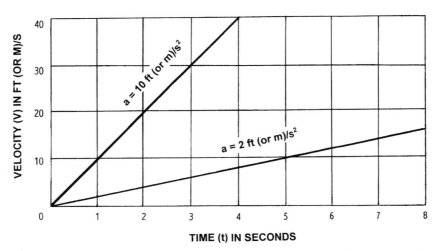

Figure 9–03. Velocity-time graph where, in applying $V = at$ (Formula 0–06), V is velocity in ft/s (m/s); a is ft/s² (m/s²), and t is time in seconds.

Formula 9–10

$$\bar{V} = \frac{V}{2}$$

where $\bar{V}$ = average velocity
V_o = initial velocity
V = final velocity

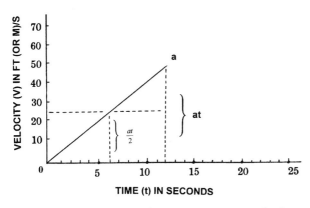

Figure 9–04. Average velocity over an interval when starting from rest (0) with constant acceleration. In this figure, feet are used as an example. In SI, substitute corresponding meter measurements for feet.

9.031 In the case of *motion*, the total distance (D) covered is equal to the *average* velocity multiplied by the number of seconds (t) as shown in the following formulae:

Formula 9–11

$$D = \bar{V}t$$

and

Formula 9–12

$$t = \frac{D}{V}$$

Formula 9–13

$$\bar{V} = \frac{D}{t}$$

where t = time in seconds
$\bar{V}$ = average velocity
D = distance

In Figure 9–04, the *average velocity* of 24 ft/s (7.5 m/s) is indicated by the horizontally-placed dashed line. At any instant during the first half of the time interval, the true velocity is below this line. At a corresponding point during the last half, it is an equal amount above the line. The result is that the average represents the motion exactly as far as computing the final distance is concerned. The final velocity, as we have already shown, is given by Formula 9–06 ($V = at$). The average velocity can be calculated with Formula 9–14.

Formula 9–14

$$\bar{V} = \frac{at}{2}$$

where $\bar{V}$ = average velocity
 a = acceleration rate
 t = time in seconds

Distance and Time

9.032 It is interesting to note that in distance and time calculations, if the acceleration is constant, the distance (D) traveled is equal to one-half of the acceleration times the square of the number of seconds. Also of interest, in Formula 9–11 $(D = \bar{V}t)$, if the accelerated vehicle or other object is replaced by one moving with this constant velocity, and substituting for $\bar{V}$ the value ${}^{at}/_2$, the distance traveled can be calculated by using Formula 9–15:

Formula 9–15

$$D = \frac{at^2}{2}$$

where D = average velocity
 a = acceleration
 t = time

In this Formula and as shown in Figure 9–05, t^2 means that the distance covered increases as the *square* of time. Therefore, after 2 seconds, a constantly accelerated vehicle will travel four times as far as it would have in the first second, and at the end of 3 seconds it will have traveled nine times as far, and so on.

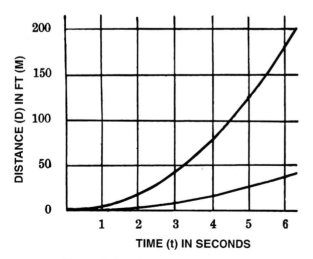

Figure 9–05. Time-distance curve.

Since $D = \frac{at^2}{2}$ (Formula 9–15) and $t = \frac{V}{a}$ (Formula 9–07), we may substitute $D = \frac{V^2}{2a}$ (***Formula 9–16***), and transposing $V^2 = 2aD$ (***Formula 9–17***), we have:

Formula 9–18

$$a = \frac{V^2}{2D}$$

where a = acceleration
 V = velocity
 D = distance

9.033 Using the foregoing as a basis in understanding acceleration, deceleration, velocity, and speed, we can say that in summary of the above, the three formulae which apply to motion with constant acceleration when the initial velocity is zero (0) are:

Formula 9–06

$$V = at$$

Formula 9–15

$$D = \frac{at^2}{2}$$

Formula 9–18

$$a = \frac{V^2}{2D}$$

where V = velocity
 a = acceleration
 D = distance
 t = time

VELOCITY AND SPEED CHANGE PROBLEM-SOLVING FORMULAE

9.034 The following is a summary of the most commonly-used formulae used in acceleration and deceleration problem-solving. In many cases, any one of these combined with other formulae found in this summary, and/or combined with formulae found elsewhere in the manual can be used in making a variety of determinations and/or in evaluating evidence. For example, a vehicle may have skidded to a stop but struck a pedestrian partway into the skid. The user can use the slide-to-stop (skid) Formula

9–31 (found under Para. 9.096) to determine the vehicle's initial speed, and then use Formula 9–20–19 to determine the vehicle's speed at the time the pedestrian was struck. It will be found that in some cases the formulae will give results in velocity, i.e., feet (meters) per second. To arrive at a speed result in miles per hour (kilometers per hour), it is then simply a matter of applying the proper conversion formula. The index provides a complete listing and location of all formulae and definitions that can be applied in any particular set of circumstances.

9.035 Speed- and velocity-change problem-solving formulae that flow from the explanation of *acceleration* set out above, include the following, wherein:

a = acceleration in ft/s (m/s) or a = acceleration rate in ft/s² (m/s²)–depending upon the context in which it is used.

D = distance in inches (cm), ft (m), miles (km)

f = drag factor

f_a = acceleration factor

g = acceleration due to gravity (32.2 ft/s/s or 9.81 m/s/s)

S = speed in mph (km/h)

t = time in seconds

μ = coefficient of friction

V = velocity in ft/s (m/s)

V_f = a final factor or result (e.g., in this example, a final velocity) denoted by a subscript f

V_0 = an initial or original factor (e.g., in this example, an initial velocity) denoted by a subscript zero

Constants

English	SI
30	254
0.249	0.45
1.466	0.278
0.682	3.6

Vehicle Acceleration Rate: Maximum acceleration rates are expressed as a function of mass/power ratio. It can be seen therefore that because of the various differences in modern vehicle models that are in use, rates can vary considerably. When the actual acceleration rate for a passenger car, on a level surface is unknown, it is reasonable, for routine investigation purposes, to use a an acceleration rate, from a stop to 20 mph (32 km/h), of 4 ft/s/s (1.2 m/s/s).

Pedestrian Walking Rates: For investigational purposes, it may be considered that the average adult and elderly move at approximately 4.5 ft/s (1.4 m/s). Children move at approximately 5.3 ft/s (1.6 m/s). For investigational purposes, when the actual rate is unknown, elderly or handicapped pedestrian walking rates can be lowered to 3.5 ft/s (1.07 m/s).

Note: For a complete list of the formulae contained in this manual, see the index under *Formulae.*

Converting Velocity (ft/sec or m/s) to Speed (mph or km/h)

In the formulae that follow, the number 1.466 (SI 0.278) is a constant. Alternatively, the constant .682 (SI 3.6) may be used, involving multiplication in place of division.

Formula 9–19–1

English	*SI*
$S = \dfrac{ft/s}{1.466}$	$S = \dfrac{m/s}{.278}$

or

$S = fts \times .682$	$S = m/s \times 3.6$

Converting Speed (mph or km/h) to Velocity (ft/s or m/s)

Formula 9–19–2

English	*SI*
$V = S \times 1.466$	$V = S \times .278$

VELOCITY AND SPEED FORMULAE

Number 9–20 Series

Distance Traveled When Speed or Velocity Is Constant

Formula 9–20–1

$$D = Vt$$

Average Speed and Velocity

Most trips are not made at a constant speed or velocity, such as when a vehicle accelerates from a stop, and accelerates or decelerates during the trip. In this formula, the symbol *V* is over-lined to denote *an average* velocity.

Formula 9–20–2

$$\overline{V} = \frac{D}{t}$$

Distance Traveled During Constant Acceleration

Constant acceleration is a term used to denote *uniform rate* of acceleration (or deceleration) of a vehicle or other object.

Formula 9–20–3

$$D = \frac{at^2}{2}$$

Speed and Velocity When Distance and Time Are Known

Formula 9–20–4

$$S = \frac{D}{t}$$

and

$$V = \frac{D}{t}$$

Formulae 9–20–5 and 9–20–6 reserved.

Time To Travel a Distance at a Constant Velocity

Formula 9–20–7

$$t = \frac{D}{V}$$

Distance Covered During Acceleration/deceleration from a Known Velocity

Formula 9–20–8

$$D = (V_o t) + (.5at^2) \quad \text{(Use + for acceleration)}$$
$$D = (V_o t) - (.5at^2) \quad \text{(Use – for deceleration)}$$

Distance Covered During Acceleration from a Stop

Formula 9–20–9

In the case of a vehicle accelerating from a stop, the term *(V$_o$t)* in Formula 9–20–8 is equal to zero (0) and may therefore be disregarded. The formula then becomes:

$$D = .5at^2$$

Speed at Any Time During Known Acceleration Rate from a Stop

Formula 9–20–10

English	*SI*
S = at × .682	S = at × 3.6

Note: The number 0.682 (SI 3.6) is a conversion factor for changing ft/s to mph (m/s to km/h).

Velocity After Acceleration from Stop at Known Acceleration Rate and Distance

Formula 9–20–11

$$V = \sqrt{2aD}$$

Time to Accelerate from Stop to a Given Velocity When Acceleration Rate Is Known

Formula 9–20–12A

$$t = \frac{V}{a}$$

Time to Decelerate to a Stop When Initial Velocity and Deceleration Rate Are Known

Formula 9–20–12B

$$t = \frac{V_o}{a}$$

where t = time in seconds
V$_o$ = initial velocity
a = deceleration rate

Acceleration Rate

Acceleration rates vary with the size, weight, and engine capability of vehicles. Heavy vehicles such as trucks and buses may have a low acceleration rate of approximately 3 ft/s (1 m/s/s/) from a stop. Late model passenger cars may have an acceleration rate as high as 10 ft/s (3 m/s/s). High-performance and modified vehicles often exceed even this acceleration rate. Therefore, in accidents involving acceleration, it is important for the investigator to determine as closely as possible the maximum or actual acceleration rate of the vehicle involved. For investigation purposes, methods of determining the *maximum acceleration rate* for a specific make and model of motor vehicle include:

a. Referring to the manufacturer's specification sheets

b. Referring to various automotive and traffic engineering publications

c. Using a vehicle similar to the one involved in the crash to test its acceleration capabilities over a measured distance.

For routine investigation purposes, a reasonable or normal acceleration rate for modern passenger cars from a stop to 20 mph (32 km/h) may be considered to be 4 ft/s/s (1.22 m/s/s). However, a reasonable acceleration can also be calculated using the following formula:

Formula 9–20–13

$$a = \frac{2D}{t^2}$$

Acceleration Factor

An acceleration factor is the ratio of an acceleration rate to the acceleration of gravity. For the purposes of this manual, the term acceleration factor is denoted by the symbol $\mathbf{f_a}$.

Formula 9–20–14

$$f_a = \frac{a}{g}$$

Speed When Acceleration Factor Is Known

When the acceleration factor has been calculated or is known for an accelerating vehicle, the speed to which the vehicle can accelerate from a stop over a known distance can be calculated with the following formula:

Formula 9–20–15

English	*SI*
$S = \sqrt{30Df_a}$	$S = \sqrt{254Df_a}$

Acceleration from a Known Speed

When a vehicle has been traveling at a known speed, and then accelerates over a certain distance at a known acceleration rate, the velocity and speed at the end of that distance can be calculated by using the following formula:

Formula 9–20–16

$$V_f = \sqrt{V_o{}^2 + (2aD)}$$

Time for Acceleration from a Known Speed

The time it takes a vehicle to travel a known distance under acceleration can be calculated with the following formula:

Formula 9–20–17

$$t = \frac{V_f - V_o}{a}$$

Deceleration Rate and Drag Factor

The deceleration rate, as related to friction between a skidding or sliding tire and the roadway surface due to the force of gravity, is usually less than the acceleration rate of gravity and therefore is usually expressed as a decimal fraction of gravity. This fraction is known as the drag factor (f) or, on a level surface, the coefficient of friction (μ) value. A drag factor or a coefficient of friction having a value of 1.00 is equal to the acceleration rate of gravity, or 32.2 ft/s/s (9.81 m/s/s), and is by definition one gravitational force (g). The coefficient of friction value may occasionally go even higher, e.g., 1.02. Drag factor and coefficient of friction are fully covered under paragraphs 9.041–9.085

When the drag factor (or coefficient of friction) is known, the acceleration or deceleration rate can be calculated using Formula 9–20–18.

Formula 9–20–18

$$a = fg$$

where a = acceleration or deceleration rate
 f = drag factor (or coefficient of friction, μ)
 g = acceleration of gravity (32.2 ft/s/s or 9.81 m/s/s)

Velocity or Speed at Any Point During Deceleration When Skid Distance and Drag Factor Are Known

Formula 9–20–19

$$V_f = \sqrt{V_o{}^2 - (2aD)}$$

where V_f = velocity after deceleration
 V_o = initial velocity
 a = deceleration rate
 D = distance or length of skid mark to point to which measured

Note: Before using this formula, it is necessary to calculate the initial speed of the vehicle based on the length of the skid marks and the drag factor by using Formula 9–31; then convert the initial speed in mph (km/h) to ft/s (m/s) with the constant 1.466 (SI .278), using Formula 9–19–2. The result will be substituted into Formula 9–20–19 for V_o. After obtaining the velocity after deceleration (V_f) with Formula 9–20–19, it is necessary to convert V_f to S_f with the constant 1.466 or .278 (Formula 19–1) to obtain an answer in mph (km/h).

Time Required to Slide (Skid) to a Given Point When Slide Distance and Drag Factor Are Known

Formula 9–20–20

$$t = \frac{V_o - V_f}{a}$$

where t = time in seconds
V_o = initial velocity
V_f = velocity at predetermined point
a = deceleration rate

Time Required to Slide (Skid) to a Stop When Slide Distance and Drag Factor Are Known

Formula 9–20–21

English	*SI*
$t = 0.249\sqrt{D/f}$	$t = 0.45\sqrt{D/f}$

Skid Distance Required to Stop When Initial Speed and Drag Factor Are Known

Formula 9–20–22

English	*SI*
$D = \dfrac{S^2}{30f}$	$D = \dfrac{S^2}{254f}$

Figures 9–06–9–10 reserved.

9.036–9.040 reserved.

COEFFICIENT OF FRICTION AND DRAG FACTOR

Coefficient of Friction and Drag Factor Defined

9.041 *Coefficient of Friction.* Coefficient of friction (designated by the Greek letter μ, pronounced "mew") represents the sliding resistance between two surfaces when one of the surfaces is level, i.e., without grade or slope, and the other slides over that surface in a continuous motion. An example of such resistance is the friction, traction, or adhesion between a tire and a level surface when the tire is skidding on that surface (see also *Friction* under Paras. 9.024 and 9.025).

9.042 Coefficient of friction is measured as a ratio based on two forces: (1) the horizontal force (i.e., pull) parallel to the level surface that is required to keep the object in continuous motion in the direction of

SKIDDING VEHICLE   **SKIDDING VEHICLE**   **SKIDDING VEHICLE**

MINUS (-) GRADE   **LEVEL SURFACE**   **PLUS (+) GRADE**

DRAG FACTOR *f*   **COEFFICIENT OF FRICTION μ**   **DRAG FACTOR *f***

(*f* = μ)

Figure 9–11. An example of the application of coefficient of friction and drag factor to a roadway having ± grades and a level surface.

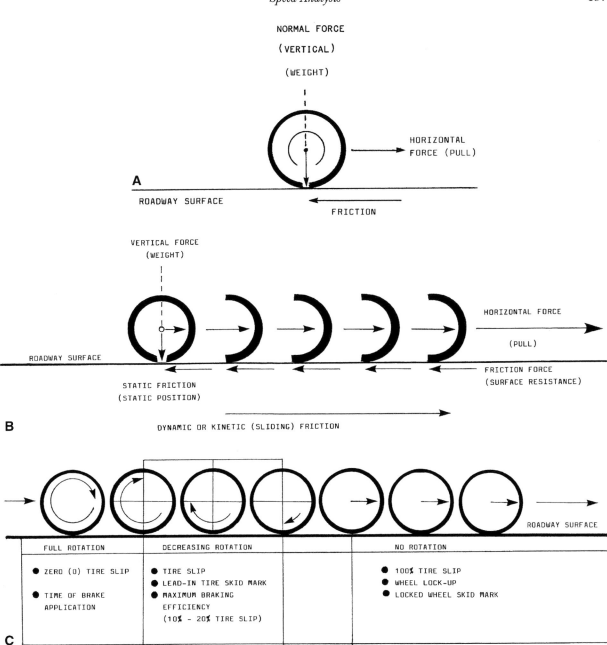

Figure 9–12. Descriptions of the forces involved in coefficient of friction and drag factor: *A* and *B*, first of all, depict the forces involved on a single wheel that is in a stationary or *static* position on a roadway, i.e., vertical force (normal force) pressing the tire against the roadway surface; and secondly, the forces then involved as a locked wheel moves along the surface. *C* depicts the effects of braking from full wheel rotation to complete lock-up. Note: The greatest braking efficiency is just prior to complete wheel lock-up.

the force divided by (2) the normal or perpendicular force exerted by the object onto the level surface over which it is sliding. Coefficient of friction applies only if vehicles have all wheels locked up, thus providing 100% braking efficiency, and are sliding on a level surface.

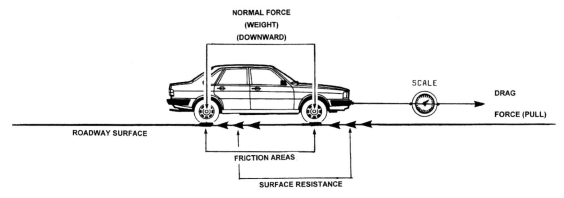

Figure 9–13. A depiction of how the forces involved in determining drag factor and/or coefficient of friction can be applied to a motor vehicle.

9.043 *Drag Factor.* In the case of *drag factor*, which is denoted by a lower case *f*, sliding need not be only on a level surface, but rather it can also be on a surface having a grade or slope. In addition to being used with vehicles having 100% braking efficiency, it can also be applied to a situation that involves any of the following:

a. Vehicles having less than 100% braking efficiency on one or more wheels;
b. Commercial-type vehicles, particularly those with attached trailers, where all wheels do not lock up at the same time;
c. Vehicles where weight shift is considered a factor;
d. Friction generated by a tire sideslipping on a roadway surface in a turn or curve;
e. Friction generated between a tire and the roadway surface when the drive wheels are under acceleration;
f. Friction generated by a body, vehicle part or any other object moving or sliding over a roadway surface or any other surface.

9.044 In a technical sense, the only time coefficient of friction and drag factor values are equal is when a four-wheel vehicle with all wheels locked up, thus providing 100% braking efficiency, skids on a level surface. However, the terms coefficient of friction and drag factor, as used in many traffic accident investigation textbooks and by investigators, are considered synonymous.

For the purposes of this manual, the terms will be treated as synonymous, that is to say, as representing the stopping force expressed as a numerical value of slipperiness (written as a decimal fraction), and unless circumstances dictate otherwise, only the term drag factor, designated with the letter *f*, will be used.

9.045 The drag sled concept is based on simple physics, i.e., calculating coefficient of friction and/or drag factor based on the ratio of force (pull) required to move an object of a given weight over a surface on which the object rests. Figure 9–13 shows how this concept can be related to a braked motor vehicle skidding over a roadway surface using Formulae 9–23 or 9–24.

Formula 9–23 *Formula 9–24*

$$\mu = \frac{F}{W} \qquad f = \frac{F}{W}$$

where μ = coefficient of friction
f = drag factor
F = force (pull) parallel to the surface required to cause an object's continuous movement across the surface. Note: The surface must be level if coefficient of friction is to be obtained
W = normal or perpendicular force pressing against a level surface (equivalent to the weight of the object)

Grade, Slope, and Superelevation

9.046 Grade or slope is the change (±) in elevation in unit distance in a specified direction along the centerline of a roadway or the path of a vehicle, expressed as a decimal fraction. For example, a 10% rise or fall is expressed as +0.10 or –0.10; a 4% rise or fall is expressed as +0.04 or –0.04, respectively–expressed in feet (meters) of rise or fall per 100 feet (meters) of level distance, or in rise or fall as a percent of the level distance. The calculation is obtained by simply dividing the difference in elevation between two points along the roadway or path by the level distance between those two points. Superelevation (bank) is the grade across the roadway at right angles to the centerline from the inside to the outside edge on a curve. The calculation for superelevation is the same as that for grade.

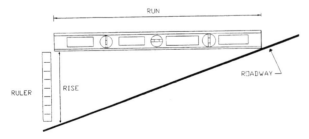

Figure 9–14A. IPTM's Grade Gauge® and carrying pouch.

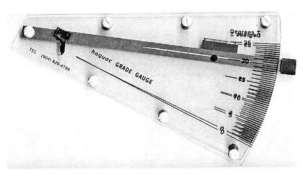

Figure 9–14B. A graphical explanation of grade or superelevation using a carpenter's level. In the absence of a more modern instrument such as a Smart Level®, which gives you the slope directly as a decimal percent, a carpenter's level, as shown here, can be used to measure the rise or fall over a short span of roadway in order to calculate the grade or suspension.

9.047 Grade and superelevation may be measured by using commercially-developed electronic instruments, or a clinometer (an instrument for determining the angular inclination of surfaces), IPTM's

Grade Gauge® which gives a grade reading in degrees that can be quickly converted to a percent reading with a pocket calculator, IPTM's *blueBlitz®* Traffic Template and a clipboard which will give a percent reading directly; or a carpenter, smart, or line level. When the grade or superelevation cannot be read directly from the instrument used, such as a carpenter's level (see Fig. 9–14B), once the required measurements are obtained, it can be calculated using Formula 9–25.

Example (see Fig. 9–14B)

A carpenter's level is used to measure the grade (or superelevation) of a roadway. The length (run) of the level is 48 in (122 cm) and the rise (or fall) is 4 in (10 cm). The percentage grade (m) or superelevation (e) is:

Formula 9–25

English	SI
$m = r/L \times 100/1$	$m = r/L \times 100/1$

where m = percentage grade (±)
　　　　[or e = superelevation (±)]
　　　r = rise or fall
　　　L = length or distance (run)

$m = 4/48 \times 100/1$	$m = 10/122 \times 100/1$
$m = .08 \times 100$	$m = .08 \times 100$
$m = 8\%$	$m = 8\%$

Note: This result will be +8% for an uphill grade and –8% for downhill.

METHODS OF DETERMINING DRAG FACTOR

9.048 Various methods can be employed to determine the drag factor of any particular surface. Existing factors at the time will often dictate which method to use to ensure tests are carried out safely and at the same time obtain the most accurate results. These methods include:

a. Conducting test skids (see also Para. 1.054)
b. Using an accelerometer
c. Using a drag sled
d. Referring to the Coefficient of Friction (Drag Factor) Guide, Table 9–02, following Paragraph 9.090.

Caution

Under no circumstances should test skids, or any other test, be made when there is a danger of causing an accident, injury, or damage. As a general rule, test skids should not be carried out at a speed greater than 35 mph (56 km/h). The prevailing conditions will often dictate how drag factor will be determined. For example, test skids usually will not be carried out on icy surfaces, but a drag sled may be used.

Test Skids

9.049 There are three methods of using test skids to determine the drag factor of a roadway surface.

1. Shot marker (also known as *bumper gun* or *chalk gun*; see Fig. 9–15)
   (When a shot marker is not used, there are two additional methods of determining the drag factor from test skids)

2. Using the longest skid mark (see Fig. 9–17)
3. Averaging skid marks (see Fig. 9–17)

Note: Depending upon the seriousness of the crash and the extent to which the investigation is to be carried out, skid tests by themselves may sometimes preclude the necessity of further calculations or determinations in respect to the speed of a crash vehicle. For example, if a crash vehicle skidded 63 ft (19 m) on a roadway where the speed limit was 25 mph (40 km/h) and test skids conducted at 25 mph (40 km/h) measured only 40 ft (12 m), it becomes obvious that the crash vehicle was exceeding the speed limit. It is recommended, however, that proper speed calculations be completed whenever possible.

Shot Marker

9.050 If possible, use a test vehicle equipped with a *shot marker*, generally a .22 caliber barrel and cartridge

Figure 9–15. A vehicle equipped with a shot marker.

Figure 9–16. The lead-in portion of a skid mark, often appearing as a cleaning action (impending or incipient skid mark) becoming a shadow on the roadway just before the dark portion.

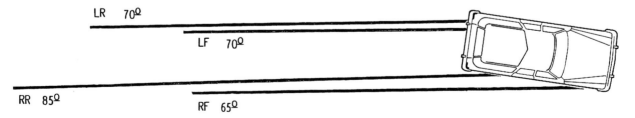

Figure 9–17. A typical skid mark pattern. (LF + RF + LR + RR)/4 equals the average skid mark length. In this example, the right rear (RR) is the longest mark.

device loaded with chalk which, when fired, leaves a chalk mark on the roadway surface at the time and place of brake application. The vehicle continues to brake until it has come to a complete stop, and the distance from the chalk mark on the pavement to the barrel of the shot marker in its stopped position is then measured giving the length of the skid.

9.051 A shot marker is very often attached the rear bumper but may be attached at other locations on the vehicle as well. There are various methods of activating the unit, including (a) on application of the brakes, a light sensor attached to the brake lights of the vehicle activates the firing mechanism of the marker; and (b) an electrical pressure sensor attached to the face of the brake pedal that activates (fires) the shot marker when pressure is placed on it by the foot in a brake application (see Fig. 9–15).

Test Skid Procedures

9.052 When test skids are carried out to determine the drag factor, certain steps and procedures should be followed to ensure safety and accuracy. These include:

a. Duplicating all environmental conditions as closely as possible, e.g.,
   1. Type of roadway surface
   2. Direction of travel
   3. Vehicle load
   4. Roadway temperature
   5. Roadway surface conditions
b. If it is possible and if permitted, use the accident vehicle with any load it may have had. If this is not possible, use a similar-type vehicle and similar load.
c. When other than the crash vehicle is used, use one with an accurate, calibrated speedometer, inasmuch as the true speed of the test vehicle must be known. Speedometer accuracy may be checked (calibrated) by radar or by determining the time it takes to travel a known distance, e.g., a measured mile or kilometer, at a constant speedometer reading (see Formula 9–26).

Speedometer Accuracy Test

Formula 9–26

$$S = \frac{3600}{t}$$

where S = actual speed
   t = time in seconds to travel measured mile or kilometer at a constant (speedometer) speed.

In a speedometer accuracy test, it is recommended that the exact or actual speed result be used, i.e., do not round the calculated speed up or down.

d. Travel in a straight path at a constant 3 to 5 mph (5 to 8 km/h) above the speed at which the test is to be made. Decelerate to the test speed. Apply the brakes quickly and hard, as in a panic stop, and let the vehicle skid to a complete stop.
e. If the speed limit allows, make test skids at 35 mph (56 km/h) or even at a substantially slower speed. However, it is recommended that test skids not be made at less than 15 mph (25 km/h) because there is a possibility of an excessively high drag factor result.
f. When a shot marker is not used, measure the length of the skid mark of each tire. Include in the overall measurement any lead-in skid mark appearing as an impending skid mark or a shadow (see Fig. 9–16).

9.053 Whenever possible, the degree of actual braking efficiency or capability of the crash vehicle should be determined. When it is determined that the vehicle had less than 100% braking efficiency or capability, the braking efficiency should, if possible, be duplicated with another vehicle in carrying out test skids. However, if this is not possible, use a test vehicle that has 100% braking efficiency and then factor in, in the drag factor calculation, the known efficiency of the crash vehicle. (See Table 9–01 and the explanation of braking capability and efficiency in Paragraph 9.081.)

9.054 When a shot marker is not used, there are two basic methods of determining the drag factor of a surface using test skids:

   1. Using the longest skid mark (see Fig. 9-17)
   2. Averaging the skid marks (see Fig. 9-17)

Both methods are considered acceptable; however, Method 1 favors the crash vehicle because it tends to result in a somewhat lower drag factor than Method 2, and of the two is the one recommended.

9.055 It is recommended that the results of test skids be rounded off as follows:

Table 9–01
BRAKING PERCENTAGES FOR VEHICLES

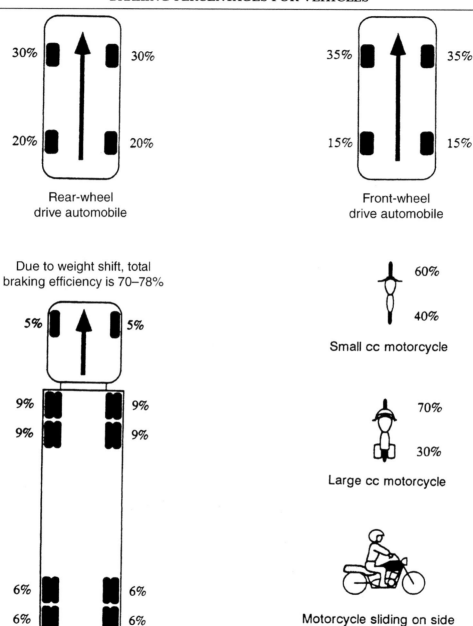

Rear-wheel
drive automobile

Front-wheel
drive automobile

Due to weight shift, total
braking efficiency is 70–78%

Small cc motorcycle

Large cc motorcycle

Truck/Trailer

Motorcycle sliding on side
concrete $f = .43 - .53$
asphalt $f = .53 - .65$

Note: Braking percentage for each
wheel must be calculated for each
individual tractor-trailor

Skid distance (D):

Round up to the nearest whole foot (.5 meters). Thus, 61.4 feet (or meters) would become 62 feet (or 61.5 meters).

Coefficient of friction (μ) or drag factor (f):

Round down to the nearest second place in the decimal fraction. Thus, 0.753 would become 0.75 and 0.608 would become 0.60.

These conventions support the practice of using always the minimum speed for the crash vehicle.

Longest Skid Mark

9.056 Use the following procedure to determine the drag factor based on the longest skid mark from test skids:

1. Conduct two (2) test skids.
2. Measure the length of the longest skid mark of each test.
3. Calculate the drag factor from the longest skid mark of each test. (Use Formula 9–27 for this purpose.) Compare these two drag factors.
4. If the drag factors are within 05% of each other, use the lower of the two in an applicable speed formula.
5. If the first two test skids fail to produce drag factors that fall within 05% of each other, conduct further test skids until two drag factors are obtained that are within 05%.
6. If circumstances are such that tests cannot or should not be made to produce results within the preferred 05%, two results within 10% can be considered acceptable.

Accelerometer-Electronic Devices

9.057 Accelerometers are designed to measure acceleration and deceleration factors. They are usually mounted inside the vehicle on the floor, dash, or on the inside of the windshield. As with other vehicle-based tests, for *deceleration* determinations, the vehicle travels at a predetermined speed and the driver simulates panic braking. During the deceleration, the instrument collects the necessary data for whatever that instrument is designed to measure, such as drag factor. Some instruments are designed to also analyze for some or all aspects of the following road travel factors: (a) acceleration ($\pm$), (b) speed, (c) cornering,

(d) time, (e) distance, (f) slope, and (g) superelevation. Additionally, some units have software that will provide for computer printouts (see Fig. 9–18).

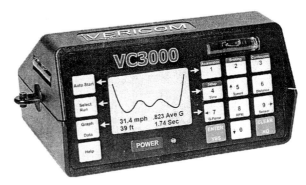

Figure 9–18. A vericom Braking Test Computer.*

9.058 As with speed measuring devices, these instruments should be checked periodically for accuracy. Such calibration can be done with radar, or be related to tests carried out with another same- or similar-type measuring device. The accuracy of these other devices must, of course, also be known.

9.059–9.065 reserved.

Drag Factor Calculation

9.066 When the vehicle test speed and the length of the skid are known, the drag factor can be calculated with the following formula:

Formula 9–27

English	SI
$f = \dfrac{S^2}{30D}$	$f = \dfrac{S^2}{254D}$

where f = drag factor
  S = speed of vehicle in making test skids
  D = skid mark distance

With this formula you can determine a vehicle's acceleration factor from a stop or deceleration factor to a stop over a given distance.

---

*Courtesy of VERICOM Computers. Website: www.vericom-computers.com; e-mail: vericom@vericomcomputers.com; Phone: 800–533–5547, (763) 428–1381, Fax (763) 428–4856.

Derivation

Start with the equation from the derivation of the following speed formula.

(Note: For the *SI* derivation, substitute 254 for 30 throughout.)

Formula 9–28

English	*SI*
$S = \sqrt{30Df}$	$S = \sqrt{254Df}$

Divide both sides by **30D** to isolate **f**.

$$\frac{1}{30D} \times \frac{30Df}{1} = \frac{S^2}{1} \times \frac{1}{30D}$$

Cancel terms.

$$\frac{1}{\cancel{30D}} \times \frac{\cancel{30D}f}{1} = \frac{S^2}{1} \times \frac{1}{30D}$$

Rewrite.

$$f = \frac{S^2}{30D} \qquad\qquad f = \frac{S^2}{254D} \,^*$$

Example

Skid tests resulted in the longest skid mark measuring 50 ft (15 m). The drag factor is (see also Para. 9.045, and Formulae 9–23 and 9–24):

English	*SI*
$f = \dfrac{S^2}{30D}$	$f = \dfrac{S^2}{254D}$
$f = \dfrac{30^2}{(30 \times 50)}$	$f = \dfrac{48^2}{(254 \times 15)}$
$f = \dfrac{900}{1500}$	$f = \dfrac{2304}{3810}$
$f = .60$	$f = .60$

Note: An investigator can check of the accuracy of the skid-to-stop procedure by obtaining a radar reading of the vehicle speed at the time of brake application and then relate that to the calculated

speed based on the drag factor and length of the skid marks.

Drag Sleds

9.067 Drag sled units fall into three categories, namely:

1. Custom-made
2. Commercially manufactured
3. Other objects

Custom-made (home-made) drag sleds can take various forms, most often it being a weight of concrete or lead with a section of tire fastened to its base (see Fig. 9–19).

Commercially-manufactured. As of 2005, a number of commercially-developed drag sleds are entering the market. Some of these provide data on the angle at which the unit is pulled, and data covering Formulae 9–23 or 9–24 (μ = F/W or *f* = F/W). Some of these are also designed with software that can be downloaded for a computer printout.

Other objects include items such as a human body, a metal fragment from a vehicle, and a tire and wheel. When a tire and wheel is to be used, select a tire and wheel from the accident vehicle if possible (see Fig. 9–21).

Custom-Made Drag Sleds

9.068 A drag sled can be constructed from a part of a tire that is then filled with a heavy material such as concrete or lead (see Fig. 9–19). The generally accepted steps are:

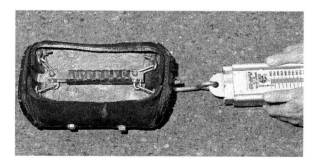

Figure 9–19. A photograph showing the basic construction of a drag sled.

*Source: Howell, Wiley L.: *Derivations Manual for Formulas Used in Traffic Accident Investigation and Reconstruction.* Institute of Police Technology and Management, University of North Florida, Jacksonville, Fl., p. 60. Reproduced with permission.

1. Cut a section of tire that includes about one-fifth the tire's outer circumference, making the cut at either end of the section at an angle that leaves the beads intact for a length of about half the length of the outer circumference along the cut section.

2. Fill the tire section with water to the desired level of the material to be added later as weight. Mark this level on the tire with a line using a grease-type pencil (chalk marks are water soluble and may readily disappear), or gently spray-paint a line on the inside of the tire along the outside edge of the water surface. In both cases, when the water is removed, the required mark at the *original* level will remain.

3. Remove the water and measure its volume, then pour half that volume back into the tire section. Mark the new water level on the tire. This line will pass through the *center of mass* of the drag sled when construction is completed.

4. Drill a hole through one end of the tire at the *center of mass line*, and then install an eye bolt by which the tire will be pulled.

5. Insert two bolts about five inches apart through and at right angles to the walls of the tire section and far enough below the beads to be covered by the weighting material. The bolts prevent the weighting material from spreading the walls when it is poured and attach the tire section firmly to the weighting material once it has hardened.

6. Fill the tire section with *concrete, lead,* etc., to the *original* water level line. Once the material has set and hardened, the construction is completed.*

Drag Sled Operation

9.069 The objective in operating a drag sled unit is, of course, to determine the coefficient of friction or drag factor of the surface over which the unit is moved. To meet this objective, the *force (pull)* and the *weight* of the unit must be established as set out in Formulae 9–23 or 9–24 ($\mu = F/W$ or $f = F/W$), where μ = coefficient of friction and f = drag factor

---

*Source: Rivers, R.W.: *Speed Analysis for Traffic Accident Investigation.* Institute of Police Technology and Management, University of North Florida (2nd ed.), 1997, pp. 28–29.

and F and W are in pounds (kilograms). Both the force (F) and the weight (W) should be established with a certifiably accurate spring or other recognized scale. The same scale should be used for obtaining both these measurements. In operating a drag sled unit, it is the number of pounds (kilograms) force (pull) required to keep an object moving (sliding) at a *constant* speed that must be used in Formulae 9–23 or 9–24, not the initial or *static* force required to start the object moving from a position of rest.

Figure 9–20. With this type of drag sled, the scale should be pulled parallel to the surface, or otherwise at a slight angle as determined through the calibration process (see Para. 9.072), in order to accurately measure the force, F, required to move the sled at a constant speed.

9.070 An advantage in using a drag sled is that the examination area can be relatively small or as large as need be, thereby making this type of unit an excellent instrument for restricted areas, or where there is a safety concern, e.g., passing traffic.

9.071 Generally accepted drag sled protocols to determine drag factor are:

1. Weigh the unit with a scale.
2. Use the same scale to pull the unit over the roadway surface.
3. Conduct test pulls alongside the accident vehicle's skid mark, in the same direction as the vehicle was traveling.
4. Carry out approximately 10 test pulls, preferably spaced over the entire length of the skid mark, as doing so will take into consideration

Figure 9–21A and B. A tire and wheel (drag sled) unit. The weight of the unit and the force (pull) required to move it along the roadway surface must be measured (as shown in A and B) and placed in Formula 9–23 or Formula 9–24 to calculate coefficient of friction or drag factor. The scale must be attached to the unit in such a say that the tire will not rotate when pulled. (Courtesy of Rivers Traffic Consultants.)

all roadway surface factors, including grade. Each test pull should be approximately 10 ft (3 m) in length.

5. Record the amount of force (pull) in pounds or kilograms required to move the unit at a constant speed. Remember, it is the force required to keep the unit moving at a constant speed that must be recorded rather than the initial force (static force) required to move the unit from its at-rest position.

6. When measuring the drag factor where a yaw mark is involved, pull the drag sled or tire and wheel across the mark from the inside to the outside of the mark at the angle of the striation. The striations show the direction the vehicle was traveling and sideslipping (see Fig. 9–22). Approximately 10 test pulls should be conducted over the length of the yaw mark, starting at the beginning of the mark, and each pull should be 3 ft (1 m) or more in length. This procedure will take into consideration all roadway surface factors, including grade or superelevation.

Drag Sled Calibration

9.072 An investigator who uses a drag sled, tire, and wheel or other device to determine drag factor should be knowledgeable about and properly trained in its use. Before using any type of drag sled to examine a roadway surface for drag factor, the investigator should properly qualify himself as well as calibrate the unit's use by carrying out field tests. To carry out these tests, he should first determine the drag factor of the roadway surface by conducting test skids with a vehicle that is equipped with a shot marker, or with an accelerometer known to

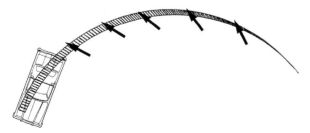

Figure 9–22. A drag sled unit should be pulled across a yaw mark in the direction of the striations in order to determine the drag factor.

give accurate results, in the manner outlined in paragraphs 9.050–9.057 above.

9.073 Knowing the correct drag factor, the investigator can then conduct several test pulls with his drag sled unit until he can consistently come up with numbers that will correspond to the known drag factor (see Example and Formula 9–29, below). Although the pull should normally be parallel to the roadway surface, it may sometimes be found through the field tests that to obtain accurate results with the unit, the pull for that unit may have to be made at an angle that may be a little off parallel ($\pm$) to the surface. This may very often be the case with a tire and wheel; and in the case of a drag sled, it could be an inherent requirement for that particular sled because of the way it was constructed, e.g., the eye bolt not being precisely aligned with the center of mass. However, when field tests for the unit point out the fact that a slight adjustment is necessary to the pull angle ($\pm$) from one that is strictly parallel to the surface, such use of that determined angle can be considered acceptable, and one that can be properly explained in evidence, if need be.

9.074 It may not, of course, be possible to calibrate in the manner described above other units such as bodies, pieces of metal, and so on. In these cases, the unit should be as similar as possible to that for which a drag factor is being determined, e.g., a piece of metal can be used that is similar to the body part of a vehicle that may have slid over a roadway surface, or a body (volunteer) of similar weight and wearing similar-type clothing as a pedestrian who might have been impacted and who slid across a roadway surface.

Example

From test skids, an investigator determines that the drag factor of a roadway surface is .65. By using Formula 9–29 below, he then calculates the force that will be required to pull his drag sled weighing 25 lbs (11 kg) over the same roadway surface. The calculated required force is 16.25 lbs (7.15 kg). He then conducts test pulls with the drag sled until the force consistently registers 16.25 lbs (7.15 kg) on the scale. Such agreement with the calculated required force would indicate that the test pulls were being properly done.

Formula 9–29

U.S.	SI
$F = Wf$	$F = Wf$

where F = force required to move unit at a constant speed
W = weight of unit
f = drag factor

$F = 25 \times .65$	$F = 11 \times .65$
$F = 16.25$ lbs	$F = 7.15$ kg

NOTE: It is of utmost importance that the drag sled operator use his drag sled as a personal-use device, i.e., he must know the intricacies of that unit. Each individual unit may have slight differences in its construction and requirements for use. An operator should not simply use any drag sled that he has access to unless he first establishes a complete familiarity with that unit in terms of how to use that unit to gain accurate results.

Drag Factor Adjustments

9.075 In cases where a crash occurs on a roadway that has a slope (grade and/or superelevation), no adjustment need be made to the calculated drag factor for use in a speed formula when drag factor skid tests are carried in a manner that equal that of the crash vehicle, i.e., conducted at the same place, in the same direction, with the same braking efficiency, and meeting all other conditions that would be reasonably expected to apply to the crash vehicle. It can be seen therefore that there is an advantage in using the crash vehicle for such tests when this is possible.

9.076 When slope is involved in determining drag factor, it must be borne in mind that the retarding effect of braking is totally independent of the effect of slope. Therefore, when an investigation involves a grade, either by the crash or the skid test vehicle, an adjustment must be made to the calculated drag factor for use in a speed formula, as well as to the drag factors set out in the Coefficient of Friction [Drag Factor] Guide (9.090, Table 9–02), when it is used. Essentially, the crux of a drag factor adjustment is that when a drag factor (f) is calculated for a grade, it must then be adjusted $\pm$ to coefficient of friction for a level surface (μ), and that factor then used as the drag factor in any further speed or velocity calculation. It should be noted here that for a level surface, $\mu = f$ (see Figure 9–23 and the examples below).

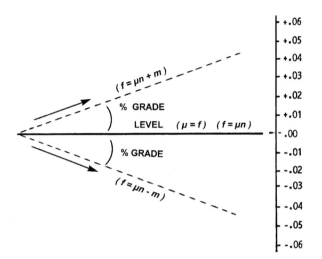

Figure 9–23. An explanation of drag factor, f value, adjustment.

9.077 When a drag sled is pulled in accordance with Paragraph 9.071(3) and (6), that operation accounts for any grade or superelevation along with the drag factor, and no drag factor adjustment is required.

9.078 The drag factor adjustment formula is (refer also to Figure 9–23):

Formula 9–30

$$f = \mu n \pm m$$

where f = adjusted drag factor
    μ = coefficient of friction (μ = drag factor f for a level surface
    n = % braking efficiency
    m = grade

When an adjusted drag factor value is determined outside any other formula (in the manner shown above), it can then be inserted into a variety of formulae where an f factor is essential, such as under the radical in calculating speed from skid marks.

9.079 See once again the definitions of coefficient of friction and drag factor in Paragraphs 9.041 and

9.043. The drag factor f is a numerical value that accounts not only for the coefficient of friction μ, but also for adjustments to other variables as demanded by the situation. These adjustments will be mainly to braking percentage, grade, and/or superelevation.

9.080 If the surface under investigation is not level, a downhill grade m will have a minus (–) value and must be *added* directly to the coefficient of friction in the formula, i.e., $\mu + m = f$. In the case of an uphill grade, the m factor will have a plus value and must be *subtracted* directly from the coefficient of friction in the formula, i.e., $\mu - m = f$. In addition, if all wheels are not braking with 100% efficiency, the coefficient of friction μ must be first multiplied by the braking percentage n, the result of which must then be added to or subtracted from the grade m in the formula to obtain f, i.e., $\mu n \pm m = f$. When braking efficiency is 100%, the n factor has a value of 1. In such cases, the n can be dropped and the formula then becomes:

Formula 9–30A

$$\mu \pm m = f$$

If only braking efficiency is involved, the symbol m can be dropped and the formula becomes:

Formula 9–30B

$$f = \mu n$$

9.081 The value of braking efficiency n is determined by the number of wheels having braking capability and/or the braking efficiency of those wheels that have braking capability (see 9.053, Table 9–01). Obviously, if a brake is disconnected, it is not capable of performing its task and its efficiency is zero. If a wheel has braking capability, but the brake is not properly adjusted, its efficiency may be somewhat less than 100%. For the purposes of this manual and in the examples set out, the braking efficiency of a wheel will be either 100% or zero, determined by the weight carried by that wheel. For example, from Table 9–01, if a front-wheel drive automobile has zero braking efficiency on its front-right wheel, the n factor for the vehicle would be (35 + 15 + 15) 65%. If, however, the investigator finds that a wheel has partial braking efficiency rather than its being100% or zero, he may wish to factor-in that efficiency. (For another example, see Para. 9.083, Fig. 9–24, Example 1.)

9.082 The order in which the adjustments are shown in Formula 9–30 is the order in which they should be calculated. Remember that the retarding effect of braking is totally independent of the effect of slope; therefore, reversing the order in the formula would make the effect of gravity caused by the grade apply to braking efficiency as well as to the effect of friction between the tires and the road surface. While reversing the order (adding/subtracting m to/from μ before multiplying μ by n) usually has a negligible effect in speed calculated, in circumstances where an acceleration or deceleration rate is based on the drag factor, a reverse order may be such as to raise or lower the rate enough to be significant.

9.083 Explanations and examples of drag factor adjustments can summarized as follows:

Example 1

At a crash site, test skids with a test vehicle having 100% braking efficiency were conducted on a roadway with a +04% grade, at the same location and traveling in the same direction as the front-wheel drive vehicle involved in the crash (see Fig. 9–24). These tests resulted in a calculated drag factor of .80. The crash vehicle, which skidded 42 ft (12.8 m), had braking capability on all wheels except one rear wheel, giving it a braking efficiency of 85% of its possible 100% braking efficiency (see 9.053, Table 9–01). Knowing this, the crash vehicle's drag factor can be calculated by first subtracting the +4% grade from

the test drag factor of .80 to bring this factor down to that of a level surface $(0.80 - .04 = 0.76)$, thus yielding a coefficient of friction of .76. By applying the f-adjustment formula, Formula 9–30, the crash vehicle's drag factor can then be calculated:

Crash Investigation Data

Test vehicle
    Braking capability and efficiency = 100%
    Test grade = +4%
    Test drag factor = .80

Crash Vehicle
    Front wheel drive
    No braking capability on one rear wheel = −15%
    Braking efficiency on three wheels = 85%
    Skid distance = 42 ft (12.8 m)
    Grade = +4%

Apply Formula 9–30 to calculate the crash vehicle's drag factor.

Formula 9–30 (f-adjustment formula)

$$f = \mu n \pm m$$

where f = adjusted drag factor
     μ = coefficient of friction on level surface
        (Note here that for a level surface,
        $\mu = f$)
     n = % braking efficiency
     m = grade

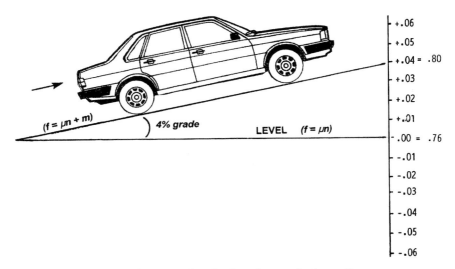

Figure 9–24. An example of a drag factor, f value, adjustment.

Calculation

$$f = (.76 \times 0.85) + .04$$

$$f = .64 + .04$$

$$f = .68$$

Using the circumstances set out above, an example of how the f-adjustment formula can be applied *inside* a formula, e.g., under a radical (in this case Speed from Skid Marks Formula 9–28), follows:

Formula 9–28

English

$$S = \sqrt{30D\ (\mu n \pm m)}$$

$$S = \sqrt{(30 \times 42) \times (.76 \times .85 + .04)}$$

$$S = \sqrt{1260 \times .686}$$

$$S = \sqrt{864.36}$$

$$S = 29 \text{ mph}$$

SI

$$S = \sqrt{254D\ (\mu n \pm m)}$$

$$S = \sqrt{(254 \times 12.8) \times (.76 \times .85 + .04)}$$

$$S = \sqrt{3251 \times .686}$$

$$S = \sqrt{2230.32}$$

$$S = 47 \text{ km/h}$$

Note: In this example, a plus (+) grade is used. In the case of a minus (–) grade, substitute minus (–) for plus (+) in the formula, but otherwise follow the same calculation procedures.

Example 2 (Downgrade adjustment)

A crash vehicle skidded to a stop on a roadway having a minus (–) 05% grade. Test vehicle drag factor skid tests conducted on a nearby *level* surface yielded a drag factor (f) value of .61 for the level surface. Both vehicles had 100% braking efficiency.

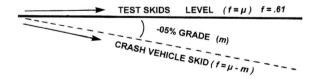

Figure 9–25. An example of an f value downgrade adjustment.

Crash Investigation Data

Test Vehicle
 Braking efficiency = 100%
 Test grade = level
 Test drag factor = .61

Crash Vehicle
 Braking efficiency = 100%
 Grade = –05%

In this example, the crash vehicle skidded on a minus (–) grade; therefore, use minus (–) in a modified adjustment formula (Formula 9–30A) to calculate its drag factor.

Formula 9–30A

$$f = \mu - m$$

where f = adjusted drag factor
 μ = coefficient of friction on level surface
   (Note here that for a level surface,
   $\mu = f$)
 m = grade

$$f = .61 - .05$$

$$f = .56$$

Example 3 (Upgrade adjustment)

A crash vehicle skidded to a stop on a roadway having a positive (+) 05%. Drag factor tests with a test vehicle conducted on a nearby *level* surface yielded a drag factor (f) value of .61. Both vehicles had 100% braking efficiency.

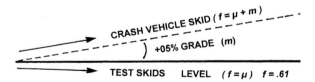

Figure 9–26. An example of an f value upgrade adjustment.

Crash Investigation Data

Test Vehicle
 Braking efficiency = 100%
 Test grade = level
 Test drag factor = .61

Crash Vehicle
    Braking efficiency $= 100\%$
    Grade $= +05\%$

In this case, the crash vehicle skidded on a plus (+) grade; therefore, use plus (+) in a modified adjustment formula (Formula 9–30B) to calculate its drag factor.

Formula 9–30B

$$f = \mu + m$$

where $f =$ adjusted drag factor
     $\mu =$ coefficient of friction on level surface
       (Note here that for a level surface,
       $\mu = f$)
     $m =$ grade

$$f = .61 + .05$$
$$f = .66$$

Example 4

A crash vehicle skidded to a stop on a minus (–) 05% grade. Drag factor skid tests with a test vehicle were performed nearby, but on a plus (+) +03% grade, resulting in a drag factor of .74. Both vehicles had 100% braking efficiency. In order to calculate the crash vehicle's drag factor, the test vehicle's drag factor must first be reduced to that for a level surface.

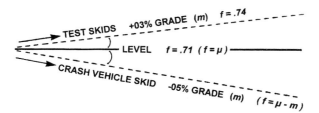

Figure 9–27. An example of f value upgrade and downgrade adjustments.

Crash Investigation Data

Test Vehicle
    Braking efficiency $= 100\%$
    Test grade $= + 03\%$
    Test drag factor $(f) = .74$

As a fist step, apply Formula 9–30C to calculate a level surface coefficient of friction μ for the test vehicle:

Formula 9–30C

$$\mu = f - m$$

where $\mu =$ coefficient of friction
     $f =$ drag factor for test vehicle
     $m =$ grade

$$\mu = .74 - .03$$
$$\mu = .71 \text{ (level)}$$

Recall here that for a level surface $\mu = f$

$\therefore f = .71$ for the level surface

In this case, the crash vehicle skidded on a minus (–) grade; therefore use minus (–) in a modified adjustment formula (Formula 9–30A) to calculate its drag factor.

Formula 9–30A

$$f = \mu - m$$
$$f = .71 \text{ (level)}$$
$$f = .71 - .05$$
$$f = .66 \text{ (crash vehicle adjusted drag factor)}$$

Note: In this example, and bearing in mind that both vehicles had 100% braking efficiency, an alternative method of calculating the crash vehicle's drag factor can be employed by simply reducing the test vehicle's drag factor of .74 by .08 (the factor of 0.08 being the combined difference in grade between the test skids and the crash vehicle skid) and carrying out a calculation as shown below.

Formula 9–30D

$$f_c = f_t + m$$

where $f_c =$ drag factor (crash vehicle)
     $f_t =$ drag factor (test vehicle)
     $m =$ grade

$$f_c = .74 - (.03 + .05)$$
$$f_c = .74 - .08$$
$$f_c = .66$$

INFLUENCES ON BRAKING SKID DISTANCE

9.084 Certain conditions and factors influence the distance tires will slide or skid on a roadway surface.

Some of these have a noticeable effect; others have a negligible effect and need not be considered in speed estimate calculations. This points out the very important requirement that when determining the drag factor for a crash vehicle, test conditions and factors duplicate as closely as possible those prevalent at the time of the crash. Roadway conditions and factors can be broken down as follows, but they, however, are not limited to these:

• *Roadway surface.* Mud, snow, ice, and wet surfaces, and hot bituminous surface are important in relation to stopping distances.
• *Tire chains.* Tire chains tend to increase the drag factor in mud, snow, or on ice. However, they tend to lessen the drag factor on hard, paved surfaces.
• *Studded tires.* Studded tires have a noticeable effect on stopping distances on most surfaces. On glare ice, studded tires on all wheels reduce stopping distances by about one-half of the distance required of studded tires on rear wheels only. On dry or wet asphalt surfaces, studded tires make virtually no difference. On both wet and dry concrete surfaces, studded tires cause an important increase in stopping distances.
• *Tire tread.* Negligible effect for stopping distance on most ordinary dry, clean surfaces. An important factor, however, on a wet surface or a surface having loose material, loose ice, or unpacked snow, where a tire with a good grooved tread will stop a vehicle more quickly than one with a smooth tread face.
• *Smooth tread face (e.g., worn).* On a hard, icy surface, a smooth tread face will most often have better stopping efficiency than a good grooved tread. This is because of the greater amount of tire face that is in contact with the surface, giving better overall traction. An exception to this, however, are tires that are specially designed for such surfaces.
• *Tire type.* Whether they be radial, bias-ply, or belted can be a factor in pre-lockup stages when the tire is still rolling. Once the tire is locked up and sliding, however, the type becomes an insignificant factor.
• *Tire air pressure.* An insignificant factor. Except in the case of a totally deflated tire, e.g., a blowout, tire air pressure makes very little difference in the stopping distance other than on ice, where a low pressure tire provides somewhat better traction because of the tire's wider than normal gripping surface or contact area with the roadway.
• *Wind direction and velocity.* Normally, these are insignificant factors. An exception is, of course, high-velocity winds such as those found under hurricane conditions.
• *Vehicle weight.* Vehicle weight is an important factor before brake lockup. Heavy-weight vehicles require slightly longer for brakes to lock up than do light-weight vehicles. During this distance, skid marks may not be visible, but may in many cases appear as an impending skid mark. Nevertheless, there are tremendous retarding forces at play during this pre-lockup time, causing loss of speed even though there may not be any visible skid marks. The stopping distances for both heavy and light vehicles, measured from the point at which the wheels lock up after the brakes are applied to the actual stop point, are approximately the same, however.

Hydroplaning

9.085 Hydroplaning may occur on a water-filmed roadway surface, particularly when the tire grooves are too shallow to disperse surface moisture effectively, causing the tire to lift from the road and ride on the film of water. Hydroplaning, which occurs only with front tires, and which pushes aside water for the trailing tires, takes place at a certain critical speed and diminishes or virtually eliminates vehicle control. When hydroplaning takes place, coefficient of friction essentially becomes non-existent, steering control is lost, and if brakes are applied, stopping must be done with only the rear tires until the speed drops below the critical hydroplaning speed when the front tires once again contact the roadway surface and normal braking can again resume.

9.086 According to Collins[1] the speed at which a tire will hydroplane depends on several things: (a) depth of the water must be between 0.2 and 0.3 in (0.5 and 0.7 cm); (b) roadway surface texture must be smooth so that water will stand easily on the roadway; (c) roadway must have a small crown; (d) tire must have a smooth tread; (e) tire inflation pressure–the lower the pressure, the more readily a tire will hydroplane. Since most automobiles use inflation pressures between 16 and 30 psi, their critical hydroplaning speeds are between 41 and 57 mph (65 and 71 km/h). Trucks and buses use tire inflation pressures of between 50 and 90 psi, and their tires will not hydroplane until they reach speed of between 73 and 98 mph (117 and 157 km/h).

9.087 A general guide to determining hydroplaning speed is governed by tire inflation pressure, using the following formula:

Formula 9–30E

English	*SI*

$$S_h = 10.35 \sqrt{p} \qquad S_h = 6.36 \sqrt{p}$$

where S_h = hydroplaning speed
   p = tire inflation pressure in psi (kPa)

For a more in-depth hydroplaning speed analysis, the following manual is recommended: Navin, Frank: *Reconstructing Truck Accidents from Tire Marks: Determining Truck Speed at Rollover.* Institute of Police Technology and Management, University of North Florida, Jacksonville, Florida, 2005, pp. 129–133.

9.088–9.089 reserved.

ROADWAY COEFFICIENT OF FRICTION (DRAG FACTOR) GUIDE

9.090 The Roadway Coefficient of Friction (Drag Factor) Guide, Table 9–02, incorporates the results of many tests conducted by different persons and organizations. There are many factors that nevertheless influence such results. When the table is used, it is recommended that speed calculations be made using the extreme drag factors at either end of the range and at least one arbitrary drag factor in the middle of the extremes. Such calculations will give the investigator a good idea of the upper and lower speed limits involved, as well as a probable average of these.

Table 9–02
POSSIBLE COEFFICIENTS OF FRICTION (DRAG FACTOR) FOR VARIOUS ROADWAY SURFACES

Concrete				
	Well-worn	*Smooth from use*	*New, Fresh pavement*	
Dry	.50 – .75	.60 – .75	.70 – 1.20	
Wet	.35 – .60	.45 – .70	.50 – .80	
Asphalt				
	Excess tar, Bleeding	*Well-worn*	*Smooth from use*	*New, Fresh pavement*
Dry	.35 – .60	.45 – .75	.55 – .80	.65 – 1.20
Wet	.25 – .55	.40 – .65	.40 – .65	.45 – .80
Gravel				
		Loose	*Packed, Well traveled*	
		.40 – .70	.50 – .85	
Ice				
	Cold, Frost	*Warm, Wet*		
	.10 – .25	.05 – .10		
Snow				
	Loose	*Packed*		
Cold, Dry	.10 – .25	.25 – .55		
Wet	.30 – .50	.30 – .60		

Large, Commercial-Type Vehicles

As a general rule, you should base drag factors for use with large, commercial-type vehicles on a range of 70 - 78% of the above drag factors. Source: Rivers, R.W.: *Training and Reference Manual for Traffic Accident Investigation.* Institute of Police Technology and Management, University of North Florida, Jacksonville, Fl, 3rd ed, 2004. Reproduced by permission.

NOTE: The values shown in this table are for information purposes only. They provide a starting point for the investigator to determine, through proper testing, the actual coefficient of friction for the surface(s) the investigator is concerned with.

Part 2

SPEED DETERMINATIONS

SPEED FROM SKID MARKS

9.091 When brakes are applied and a tire skids during wheel lockup, the temperature at the tire-roadway contact point becomes sufficiently high as to melt the tar of an asphalt roadway, drawing the tar to the roadway surface, leaving a visible, dark mark along the tire's path of travel. This mark is known as a *positive skid mark*, and allows an investigator to determine and measure most, if not all of the distance traveled during wheel lockup. However, it should be understood that on many surfaces, a vehicle will have had its brakes applied for a considerable distance in excess of that which can be measured from a visible dark skid mark. After brakes are applied and during the wheel pre-lockup phase, the skid mark may appear as a faint cleaning action–known as an *impending* or *incipient* skid mark. During daylight hours, a clearer view of an overall skid mark can be had using polarized sunglasses and the sun at the back (See Figs. 7–52 and 9–16 and Para. 8.053).

9.092 On softer surfaces, such as asphalt or oily surfaces, a skidding tire may pull up small, thin needle-like sticky material, known as *stippling*. This usually occurs in the dark or positive portion of the skid mark. In the case of a very hard surface, such as on cement or concrete, in addition to the impending skid mark and even after lockup, the mark may appear as a cleaning action throughout–not necessarily leading into the common identifying positive skid mark. Additionally, during full-wheel lockup on such hard surfaces, the tire tread may abrade, leaving residue on the roadway surface. These residues (stippling and abrade debris) are normally short-term evidence inasmuch as they can easily be displaced by passing traffic, inclement weather conditions, and so on.

9.093 After brakes are applied and during the pre-lockup stage where a complete impending skid mark may or may not be visible, there are considerable retarding forces at work causing a decrease in speed prior to the point where a positive skid mark becomes visible (see Fig. 9–12C). Therefore, in speed from skid mark calculations, it is evident that when the skid mark measurement is taken from somewhere at the beginning of or in the impending skid mark area, or at the beginning of the positive skid mark, the calculated speed will be a *minimum speed* at which the vehicle was traveling at the time the brakes were applied. It is important, therefore, when skid mark measurements are made, every effort should be made to include as much as possible of any impending skid mark in the overall skid mark length in order to provide a more accurate speed of the vehicle at the time the brakes were applied.

9.094 In order to calculate speed from skid marks (known as skid-to-stop or slide-to-stop speeds), the following points must be known:

a. Skid distance
b. Drag factor (adjusted when required)
c. That the vehicle did not strike a substantial object while sliding to a stop.

Skid Mark Measurements

9.095 Measurements should be made of all skid marks, the primary purpose of which is to determine and to record as accurately as possible how far the vehicle skidded (see also Para. 1.054). Factors and procedures in making skid mark measurements include:

a. *Markers.* Markers may be used to show specific locations along a skid mark or to identify any point of interest at the scene, e.g., the beginning and end of an impending skid mark, or the beginning and end of a positive skid mark. When photographs are to be taken at the scene, they should be taken before the placement of any marker in order to avoid the possibility of argument in court that the photograph is not a true representation of what was there at the time of the investigator's arrival (see examples of markers in Fig. 7–34.)

b. *Accuracy.* Do not guess the length of any skid mark or any other distance. Always use a tape or other accurate measuring device (see Tolerances, Para. 1.055 and Table 1–02). Make measurements to at least the closest 6 in (15 cm), and closer if possible. Use an easily understood and explainable recording format for the measurements taken at the scene from which a scale diagram may later be prepared to assist in the reconstruction of the accident, and to be able to present the measurements in a professional, factual manner in any subsequent legal proceeding.

c. *Measurement Procedures.* There are various types of skid marks, each of which sometimes require special consideration in making their measurements:

   i. *Straight Skids.* In a straight-line skid, the measurement should be made from the beginning of the skid mark to its very end. When skid marks overlap (see Para. 7.087 and Fig. 7–53), the total length of the skid will be the length of the overlapping skid marks from the start of the mark made by the rear tires straight through the end of the marks made by the front tires—*minus the length of the vehicle's wheelbase.* If upon investigation at the scene, the vehicle is still located at the end of the skid marks, the total skid distance will be from the start of the skid marks to the rear wheels of the vehicle [see also sub-para. (k) following].

   ii. *Curved Skid Mark.* Measure a curved skid mark by letting the measuring device follow the path of the skid mark around its curve. A skidding vehicle may often drift to the lower side of a roadway, giving the appearance of a curved skid mark. **Important**: Do not confuse a curved skid mark with a yaw mark. (See Fig. 7–36B where there is a combination: a yaw mark followed by a skid mark.)

   iii. *Spin Skid Marks.* Spin skid marks are sometimes difficult to measure. It is often better to measure the length of the skid by following the center-of-mass path throughout the entire spin, rather than measuring the actual path of each tire mark. As a rule-of-thumb, however, when a measurement of the center-of-mass path is to be measured as the skid distance, it can be considered to be the distance in a straight line from the center-of-mass point where the spin begins to the center-of-mass point where the vehicle comes to rest at the end of the spin. Notwithstanding a measurement is taken between center-of-mass points; whenever possible, measurements should also be taken of the actual tire mark paths for record purposes.

   Alternative. As an alternative, the distance of the path followed by each wheel in a spin skid on the roadway may be measured and an average of the skid mark distances then used as the skid distance.

d. *Use of Longest Skid Mark in Straight Skids.* In a straight skid, the longest skid mark may be used as the skid distance when it has been established that all wheels locked up at about the same time. It can then be assumed that the longest skid mark is the total distance that the vehicle skidded. Nevertheless, measure and record the lengths of all skid marks separately for record purposes (see Fig. 9–17).

e. *When All Wheels Do Not Lock Up or There Are Varied Skid Mark Lengths.* When all wheels do not lock up at the same time, or when there are considerable differences in skid-mark lengths, measure all skid marks separately. In these circumstances, the average length of the skid marks may be used as the skid distance, the result of which provides a conservative measurement of the actual skid distance (see Fig. 9–17.)

f. *Commercial Vehicle Dual-Wheel Skid Marks.* A dual wheel will cause two side-by-side skid marks, which should be measured as a single skid mark. When one of dual-wheel skid marks is longer than the other, the longer mark should be used as the skid distance; if the two marks do not begin and end at the same place, the length of the skid for that dual wheel should be measured from the first indication of a skid mark to the last indication of a skid mark, regardless of which of the two side-by-side tires left the first or last mark (see Fig. 7–58A.)

g. *Gap or Intermittent Skid Marks.* Intermittent skid marks appear with gaps between them. These gaps occur when wheels are locked up, released and then re-locked through braking action. Each blank space or gap between intermittent skid marks is usually a minimum of 15 ft to 20 ft (5 m to 7 m) in length, depending upon the speed of the vehicle and the driver's reaction time. Measure each individual mark (excluding the blank spaces) as a single skid and use their sum as the total skid distance (see Para. 7.091 and Fig. 7–57).

h. *Skip Skid Marks.* Skip skid marks are most often caused by a (1) locked wheel on an unloaded or lightly loaded trailer, particularly a semi-trailer; and (2) a locked wheel striking a hole or a bump in the roadway. The blank spaces between the skid marks are usually not longer than 3 ft (1 m). Measure skip skid marks as one continuous skid mark from the beginning of the first skid mark to the end of the last skid mark for each wheel (see Fig. 7–58B).

i. *Offset Skid Marks.* Measure the entire length of the skid mark, including the offset. When using the length of a skid mark for speed calculation purposes and when the skid mark is offset because the vehicle was struck while sliding, the vehicle's energy loss during its skid may not necessarily include that portion involving the offset mark. Under these circumstances, measure the length of the actual skid mark and the offset separately (see Fig. 7–54).

j. *Motorcycle Skid Marks.* Measure each skid mark separately.

k. *Various-Surface Skid Marks.* When a skid mark traverses different kinds of roadway surfaces, use the following as general guidelines in measuring the skid distances:

    i. Measure the skid distance on each surface separately because of different drag factor (*f*) values.

    ii. If the skid distance on the first surface is less than the length of the wheelbase, consider that skid distance to be part of the following surface.

    iii. If the skid distance on any one surface is less than the length of the wheelbase,

consider that skid distance to be part of the skid distance on the preceding surface, and use the drag factor of the preceding surface also for this part of the skid.

    iv. In the case of a straight, overlapping skid mark, measure from the beginning to the end of the marks, but subtract the length of the wheel base from the length of the skid on the last surface [see also Para. 9.095(c)(i)].

Slide (Skid)-to-Stop Speed Calculations

9.096 Formula 9–31 is a basic equation used to calculate the speed of a vehicle based on skid marks. If the procedures outlined in this chapter relating to determining drag factor and measuring the length of skid marks are followed, the calculated speed will be the vehicle's minimum speed at the beginning of the skid marks. Recall that there are many circumstances requiring that the drag factor be adjusted before using it in a speed formula, such as in the cases of grade or braking deficiencies, most often determined through a close examination of skid marks and/or a mechanical inspection. An examination of the roadway will determine the need for a grade or superelevation calculation (see also Para. 1.054, and under Drag Factors, Paras. 9.041–9.083).

Formula 9–31

English	*SI*
$S = \sqrt{30Df}$	$S = \sqrt{254Df}$

where S = minimum speed in mph (km/h) at the beginning of the skid marks
      D = length of skid in feet (meters)
      f = drag factor (adjusted when required)

The numbers 30 and 254 are constants.

For the derivation of this formula, see Formula 9–28 under Paragraph 9.066.

Example

A vehicle skidded 144 ft (44 m) to a stop on an asphalt surface. The drag factor was calculated to be 0.75. The vehicle's minimum speed at the beginning of its skid marks would have been:

English	SI
$S = \sqrt{30Df}$	$S = \sqrt{254Df}$
$S = \sqrt{30 \times 144 \times .75}$	$S = \sqrt{254 \times 44 \times .75}$
$S = \sqrt{3240}$	$S = \sqrt{8382}$
$S = 56.92$	$S = 91.55$
$S = 56$ mph	$S = 91$ km/h

9.097 A statement is made in Paragraph 9.094(c) that the investigator should know that when using the slide-to-stop Formula 9–31, the vehicle did not strike a *substantial* object. Notwithstanding this statement, Formula 9–31 can be used to calculate an initial *low speed* of a vehicle that skids up to a point where it strikes a substantial object and stops as the result of the collision. The speed will, of course, be based on a shorter length of skid marks than that which there would have been should the vehicle not have struck the object. Therefore, the speed calculated will be less than the actual minimum speed at the beginning of the skid marks. In this type of calculation, it can be safely said that the actual minimum speed of the vehicle was something in excess of the speed calculated. A pedestrian or similar-type object is not generally considered a substantial object for these purposes. There are many energy-loss equations that can be used to determine the actual speed when a substantial object is struck, such as a collision between two vehicles. The most common calculation procedure in these instances is the use of *Momentum*, which is outside the scope of this manual. The procedure is, however, fully explained in: *Technical Traffic Accident Investigators' Handbook. A Level 3 Reference, Training and Investigation Manual* (2nd ed.) by R.W. Rivers (Springfield, IL: Charles C Thomas, 1997, pp. 257–316.

Speed Calculation When Skid is on Different Types of Roadway Surfaces

9.098 When a vehicle skids to a stop over different types of roadway surfaces, the initial speed at the beginning of the skid marks can be calculated as follows:

Example 1

A vehicle skidded 96 ft (29 m) to a stop with its left wheels (side 1) on an asphalt surface having a drag factor of 0.75, and its right wheels (side 2) on a gravel surface having a drag factor of 0.40. The speed at the beginning of its skid was:

Formula 9–32

English	SI
$S = \sqrt{15\,(f_1 + f_2)\,D}$	$S = \sqrt{127\,(f_1 + f_2)\,D}$

where S = speed in mph (km/h)
f_1 = drag factor on side 1
f_2 = drag factor on side 2
D = skid distance

$S = \sqrt{15\,(f_1 + f_2)\,D}$	$S = \sqrt{127\,(f_1 + f_2)\,D}$
$S = \sqrt{15\,(.75 + .40)\,96}$	$S = \sqrt{127\,(.75 + .40)\,29}$
$S = \sqrt{15 \times 1.15 \times 96}$	$S = \sqrt{127 \times 1.15 \times 29}$
$S = \sqrt{1656}$	$S = \sqrt{4235.45}$
$S = 40.69$ mph	$S = 65.08$
$S = 40$ mph	$S = 65$ km/h

Note: For skid-to-stop speed calculations involving a continuous skid over different-type roadway surfaces, see Paragraphs 9.133 and 9.134.

Brakeless Utility Trailers

9.099 Some utility trailers that are under tow are not equipped with brakes. When calculating speed from slide-to-stop skid marks of the towing vehicle, the braking efficiency for use in calculating an adjusted drag factor must be considered in terms of (a) the braking efficiency of the towing vehicle and (b) the ratio between the weights of the two vehicles. For example, if a vehicle that weighed 3,000 lbs (1350 kg) with 100% braking efficiency was towing a trailer that was not equipped with brakes, and which also weighed 3,000 lbs (1350 kg), the braking efficiency in the adjusted drag factor formula would be (3,000/6,000) 0.50% (see Paras. 9.078 and 9.081).

Special Drag Factor Problems

9.100 The principles for calculating speed from sliding or skidding tires can be applied to any sliding object for which the sliding distance and the drag factor are known. Such objects include vehicles that overturn and slide on their side or roof, motorcycles that slide on their side, and pedestrians who are struck by a vehicle and then slide across a surface after disengagement with the vehicle. To duplicate the slide taken by a body, investigators often use a spring scale to pull an assistant along the roadway. In these circumstances, the assistant should be clothed in material similar to that worn by the accident victim. In these calculations, for purposes of determining the drag factor, the object is treated the same as a drag sled, i.e., by using Formula 9–24, $f = F/W$ (see Paras. 9.069 and 9.074).

9.101–9.105 reserved.

SPEED FROM VEHICLE YAW

9.106 For speed analysis purposes, *yaw* is a term used to identify a vehicle movement that involves the vehicle revolving around its center of mass, resulting in (a) an angular displacement about its vertical axis, most often causing a forward-sideways (sideslip) movement; or (b) a deviation from its intended path in a curve (fishtailing), such as when the rear of a vehicle rounding a corner sideslips and moves out from the intended curved path in which the vehicle has been moving (see Fig. 9–28).

9.107 At safe and reasonable speeds on curves, rear tires always track *inside* the front tires (see Fig. 9–28). At excessive speeds, however, the vehicle will go into yaw. Yaw actually begins when the rear tires start to sideslip to a greater extent than the front tires so that they then come to track *outside* the front tires. Yaw is considered *definite* once the paths of the rear tires have crossed over the paths of the front tires (see Figs. 7–36C and 9–29).

9.108 Each curve in a roadway has a radius that, when coupled with the roadway drag factor, has a *critical speed* above which a vehicle cannot safely negotiate the curve and it will go into yaw, sideslip and leave the intended path of travel, often leaving the roadway and overturning. When this occurs, it is most often because the vehicle's speed was too great for the curve, considering its radius and drag factor.

9.109 *Centrifugal force* (best explained by the term *inertia*) and *centripetal force* are two forces that act

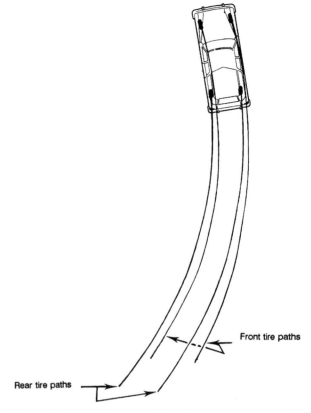

Figure 9–28. Under normal conditions, rear tires track inside front tires on a curve, i.e., each rear tire tracks inside its respective front tire. (Courtesy Rivers Traffic Consultants Ltd.)

upon a vehicle traveling around a curve. It is the centripetal force supplied by friction between the tires and the road surface (and determined by the type of surface and any superelevation present) that holds the vehicle on the roadway and allows it to follow the curve. At safe speeds, there is balance or equilibrium between the two forces; however, when the speed is too great, there becomes an imbalance between the forces, allowing centrifugal force (inertia) to overcome the centripetal force which can then result in the vehicle traveling in a straight path tangent to the curve rather than following its intended travel path in the curve. When this happens, the vehicle will sideslip or go into yaw and possibly spin or overturn (see also 9.008, 9.009).

9.110 When a roadway is icy or superelevation is nonexistent, a vehicle may leave the road at a much

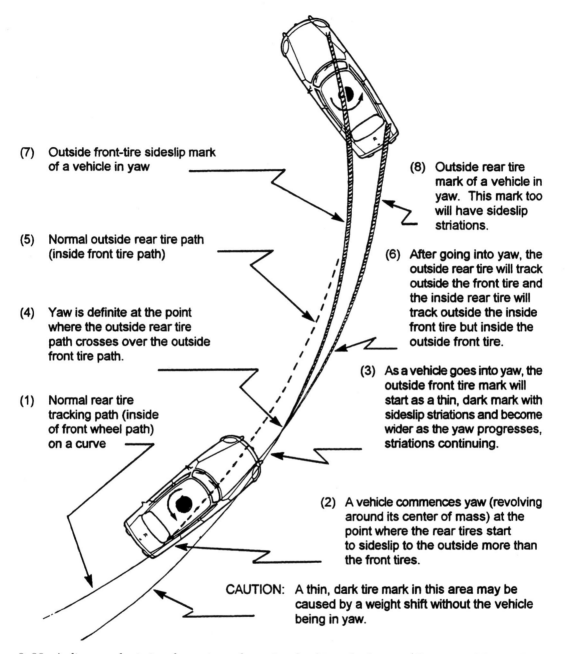

(7) Outside front-tire sideslip mark of a vehicle in yaw

(8) Outside rear tire mark of a vehicle in yaw. This mark too will have sideslip striations.

(5) Normal outside rear tire path (inside front tire path)

(4) Yaw is definite at the point where the outside rear tire path crosses over the outside front tire path.

(6) After going into yaw, the outside rear tire will track outside the front tire and the inside rear tire will track outside the inside front tire but inside the outside front tire.

(1) Normal rear tire tracking path (inside of front wheel path) on a curve

(3) As a vehicle goes into yaw, the outside front tire mark will start as a thin, dark mark with sideslip striations and become wider as the yaw progresses, striations continuing.

(2) A vehicle commences yaw (revolving around its center of mass) at the point where the rear tires start to sideslip to the outside more than the front tires.

CAUTION: A thin, dark tire mark in this area may be caused by a weight shift without the vehicle being in yaw.

Figure 9–29. A diagram depicting the various phases involved in vehicle yaw. (Courtesy of Rivers Traffic Consultants Ltd.)

lower speed and as the result of a much smaller inertial force than would otherwise be the case. Under slippery conditions, such as roadway having an icy surface, yaw speed calculations are not recommended.

9.111 As a vehicle travels into a curve, centrifugal force causes a weight shift onto the front outside (leading) tire. This lead tire may then leave a very narrow continuous dark mark, usually 1–2 in (2.5–5 cm) in width, known as a *weight-shift mark*. Often appearing before the vehicle goes into definite yaw, this mark has no forward-sideways striations and must not be confused with the beginning of a yaw mark (see Fig. 7–36D, and "Caution" in Fig. 9–29).

9.112 When centrifugal force acting on the lead tire is great enough to overcome the lateral resistance provided by the friction between the tire patch and the roadway surface, the tire will sideslip in the outward direction of the centrifugal force. The thin, dark weight-shift mark then begins to leave striations that are usually visible unless obliterated by passing traffic, wind, or rain. When the vehicle goes into yaw, this mark becomes a *yaw mark* of approximately 2 in (5 cm) width at the beginning stage. The extra weight and sideways thrust will cause the *front lead tire* to leave the most visible and distinguishable yaw mark. This front outside tire mark is normally used by investigators and is the one recommended to determine the radius of the yaw-mark curve. If, however, this mark is not adequate for some reason, use whatever other tire yaw mark from the vehicle that is visible and otherwise suitable for yaw radius measurements (see Fig.9–29), or improvise for radii measurements as shown in Figures 9–29, 9–30, 9–31, and 9–32.

9.113 The further the vehicle travels in yaw, the thin or narrow yaw mark initially left by the outer edge of a tire broadens to the width of the portion

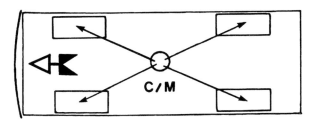

Figure 9–30. When a vehicle's center-of-mass path is used to determine a vehicle's speed in yaw, measurements must be made from the location of the center of the mass on the vehicle to the roadway contact area of each tire in the manner shown in this figure. All these measurements must in turn be related to the tire marks on the roadway by further measurements in order to plot the vehicle center-of-mass path. For practical investigation purposes, a vehicle's center of mass can be considered to be located at some point on the central axis, usually halfway between the front and rear axles.

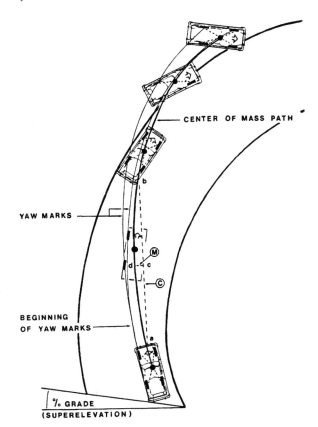

Figure 9–31. A method of plotting the radius of a yaw mark or the center-of-mass path for purposes of calculating the speed of a vehicle in yaw. Note: For record purposes, other tire marks found at the scene should also be included in the actual field measurements. However, in this example, possible marks from other tires have been excluded to simplify the explanation of yaw-mark and vehicle-path measurements.

of the tire tread that is in contact with the roadway. As this mark broadens, striation marks become and remain very prominent and are normally not lost to environmental factors.

Yaw Mark Measurements

9.114 The initial, thin sideslip mark from the lead tire, being the most prominent, is very important in an investigation (see Fig. 9–29). Most often this will be a front tire. It should be emphasized once again, however, that yaw is not considered to be definite until the point where the rear tire path crosses over the front tire path (see Para. 7.066 and Fig. 7–36C).

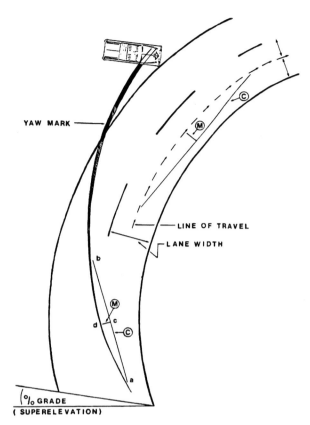

Figure 9–32. Methods of plotting the radius of a yaw mark, the center line, roadway, and normal path of travel, where: a-b = chord (C), c-d = middle ordinate (M).

For investigation purposes, this point should be used as the beginning of the yaw mark, particularly for radius measurement purposes. Three consecutive radius measurements along the yaw mark are recommended: (a) first measurement in the first one-third of the yaw mark, and (b) two subsequent ones taken further along the mark. Although under most circumstances, the first radius measurement is sufficient, two subsequent calculated radii can be used as evidence to show a decrease in size and consequently proof that the vehicle was slowing as it traveled along its path. If the two additional radii do not show a decrease in size, the mark should not be used for a yaw speed calculation.

IMPORTANT: Review once again, Paragraph 7.066 and Figures 7–36A, B, C and D.

9.115 To calculate the radius of a yaw mark, the following measurements must be made available (see Figs. 9–31 and 9–32):

    a. Length of the chord (C)
    b. Length of the middle ordinate (M)

9.116 The following procedures are recommended when measuring for a radius calculation (see Figs. 9–31 and 9–32):

    a. Use a chord of at least 30 ft (10 m). A short chord will compound any error made in measuring the middle ordinate.
    b. In the case of a yaw mark, ensure that all three measuring points, i.e., the two chord ends and the chord midpoint, are on the same edge (side) of the mark.
    c. Ensure that the middle ordinate is measured at a point midway between the ends of the chord, and at 90 degrees to the chord.

Speed Calculations Based on Vehicle Yaw

9.117 When a vehicle fails to safely negotiate a curve, the investigator should give consideration to the following two speed calculations:

    1. *Critical vehicle curve speed.* This is the speed at which a vehicle slides off the roadway when driven around a curve. This speed calculation is most often based on yaw marks.
    2. *Critical curve speed.* This is *the speed above which a vehicle will slide out of its lane of travel when driven around a curve, i.e., a speed at which the vehicle cannot stay in its intended path of travel.* This speed can be calculated by determining the radius of the center or middle line of the vehicle's proper or normal lane of travel. When necessary, the roadway center line or roadway edge may be used to calculate *indirectly* the radius of the center line of the lane or normal path of travel (See Figs. 9–31 and 9–32).

9.118 To calculate a critical speed, the following information is needed (see Figs. 9–31 and 9–32):

    1. The *radius* of the
       a. *Yaw mark* (if the speed is to be calculated from the yaw mark), or

b. *Center of mass path* (if the center-of-mass path is to be used for the calculation), or

c. *Center line of the proper lane of travel* of the vehicle (if the critical curve speed is to be calculated)

2. *Drag factor.* **Note**: If possible, drag factor skid tests should be conducted traveling in the same direction as the crash vehicle, alongside the yaw mark or as near as possible to the yaw mark. When a drag sled is used, it should be pulled across the yaw mark in the manner shown in Figure 9–22.

3. Roadway *superelevation*

Example (Using a Yaw Mark)

A vehicle traveled into a curve at a high rate of speed and sideslipped, leaving a yaw mark which measured 300 ft (90 m) in length. The first one-third (100 ft or 30 m) of the yaw mark was used and a chord 75 ft (23 m) and a middle ordinate of 3 ft (1 m) were measured. A .70 drag factor was obtained by conducting test skids alongside the yaw mark. The curve had a superelevation of +05%.

Step 1: Calculate the radius of the yaw mark by applying the following formula:

Formula 9–33

$$R = \frac{C^2}{8M} + \frac{M}{2}$$

where R = radius
C = chord
M = middle ordinate

The numbers 8 and 2 are constants used in calculating radius.

English	*SI*
$R = \dfrac{75^2}{8 \times 3} + \dfrac{3}{2}$	$R = \dfrac{23^2}{8 \times 1} + \dfrac{1}{2}$
$R = \dfrac{5625}{24} + \dfrac{3}{2}$	$R = \dfrac{529}{8} + \dfrac{1}{2}$
$R = 234.38 + 1.5$	$R = 66.125 + 0.5$
$R = 235.88$	$R = 66.625$
$R = 235 \text{ ft}$	$R = 66 \text{ m}$

Step 2: Calculate the critical vehicle curve speed from the yaw mark with:

Formula 9–34

English	*SI*
$S = 3.86 \sqrt{R (f \pm e)}$	$S = 11.27 \sqrt{R (f \pm e)}$

where S = speed in mph (km/h)
f = drag factor
e = superelevation
R = radius

The number 3.86 (SI 11.27) is a constant.

$S = 3.86 \sqrt{R (f \pm e)}$	$S = 11.27 \sqrt{R (f \pm e)}$
$S = 3.86 \sqrt{235 (.70 + .05)}$	$S = 11.27 \sqrt{66 (.70 + .05)}$
$S = 3.86 \sqrt{235 \times .75}$	$S = 11.27 \sqrt{66 \times .75}$
$S = 3.86 \sqrt{176.25}$	$S = 11.27 \sqrt{49.50}$
$S = 3.86 \times 13.27$	$S = 11.27 \times 7.03$
$S = 51.22$	$S = 79.22$
$S = 51 \text{ mph}$	$S = 79 \text{ km/h}$

9.119 If the path of a vehicle around a curve cannot be adequately established from yaw marks or if the marks appear confusing, an investigator may use the *critical curve speed.* The critical curve speed is much lower than the critical vehicle curve speed because it has a shorter radius. Since the vehicle had to be traveling at least at the critical curve speed in order to leave the roadway, determining this speed is frequently sufficient to prove that the vehicle was traveling at an excessive speed. The same procedures used to calculate speed based on a yaw mark *(critical vehicle curve speed)* can be used to calculate a *critical curve speed.*

9.120 To confirm the validity of a yaw mark speed calculation, the investigator may calculate the critical curve speed for the curve involved to determine whether or not the vehicle exceeded the speed at which it could have stayed in its lane of travel. The critical curve speed should be less than the yaw mark speed because of the shorter radius that will be used in the critical curve speed calculation.

9.121 Before using a mark as a yaw mark for a speed calculation, the investigator must know that:

1. The vehicle was in yaw, with the rear wheels tracking outside the front wheels (see Para. 9.107 and Fig. 9–28).

2. The vehicle was sideslipping. (Striations were present in the marks; see Paras. 9.111–9.113.)

3. There was no excessive acceleration.
Examine the angle of the striations made by either of the vehicle's driving wheels. If the striation marks appear as parallel spin marks caused by the tire tread of the wheels as it was rotating and are longitudinal to the wheel's direction of travel rather than at an angle to this direction, as would be the case if these marks were sideslip striations, suspect acceleration and do not use the tire mark for a yaw speed calculation.

4. There was no appreciable braking.
If there was braking, striations in the yaw mark will show a change of angle and what can be described as *hooks* at the ends of the striations. Additionally, braking will often cause the wheels on the lighter side (the side with the inside wheels) to lock up, leaving skid marks from that side of the vehicle.

5. All wheels were on at least similar-type surfaces.

9.122 A *side-scuff mark* is similar in appearance to a weight-shift mark that leads into a yaw mark. Such a mark is most often caused by an underinflated or overloaded tire and does not have the sideslip striations found in a yaw mark. A side-scuff mark will normally follow a path within the lane of travel of the vehicle and may continue on for great distances. This type of mark may occur at relatively low speeds and should not be confused with a high-speed sideslip or yaw mark. (See Para. 9.111 and the CAUTION included in Fig. 9–29.)

9.123 In the absence of definite yaw marks, the investigator should look for other factors that might

have caused the vehicle to go out of control. These include oversteering after a wheel has dropped off the edge of the pavement, the actions of an inexperienced driver, or a mechanical malfunction related to the vehicle.

9.124–9.125 reserved.

FALLS, FLIPS, AND VAULT SPEEDS

9.126 A vehicle may leave the highway for a variety of reasons in addition to its losing control in yaw. A vehicle may fall from a highway, such as when as traveling too fast in a curve; or it may vault or flip and vault from a highway when it strikes a substantial object, such as hitting a curb. In these cases, the vehicle's speed at the point of takeoff can be calculated if the following are known (see Figs. 9–33 and 9–34):

a. In the case of a fall, the angle of area leading up to point of takeoff.

b. *Horizontal* and *vertical* distances of the vehicle's center-of-mass travel from the *point of takeoff* to the *first point of landing* or *first touching of a surface.*

c. The landing is higher (+) or lower (–) than the point of takeoff.

d. That any bounce, roll, or skid after the vehicle first touches down on another surface is disregarded for purposes of the speed calculation. In some instances, the precise measurements of the center-of-mass location at the point of takeoff and the point of landing, is difficult to obtain. Therefore, for the purposes of this manual and fall and other airborne speed calculation investigations, the approximate

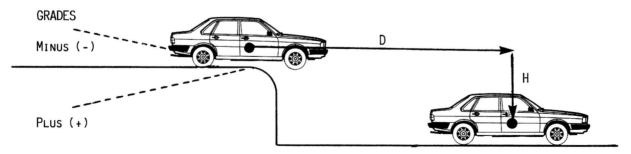

Figure 9–33. A fall.

location is considered sufficient. It is important, however, to obtain as precisely as possible the *horizontal* and *vertical* distances from the approximate location of the center of mass in a vehicle at the *point of takeoff* to its approximate location at the *first point of landing* or *first touching of a surface* in the manner shown in Figures 9–33 and 9–34.

Falls

9.127 A *fall* is a situation where a vehicle leaves the roadway and falls to a point below its point of takeoff. An example is when a vehicle fails to negotiate a curve and is projected off the highway, frequently over an embankment. Any *takeoff angle* (grade), plus or minus (±), of the roadway or area leading up to the point of takeoff must be known for a fall speed calculation. Takeoff angle is defined as the angle between the level plane and the plane of the grade on which the vehicle is positioned at the point of takeoff. This area may be level or have a positive (+) or negative (–) grade. A positive grade will give a positive takeoff angle; a negative grade will give a negative takeoff angle.

9.128 The principles relating to points of departure, i.e., the height (H), and the point of landing as set out herein for calculating speed based on falls for vehicles can also be applied to airborne objects other than vehicles, such as in the case of an item, e.g., luggage or freight, being carried on a vehicle that stops suddenly, causing the item to break loose, and which then lands some distance away. Another example is when a vehicle comes to an abrupt stop after striking a utility pole, causing debris or vehicle parts to disengage from the vehicle, which then land some distance away from the vehicle. In such instances, the speed determined for the projected item at the time it left the vehicle is also the speed of the vehicle at the time of such departure.

Note: Always remember that the grade of the takeoff point is not necessarily the roadway grade, but rather the grade of the path followed by the vehicle before it leaves the highway, e.g., a shoulder area.

9.129 If the takeoff area in a fall is level, use Formula 9–35:

Formula 9–35

English	*SI*
$S = \dfrac{2.73D}{\sqrt{H}}$	$S = \dfrac{7.97D}{\sqrt{H}}$

where S = speed at takeoff in mph (km/h) with zero grade
　　　 D = horizontal distance
　　　 H = vertical distance

Example (Fall with level takeoff area)

A vehicle veered off the highway. The immediate area leading up to the point where the vehicle left the highway was level, i.e., it had a zero grade. Measurements taken from the vehicle's center of mass at the point of takeoff to its center of mass at the first touching of the ground after takeoff revealed that the vehicle had traveled a horizontal distance (D) of 40 ft (12 m) and a vertical distance (H) of 10 ft (3 m) *below* the takeoff point.

Applying Formula 9–35, we can calculate the vehicle's speed at its point of takeoff as follows:

English	*SI*
$S = \dfrac{2.73D}{\sqrt{H}}$	$S = \dfrac{7.97D}{\sqrt{H}}$
$S = \dfrac{2.73 \times 40}{\sqrt{10}}$	$S = \dfrac{7.97 \times 12}{\sqrt{3}}$
$S = \dfrac{109.2}{3.16}$	$S = \dfrac{95.64}{1.732}$
$S = 34.55$	$S = 55.22$
$S = 34$ mph	$S = 55$ km/h

9.130 In a fall, when the immediate area leading up to the point of takeoff has a ± grade (m), use Formula 9–36:

Note: When the grade is positive (+), add it within the formula; when it is negative (–), subtract it within the formula. Formula 9–36 provides minimum speeds for takeoff angles up to ± 10%. For takeoff angles greater than ±10%, the speed calculation will be quite conservative, i.e., somewhat less than the actual speed.

Formula 9–36

$$S = \frac{2.73D}{\sqrt{H \pm (Dm)}} \qquad S = \frac{7.97D}{\sqrt{H \pm (Dm)}}$$

English   *SI*

where   S = speed in mph (km/h) at takeoff
    H = vertical distance of fall or rise
    D = horizontal distance
    m = grade (%)
The number English 2.73 (SI 7.97) is a constant.
    + Dm designates positive takeoff grade
    – Dm designates negative takeoff grade

Example   [A fall with minus (–) grade leading up to the point of takeoff (see Fig. 9–33).]

A vehicle failed to negotiate a curve in a highway, falling over an embankment. The immediate area leading up to the point of takeoff had a grade (m) of minus 8 percent (–0.08). The vehicle became airborne, first striking a point on a tree at a horizontal distance (D) of 40 ft (12 m) beyond and a vertical distance (H) of 10 ft (3 m) below the point of takeoff. Measurements were taken to the vehicle's center of mass at both points.

Applying Formula 9–36:

English   *SI*

$$S = \frac{2.73D}{\sqrt{H \pm (Dm)}} \qquad S = \frac{7.97D}{\sqrt{H \pm (Dm)}}$$

Note: In this case, the ± factor will be minus (–)

$$S = \frac{2.73 \times 40}{\sqrt{10 - (40 \times .08)}} \qquad S = \frac{7.97 \times 12}{\sqrt{3 - (12 \times .08)}}$$

$$S = \frac{109.2}{\sqrt{10 - 3.2}} \qquad S = \frac{95.64}{\sqrt{3 - .96}}$$

$$S = \frac{109.6}{\sqrt{6.8}} \qquad S = \frac{95.64}{\sqrt{2.04}}$$

$$S = \frac{109.6}{2.6} \qquad S = \frac{95.64}{1.428}$$

$$S = 42.15 \qquad S = 66.97$$

$$S = 42 \text{ mph} \qquad S = 66 \text{ km/h}$$

Note: If in this case the immediate area leading up to the point of departure, i.e., the grade, had been positive (+), the calculation procedures would be the same, except that the minus symbol (–) in the formula would be replaced with a plus symbol (+) and the subsequent calculation carried out accordingly.

Flips and Vaults

9.131   A *flip* and *vault* is a situation where a vehicle strikes a substantial object head-on or sideways, at a collision point below its center of mass, which causes it to stop, pivot and flip and vault through the air, landing some distance away. The takeoff angle for a vault will always be positive. The landing point can be either level with or higher or lower (±) than the point of takeoff.

9.132   The flip and vault formulae that follow are intended for an approximate takeoff angle of 45 degrees, which is adequate for most flip and vault speed calculations. When the actual takeoff angle is either greater or lesser than 45 degrees, speed calculations using these formulae will be conservative, i.e., somewhat less than what can be considered actual minimum speeds. Also, in these formulae, when landings are below the level of takeoff, the vertical distance *(H)* is considered to be *plus* (+) and must be added to the horizontal distance *(D)* inside the formula. When these landings are above the level of takeoff, the vertical distance *(H)* is considered to be minus (–) and must be subtracted from the horizontal distance *(D)* inside the formula.

Example 1   (Points of takeoff and landing are at the same level–see Figure 9–34A.)

A vehicle struck a substantial object, flipped and vaulted through the air. From the point of takeoff to the point of landing (measured between the centers of mass) was a horizontal, level distance of 46 ft (14m). The vehicle's speed at the point of take off can be calculated as follows:

Formula 9–37

English   *SI*

$$S = \sqrt{15D} \qquad S = \sqrt{127D}$$

or

$$S = 3.86 \sqrt{D} \qquad S = 11.27 \sqrt{D}$$

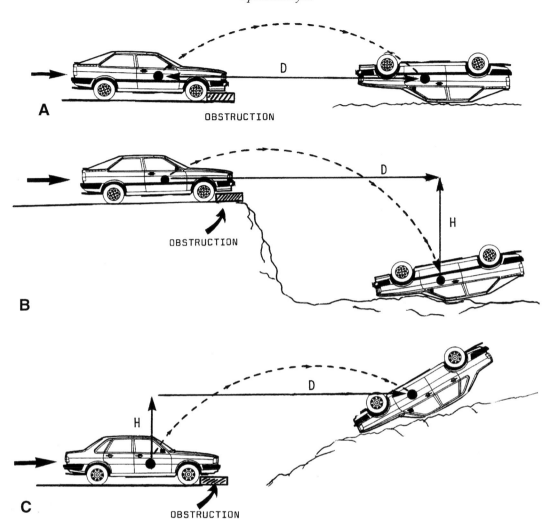

Figure 9–34. Examples of flips and vaults. *A* represents a flip and vault having a level takeoff and landing; *B* a flip and vault with a landing lower than the point of takeoff, and *C* a flip and vault with a landing that is higher than the point of takeoff.

where S = speed in mph (km/h) at takeoff
        D = horizontal distance between mass centers

Note: The formula here is shown in two different forms. Both are correct. The constant 15 (SI 127) simply represents the square of 3.86 (SI 11.27).

English	*SI*
$S = \sqrt{15D}$	$S = \sqrt{127D}$
$S = \sqrt{15 \times 46}$	$S = \sqrt{127 \times 14}$
$S = \sqrt{690}$	$S = \sqrt{1778}$

$S = 26.27$ $S = 42.17$

$S = 26$ mph $S = 42$ km/h

Example 2 (Landing higher or lower than point of takeoff–see Figures 9–34B and C)

Circumstances: Landing Lower Than Point of Takeoff. A vehicle struck a substantial object, flipped and vaulted through the air, landing at a horizontal distance of 46 ft (14 m) beyond the point of takeoff and 10 ft (3 m) below the level of takeoff. Applying Formula 9–38, the vehicle's speed at its point of takeoff can be calculated as follows:

Formula 9–38

English	SI
$S = \dfrac{3.86D}{\sqrt{D \pm H}}$	$S = \dfrac{11.27D}{\sqrt{D \pm H}}$

where S = speed in mph (km/h) at takeoff
   D = horizontal distance between center-of-mass positions
   H = vertical distance (rise or fall) between center-of-mass positions
Note: Use +H when landing is lower than takeoff; use –H when landing is higher than takeoff.

English	SI
$S = \dfrac{3.86 \times 46}{\sqrt{46 + 10}}$	$S = \dfrac{11.27 \times 14}{\sqrt{14 + 3}}$
$S = \dfrac{177.56}{\sqrt{56}}$	$S = \dfrac{157.78}{\sqrt{17}}$
$S = \dfrac{178.02}{7.483}$	$S = \dfrac{157.78}{4.123}$
$S = 23.72$	$S = 38.27$
$S = 23$ mph	$S = 38$ km/h

Because in the circumstances of this case, the landing is lower than the point of takeoff, we will use plus (+) in the formula. If in these circumstances, the landing would have been higher than the point of takeoff, we would use minus (–) in the formula and would have carried out the calculation accordingly.

COMBINED SPEEDS

9.133 When a vehicle skids only part-way to a stop because the skid is interrupted by another event (one from which an independent speed can be calculated), such as:

   a. Yaw
   b. Fall
   c. Flip and vault
   d. Continuous skid from one type of surface to another when each surface has a different drag factor [see also Various Skid Measurements, paragraph 9.095 (k)].

e. Crush, such as when the vehicle collides with a firmly-fixed utility pole or other object from which an energy loss speed can be calculated, but stops at the end of or because of the last event, the vehicle's initial speed, i.e., the speed at the beginning of the first event (the initial skid mark) can be calculated using the Combined Speed Formula, Formula 9–39.

It is important to understand that to calculate the initial speed at the beginning of the first event, the various calculated speeds involved *must not be added together*. Rather, they should be placed in the combined speed formula and the initial speed then calculated as the square root of the sum of the squares of the various individual speeds.

9.134 The most commonly-made use of the combined speed formula, Formula 9–39, is to establish the initial speed at the beginning of a skid mark when that skid precedes some other happening (event), as in a fall or flip and vault. Each event should be designated with a small subscript: S_1, S_2, S_3, and so on (see Para. 9.133, above).

Formula 9–39

$$S_c = \sqrt{S_1{}^2 + S_2{}^2 \ldots + S_n{}^2}$$

where S_c = speeds combined (initial speed, i.e., speed at the beginning of the first event, e.g., where skid marks start on the 1st surface)
   S_1 = speed calculated for the 1st surface
   S_2 = speed calculated for the 2nd surface or speed from the 2nd event, e.g., fall, flip and vault, collision with substantial object, etc.
   S_n = expanded to include additional speed (variables) as might be necessary to meet the circumstances of the case.

Note: When an individual, independent speed calculation in the combined speed formula is based on skid marks, the calculation must be carried out in the manner set out in Paragraph 9.096, as if that speed, e.g., S_1, S_2, and so on, were for a slide-to-stop speed.

SPECIAL SPEED PROBLEMS

Crush Speed Estimates

9.135 Speed calculations, such as those establishing speed in impacts with substantial objects, e.g.,utility poles, commonly referred to as crush speed calculations, are beyond the scope of this manual. There are, however, various computer-based programs that can be used to properly establish these crush-type speeds. In some cases, when during a skid, the vehicle impacts a substantial object, a rough estimate of the speed at the point of impact may be made by qualified people based on the resultant damage(s), and/or information obtained in other ways, e.g., from a witness who observed the vehicle's speed as it traveled up to and at the time of the impact. It must be cautioned, however, that such speed estimates by observer-witnesses are just that–purely estimates, and their reliability can be open to question.

Commercial Vehicle Crash Investigations

9.136 The procedures outlined in this manual are generally valid for investigation of all types of vehicle collisions. Passenger car collision procedures can be applied without difficulty in relation to small, light-type trucks, such as pick-ups and delivery vans. However, in a general sense, in-depth investigation and reconstruction of large, commercial-type vehicle crashes–those that have a laden unit weight that exceed 60,000 lbs (27,000 kg)–and particularly those involving a combination of units, require some procedures that are beyond the scope of this manual. These special procedures fall within the purview of and should be referred to qualified traffic crash reconstructionists who have the educational background and specialized training to investigate and reconstruct collisions in this very specialized area.

9.137 *Commercial Vehicle Speed Estimates.* Many modern commercial vehicles are equipped with on-board computers and/or tachographs that register and/or document the vehicle's speed at all times during travel. These instruments can be useful in determining speed at any time during the trip, and at the time of a crash. For further information on these instruments, see paragraphs 8.083–8.087.

9.138 For in-depth commercial vehicle crash investigation and reconstruction, it is recommended that the following manual be referred to: *Reconstructing Truck Accidents from Tire Marks: Determining Truck Speed at Rollover* by Frank Navin (Jacksonville, Florida, Institute of Police Technology and Management, University of North Florida, 2005).

REFERENCE

1. Collins, James C.: *Accident Reconstruction.* Charles C Thomas, Publisher, Springfield, Illinois, 1979, p. 167.

RECOMMENDED READING

Rivers, R.W.: *Technical Traffic Accident Investigators' Handbook. A Level 3 Reference, Training and Investigation Manual* (2nd ed.). Charles C Thomas, Springfield, Illinois, 1997, pp. 257–316.

Rivers, R.W.: *Speed Analysis for Traffic Accident Investigation* (2nd ed.). Institute of Police Technology and Management, University of North Florida, Jacksonville, Florida, 1997.

Rivers, R.W.: *Seat Belt and Air Bag Systems Manual for Traffic Crash Investigation and Reconstruction.* Institute of Police Technology and Management, University of North Florida, Jacksonville, Florida, 2001.

Rivers, R.W.: *Basic Physics, Notes for Traffic Crash Investigators and Reconstructionists.* Charles C Thomas, Springfield, Illinois, 2004. Excerpts have been used with permission of the author and/or the publisher.

Chapter 10

EVIDENCE MANUAL
MOTORCYCLE CRASH INVESTIGATION

Albert T. Baxter

INTRODUCTION

10.001 The motorcycle has existed for over one hundred years. Initially a gasoline-powered bicycle, the motorcycle has evolved into a means of transportation and recreation around the world. In the 1970s, motorcycle sales peaked to approximately seven million where they have remained relatively level at that number to the present time (2005). The vehicles handle differently than a passenger car. They have greater acceleration and braking performance, and are more agile. To operate a motorcycle requires much more skill than a passenger car. As a trade-off for performance, the rider has no steel beams or metal protecting his entire body from injury or weather, nor as protection in the event of a crash. Having only two wheels for stability, the motorcycle is very sensitive to road and weather conditions. Also, the rider must endure being exposed to wind, rain, heat, cold, and debris.

TYPES OF MOTORCYCLES

10.002 There are three basic classes of motorcycles for the riding public:

1. Street
2. Off-road
3. Combination

Street. Street or on-highway motorcycles are designed to be equipped with all applicable safety equipment and state light and registration requirements.

Off-Road. Off-road motorcycles are built to withstand the rigors of operating cross-country, through woods, in deserts, and over hills. They are usually not equipped with lights or turn signals. The tires and suspension and gearing are engineered to meet the demand of the terrain.

Combination. The combination motorcycle is a cross between the street and off-road classes. Although equipped with all required safety equipment, the combination motorcycle has a modified suspension and tires to permit riding off-street.

10.003 Within the three classes, there are different styles and applications for the rider. For example, street motorcycles can be further divided into the following styles:

- *Touring.* Designed for long distance riding and carrying passengers and gear. This style is usually operated by older males.
- *Cruiser.* Designed for short trips. This style exhibits pull back handlebars, a step seat, slightly extended fork, and is customized to the owner's taste.
- *Sport.* Designed with colorful aerodynamic body panels, this high performance machine has a short rake angle for responsive steering and high power-to-weight ratio. It is usually operated by young males.
  - *Standard.* The basic familiar design for street riding and commuting.
  - *Scooter.* Small, low-powered machine, designed for low-cost transportation. Frequently

found in resort areas and around schools and colleges.

- *Moped.* A low-powered bicycle-style vehicle. Many states include mopes as part of their motorcycle laws.
- *Off-Road Motorcycles.* The machines are classified for their intended purpose.
  - *Enduro* (Endurance). Riders operate long distances over an off-road course for a specified period of time.
  - *Motocross* (Cross-country). Riders ride courses on earth race tracks or over short distances.
  - *Although All Terrain Vehicles* (ATV) are included in this category, they are actually a four-wheel vehicle with different handling characteristics.

CONTROLS

10.004 Five controls are standardized in accordance with Federal Motor Vehicle Safety Standard #123, being the rear brake, front brake, throttle, clutch, and gearshift levers. Many of the other controls are also placed in the same locations by all manufacturers. Generally, they are located as follows (see Fig. 10–9):

- *Rear Brake Pedal.* Located on the right side of the motorcycle near the operator's footrest. For a rear-disc brake unit, it is connected to a master cylinder. In the case of a drum brake, a rod or cable is used to operate the brake.
- *Front Brake Lever.* Located on the right hand-grip, this lever controls the front brake. If the

Figure 10–01. Touring style motorcycle.

Figure 10–02. Cruiser style motorcycle.

Figure 10–03. Sport style motorcycle.

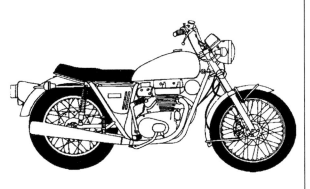

Figure 10–04. Standard style motorcycle.

Figure 10–05. Scooter.

Figure 10–06. Moped.

Figure 10–07. Combination style motorcycle.

Figure 10–08. Off-road style motorcycle.

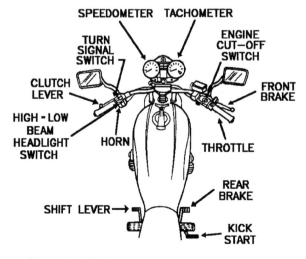

Figure 10–09. Standard motorcycle controls.

front wheel is equipped with a disc brake system, there will be a master cylinder with brake line(s) to the front calipers. If the front brake is a drum, it will have a cable with an adjustable thumb-wheel for cable tension.

• *Throttle.* Located on the right handgrip, the throttle controls the amount of fuel to the carburetor(s). Twisting it counterclockwise or to the rear increases engine speed. The system usually contains a return spring on the carburetor which is activated when the grip is released or grip pressure is reduced. The spring returns the throttle setting to the idle position. Some motorcycles can be equipped with an after-market cruise control device to lock the throttle into a desired position, or an electronic cruise control can also be provided by the manufacturer.

• *Clutch Lever.* Located on the left handlebar grip. When the lever is pulled toward the operator, it disengages the clutch. The lever may be connected to a cable or a hydraulic system.

• *Gear Shift Lever.* Located at the left footrest, it can be a single lever or a rocker-type lever operated by both the heel and toe of the operator.

• *Horn.* A push-button located on the left handlebar grip; pushed in to be activated.

• *Turn Signal Switch.* Located on the left handlebar. It may be a push-button type, which must be held in to keep the signal activated, or it may be a rocker-type switch. The switch is moved either right or left, depending upon the signal direction intended. Some turn signal systems are self-canceling, where the signal stops after a specific amount of time. Others must be manually moved back to center to cancel the signal.

• *High and Low Beam Headlamp Switch.* A rocker switch, located on the left handlebar grip. It is designed to be pressed to activate the high beam.

• *Engine Cut-Off Switch.* Located on the right handlebar grip, and is usually red in color. It is strictly a safety device for stopping the engine in an emergency. When activated, it grounds electrical power to the engine's coil, causing an immediate stall.

• *Speedometer and Odometer.* This instrument is standard on all street motorcycles. It may also contain an indicator light for neutral gear lever position (usually green), turn signal operation (yellow), and headlamp high beam use (blue). The odometer records the actual mileage accumulated on the motorcycle. Some motorcycles also have a trip odometer to measure specific mileage. This odometer can be reset after each trip or segment of travel for which mileage is desired. Some motorcycles use a digital speedometer and tachometer mounted in a dashboard configuration.

• *Tachometer.* This is an indicator of the engine revolutions per minute in a specific gear. It is an optional piece of equipment and does not appear on lower-priced models. Beyond a certain *rpm* value, the numbers on the face plate are in red to show that the engine revolution limit is being exceeded, or there may be a line on the face plate to mark the limit. If this point is exceeded, engine damage could result.

• *Kick Starter.* Located on the right side of the motorcycle, to the rear of the operator's footrest. It is a lever that folds out for use and can be retracted against the side of the motorcycle when not in use. Most motorcycles are not equipped with this device. Rather, many start the engine by using an electrical motor activated by push button type switch on the right handlebar grip.

• Some motorcycles may have additional equipment for operator use, such as a citizen-band radio, radio and tape deck, various additional switches, and so on.

Two exceptions apply to FMVSS #123 Motorcycle Controls. First, motorcycles built specifically for police use do not have to comply with the standard if requested by the purchasing agency. Second, on scooters with automatic transmissions where no shift lever is required, waivers to the standard have been granted to manufacturers to move the rear brake application from the right side pedal to the left handlebar end.

The investigator should consult the owner's manual for the motorcycle under investigation for additional details and descriptions.

BASICS

10.005 Three very important aspects of any traffic crash investigation are:

1. Roadway
2. Vehicle(s) involved
3. Operator

Roadway Conditions. The roadway (including weather conditions) plays an important part in the safe operation of a motorcycle. It should be examined for debris; surface contamination, such as sand, ice, and/or oil; and defects in the surface itself, such as holes, grooves, edge drop-off, etc. (see Figs. 7–12 and 7–13). Any interference with the tires, such as these, can upset the balance of the motorcycle. Since the motorcycle offers a small profile, examine for objects or other vehicles which may have obstructed the view of the driver(s) involved.

Vehicles. The motorcycle itself should be examined and all identifying information recorded. This examination should include (*review* also Chapter 8, Vehicle Examinations):

a. Vehicle identification number (VIN)
b. Tire size
c. Final drive type (chain, shaft, or belt)
d. Engine type and style
e. Lighting system
f. Accumulated mileage
g. Brakes
h. Tire tread-depth
i. Controls and levers (examined for any mechanical malfunction that could have contributed to the crash)
j. Complete description of damages sustained, including a match-up with damage evidence on other vehicle or object involved

Operator. The operator should be examined and interviewed to determine why and how the crash took place:

a. Type and color of clothing
b. Style of helmet
c. Type and extent of injury (see also Para. 4.055 and Fig. 4–01)

DYNAMICS

10.006 The motorcycle, by nature of its design, is a single-track vehicle. If viewed from above, the rear tire tracks behind the path of the front tire in a single line. The motorcycle is also an articulated vehicle.

The front fork and handlebar assembly pivot around the leading section of the frame which contains the engine, transmission, seat, and rear swingarm and tire. While in operation, in essence, there are three masses to the unit: (1) front fork and tire, (2) rear section, and (3) these two combined with the rider and/or passenger. At rest, the motorcycle is very unstable, requiring a sidestand or centerstand for support. At slow speeds, the stability improves but requires the skill of the rider to maintain balance. Only at speeds above 15–20 mph (24–30 km/h) does the motorcycle become a relatively stable platform.

10.007 The motorcycle can be maneuvered much faster than the passenger car. As a single track vehicle, the motorcycle must be leaned to execute a turn at speeds greater than 15–20 mph (24–30 km/h). The amount of lean depends on the speed of the motorcycle and radius of the turn. Initially, the front tire is turned slightly opposite to the direction of the intended turn. This causes the front wheel to out-track the path taken by the rear wheel. Turning the front wheel reduces the wheelbase length on the side of the intended turn. This coupled with the gyroscopic effect of the front and rear wheels, coupled with the lean of the rider causes the motorcycle to roll about its center of mass. The rider reverses the process to recover from the turn and bring the motorcycle upright. An important part of the design and ultimate handling of the motorcycle are two components called rake and trail.

While it does appear that a motorcycle has better maneuverability, in an emergency swerve situation, when compared with an automobile, the motorcycle does not change lane positioning any faster than the car. In fact, the distance is slightly longer.[1]

Rake

10.008 Rake is the angle at which the front fork is set forward on an imaginary line perpendicular to the ground through the steering head. If the rake is too small or is non-existent, the front wheel will have little resistance to any steer input—a hazardous condition for a moving motorcycle. The rake angle found on production motorcycles varies between 21° and 36°. The smaller value is found on sport motorcycles where rapid directional response is required under racing conditions. The latter value is found on cruiser/touring motorcycles. A large rake angle results in better straight line stability at highway speeds. Steering becomes difficult and requires additional operator skill at slow speeds. On occasion, motorcycle owners alter the stock rake angle by rewelding the steering head angle to the frame. This creates the *chopper* appearance (a long fork and extended front wheel). If the owner only places extensions on the slider tube, the fork is extended, but the actual rake angle at the steering head is not affected. This scenario creates a very sensitive steer input and shifts the mass center of the motorcycle slightly to the rear (see Fig. 10–10.)

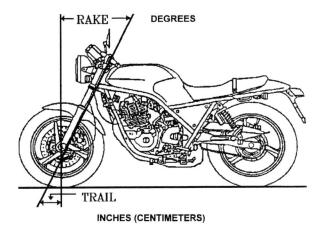

Figure 10–10. Rake.

Trail

10.009 Trail is the measurement of the imaginary rake angle line where it bisects the ground and an imaginary vertical line between the front wheel axle center and the contact patch. It is directly related to the rake angle. The value is always positive, and varies between 3 and 6.5 in (7.6 cm and 16.5 cm) on production models. The trail acts as a resistant force on the turning movement, imposing a self-centering action on the front wheel. This action increases as speed increases which in turn increases the stability of the motorcycle. Because the front tire contact patch is behind this imaginary point where the steering axis intersects the ground plane, the resulting resistance allows additional time to move the fork to execute a turn.

Turning

10.010 Except at very slow speeds, a motorcycle must be placed into a lean to execute a turn. New riders are reluctant to lean the motorcycle while making a turn due to the fear of falling over. Studies have show that the novice rider will only lean the motorcycle 15° to 25° while experienced riders can lean the motorcycle as much as 40°. Failure to lean sufficiently can cause the motorcycle to run off the curve or cross into an oncoming traffic lane. The time for the motorcycle to fully enter a lean condition is approximately 1.5 to 2 seconds and does not vary by the radius of the turn or speed of the motorcycle. The basic formula can be used to calculate the curve radius as well as the critical speed for the curve. To determine the amount of lean required to successfully negotiate a curve, the follow formula may be used:

Formula 10–01

English	*SI*
$L\phi = \dfrac{S^2}{15\,R}$	$L\phi = \dfrac{S^2}{127\,R}$

where $L\phi$ = Tangent value of lean angle
S = speed in mph (km/h)
R = radius of curve
15 (127) = a constant

Example:

If a motorcycle is to negotiate a turn radius of 200 ft (61 m) at 40 mph (64 km/h), how far would the rider have to lean the machine?

English	*SI*
$L\phi = \dfrac{40^2}{15 \times 200}$	$L\phi = \dfrac{64^2}{127 \times 61}$
$L\phi = \dfrac{1600}{3000}$	$L\phi = \dfrac{4096}{7747}$

$L\phi = 0.53$ Inverse tangent = 28°

Note: Lateral acceleration factor = tangent value of the lean angle. To obtain the lean angle in degrees, use the reverse tangent key on your calculator.

10.011 To determine the radius of a curve that a motorcycle can successfully negotiate at a given speed and lean angle (or with a given lateral acceleration factor), use the following formula:

Formula 10–02

$$R = \frac{V^2}{f_L\, g}$$

where R = radius of curve in ft (m)
V^2 = velocity in ft/s (m/s)
f_L = lateral acceleration factor
g = acceleration due to gravity

Example

A motorcycle, traveling at 50 mph or 73.3 ft/s (80 km/h or 22.2 m/s) on a road surface having a lateral acceleration factor of 0.65, would require a minimum curve radius, calculated as follows, to successfully negotiate the curve:

English	SI
$R = \dfrac{73.3^2}{.65 \times 32.2}$	$R = \dfrac{22.2^2}{.65 \times 9.81}$
$R = \dfrac{5372.89}{20.93}$	$R = \dfrac{492.8}{6.37}$
$R = 256$ ft	$R = 77$ m

Table 10–1

Converting Velocity (ft/s or m/s) to Speed (mph or km/h)

In the formulae that follow, the number 1.466 (SI 0.278) is a constant. Alternatively, the constant .682 (SI 3.6) may be used, involving multiplication in place of division.

English	SI
$S = \dfrac{V}{1.466}$	$S = \dfrac{V}{.278}$
or	
$S = V \times .682$	$S = V \times 3.6$

Converting Speed (mph or km/h) to Velocity (ft/s or m/s)

English	SI
$V = S \times 1.466$	$V = S \times .278$

where S = speed in mph (km/h)
V = velocity in ft/s (m/s)

10.012 When the curve radius and lateral acceleration factor are known, the following formula can be used to calculate the maximum speed at which a motorcycle can negotiate the curve:

Formula 10–3

$$V = \sqrt{f_L\, g\, R}$$

where V = velocity
R = radius
f_L = lateral acceleration factor
g = acceleration due to gravity

Example

An operator leans his motorcycle 20° (lateral acceleration factor = .355) to negotiate a curve having a radius of 300 ft (91 m). The maximum speed at which this curve can be negotiated by the operator can be calculated as follows:

English	SI
$V = \sqrt{.355 \times 32.2 \times 300}$	$V = \sqrt{.355 \times 9.81 \times 91}$
$V = \sqrt{3429.3}$	$V = \sqrt{316.9}$
$V = 58.56$ ft/s	$V = 17.8$ m/s
$S = 58.56 \times .682 = 39.9$	$S = 17.8 \times 3.6 = 64$
$S = 40$ mph	$S = 64$ km/h

ACCELERATION

10.013 When compared to the standard passenger vehicle, the motorcycle: (a) has exceptional acceleration performance due to the engine power to the overall weight ratio; (b) requires less room to maneuver in traffic; and (c) when properly used, can brake more efficiently than the passenger vehicle. It is usually one of these three situations that causes difficulty for the inexperienced operator. For example, some motorcycles can accelerate from 0 to 60 mph (96 km/h) in just under 4 seconds. This performance can help a rider to extricate himself from a potential crash and can also cause a hazardous situation. Due to the smaller size and profile of the motorcycle and its corresponding performance, an automobile driver may not see the motorcycle until a collision is inevitable or he may misjudge its approach speed.

10.014 Motorcycle acceleration is calculated in the same manner as for other vehicles. In determining motorcycle acceleration, a combination of time, distance, and speed in feet (meters) per second is used. (For complete coverage of acceleration and acceleration-solving problems, see Paras. 9.026–9.034.) Acceleration tests can be conducted using the involved machine or a similar-type motorcycle. If this is not practical, data can be obtained from various road-test sources, such as those available from motorcycle manufacturers, data published almost annually by traffic crash investigation schools or organizations, and scientific papers (e.g., SAE publications). *Caution: If a road test is conducted, it should be done only by a professional rider, capable of controlling the machine under the variety of circumstances that might be encountered.* Normal acceleration factors (see Formula 9–20–14) using an average application of engine power, range between 0.15 and 0.4. These values are dependent on engine horsepower and size along with the operational considerations of the rider. As with any other vehicle, the motorcycle starts out with a high acceleration rate or factor, but as time and distance progress, the rate/factor decreases.

10.015 *Acceleration Factor.* An acceleration factor is the ratio of an acceleration rate to the acceleration of gravity. For the purposes of this manual, the term acceleration factor is denoted by the symbol f_a.

Formula 10–04

$$f_a = \frac{a}{g}$$

where f_a = acceleration factor
   a = acceleration rate
   g = acceleration due to gravity

10.016 *Acceleration Rate.* To determine a motorcycle's uniform acceleration rate from a stop, apply Formula 10–05:

Formula 10–05

$$a = \frac{V}{t}$$

where a = acceleration rate
   V = velocity
   t = time

Example

A motorcycle accelerates from a stop to 40 mph or 58.68 ft/s (64 km/h or 17.79 m/s) in 6 seconds. Its acceleration rate is:

English	*SI*
$a = \dfrac{V}{t}$	$a = \dfrac{V}{t}$
$a = \dfrac{58.68}{6}$	$a = \dfrac{17.79}{6}$
a = 9.78 ft/s/s	a = 2.96 m/s/s

In this case, the acceleration factor (f_a) can be calculated as follows:

$$f_a = 9.78/32.2 = .30 \qquad f_a = 2.96/9.81 = .30$$

10.017 *Distance.* The distance traveled when the acceleration rate and time are known can be calculated using Formula 10–06:

Formula 10–06

$$D = .5 \, at^2$$

where D = distance
   a = acceleration rate
   t = time in seconds

Example

A motorcycle that accelerates at a rate of 9.78 ft/s/s (2.96 m/s/s), will travel the following distance in 6 seconds:

English	*SI*
$D = .5 \, at^2$	$D = .5 \, at^2$
$D = .5 \times 9.78 \times 6^2$	$D = .5 \times 2.96 \times 6^2$
$D = .5 \times 9.78 \times 36$	$D = .5 \times 2.96 \times 36$
D = 176 ft	D = 53.6 m

10.018 An acceleration rate can be changed into an acceleration factor by dividing the rate by the acceleration due to gravity, i.e. 32.2 ft/s/s (9.81 m/s/s). This factor can then be placed in the minimum speed formula to determine speed over a specified distance.

Example

From circumstances outlined under Para. 10.016.

English	SI
$f_a = 9.78/32.2 = .30$	$f_a = 2.96/9.81 = .30$

Formula 10-07 (Minimum Speed Formula)

$$S = \sqrt{30\,D\,f_a}$$

where S = minimum speed
D = distance
f_a = acceleration factor

English	SI
$S = \sqrt{30 \times 176 \times .30}$	$S = \sqrt{254 \times 53.6 \times .30}$
$S = \sqrt{1584}$	$S = \sqrt{4084.32}$
$S = 39.79$	$S = 63.9$
$S = 40$ mph	$S = 64$ km/h

10.019 *Passing Potential.* To establish the passing potential of a motorcycle, the acceleration factor/rate over the distance is required. Some motorcycle magazines publish what is called a *roll-on (R/O)* acceleration tests. This is where the motorcycle travels in a known speed and gear and then is accelerated over a measured distance and time. If this information is not available, it will require tests with a similar motorcycle. This information is required to determine if a motorcycle can initiate a passing maneuver within a certain distance or time. For example, many tests have shown that between 45–70 mph (72–112 km/h), the average acceleration factors are: In 3rd gear = .33; 4th gear = .26; 5th gear = .21; 6th gear = .20.

To determine the speed of a motorcycle after a certain period of time, under uniform acceleration, use Formula 10-8:

Formula 10-08

$$V_f = V_o + (at)$$

where V_f = final velocity
V_o = initial velocity
a = acceleration rate
t = time

Example

A motorcycle traveling at 40 mph or 58.68 ft/s (64 km/h or 17.8 m/s) accelerates at a *uniform* rate of 9.7 ft/s (2.9 m/s) for 4 seconds. Its speed at the end of the 4 seconds would be:

English

$$V_f = 58.68 + (9.7 \times 4) = 97.48 \text{ ft/s}$$

$$S = 97.48 \times 0.6818 = 66 \text{ mph}$$

SI

$$V_f = 17.8 + (2.9 \times 4) = 29.4 \text{ m/s}$$

$$S = 29.4 \times 3.6 = 105 \text{ km/h}$$

10.020–10.025 reserved.

10.026 *Acceleration Factor During Acceleration.* Use Formula 10–9 to calculate the acceleration factor for a motorcycle during acceleration:

Formula 10-09

English	SI
$f_a = \dfrac{D - (V_o\,t)}{16.1\,t^2}$	$f_a = \dfrac{D - (V_o\,t)}{4.9\,t^2}$

where f_a = acceleration factor
V_o = initial velocity
D = distance
t = time
16.1 (4.9) = ½ acceleration due to gravity

Example

A motorcycle is given 4 seconds to accelerate from 40 mph (64 km/h) to travel 300 ft (91 m). What acceleration factor is required to perform this maneuver?

English	SI
$f_a = \dfrac{300 - (58.68 \times 4)}{16.1 \times 4^2}$	$f_a = \dfrac{91 - (17.8 \times 4)}{4.9 \times 4^2}$
$f_a = \dfrac{300 - 234.72}{257.6}$	$f_a = \dfrac{91 - (17.8 \times 4)}{78.4}$
$f_a = \dfrac{65.28}{257.6}$	$f_a = \dfrac{19.8}{78.4}$
$f_a = 0.25$	$f_a = 0.25$

10.027 *Passing Distance.* When the acceleration factor, time, and speeds are known, the passing distance required to carry out this maneuver can be calculated as follows:

Formula 10-10

English	SI
$D = [(V_o t) + (16.1\,f_a\,(t^2)]$	$D = [(V_o t) + (4.9\,f_a\,(t^2)]$

where D = distance
  V_o = velocity
  t = time
  f_a = acceleration factor
16.1 (4.9) = ½ acceleration due to gravity

Example

A motorcycle traveling at 40 mph (64 km/h), accelerates for 4 seconds with an acceleration factor of 0.25. The distance covered during this period of time is:

English

$$D = [(V_o t) + (16.1\ f_a\ (t^2)]$$

$$D = [(58.68 \times 4) + (16.1 \times .25 \times 4^2)]$$

$$D = [(58.68 \times 4) + (16.1 \times .25 \times 16)]$$

$$D = 234.72 + 64.4$$

$$D = 299\ \text{ft}$$

SI

$$D = [(V_o t) + (4.9\ f_a\ (t^2)]$$

$$D = [(17.8 \times 4) + (4.9 \times .25 \times 4^2)]$$

$$D = [(17.8 \times 4) + (4.9 \times .25 \times 16)]$$

$$D = 71.2 + 19.6$$

$$D = 91\ \text{m}$$

10.028 *Initial Speed.* When the final speed, distance covered, and the acceleration factor are known, the initial speed can be calculated as follows (see also Formula 9–20–19):

Formula 10–11

$$V_f = \sqrt{V_o^2 - (2aD)}$$

where V_f = velocity after deceleration
  V_o = initial velocity
  a = acceleration rate [calculated from acceleration factor, i.e., $a = f_a \times 32.2$ $(f_a \times 9.81)$]
  D = distance
  2 = constant

Example

A motorcycle traveling at an initial speed of 40 mph (64 km/h) accelerates for 4 seconds with an acceleration factor (f_a) of 0.25. The final speed after

traveling a distance of 300 ft (91 m) can be calculated as follows:

English

$$V_f = \sqrt{V_o^2 - (2aD)}$$

$$V_f = \sqrt{58.68^2 + (2 \times .25 \times 32.2 \times 300)}$$

$$V_f = \sqrt{3443.34 + 4830}$$

$$V_f = \sqrt{8273.34}$$

$$V_f = 90.95\ \text{ft/s}$$

$$S = 62\ \text{mph}$$

SI

$$V_f = \sqrt{V_o^2 - (2aD)}$$

$$V_f = \sqrt{17.8^2 + (2 \times .25 \times 9.81 \times 91)}$$

$$V_f = \sqrt{316.84 + 446.35}$$

$$V_f = \sqrt{763.19}$$

$$V_f = 27.62\ \text{m/s}$$

$$S = 99\ \text{km/h}$$

BRAKING

10.029 Stopping a motorcycle to avoid a collision requires the full application of both the front and rear brakes by the operator. The front brake accounts for 60–70% of the total braking capability of a motorcycle. The rider *must* utilize the front brake to decelerate the motorcycle efficiently. The weight shift encountered during heavy front and rear brake application reduces the load carried on the rear tire. If the front braked is applied with substantial force, a forward weight shift takes place. The fork and front suspension compress, and the rider's weight shifts forward from the inertia. As a result of this weight shift from the rear wheel, it ceases rotation faster and the rear suspension extends. This weight shifting forward places more force on the front wheel. This pressure effectively allows the front wheel to continue rotating.

10.030 If no front brake is used, the rear section of the motorcycle, due to its articulated construction, will begin to swing left or right. The rider will usually overinitiate a steering correction to compensate for the swing. This will leave a curving skid mark on the road surface. If the rear brake is released when the front and rear wheels are out of alignment, the rear tire will regain traction and snap back into alignment. This can throw the rider from the machine. This effect, called *high-siding*, can occur either in a straight or curved section of a road under hard application fo the rear brake with no front brake use.

10.031 The operator's failure to properly use a motorcycle's full braking potential is a continuing problem. If both brakes were used, many collisions could be avoided. The speed estimate from a skidding motorcycle can be determined as effectively as from an automobile. In an emergency braking situation, when the full braking potential of a motorcycle is utilized, there is the ability to stop as quickly, if not more quickly than for an automobile. This is, of course, the rider's dependent skill on maximum brake application without locking the front wheel. The motorcycle operator has tactile feedback in weight shift, lever pressure application as well as sound from the tire under maximum deceleration. Unless equipped with anti-lock brakes, automobile drivers cannot establish the pending lock of all four wheels simply by pedal application pressure or sound from the tires.

10.032 The design of the motorcycle will not allow it to remain in an upright position for any distance with a locked front wheel. It will crash. Side force capability of the front tire while skidding will be minimal, therefore the tire will rapidly slide out to one side or the other in about 0.2–0.3 seconds, too fast for an operator to make a steering correction. Novice riders ignore the front brake and usually overbrake and skid the rear tire. In an emergency situation, the rider instinctively presses down on the rear brake pedal. If only the rear brake is locked and sliding, the actual rate of deceleration is low and the rider does not experience the sensation of slowing. As a result, the rider, sensing no deceleration, will lay the motorcycle onto its side in a last-ditch attempt to avoid the collision. The motorcycle then has less deceleration as friction between metal parts and the road surface is lower than rubber from the tires.

REACTION TIME

10.033 The operator's reaction time is relatively faster on a motorcycle when compared to that of an automobile driver. The motorcycle operator's right foot is in immediate proximity to the rear brake pedal. This position allows immediate application of the pedal. The front brake lever on the right handgrip is within easy reach. The time required for the fingers to move from the handgrip to the lever is also very short, generally considered to be in the range of 0.5 second in traffic conditions.

MECHANICAL CONSIDERATIONS

10.034 *Gear Shift Lever Position.* An important part of motorcycle acceleration during passing is to establish the gear ratio used when the passing maneuver was executed. This is why it is imperative not to disturb the gear shift lever before an examination of the machine and the circumstances surrounding the incident has been completed by a qualified examiner. If the gear shift lever is inadvertently moved, a range of possible speeds based on gear ratios will have to be calculated in order to determine time and distances available to the motorcycle operator to execute a passing maneuver.

10.035 It is important for the investigator to know that if the motorcycle has been customized, the front wheel and brake system could be altered. In some cases, in order to customize the appearance, the front brake is removed and replaced by a straight axle; or a smaller brake system might installed to meet minimum vehicle equipment requirements. This practice can result in the overall effective braking capability of the motorcycle being reduced.

10.036 *Integrated Brake Systems.* An integrated brake system uses partial application of the front brake (on a two-rotor front wheel system) when the rear brake is activated. Tests of motorcycles equipped with this system have shown that there is 14% greater deceleration values on dry roads when the rear brake pedal alone is used in stopping. ABS, on the other hand, showed an improvement from 8–14% on dry surfaces and even higher on wet or slippery surfaces. These test results indicate that integrated braking improves the stopping ability of motorcycles and braking is most effective when the front brake is used to its maximum capability. However, since both front and rear brakes are activated using the pedal, on soft-loose surfaces (sand, gravel), unanticipated front wheel lock can occur.

10.037 *Anti-Lock Brake Systems.* Anti-lock braking systems (ABS) have been on production automobile for several years and now appear on some production motorcycles. ABS technology is designed to provide an emergency safety system in low traction conditions or where traction changes rapidly. It is not designed to allow a motorcycle operator higher entry speeds into curves or to shorten a safe following distance. ABS brake application while in a lean mode can cause a *slide-out* or failure to maintain lane placement. ABS systems on automobiles allow the driver to input steering actions under a heavy braking demand. This is primarily due to the vehicle having a dual track design and maximum braking traction on the road surface. This reduces the possibility of the automobile going into yaw. However, the motorcycle, by virtue of being a single-track vehicle, cannot change steering input under maximum braking application.

The ABS-equipped motorcycle will brake in a straight line. Some facts to consider regarding ABS systems on motorcycles are:

   a. A braking application must be hard in order to activate an ABS system. A gradual increase of brake pressure results in a longer stopping distance. The ABS system functions best under emergency application.

   b. ABS will not help the operator who does not undertake a collision avoidance maneuver or fails to use brakes.

   c. Even if only the rear brake is applied, it will prevent a lockup of the rear wheel and a possible slide-out but will render only 30–40% of the motorcycle's braking capability.

   d. Some motorcycles have an integral ABS system that functions similar to the linked system. Operation of either the pedal or lever activates brakes on both front and rear.

10.038. *Linked (or combined) Brake Systems.* This is a proprietary system designed by Honda and found on several of their models. Depending on the design generation, application of the front brake lever also activates caliper piston movement on the rear brake, and vice-versa. Use of either braking control points activates brake action on both the front and rear wheels.

Note: See also motorcycle examination information under Paragraph 10.005, and Vehicle Examinations, Chapter 8.

SLIDE-TO-STOP SPEED

10.039 An adjusted basic slide-to-stop speed formula (Formula 10–12), can be used to calculate a *minimum* speed from a skidding or sliding motorcycle.

Formula 10–12 (Adjusted Minimum Speed Formula)

$$S = \sqrt{30\ D\ f\ f_b} \qquad S = \sqrt{254\ D\ f\ f_b}$$

where S = minimum speed
      D = distance of skid or slide
      f = drag factor
      f_b = braking percent adjustment factor

Example

A motorcycle that had a braking efficiency of 0.30 skidded 125 ft (38.1 m) to a stop on a roadway that had a known drag factor of 0.70. It minimum speed at the beginning of the skid can be calculated as follows:

$$S = \sqrt{30 \times 125 \times .70 \times .30} \qquad S = \sqrt{254 \times 38.1 \times .70 \times .30}$$

$$S = \sqrt{787.5} \qquad\qquad S = \sqrt{2032.25}$$

$$S = 28\ mph \qquad\qquad S = 45\ km/h$$

10.040 *Sliding.* Immediately before or after a collision, a motorcycle may fall on its side and/or the operator may be thrown off the machine; both of which may slide over the roadway surface. Tests conducted over the past several years indicate that the following drag factor ranges may be used to calculate speed at the starting point where these take place:

Clothing:	
Leathers (not tumbling)	0.60–0.70
Polyesters, other synthetics (not tumbling)	0.70
Motorcycle:	
Standard street, light pavement scratching	0.35–0.45
Significant pavement scratches, $^{1}/_{4}$ in deep	0.45–0.55
Sports Motorcycles:	
With plastic intact or if equipped with frame sliders	0.30–0.35

Note: See also motorcycle examination information under Paragraph 10.005, and Vehicle Examinations, Chapter 8.

To determine a speed in these cases, simply enter the appropriate drag factor into Formula 10–07 and carry out the calculation.

Formula 10–07 (Minimum Speed Formula)

$$S = \sqrt{30\,D\,f} \qquad\qquad S = \sqrt{254\,D\,f}$$

where S = minimum speed
D = distance of slide
f = drag factor

10.041 *Determining Speed from Engine Revolution Values.* A determination of the gear-shift lever position during the examination of the motorcycle can provide information to develop a range of speeds available which can be used for particular gear position. During normal operation, the majority of riders, when slowing, downshift from higher gear to the next lower gear and use the engine as part of the braking process. There are also riders who will utilize brakes only, downshifting when at or near a stop.

10.042 During an emergency situation, the rider does not have time to downshift and utilize engine braking. Only the brakes of the motorcycle are used until it has stopped or becomes involved in a collision. Establishing the gear position will allow a determination of range of speeds for that position. That is why it is so important to establish the gear position before the motorcycle is moved after a crash.

10.043 To reach a speed determination from the gear position, three items from the motorcycle are required:

1. *The position of the gear shift lever indicating which gear it is in.* Information on the gear ratio can be obtained from manufacturer's data, a shop repair manual, owner's manual, or from published road tests of the motorcycle.
2. *The radius of the rear wheel of the motorcycle.* The radius can be measured or recorded from the tire sidewall information.
3. *An engine revolution per minute (RPM) value.* The RPM value is the most difficult value to obtain—an interpretation by the investigator is required. If equipped with a tachometer, the upper limit of the RPM can be recorded

from the redline or warning position on the gauge. However, very few motorcycles are operated approaching this zone unless involved under maximum acceleration. There are ranges of engine RPM values for each gear position. The minimum RPM value will be the stalling point of the engine or where the engine lugs and there is hesitation in the driveline. The maximum RPM is slightly higher than the redline value. There is some point in engine RPM during normal acceleration where the engine begins to labor. This is normally where a gear shift would be initiated. It is at this value, during normal operation, where the rider would change to the next higher gear to reduce the RPM to a more comfortable level. Each motorcycle will have a different shift point. Use of the RPM level in this area in calculation will provide a reasonable estimate of speed. An estimate for the shift point would be approximately 1000–1,500 rpm's higher than the value for the motorcycle in its highest gear while traveling at approximately 60 mph (100 km/h).

10.044 Formula 10–13 can be used to calculate the speed of a motorcycle involved in a crash when the (a) rpm, (b) rear wheel radius, and (c) final gear ratio can be determined. This might apply to any point before the crash, or at the time of the crash should the speedometer needle be jammed from impact.

Note: Be sure to use the overall gear ratio—not the internal or transmission ratio—in the formula.

Formula 10–13

English

$$\text{mph} = \frac{\text{engine rpm} \times \text{rear wheel radius}}{\text{final gear ratio} \times 168}$$

SI

$$\text{km/h} = \frac{\text{engine rpm} \times \text{rear wheel radius}}{\text{final gear ratio} \times 265.1}$$

Example

A small version of a Yamaha sport-style motorcycle was involved in a crash. Investigation revealed the following unit information:

a. Powered by a 49cc engine that develops a maximum power of about 1350 rpm, giving a maximum speed of about 45–50 mph (72–80 km/h).
b. Rear wheel radius = 6 in (15.24 cm).
c. Traveling in 3rd gear.
d. Owner's manual indicates that the final drive ratio for 3rd gear is 1.42.

English

$$\text{mph} = \frac{\text{engine rpm} \times \text{rear wheel radius}}{\text{final gear ratio} \times 168}$$

$$\text{mph} = \frac{1350 \times 6}{1.42 \times 168}$$

$$\text{mph} = \frac{8100}{238.56}$$

$$\text{mph} = 33.95$$

$$\text{mph} = 34$$

SI

$$\text{km/h} = \frac{\text{engine rpm} \times \text{rear wheel radius}}{\text{final gear ratio} \times 265.1}$$

$$\text{km/h} = \frac{1350 \times 15.24}{1.42 \times 265.1}$$

$$\text{km/h} = \frac{20574}{376.44}$$

$$\text{km/h} = 54.72$$

$$\text{km/h} = 55$$

VAULTS

10.045 Motorcycle occupants involved in collisions are often thrown through the air, landing and sliding to a stop on the highway surface. For the operator, the only resistance offered by the motorcycle to his trajectory is the fuel tank, handlebars, and windscreen (if so equipped). Other than striking any of these items or the other vehicle, there is nothing preventing forward motion. In a motorcycle-vehicle collision, the operator will contact the higher areas of the automobile, such as the side-door glass, a, b, or c pillar, roof gutter. If impact is in the area of the front fenders or rear deck, he may pass completely over the vehicle. Much depends on the relative impact speeds, angles of approach, and the portion of the vehicle contacted.

10.046 Passengers occupying the rear portion of the motorcycle seat will have less objects to obstruct their forward trajectory. Often the body of the operator acts as a ramp for the passenger to depart the motorcycle.

10.047 To accurately determine departure speed of motorcycle occupants in vault or fall situations requires several items of evidence, including (a) coefficient of friction value of the clothing worn in relation to the highway surface, (b) height of the motorcycle occupant's center of mass above ground level, and (c) departure or takeoff angle from the motorcycle (see also Paras. 9.131 and 10.040).

10.048 During collisions, motorcycle operators depart the motorcycle at an angle of between 15° and 20°. The values are influenced by the speed of the motorcycle, the other vehicle involved, and any interference by the handlebars or windscreen. Cases involving a motorcycle passenger are different due to the various configurations of the occupant at departure. In these cases, the departure angle can be as little as 18° and 20°, to as much as 45°. Because there are many factors that will influence calculated departure speeds, it is recommended that speed calculations be made using the extreme factors at either end of the ranges mentioned, and at least one arbitrary factor in the middle of the extremes. Such calculations will give the investigator a good idea of the upper and lower departure speeds involved as well as a probable average of these.

10.049 In a vault situation, the following formula may be used to calculate a departure speed:

Formula 10–14

English

$$S = \frac{2.73D}{(\cos\theta) \sqrt{\pm h \pm (D \tan\theta)}}$$

SI

$$S = \frac{7.97D}{(\cos\theta) \sqrt{\pm h \pm (D \tan\theta)}}$$

where S = speed in mph (km/h)
D = horizontal vault distance
h = vertical distance
θ = takeoff angle in degrees

When applying this formula, the *h* value (*tan* angle) is usually positive inasmuch as the rider generally lands at a point lower than his point of takeoff. For the rider, the "±" variable between *h* and *D* should always be considered positive (+) because the ramp effect of the tank is always upwards.

It should be noted that a motorcycle rider would never normally vault from the machine with a negative (–) takeoff; whereas the machine itself or a car could very well experience a downward takeoff angle, depending upon the terrain.

Use $+[h \times (\cos\theta)^2]$ when the body lands lower than takeoff.
Use $-[h \times (\cos\theta)^2]$ when the body lands higher than takeoff.

Note: This standard vault formula used in basic vehicle crash investigation will work for the speed of the motorcycle at impact. However, the calculation results in a lower speed for the motorcycle. Using this formula requires precise establishment of the departure angle, often difficult to obtain (see recommended ranges in Para. 10.048). It is provided here for general information purposes, only.

REFERENCE

1. Watanabe Yoshinori & Yoshida Keigo: *Motorcycle Handling Performance for Obstacle Avoidance.* Honda R & D Company Ltd., Technical Paper No. 73044, Presented at the Second International Congress on Automotive Safety, San Francisco, CA, July 16–18, 1973.

APPENDICES

Source: R. W. Rivers, *Traffic Accident Investigators' and Reconstructionists' Book of Formulae and Tables* (2nd ed.). Springfield, Illinois, Charles C Thomas Publisher, Ltd., 1999.

Appendix A

**ENGLISH (U.S.) AND METRIC (S.I.)
MEASUREMENT SYSTEMS
CONVERSION TABLES**

Table A–1
UNIT DESIGNATIONS AND ABBREVIATIONS

The following are units with abbreviations that are of particular interest to traffic accident investigators and reconstructionists.

U.S.			*S.I.*	
		Length		
			Millimeter	mm
Inch	in		Centimeter	cm
Foot	ft		Meter	m
Mile	mi		Kilometer	km

Weight/Mass

Some confusion exists in the use of the term "weight" to mean either "force of gravity" or "mass." In everyday use, the term "weight" has nearly always meant "mass." For the purposes of this manual, the two terms may be considered to be synonymous.

Ounce	oz		Gram	g
Pound	lb		Kilogram	kg
Ton			Tonne	

Time

Second	sec or s		Second	sec or s
Minute	min		Minute	min
Hour	hr		Hour	hr

Force

Pound-force per square inch	psi		One newton per square meter	Pa or kPa

Volume

Quart	qt		Liter	L
Gallon	gal			

Velocity/Speed

Feet per second	ft/s		Meters per second	m/s
Miles per hour	mph		Kilometers per hour	km/h

Temperature

Degrees Fahrenheit	°F		Degrees Centigrade	°C

Table A–2
DISTANCE, SPEED AND VELOCITY CONVERSION TABLE

Known Factor		*Multiplied By* *(A constant Factor)*		*Equals or Result* *(Required)*
		Feet per Second		
Feet per second	×	0.01136	=	Miles per minute
Feet per second	×	0.6818	=	Miles per hour
Feet per second	×	0.3048	=	Meters per second
		Feet per Minute		
Feet per minute	×	0.01667	=	Feet per second
Feet per minute	×	0.01136	=	Miles per hour
Feet per minute	×	0.3048	=	Meters per minute
		Miles per Minute		
Miles per minute	×	88	=	Feet per second
Miles per minute	×	1.609 344	=	Kilometers per minute
Miles per minute	×	26.8224	=	Meters per second
		Miles per Hour		
Miles per hour	×	1.466 67	=	Feet per second
Miles per hour	×	88	=	Feet per minute
Miles per hour	×	0.447 04	=	Meters per second
Miles per hour	×	1.609 344	=	Kilometers per hour
		Meters per Second		
Meters per second	×	0.06	=	Kilometers per minute
Meters per second	×	3.6	=	Kilometers per hour
Meters per second	×	3.2808	=	Feet per second
		Meters per Minute		
Meters per minute	×	0.06	=	Kilometers per hour
Meters per minute	×	3.2808	=	Feet per minute
		Kilometers per Hour		
Kilometers per hour	×	0.2778	=	Meters per second
Kilometers per hour	×	16.67	=	Meters per minute
Kilometers per hour	×	0.6214	=	Miles per hour

Table A–3
LINEAR RELATIONSHIPS

Length		Km		m		ft		mi
1 km	=	1	=	1000	=	3280.83	=	0.62137
1 m	=	0.00100	=	1	=	3.28083	=	6.21×10^{-4}
1 mile	=	1.60935	=	1609.35	=	5280	=	1

Table A–4
VELOCITY AND SPEED RELATIONSHIPS

Velocity		m/s		ft/s		km/h		mph
1 m/s	=	1	=	3.282	=	3.6	=	2.240
1 ft/s	=	0.30480	=	1	=	1.0973	=	0.6818
1 km/h	=	0.27778	=	0.9113	=	1	=	0.6214
1 mph	=	0.44704	=	1.46667	=	1.6093	=	1

Table A–5
COMMONLY-USED CONSTANTS

U.S.		S.I.
0.031	=	0.102
0.033	=	0.0039
0.062	=	0.203
0.249	=	0.45
0.25	=	0.45
0.366	=	0.124
0.455	=	0.028
0.537	=	0.0625
0.682	=	3.6
0.732	=	0.248
1.466	=	0.277
2.14	=	0.077
2.73	=	7.97
3.86	=	11.27
5.67	=	3.13
10.35	=	6.36
15	=	127
16.1	=	4.9
30	=	254
32.2	=	9.81
64.4	=	19.62

Table A–6
ACCELERATION FT/S AND M/S

U.S.	*S.I.*
1 ft/s^2 = 0.3048 m/s^2	1 m/s^2 = 3.2808 ft/s^2

Table A–7
ACCELERATION OF GRAVITY

In foot second units, the value conventionally taken for standard gravity or standard acceleration, namely 32.1740 ft/s^2, is derived by rounding to the nearest 0.0001 ft/s^2 from the internationally accepted metric value 9.806 65 m/s^2.

U.S.	*S.I.*
32.174 ft/s^2	9.806 65 m/s^2

Table A–8
LENGTH

U.S.		to		*S.I.*
Inches	×	2.54	=	centimeters
Feet	×	0.3048	=	meters
Miles	×	1.609344	=	kilometers
S.I.		to		*U.S.*
Centimeters	×	0.3937008	=	inches
Meters	×	3.280840	=	feet
Kilometers	×	0.621371	=	miles

Table A–9
WEIGHT

U.S.		to		*S.I.*
Pounds	×	0.45359237	=	kilograms
Short ton	×	0.90718474	=	tonnes
S.I.		to		*U.S.*
Kilograms	×	2.204623	=	pounds
Tonnes	×	1.1023113	=	short tons

Table A–10
VOLUME

U.S.		to		S.I.
Quart	×	0.946352946	=	liters
Gallon	×	3.785411784	=	liters
IMPERIAL		to		*S.I.*
Quart	×	1.136	=	liters
Gallon	×	4.546	=	liters
S.I.		to		*U.S.*
Liters	×	2.113376	=	pints
Liters	×	1.056688	=	quarts
Liters	×	0.264172 05	=	gallons

Table A–11
WEIGHT – MASS

English (U.S.)

1 short ton or 2,000 lbs (U.S.)	=	0.9072 metric tonne
1 long ton or 2,240 lbs (Imperial)	=	1.016 metric tonnes
1 short ton or 2,000 lbs (U.S.)	=	907.18474 kg
1 long ton or 2,240 lbs (Imperial)	=	1016.0469 kg
1 pound (avoirdupois)	=	0.45359 kg

S.I.

1 metric tonne	=	2205 lbs
1 metric tonne	=	1.1023 short tons (U.S.)
1 metric tonne	=	0.9842 long ton (Imperial)
1 metric tonne	=	1,000 kg
1 kilogram	=	2.205 lbs (avoirdupois)

Table A–12
FORCE, POWER, PRESSURE, ENERGY OR WORK

Force

Kilogram × 9.807 = N
1 pound-force = 4.448 2222 N

Power

Horsepower × 0.746 = Kilowatts(kw)

Pressure and Stress

1 pound-force per square inch (psi) = 6.894757 kPa

Energy or Work

Foot-pound × 1.3558 = joules

Table A–13
MOMENTUM

1 pound-foot per second = 0.138 255 kg m/s

Table A–14
HORSEPOWER

1 horsepower (550 ft.lbf/s) = 745.6999 W
1 horsepower (electric) = 746 W

Table A–15
TORQUE

Pound-foot × 1.355 8 = newton-meters

Table A–16
INTERNATIONAL NAUTICAL MILES AND KILOMETERS

1 nautical mile = 1.1508 miles = 1,852 m

Table A–17
SPEED OF SOUND IN AIR

U.S.	*S.I.*
1,087 ft/s	331.5 m/s

Table A–18
SPEED OF LIGHT

U.S.	*S.I.*
186,300 miles per second	300,000 kilometers per second

Appendix B

ENGLISH (U.S.) CONVERSION TABLES

Table B-1

MILES-PER-HOUR TO FEET-PER-SECOND CONVERSION TABLE

mph	ft/sec	mph	ft/sec	mph	ft/sec	mph	ft/sec
1.0	1.467	31.0	45.477	61.0	89.487	91.0	133.497
1.5	2.201	31.5	46.211	61.5	90.221	91.5	134.231
2.0	2.934	32.0	46.944	62.0	90.954	92.0	134.964
2.5	3.668	32.5	47.678	62.5	91.688	92.5	135.698
3.0	4.401	33.0	48.411	63.0	92.421	93.0	136.431
3.5	5.135	33.5	49.145	63.5	93.155	93.5	137.165
4.0	5.868	34.0	49.878	64.0	93.888	94.0	137.898
4.5	6.602	34.5	50.612	64.5	94.622	94.5	138.632
5.0	7.335	35.0	51.345	65.0	95.355	95.0	139.365
5.5	8.069	35.5	52.079	65.5	96.089	95.5	140.099
6.0	8.802	36.0	52.812	66.0	96.822	96.0	140.832
6.5	9.536	36.5	53.546	66.5	97.556	96.5	141.566
7.0	10.269	37.0	54.279	67.0	98.289	97.0	142.299
7.5	11.003	37.5	55.013	67.5	99.023	97.5	143.033
8.0	11.736	38.0	55.746	68.0	99.756	98.0	143.766
8.5	12.470	38.5	56.480	68.5	100.490	98.5	144.500
9.0	13.203	39.0	57.213	69.0	101.223	99.0	145.233
9.5	13.937	39.5	57.947	69.5	101.957	99.5	145.967
10.0	14.670	40.0	58.680	70.0	102.690	100.0	146.700
10.5	15.404	40.5	59.414	70.5	103.424	100.5	147.434
11.0	16.137	41.0	60.147	71.0	104.157	101.0	148.167
11.5	16.871	41.5	60.881	71.5	104.891	101.5	148.901
12.0	17.604	42.0	61.614	72.0	105.624	102.0	149.634
12.5	18.338	42.5	62.348	72.5	106.358	102.5	150.368
13.0	19.071	43.0	62.081	73.0	107.091	103.0	151.101
13.5	19.805	43.5	68.815	73.5	107.825	103.5	151.835
14.0	20.538	44.0	64.548	74.0	108.558	104.0	152.568
14.5	21.272	44.5	65.282	74.5	109.292	104.5	153.302
15.0	22.005	45.0	66.015	75.0	110.025	105.0	154.035
15.5	22.739	45.5	66.749	75.5	110.759	105.5	154.769
16.0	23.472	46.0	67.482	76.0	111.492	106.0	155.502
16.5	24.206	46.5	68.216	76.5	112.226	106.5	156.236
17.0	24.939	47.0	68.949	77.0	112.959	107.0	156.969
17.5	25.673	47.5	69.683	77.5	113.693	107.5	157.703
18.0	26.406	48.0	70.416	78.0	114.426	108.0	158.436
18.5	27.140	48.5	71.150	78.5	115.160	108.5	159.170
19.0	27.873	49.0	71.883	79.0	115.893	109.0	159.903
19.5	28.607	49.5	72.617	79.5	116.627	109.5	160.637
20.0	29.340	50.0	73.350	80.0	117.360	110.0	161.370
20.5	30.074	50.5	74.084	80.5	118.094	110.5	162.104
21.0	30.807	51.0	74.817	81.0	118.827	111.0	162.837
21.5	31.541	51.5	75.551	81.5	119.561	111.5	163.571
22.0	32.274	52.0	76.284	82.0	120.294	112.0	164.304
22.5	33.008	52.5	77.018	82.5	121.028	112.5	165.038
23.0	33.741	53.0	77.751	83.0	121.761	113.0	165.771
23.5	34.475	53.5	78.485	83.5	122.495	113.5	166.505
24.0	35.208	54.0	79.218	84.0	123.228	114.0	167.238
24.5	35.942	54.5	79.952	84.5	123.962	114.5	167.972
25.0	36.675	55.0	80.685	85.0	124.695	115.0	168.705
25.5	37.409	55.5	81.419	85.5	125.429	115.5	169.439
26.0	38.142	56.0	82.152	86.0	126.162	116.0	170.172
26.5	38.876	56.5	82.886	86.5	126.896	116.5	170.906
27.0	39.609	57.0	83.619	87.0	127.629	117.0	171.639
27.5	40.343	57.5	84.353	87.5	128.363	117.5	172.373
28.0	41.076	58.0	85.086	88.0	129.096	118.0	173.106
28.5	41.810	58.5	85.820	88.5	129.830	118.5	173.840
29.0	42.543	59.0	86.553	89.0	130.563	119.0	174.573
29.5	43.277	59.5	87.287	89.5	131.297	119.5	175.307
30.0	44.010	60.0	88.020	90.0	132.030	120.0	176.040
30.5	44.744	60.5	88.754	90.5	132.764		

Table B-2

COEFFICIENT OF FRICTION TO DECELERATION RATE IN
FEET-PER-SECOND-PER-SECOND CONVERSION TABLE

(*g* = 32.2 ft/sec/sec)

Deceleration Rate (a) (ft/sec/sec)	Coefficient of Friction (f)	Deceleration Rate (a) (ft/sec/sec)	Coefficient of Friction (f)
32.20	1.00	16.10	.50
31.88	.99	15.78	.49
31.56	.98	15.46	.48
31.23	.97	15.13	.47
30.91	.96	14.81	.46
30.59	.95	14.49	.45
30.27	.94	14.17	.44
29.95	.93	13.85	.43
29.62	.92	13.52	.42
29.30	.91	13.20	.41
28.98	.90	12.88	.40
28.66	.89	12.56	.39
28.34	.88	12.24	.38
28.01	.87	11.91	.37
27.69	.86	11.59	.36
27.37	.85	11.27	.35
27.05	.84	10.95	.34
26.73	.83	10.63	.33
26.40	.82	10.30	.32
26.08	.81	9.98	.31
25.76	.80	9.66	.30
25.44	.79	9.34	.29
25.12	.78	9.02	.28
24.79	.77	8.69	.27
24.47	.76	8.37	.26
24.15	.75	8.05	.25
23.83	.74	7.73	.24
23.51	.73	7.41	.23
23.18	.72	7.08	.22
22.86	.71	6.76	.21
22.54	.70	6.44	.20
22.22	.69	6.12	.19
21.90	.68	5.80	.18
21.57	.67	5.47	.17
21.25	.66	5.15	.16
20.93	.65	4.83	.15
20.61	.64	4.51	.14
20.29	.63	4.19	.13
19.96	.62	3.86	.12
19.64	.61	3.54	.11
19.32	.60	3.22	.10
19.00	.59	2.90	.09
18.68	.58	2.58	.08
18.35	.57	2.25	.07
18.03	.56	1.93	.06
17.71	.55	1.61	.05
17.39	.54	1.29	.04
17.07	.53	.97	.03
16.74	.52	.64	.02
16.42	.51	.32	.01
		.00	.00

Table B-3

INCHES-TO-CENTIMETERS CONVERSION TABLE

Inches	=	Centimeters	Inches	=	Centimeters
1	=	2.54	51	=	129.54
2	=	5.08	52	=	132.08
3	=	7.62	53	=	134.62
4	=	10.16	54	=	137.16
5	=	12.70	55	=	139.70
6	=	15.24	56	=	142.24
7	=	17.78	57	=	144.78
8	=	20.32	58	=	147.32
9	=	22.86	59	=	149.86
10	=	25.40	60	=	152.40
11	=	27.94	61	=	154.94
12	=	30.48	62	=	157.48
13	=	33.02	63	=	160.02
14	=	35.56	64	=	162.56
15	=	38.10	65	=	165.10
16	=	40.64	66	=	167.64
17	=	43.18	67	=	170.18
18	=	45.72	68	=	172.72
19	=	48.26	69	=	175.26
20	=	50.80	70	=	177.80
21	=	53.34	71	=	180.34
22	=	55.88	72	=	182.88
23	=	58.42	73	=	185.42
24	=	60.96	74	=	187.96
25	=	63.50	75	=	190.50
26	=	66.04	76	=	193.04
27	=	68.58	77	=	195.58
28	=	71.12	78	=	198.12
29	=	73.66	79	=	200.66
30	=	76.20	80	=	203.20
31	=	78.74	81	=	205.74
32	=	81.28	82	=	208.28
33	=	83.82	83	=	210.82
34	=	86.36	84	=	213.36
35	=	88.90	85	=	215.90
36	=	91.44	86	=	218.44
37	=	93.98	87	=	220.98
38	=	96.52	88	=	223.52
39	=	99.06	89	=	226.06
40	=	101.60	90	=	228.60
41	=	104.14	91	=	231.14
42	=	106.68	92	=	233.68
43	=	109.22	93	=	236.22
44	=	111.76	94	=	238.76
45	=	114.30	95	=	241.30
46	=	116.84	96	=	243.84
47	=	119.38	97	=	246.38
48	=	121.92	98	=	248.92
49	=	124.46	99	=	251.46
50	=	127.00	100	=	254.00

Table B-4

FEET-TO-METERS CONVERSION TABLE

Feet	=	Meters	Feet	=	Meters
1	=	.3048	51	=	15.5448
2	=	.6096	52	=	15.8496
3	=	.9144	53	=	16.1544
4	=	1.2192	54	=	16.4592
5	=	1.5240	55	=	16.7640
6	=	1.8288	56	=	17.0688
7	=	2.1336	57	=	17.3736
8	=	2.4384	58	=	17.6784
9	=	2.7432	59	=	17.9832
10	=	3.0480	60	=	18.2880
11	=	3.3528	61	=	18.5928
12	=	3.6576	62	=	18.8976
13	=	3.9624	63	=	19.2024
14	=	4.2672	64	=	19.5072
15	=	4.5720	65	=	19.8120
16	=	4.8768	66	=	20.1168
17	=	5.1816	67	=	20.4216
18	=	5.4864	68	=	20.7264
19	=	5.7912	69	=	21.0312
20	=	6.0960	70	=	21.3360
21	=	6.4008	71	=	21.6408
22	=	6.7056	72	=	21.9456
23	=	7.0104	73	=	22.2504
24	=	7.3152	74	=	22.5552
25	=	7.6200	75	=	22.8600
26	=	7.9248	76	=	23.1648
27	=	8.2296	77	=	23.4696
28	=	8.5344	78	=	23.7744
29	=	8.8392	79	=	24.0792
30	=	9.1440	80	=	24.3840
31	=	9.4488	81	=	24.6888
32	=	9.7536	82	=	24.9936
33	=	10.0584	83	=	25.2984
34	=	10.3632	84	=	25.6032
35	=	10.6680	85	=	25.9080
36	=	10.9728	86	=	26.2128
37	=	11.2776	87	=	26.5176
38	=	11.5824	88	=	26.8224
39	=	11.8872	89	=	27.1272
40	=	12.1920	90	=	27.4320
41	=	12.4968	91	=	27.7368
42	=	12.8016	92	=	28.0416
43	=	13.1064	93	=	28.3464
44	=	13.4112	94	=	28.6512
45	=	13.7160	95	=	28.9560
46	=	14.0208	96	=	29.2608
47	=	14.3256	97	=	29.5656
48	=	14.6304	98	=	29.8704
49	=	14.9352	99	=	30.1752
50	=	15.2400	100	=	30.4800

Table B-5

MILES-TO-KILOMETERS CONVERSION TABLE

Miles	Kilometers	Miles	Kilometers	Miles	Kilometers	Miles	Kilometers
1.0	1.609	31.0	49.879	61.0	98.149	91.0	146.419
1.5	2.414	31.5	50.684	61.5	98.954	91.5	147.224
2.0	3.218	32.0	51.488	62.0	99.758	92.0	148.028
2.5	4.023	32.5	52.293	62.5	100.563	92.5	148.833
3.0	4.827	33.0	53.097	63.0	101.367	93.0	149.637
3.5	5.632	33.5	53.902	63.5	102.172	93.5	150.442
4.0	6.436	34.0	54.706	64.0	102.976	94.0	151.246
4.5	7.241	34.5	55.511	64.5	103.781	94.5	152.051
5.0	8.045	35.0	56.315	65.0	104.585	95.0	152.855
5.5	8.850	35.5	57.120	65.5	105.390	95.5	153.660
6.0	9.654	36.0	57.924	66.0	106.194	96.0	154.464
6.5	10.459	36.5	58.729	66.5	106.999	96.5	155.269
7.0	11.263	37.0	59.533	67.0	107.803	97.0	156.073
7.5	12.068	37.5	60.338	67.5	108.608	97.5	156.878
8.0	12.872	38.0	61.142	68.0	109.412	98.0	157.682
8.5	13.677	38.5	61.947	68.5	110.217	98.5	158.487
9.0	14.481	39.0	62.751	69.0	111.021	99.0	159.291
9.5	15.286	39.5	63.556	69.5	111.826	99.5	160.096
10.0	16.090	40.0	64.360	70.0	112.630	100.0	160.900
10.5	16.895	40.5	65.165	70.5	113.435	100.5	161.705
11.0	17.699	41.0	65.969	71.0	114.239	101.0	162.509
11.5	18.504	41.5	66.774	71.5	115.044	101.5	163.314
12.0	19.308	42.0	67.578	72.0	115.848	102.0	164.118
12.5	20.113	42.5	68.383	72.5	116.653	102.5	164.923
13.0	20.917	43.0	69.187	73.0	117.457	103.0	165.727
13.5	21.722	43.5	69.992	73.5	118.262	103.5	166.532
14.0	22.526	44.0	70.796	74.0	119.066	104.0	167.336
14.5	23.331	44.5	71.601	74.5	119.871	104.5	168.141
15.0	24.135	45.0	72.405	75.0	120.675	105.0	168.945
15.5	24.940	45.5	73.210	75.5	121.480	105.5	169.750
16.0	25.744	46.0	74.014	76.0	122.284	106.0	170.554
16.5	26.549	46.5	74.819	76.5	123.089	106.5	171.359
17.0	27.353	47.0	75.623	77.0	123.893	107.0	172.163
17.5	28.158	47.5	76.428	77.5	124.698	107.5	172.968
18.0	28.962	48.0	77.232	78.0	125.502	108.0	173.772
18.5	29.767	48.5	78.037	78.5	126.307	108.5	174.577
19.0	30.571	49.0	78.841	79.0	127.111	109.0	175.381
19.5	31.376	49.5	79.646	79.5	127.916	109.5	176.186
20.0	32.180	50.0	80.450	80.0	128.720	110.0	176.990
20.5	32.985	50.5	81.255	80.5	129.525	110.5	177.795
21.0	33.789	51.0	82.059	81.0	130.329	111.0	178.599
21.5	34.594	51.5	82.864	81.5	131.134	111.5	179.404
22.0	35.398	52.0	83.668	82.0	131.938	112.0	180.208
22.5	36.203	52.5	84.473	82.5	132.743	112.5	181.013
23.0	37.007	53.0	85.277	83.0	133.547	113.0	181.817
23.5	37.812	53.5	86.082	83.5	134.352	113.5	182.622
24.0	38.616	54.0	86.886	84.0	135.156	114.0	183.426
24.5	39.421	54.5	87.691	84.5	135.961	114.5	184.231
25.0	40.225	55.0	88.495	85.0	136.765	115.0	185.035
25.5	41.030	55.5	89.300	85.5	137.570	115.5	185.840
26.0	41.834	56.0	90.104	86.0	138.374	116.0	186.644
26.5	42.639	56.5	90.909	86.5	139.179	116.5	187.449
27.0	43.443	57.0	91.713	87.0	139.983	117.0	188.253
27.5	44.248	57.5	92.518	87.5	140.788	117.5	189.058
28.0	45.052	58.0	93.322	88.0	141.592	118.0	189.862
28.5	45.857	58.5	94.127	88.5	142.397	118.5	190.667
29.0	46.661	59.0	94.931	89.0	143.201	119.0	191.471
29.5	47.466	59.5	95.736	89.5	144.006	119.5	192.276
30.0	48.270	60.0	96.540	90.0	144.810	120.0	193.080
30.5	49.075	60.5	97.345	90.5	145.615		

Appendix C

METRIC (S.I.) CONVERSION TABLES

Table C-1

KILOMETERS-PER-HOUR TO METERS-PER-SECOND CONVERSION TABLE

km/h	m/s	km/h	m/s	km/h	m/s	km/h	m/s
1.0	0.278	26.0	7.228	51.0	14.178	76.0	21.128
1.5	0.417	26.5	7.367	51.5	14.317	76.5	21.267
2.0	0.556	27.0	7.506	52.0	14.456	77.0	21.406
2.5	0.695	27.5	7.645	52.5	14.595	77.5	21.545
3.0	0.834	28.0	7.784	53.0	14.734	78.0	21.684
3.5	0.973	28.5	7.923	53.5	14.873	78.5	21.823
4.0	1.112	29.0	8.062	54.0	15.012	79.0	21.962
4.5	1.251	29.5	8.201	54.5	15.151	79.5	22.101
5.0	1.390	30.0	8.340	55.0	15.290	80.0	22.240
5.5	1.529	30.5	8.479	55.5	15.429	80.5	22.379
6.0	1.668	31.0	8.618	56.0	15.568	81.0	22.518
6.5	1.807	31.5	8.757	56.5	15.707	81.5	22.657
7.0	1.946	32.0	8.896	57.0	15.846	82.0	22.796
7.5	2.085	32.5	9.035	57.5	15.985	82.5	22.935
8.0	2.224	33.0	9.174	58.0	16.124	83.0	23.074
8.5	2.363	33.5	9.313	58.5	16.263	83.5	23.213
9.0	2.502	34.0	9.452	59.0	16.402	84.0	23.352
9.5	2.641	34.5	9.591	59.5	16.541	84.5	23.491
10.0	2.780	35.0	9.730	60.0	16.680	85.0	23.630
10.5	2.919	35.5	9.869	60.5	16.819	85.5	23.769
11.0	3.058	36.0	10.008	61.0	16.958	86.0	23.908
11.5	3.197	36.5	10.147	61.5	17.097	86.5	24.047
12.0	3.336	37.0	10.286	62.0	17.236	87.0	24.186
12.5	3.475	37.5	10.425	62.5	17.375	87.5	24.325
13.0	3.614	38.0	10.564	63.0	17.514	88.0	24.464
13.5	3.753	38.5	10.703	63.5	17.653	88.5	24.603
14.0	3.892	39.0	10.842	64.0	17.792	89.0	24.742
14.5	4.031	39.5	10.981	64.5	17.931	89.5	24.881
15.0	4.170	40.0	11.120	65.0	18.070	90.0	25.020
15.5	4.309	40.5	11.259	65.5	18.209	90.5	25.159
16.0	4.448	41.0	11.398	66.0	18.348	91.0	25.298
16.5	4.587	41.5	11.537	66.5	18.487	91.5	25.437
17.0	4.726	42.0	11.676	67.0	18.626	92.0	25.576
17.5	4.865	42.5	11.815	67.5	18.765	92.5	25.715
18.0	5.004	43.0	11.954	68.0	18.904	93.0	25.854
18.5	5.143	43.5	12.093	68.5	19.043	93.5	25.993
19.0	5.282	44.0	12.232	69.0	19.182	94.0	26.132
19.5	5.421	44.5	12.371	69.5	19.321	94.5	26.271
20.0	5.560	45.0	12.510	70.0	19.460	95.0	26.410
20.5	5.699	45.5	12.649	70.5	19.599	95.5	26.549
21.0	5.838	46.0	12.788	71.0	19.738	96.0	26.688
21.5	5.977	46.5	12.927	71.5	19.877	96.5	26.827
22.0	6.116	47.0	13.066	72.0	20.016	97.0	26.966
22.5	6.255	47.5	13.205	72.5	20.155	97.5	27.105
23.0	6.394	48.0	13.344	73.0	20.294	98.0	27.244
23.5	6.533	48.5	13.483	73.5	20.433	98.5	27.383
24.0	6.672	49.0	13.622	74.0	20.572	99.0	27.522
24.5	6.811	49.5	13.761	74.5	20.711	99.5	27.661
25.0	6.950	50.0	13.900	75.0	20.850	100.0	27.800
25.5	7.089	50.5	14.039	75.5	20.989	100.5	27.939

Table C-1 *(Continued)*

KILOMETERS-PER-HOUR TO METERS-PER-SECOND CONVERSION TABLE

km/h	m/s	km/h	m/s	km/h	m/s	km/h	m/s
101.0	28.078	126.0	35.028	151.0	41.978	176.0	48.928
101.5	28.217	126.5	35.167	151.5	42.117	176.5	49.067
102.0	28.356	127.0	35.306	152.0	42.256	177.0	49.206
102.5	28.495	127.5	35.445	152.5	42.395	177.5	49.345
103.0	28.634	128.0	35.584	153.0	42.534	178.0	49.484
103.5	28.773	128.5	35.723	153.5	42.673	178.5	49.623
104.0	28.912	129.0	35.862	154.0	42.812	179.0	49.762
104.5	29.051	129.5	36.001	154.5	42.951	179.5	49.901
105.0	29.190	130.0	36.140	155.0	43.090	180.0	50.040
105.5	29.329	130.5	36.279	155.5	43.229	180.5	50.179
106.0	29.468	131.0	36.418	156.0	43.368	181.0	50.318
106.5	29.607	131.5	36.557	156.5	43.507	181.5	50.457
107.0	29.746	132.0	36.696	157.0	43.646	182.0	50.596
107.5	29.885	132.5	36.835	157.5	43.785	182.5	50.735
108.0	30.024	133.0	36.974	158.0	43.924	183.0	50.874
108.5	30.163	133.5	37.113	158.5	44.063	183.5	51.013
109.0	30.302	134.0	37.252	159.0	44.202	184.0	51.152
109.5	30.441	134.5	37.391	159.5	44.341	184.5	51.291
110.0	30.580	135.0	37.530	160.0	44.480	185.0	51.430
110.5	30.719	135.5	37.669	160.5	44.619	185.5	51.569
111.0	30.858	136.0	37.808	161.0	44.758	186.0	51.708
111.5	30.997	136.5	37.947	161.5	44.897	186.5	51.847
112.0	31.136	137.0	38.086	162.0	45.036	187.0	51.986
112.5	31.275	137.5	38.225	162.5	45.175	187.5	52.125
113.0	31.414	138.0	38.364	163.0	45.314	188.0	52.264
113.5	31.553	138.5	38.503	163.5	45.453	188.5	52.403
114.0	31.692	139.0	38.642	164.0	45.592	189.0	52.542
114.5	31.831	139.5	38.781	164.5	45.731	189.5	52.681
115.0	31.970	140.0	38.920	165.0	45.870	190.0	52.820
115.5	32.109	140.5	39.059	165.5	46.009	190.5	52.959
116.0	32.248	141.0	39.198	166.0	46.148	191.0	53.098
116.5	32.387	141.5	39.337	166.5	46.287	191.5	53.237
117.0	32.526	142.0	39.476	167.0	46.426	192.0	53.376
117.5	32.665	142.5	39.615	167.5	46.565	192.5	53.515
118.0	32.804	143.0	39.754	168.0	46.704	193.0	53.654
118.5	32.943	143.5	39.893	168.5	46.843	193.5	53.793
119.0	33.082	144.0	40.032	169.0	46.982	194.0	53.932
119.5	33.221	144.5	40.171	169.5	47.121	194.5	54.071
120.0	33.360	145.0	40.310	170.0	47.260	195.0	54.210
120.5	33.499	145.5	40.449	170.5	47.399	195.5	54.349
121.0	33.638	146.0	40.588	171.0	47.538	196.0	54.488
121.5	33.777	146.5	40.727	171.5	47.677	196.5	54.627
122.0	33.916	147.0	40.866	172.0	47.816	197.0	54.766
122.5	34.055	147.5	41.005	172.5	47.955	197.5	54.905
123.0	34.194	148.0	41.144	173.0	48.094	198.0	55.044
123.5	34.333	148.5	41.283	173.5	48.233	198.5	55.183
124.0	34.472	149.0	41.422	174.0	48.372	199.0	55.322
124.5	34.611	149.5	41.561	174.5	48.511	199.5	55.461
125.0	34.750	150.0	41.700	175.0	48.650	200.0	55.600
125.5	34.889	150.5	41.839	175.5	48.789		

Table C-2

COEFFICIENT OF FRICTION TO DECELERATION RATE IN METERS-PER-SECOND-PER
SECOND CONVERSION TABLE

(g = 9.81 m/s/s)

Deceleration Rate (a) (m/s/s)	Coefficient of Friction (f)	Deceleration Rate (a) (m/s/s)	Coefficient of Friction (f)
9.81	1.00	4.91	.50
9.71	.99	4.81	.49
9.61	.98	4.71	.48
9.52	.97	4.61	.47
9.42	.96	4.51	.46
9.32	.95	4.41	.45
9.22	.94	4.32	.44
9.12	.93	4.22	.43
9.03	.92	4.12	.42
8.93	.91	4.02	.41
8.83	.90	3.92	.40
8.73	.89	3.83	.39
8.63	.88	3.73	.38
8.53	.87	3.63	.37
8.44	.86	3.53	.36
8.34	.85	3.43	.35
8.24	.84	3.34	.34
8.14	.83	3.24	.33
8.04	.82	3.14	.32
7.95	.81	3.04	.31
7.85	.80	2.94	.30
7.75	.79	2.84	.29
7.65	.78	2.75	.28
7.55	.77	2.65	.27
7.46	.76	2.55	.26
7.36	.75	2.45	.25
7.26	.74	2.35	.24
7.16	.73	2.26	.23
7.06	.72	2.16	.22
6.97	.71	2.06	.21
6.87	.70	1.96	.20
6.77	.69	1.86	.19
6.67	.68	1.77	.18
6.57	.67	1.67	.17
6.47	.66	1.57	.16
6.38	.65	1.47	.15
6.28	.64	1.37	.14
6.18	.63	1.28	.13
6.08	.62	1.18	.12
5.98	.61	1.08	.11
5.89	.60	0.98	.10
5.79	.59	0.88	.09
5.69	.58	0.78	.08
5.59	.57	0.69	.07
5.49	.56	0.59	.06
5.40	.55	0.49	.05
5.30	.54	0.39	.04
5.20	.53	0.29	.03
5.10	.52	0.20	.02
5.00	.51	0.10	.01

Table C-3

CENTIMETERS-TO-INCHES CONVERSION TABLE

Centimeters	=	Inches	Centimeters	=	Inches
1	=	0.394	51	=	20.094
2	=	0.788	52	=	20.488
3	=	1.182	53	=	20.882
4	=	1.576	54	=	21.276
5	=	1.970	55	=	21.670
6	=	2.364	56	=	22.064
7	=	2.758	57	=	22.458
8	=	3.152	58	=	22.852
9	=	3.546	59	=	23.246
10	=	3.940	60	=	23.640
11	=	4.334	61	=	24.034
12	=	4.728	62	=	24.428
13	=	5.122	63	=	24.822
14	=	5.516	64	=	25.216
15	=	5.910	65	=	25.610
16	=	6.304	66	=	26.004
17	=	6.698	67	=	26.398
18	=	7.092	68	=	26.792
19	=	7.486	69	=	27.186
20	=	7.886	70	=	27.580
21	=	8.274	71	=	27.974
22	=	8.668	72	=	28.368
23	=	9.062	73	=	28.762
24	=	9.456	74	=	29.156
25	=	9.850	75	=	29.550
26	=	10.244	76	=	29.944
27	=	10.638	77	=	30.338
28	=	11.032	78	=	30.732
29	=	11.426	79	=	31.126
30	=	11.820	80	=	31.520
31	=	12.214	81	=	31.914
32	=	12.608	82	=	32.308
33	=	13.002	83	=	32.702
34	=	13.396	84	=	33.096
35	=	13.790	85	=	33.490
36	=	14.184	86	=	33.884
37	=	14.578	87	=	34.278
38	=	14.972	88	=	34.672
39	=	15.366	89	=	35.066
40	=	15.760	90	=	35.460
41	=	16.154	91	=	35.854
42	=	16.548	92	=	36.248
43	=	16.942	93	=	36.642
44	=	17.336	94	=	37.036
45	=	17.730	95	=	37.430
46	=	18.124	96	=	37.824
47	=	18.518	97	=	38.218
48	=	18.912	98	=	38.612
49	=	19.306	99	=	39.006
50	=	19.700	100	=	39.400

Table C-4

METERS-TO-FEET CONVERSION TABLE

Meters	=	Feet	Meters	=	Feet
1	=	3.281	51	=	167.331
2	=	6.562	52	=	170.612
3	=	9.843	53	=	173.893
4	=	13.124	54	=	177.174
5	=	16.405	55	=	180.455
6	=	19.686	56	=	183.736
7	=	22.967	57	=	187.017
8	=	26.248	58	=	190.298
9	=	29.529	59	=	193.579
10	=	32.810	60	=	196.860
11	=	36.091	61	=	200.141
12	=	39.372	62	=	203.422
13	=	42.653	63	=	206.703
14	=	45.934	64	=	209.984
15	=	49.215	65	=	213.265
16	=	52.496	66	=	216.546
17	=	55.777	67	=	219.827
18	=	59.058	68	=	223.108
19	=	62.339	69	=	226.389
20	=	65.620	70	=	229.670
21	=	68.901	71	=	232.951
22	=	72.182	72	=	236.232
23	=	75.463	73	=	239.513
24	=	78.744	74	=	242.794
25	=	82.025	75	=	246.075
26	=	85.306	76	=	249.356
27	=	88.587	77	=	252.637
28	=	91.868	78	=	255.918
29	=	95.149	79	=	259.199
30	=	98.430	80	=	262.480
31	=	101.711	81	=	265.761
32	=	104.992	82	=	269.042
33	=	108.273	83	=	272.323
34	=	111.554	84	=	275.604
35	=	114.835	85	=	278.885
36	=	118.116	86	=	282.166
37	=	121.397	87	=	285.447
38	=	124.678	88	=	288.728
39	=	127.959	89	=	292.009
40	=	131.240	90	=	295.290
41	=	134.521	91	=	298.571
42	=	137.802	92	=	301.852
43	=	141.083	93	=	305.133
44	=	144.364	94	=	308.414
45	=	147.645	95	=	311.695
46	=	150.926	96	=	314.976
47	=	154.207	97	=	318.257
48	=	157.488	98	=	321.538
49	=	160.769	99	=	324.819
50	=	164.050	100	=	328.100

Table C-5

KILOMETERS-TO-MILES CONVERSION TABLE

Kilometers	Miles	Kilometers	Miles	Kilometers	Miles	Kilometers	Miles
1.0	0.621	26.0	16.146	51.0	31.671	76.0	47.196
1.5	0.932	26.5	16.457	51.5	31.982	76.5	47.507
2.0	1.242	27.0	16.767	52.0	32.292	77.0	47.817
2.5	1.553	27.5	17.078	52.5	32.603	77.5	48.128
3.0	1.863	28.0	17.388	53.0	32.913	78.0	48.438
3.5	2.174	28.5	17.699	53.5	33.224	78.5	48.749
4.0	2.484	29.0	18.009	54.0	33.534	79.0	49.059
4.5	2.795	29.5	18.320	54.5	33.845	79.5	49.370
5.0	3.105	30.0	18.630	55.0	34.155	80.0	49.680
5.5	3.416	30.5	18.941	55.5	34.466	80.5	49.991
6.0	3.726	31.0	19.251	56.0	34.776	81.0	50.301
6.5	4.037	31.5	19.562	56.5	35.087	81.5	50.612
7.0	4.347	32.0	19.872	57.0	35.397	82.0	50.922
7.5	4.658	32.5	20.183	57.5	35.708	82.5	51.233
8.0	4.968	33.0	20.493	58.0	36.018	83.0	51.543
8.5	5.279	33.5	20.804	58.5	36.329	83.5	51.854
9.0	5.589	34.0	21.114	59.0	36.639	84.0	52.164
9.5	5.900	34.5	21.425	59.5	36.950	84.5	52.475
10.0	6.210	35.0	21.735	60.0	37.260	85.0	52.785
10.5	6.521	35.5	22.046	60.5	37.571	85.5	53.096
11.0	6.831	36.0	22.356	61.0	37.881	86.0	53.406
11.5	7.142	36.5	22.667	61.5	38.192	86.5	53.717
12.0	7.452	37.0	22.977	62.0	38.502	87.0	54.027
12.5	7.763	37.5	23.288	62.5	38.813	87.5	54.338
13.0	8.073	38.0	23.598	63.0	39.123	88.0	54.648
13.5	8.384	38.5	23.909	63.5	39.434	88.5	54.959
14.0	8.694	39.0	24.219	64.0	39.744	89.0	55.269
14.5	9.005	39.5	24.530	64.5	40.055	89.5	55.580
15.0	9.315	40.0	24.840	65.0	40.365	90.0	55.890
15.5	9.626	40.5	25.151	65.5	40.676	90.5	56.201
16.0	9.936	41.0	25.461	66.0	40.986	91.0	56.511
16.5	10.247	41.5	25.772	66.5	41.297	91.5	56.822
17.0	10.557	42.0	26.082	67.0	41.607	92.0	57.132
17.5	10.868	42.5	26.393	67.5	41.918	92.5	57.443
18.0	11.178	43.0	26.703	68.0	42.228	93.0	57.753
18.5	11.489	43.5	27.014	68.5	42.539	93.5	58.064
19.0	11.799	44.0	27.324	69.0	42.849	94.0	58.374
19.5	12.110	44.5	27.635	69.5	43.160	94.5	58.685
20.0	12.420	45.0	27.945	70.0	43.470	95.0	58.995
20.5	12.731	45.5	28.256	70.5	43.781	95.5	59.306
21.0	13.041	46.0	28.566	71.0	44.091	96.0	59.616
21.5	13.352	46.5	28.877	71.5	44.402	96.5	59.927
22.0	13.662	47.0	29.187	72.0	44.712	97.0	60.237
22.5	13.973	47.5	29.498	72.5	45.023	97.5	60.548
23.0	14.283	48.0	29.808	73.0	45.333	98.0	60.858
23.5	14.594	48.5	30.119	73.5	45.644	98.5	61.169
24.0	14.904	4910	30.429	74.0	45.954	99.0	61.479
24.5	15.215	49.5	30.740	74.5	46.265	99.5	61.790
25.0	15.525	50.0	31.050	75.0	46.575	100.0	62.100
25.5	15.836	50.5	31.361	75.5	46.886	100.5	62.411

Table C-5 *(Continued)*
KILOMETERS-TO-MILES CONVERSION TABLE

Kilometers	Miles	Kilometers	Miles	Kilometers	Miles	Kilometers	Miles
101.0	62.721	126.0	78.246	151.0	93.771	176.0	109.296
101.5	63.032	126.5	78.557	151.5	94.082	176.5	109.607
102.0	63.342	127.0	78.867	152.0	94.392	177.0	109.917
102.5	63.653	127.5	79.178	152.5	94.703	177.5	110.228
103.0	63.963	128.0	79.488	153.0	95.013	178.0	110.538
103.5	64.274	128.5	79.799	153.5	95.324	178.5	110.849
104.0	64.584	129.0	80.109	154.0	95.634	179.0	111.159
104.5	64.895	129.5	80.420	154.5	95.945	179.5	111.470
105.0	65.205	130.0	80.730	155.0	96.255	180.0	111.780
105.5	65.516	130.5	81.041	155.5	96.566	180.5	112.091
106.0	65.826	131.0	81.351	156.0	96.876	181.0	112.401
106.5	66.137	131.5	81.662	156.5	97.187	181.5	112.712
107.0	66.447	132.0	81.972	157.0	97.497	182.0	113.022
107.5	66.758	132.5	82.283	157.5	97.808	182.5	113.333
108.0	67.068	133.0	82.593	158.0	98.118	183.0	113.643
108.5	67.379	133.5	82.904	158.5	98.429	183.5	113.954
109.0	67.689	134.0	83.214	159.0	98.739	184.0	114.264
109.5	68.000	134.5	83.525	159.5	99.050	184.5	114.575
110.0	68.310	135.0	83.835	160.0	99.360	185.0	114.885
110.5	68.621	135.5	84.146	160.5	99.671	185.5	115.196
111.0	68.931	136.0	84.456	161.0	99.981	186.0	115.506
111.5	69.242	136.5	84.767	161.5	100.292	186.5	115.817
112.0	69.552	137.0	85.077	162.0	100.602	187.0	116.127
112.5	69.863	137.5	85.388	612.5	100.913	187.5	116.438
113.0	70.173	138.0	85.698	163.0	101.223	188.0	116.748
113.5	70.484	138.5	86.009	163.5	101.534	188.5	117.059
114.0	70.794	139.0	86.319	164.0	101.844	189.0	117.369
114.5	71.105	139.5	86.630	164.5	102.155	189.5	117.680
115.0	71.415	140.0	86.940	165.0	102.465	190.0	117.990
115.5	71.726	140.5	87.251	165.5	102.776	190.5	118.301
116.0	72.036	141.0	87.561	166.0	103.086	191.0	118.611
116.5	72.347	141.5	87.872	166.5	103.397	191.5	118.922
117.0	72.657	142.0	88.182	167.0	103.707	192.0	119.232
117.5	72.968	142.5	88.493	167.5	104.018	192.5	119.543
118.0	73.278	143.0	88.803	168.0	104.328	193.0	119.853
118.5	73.589	143.5	89.114	168.5	104.639	193.5	120.164
119.0	73.899	144.0	89.424	169.0	104.949	194.0	120.474
119.5	74.210	144.5	89.735	169.5	105.260	194.5	120.785
120.0	74.520	145.0	90.045	170.0	105.570	195.0	121.095
120.5	74.831	145.5	90.356	170.5	105.881	195.5	121.406
121.0	75.141	146.0	90.666	171.0	106.191	196.0	121.716
121.5	75.452	146.5	90.977	171.5	106.502	196.5	122.027
122.0	75.762	147.0	91.287	172.0	106.812	197.0	122.337
122.5	76.073	147.5	91.598	172.5	107.123	197.5	122.648
123.0	76.383	148.0	91.908	173.0	107.433	198.0	122.958
123.5	76.694	148.5	92.219	173.5	107.744	198.5	123.268
124.0	77.004	149.0	92.529	174.0	108.054	199.0	123.579
124.5	77.315	149.5	92.840	174.5	108.365	199.5	123.890
125.0	77.625	150.0	93.150	175.0	108.675	200.0	124.200
125.5	77.936	150.5	93.461	175.5	108.986		

Appendix D

SPEEDOMETER ACCURACY

Table D–1

SPEEDOMETER ACCURACY CHECKLIST

Time (in seconds)	Speed (mph or km/h)	Time (in seconds)	Speed (mph or km/h)	Time (in seconds)	Speed (mph or km/h)
40	90.00	88	40.91	136	26.47
41	87.80	89	40.45	137	26.28
42	85.71	90	40.00	138	26.09
43	83.72	91	39.56	139	25.90
44	81.82	92	39.13	140	25.71
45	80.00	93	38.71	141	25.53
46	78.26	94	38.30	142	25.35
47	76.60	95	37.89	143	25.17
48	75.00	96	37.50	144	25.00
49	73.47	97	37.11	145	24.83
50	72.00	98	36.73	146	24.66
51	70.59	99	36.36	147	24.49
52	69.23	100	36.00	148	24.32
53	67.92	101	35.64	149	24.16
54	66.67	102	35.29	150	24.00
55	65.45	103	34.95	151	23.84
56	64.29	104	34.62	152	23.68
57	63.16	105	34.29	153	23.53
58	62.07	106	33.96	154	23.38
59	61.02	107	33.64	155	23.23
60	60.00	108	33.33	156	23.08
61	59.02	109	33.03	157	22.93
62	58.06	110	32.73	158	22.78
63	57.14	111	32.43	159	22.64
64	56.25	112	32.14	160	22.50
65	55.38	113	31.86	161	22.36
66	54.55	114	31.58	162	22.22
67	53.73	115	31.30	163	22.09
68	52.94	116	31.03	164	21.95
69	52.17	117	30.77	165	21.82
70	51.43	118	30.51	166	21.69
71	50.70	119	30.25	167	21.56
72	50.00	120	30.00	168	21.43
73	49.32	121	29.75	169	21.30
74	48.65	122	29.51	170	21.18
75	48.00	123	29.27	171	21.05
76	47.37	124	29.03	172	20.93
77	46.75	125	28.80	173	20.81
78	46.15	126	28.57	174	20.69
79	45.57	127	28.35	175	20.57
80	45.00	128	28.13	176	20.45
81	44.44	129	27.91	177	20.34
82	43.90	130	27.69	178	20.22
83	43.37	131	27.48	179	20.11
84	42.86	132	27.27	180	20.00
85	42.35	133	27.07	181	19.89
86	41.86	134	26.87		
87	41.38	135	26.67		

Appendix E

SYMBOLS

The following table provides a ready reference of symbols, with descriptions, commonly used in traffic accident investigation and reconstruction. These symbols and definitions will assist the reader in gaining a better understanding of the more complex formulae found in the text, as well as those used in other traffic accident investigation and reconstruction textbooks.

GENERAL SYMBOLS, DEFINITIONS, AND MEASUREMENT UNITS

Symbols and Descriptions		Measurement Units	
		U.S.	*S.I.*
General			
a	= acceleration ($\pm$)	ft/s^2	m/s^2
C	= chord	ft, in	m, cm
CG	= center of gravity	ft, in	m, cm
CM	= center of mass	ft, in	m, cm
d	= distance, displacement	ft, in	m, cm
e	= superelevation	percent	percent
	(See also lower case *m*)		
f	= drag factor	decimal fraction	decimal fraction
μ	= coefficient of friction	decimal fraction	decimal fraction
f	= acceleration (drag) factor ($\pm$)	Usually expressed as a decimal fraction	Usually expressed as a decimal fraction
f$_a$	= acceleration factor	Usually expressed as a decimal fraction	Usually expressed as a decimal fraction
f$_d$	= deceleration factor	Usually expressed as a decimal fraction	Usually expressed as a decimal fraction
f$_L$	= lateral acceleration factor	Usually expressed as a decimal fraction	Usually expressed as a decimal fraction
F	= force in pounds (newtons)	lbf	N kgf
g	= acceleration due to gravity	32.2 ft/s^2	9.81 m/s^2
h	= height	ft, in	m, cm
I	= inertia	slugs	kg, grams
kg	= kilograms		
Ke	= kinetic energy		
L	= length	ft, in	m, cm
l	= length	ft, in	m, cm
M	= mass	lb	kg
M	= middle ordinate	ft, in	m, cm
Mom	= momentum	lb.ft/s	kg.m/s
p	= momentum	lb.ft/s	kg.m/s
m	= grade, slope	percent	percent
	(See also lower case *e*)		
n	= percentage factor	e.g., percent braking efficiency	e.g., percent braking efficiency
R	= radius	ft, in	m, cm
r	= run, rise or fall	ft, in	m, cm
	(Used in measuring grade, slope or superelevation)		
S	= speed	mph	km/h
t	= time	hr, min, sec	hr, min, sec
t$_w$	= track width	Usually expressed in inches	Usually expressed in cm
Mu	= Coefficient of friction	Usually expressed as a decimal fraction	Usually expressed as a decimal fraction
	(See also *f*, drag factor)		
V	= velocity	ft/s	m/s
W	= weight	lb	kg

(continued)

GENERAL SYMBOLS, DEFINITIONS, AND MEASUREMENT UNITS *(Continued)*

Symbols and Descriptions

Symbols to Denote Specific Angles

α	= *alpha*	Angle in degrees
θ	= *theta*	Angle in degrees
ϕ	= *phi*	Angle in degrees
ψ	= *psi*	Angle in degrees
Ω	= *omega*	Any other specific angle

Common Symbols in Solving for Momentum Speed

α	= *alpha*	Vehicle 1's approach angle
θ	= *theta*	Vehicle 1's departure angle
ϕ	= *phi*	Vehicle 2's departure angle
ψ	= *psi*	Vehicle 2's approach angle
Ω	= *omega*	Any other specific angle

General Symbols in Traffic Accident Reconstruction

tan	= tangent		
tan Θ	= tangent of angle Θ		
$\in$	= coefficient of restitution		
Δ	= delta (Used to indicate change, e.g., ΔV = change in velocity)		
$\propto$	= directly proportional to		
$\cong$	= approximately equal; congruent		
$\sim$	= similar to; equivalent		
∞	= infinity		
π	= *pi* (3.14159) The ratio of the circumference and a diameter of the same circle.		
$\sqrt{}$	= radical sign		
Σ	= sigma; summation of		
$\pm$	= plus or minus		
cos	= cosine		
sin	= sine		
tan	= tangent		
n	= ad infinitum		
$\therefore$	= therefore		
W	= work	ft-lb	N-m or j
Y	= Y axis; vertical axis		
X	= X axis; horizontal axis		

Subscripts

X_o	=	subscript o denoting the original or initial factor for the component to which it is attached.
X_1	=	subscript 1 denoting an initial factor, such as speed or velocity, or number 1 for the component to which it is attached when two or more factors are involved. Additional factors may be denoted by subscripts 2 and 3 and so on.
X_f	=	subscript f denoting the final factor for the component to which it is attached.

Overline

$\overline{S}$	=	average speed. The small bar (overline) denotes average for the component to which it is attached.

RECOMMENDED READING

The following bibliography works are recommended by the author as material for further reading and study, and as acquisitions to form part of the practitioner's library.

Baxter, Albert J.: *Motorcycle Accident Investigation* (2nd ed.). Institute of Police Technology and Management, University of North Florida, Jacksonville, Florida, 1997.

Becker, Tony L.: *Vehicle-Pedestrian Collision Investigation Manual.* Institute of Police Technology and Management, University of North Florida, Jacksonville, Florida, 1997.

Bonnett, George M.: *Anatomy of a Collision: Energy, Momentum, Restitution and the Reconstructionist.* Institute of Police Technology and Management, University of North Florida, Jacksonville, Florida, 1999.

Brown, John Fiske & Obenski, Kenneth S.: *Forensic Engineering Reconstruction of Accidents.* Charles C Thomas, Springfield, Illinois, 1990.

Collins, J.C. & Morris, J.L.: *Highway Collision Analysis.* Charles C Thomas, Springfield, Illinois, 1974.

Craig, Victor (Ed.): *Accident Investigation Quarterly.* Published by the Accident Reconstruction Journal, PO Box 234, Waldorf, Maryland. Available by subscription.

Craig, Victor (Ed.): *Accident Reconstruction Journal.* Published by the Accident Reconstruction Journal, PO Box 234, Waldorf, Maryland. Available by subscription.

Daily, John.: *Fundamentals of Traffic Accident Reconstruction.* Institute of Police Technology and Management, University of North Florida, Jacksonville, Florida, 1988.

Daily, John & Shigemura, Nathan S.: *Fundamentals of Applied Physics for Traffic Accident Investigators* (Vol.1). Institute of Police Technology and Management, University of North Florida, Jacksonville, Florida, 1997.

DuBois, Robert A.: *Insurance Fraud and Motor Vehicle Collisions* (rev. ed.). Institute of Police Technology and Management, University of North Florida, Jacksonville, Florida, 1993.

Lynn B. Fricke et al.: *Traffic Accident Reconstruction, Vol. 2* (1st ed.). Northwestern University Center for Public Safety, Evanston, Illinois, 1990.

Homburger, Wolfgang S. & Kell, James H.: *Fundamentals of Traffic Engineering* (11th ed.). Institute of Transportation Studies, University of California, Berkeley, California, 1984.

Howell, Wiley L.: *Derivation Manual for Formulas Used in Traffic Accident Investigation and Reconstruction.* Institute of Police Technology and Management, University of North Florida, Jacksonville, Florida, 1994.

Pine, James L. (Ed.): *Traffic Engineering Handbook* (5th ed.). Institute of Transportation Engineers, Washington, DC, 1999.

Limpert, Rudolph: *Motor Vehicle Accident Reconstruction and Cause Analysis* (4th ed.). The Mitchie Company, Charlottesville, Virginia, 1994.

Lofgren, M.J.: *Handbook for the Reconstructionist* (3rd ed.). Institute of Police Technology and Management, University of North Florida, Jacksonville, Florida, 1983.

Mitchell, J.F.: *International Guide Book for Traffic Accident Reconstruction* (3rd ed.). New World Publishing, P. O. Box 36075 Halifax, N.S., B3J 3S9, Canada, 2002.

Navin, Francis P.D.: *Estimating Truck's Critical Cornering Speed and Factor of Safety.* Department of Civil Engineering, University of British Columbia, Vancouver, British Columbia, Canada, 1990.

Navin, Frank: *Reconstructing Truck Accidents from Tire Marks: Determining Truck Speed at Rollover.* Institute of Police Technology and Management, University of North Florida, Jacksonville, Florida, 2005.

Navin, Francis P.D.: Truck Braking Distance and Speed Estimates. *Canadian Journal of Civil Engineering,* 1986.

Noon, Randall K.: *Engineering Analysis of Vehicular Accidents.* CRC Press, Boca Raton, Florida, 1994.

Parkka, Daniel J.: *Equation Directory for the Reconstructionist* (2nd ed.). Institute of Police Technology and Management, University of North Florida, Jacksonville, Florida, 1996.

Rivers, R.W.: *Basic Physics. Notes for Traffic Crash Investigators and Reconstructionists. An Introduction for Some, A Review for Others.* Charles C Thomas, Springfield, Illinois, 2004.

Rivers, R.W.: *Traffic Accident Investigators' Lamp Analysis Manual.* Charles C Thomas, Springfield, Illinois, 2001.

Rivers, R.W.: *Speed Analysis for Traffic Accident Investigation.* Institute of Police Technology and Management, University of North Florida, Jacksonville, Florida, 1997.

Rivers, R.W.: *Traffic Accident Field Measurements and Scale Diagrams Manual.* Charles C Thomas, Springfield, Illinois, 1983.

Rivers, R.W.: *Traffic Accident Investigators' Book of Formulae and Tables.* Charles C Thomas, Springfield, Illinois, 1981.

Rivers, R.W.: *Traffic Accident Investigation Manual (A Levels 1 and 2 Reference, Training and Investigation Manual).* Charles C Thomas, Springfield, Illinois, 1995.

Rivers, R.W.: Tire *Failures and Evidence Manual.* Charles C Thomas, Springfield, Illinois, 2001.

Rivers, R.W.: *Technical Traffic Accident Investigators' Handbook (A Level 3 Reference, Training and Investigation Manual).* Charles C Thomas, Springfield, Illinois, 1997.

Rivers, R.W.: *Training and Reference Manual for Traffic Accident Investigation.* (3rd ed.). Institute of Police Technology and Management, University of North Florida, Jacksonville, Florida, 2005.

Stephens, Gary L.: *Formula Workbook for Traffic Accident Investigation and Reconstruction.* Institute of Police Technology and Management, University of North Florida, Jacksonville, Florida, 1989.

INDEX

A

Abbreviations and unit designations, Appendix A, Table A–1. *See also* 6.062, 9.035

ABS (MC), 10.037

Acceleration, 9.026
    defined, 9.027, 9.035
    due to gravity, Appendix A, Table A–7
    factor, 10.015; *see also* p. 195, Formula 9–20–14
    marks, 7.071, 7.072
    rate, normal, vehicle, 9.035, 10.016
    related to series of events, 9.028

Acceleration/deceleration, 9.026–9.033. *See also* Figs. 9.03–9.05
    constant, 9.027
    deceleration, 9.027
    defined, 9.027, 9.035
    rates, 9.027
    time, acceleration and velocity relationships explained, 9.029
    time and distance relationships explained, 9.030
    velocity and time, 9.029
    velocity, acceleration and time, 9.029

Accident. *See* Crash
    defined, 1.004
    Investigation Summary and *Evidence Check List, see* 1.030

Accreditation Commission for Traffic Crash Reconstruction (ACTAR), 1.131

ACTAR, 1.131

Action point, 1.018(I)

Acuity, visual, 3.032

Accuracy, errors and tolerances in the investigation process, 1.051–1.061, 2.006, 2.017
    in measurements (6 in or 15 cm), 9.095(b)
    rounding off, 1.065, 9.055
    speedometer, 9.052
    skid marks and speed, 1.054

Age, 3.050

Air bags, 8.113, Figs. 8–36, 8–37, 8–38. *See also* Safety Restraints
    NHTSA Executive Summary, 8.120

Air brakes, 8.060, Fig. 8–24
    Evidence and Investigation Check List, 8.064

Air-conditioning unit, 8.066
    recirculation, 8.066
    Evidence and Investigation CheckList, 8.067

Air, speed of sound in, Appendix A, Table A–17

Alcohol, 3.052

Analyst services, various, 1.071, 1.074

Analyzing series of events, 1.026–1.029

Appendices
    A English (U.S.) and Metric (SI) Measurement Systems Conversion Tables
    B English (U.S.) Conversion Tables
    C Metric (SI) Conversion Tables
    D Speedometer Accuracy Check List
    E General Symbols, Definitions and Measurement Units

At-scene overview, 7.038, 7.039

Note: This index is prepared as a *Quick-Find Index*. Terms used are intended to serve as prompters for locating items of interest. The paragraph numbering system takes the reader directly to an item's precise location without the necessity of having to search an entire page to locate the subject matter. In the references quoted, the number preceding the decimal point designates the chapter number and the following numbers designate the paragraph sequence in the chapter. For example, in the case of reference number *1.003*, the *1* designates Chapter *1* and *.003* designates the third paragraph of that chapter. Similarly, in the case of the number *4.035*, reference is made to Chapter *4* and paragraph *35* thereof. In the case of figures and formulae, *Figure 1-03* (or formula), for example, indicates the *third figure* (or formula) in *Chapter 1.*

At-rest position, 1.018(w)

B

Behavioral science resources, 1.086
Bias, 1.052
Black boxes, 8.082
   Evidence and Investigation Check List, 8.082
Blind spot, 3.015
Blow-out, 8.041
   tire remnants, Fig. 8–17
Bloodstain pattern analysis. *See* Chapter 5
   analyst assistance in investigations, 5.021
   analyst information, 5.018–5.019
   blood sample collection, 5.028
   categories, 5.017
   determining direction, 5.011
   DNA exhibit collection, 5.030
   examination, 5.003
   exhibits, handling of, 5.034
   history, 5.005, 5.012
   hit-and-run cases, 5.020
   introduction, 5.001
   objectives, 5.003
   pedestrian collisions, 5.022
   photography and stains, 5.026
   physical properties, 5.008
   purpose, 5.003
   seating positions, determination, 5.022
   traffic collision evidence, 5.021
Body repair shops, assistance of, 1.093
Bounce tire marks, 7.092, Fig. 7–59
Braked wheel tire evidence, 7.089, Fig. 7.55
Brakes, 8.051
   ABS (MC), 10.037
   assumption if no skid marks, 8.053
   extended use on down grades, 8.058
      overheating, 8.058
   fluid loss, 8.054
   inspections, 8.053
   low pedal reserve, 8.057
   Evidence and Investigation Guide, 8.057
lining wear, 8.055
steering loss, 8.056
types of systems, 8.051, Fig. 8–22
   ABS (MC) 10.037
   air brakes, 8.060, Fig. 24
      chamber, Fig. 8–25
      operation, 8.061–8.064, Fig. 8–24

Evidence and Investigation Check List, 8.064
   disc, 8.051(2), Figs. 8–20, 8–21
   drum, 8.051(1), Figs. 8–19, 8–21
   parking brake, 8.052, Fig. 8–23
Braking and skid distance
   influences, 9.084
Braking, 9.053, 9.081
   Efficiency, Table 9–01
   fading, 8.058
   on hills, 8.058
Bright lights, 8.007
Business forensic specialist, 1.093

C

Carbon-monoxide poisoning, 8.066
Cause analysis, 1.029, *see also* Chapter 2
   proximate cause explained, Chapter 2
   traffic engineering, 7.027, 7.032
Center of gravity (CG), defined, 9.019
   path, in yaw, 9.116, Fig. 9–30
Center of mass (C/M), defined, 9.019
   path, in yaw, 9.116, Fig. 9–30
Centrifugal and centripetal forces, 9.008, 9.009, 9.109, 9.112
Chip, defined, 7.047, Fig. 7–18
Child safety restraints, 8.111
   Investigation and Evidence Guide, 8.112
Chop, 7.047, Fig. 7–18
Chopper, 10.008
Coefficient of friction, 9.041, 9.042. *See also* drag factor
   defined, 9.041
   examples, Figs. 9–11, 9–12, 9–13
   Formula 9–23 (*see* 9.045)
   rounding off, 9.055
Coefficient of friction and drag factor, 9.041–9.090, Figs. 9–11, 9–12, 9–13
   Coefficient of Friction and Drag Factor Guide, Table 9–02 (*see* 9.090)
Clothing, pedestrian, 3.057
Collision, defined, 1.004
Color blindness, 3.049
Combined speeds, 9.133
   explained, 9.133
   Formula 9–39 (9.134)
Commercial vehicle crash investigations, 9.136
   skid mark measurements, 9.095(f)
   skid marks, 7–092, Fig. 7–58
   speed estimates, 9.137

websites, following, 8.155

Complex, inferiority, 1.130

Complex reaction, 1.018(e)(ii)

Computers, on-board, 8.083

Constants, English and SI, 9.035, Appendix A, Table A–5

Constant acceleration, defined, 9.027

Contact points, 8.154

Conversion tables, *see* Appendices

Conversions

    acceleration due to gravity, Appendix A, Table A–7

    acceleration ft/s and m/s, Appendix A, Table A–6

    centimeters-to-inches, Appendix C, Table C–3

    coefficient of friction to deceleration rate (English), Appendix B, Table B–2

    coefficient of friction to deceleration rate (SI), Appendix C, Table C–2

    definitions and factors, 9.035

    distance, speed and velocity, Appendix A, Table A–2

    factors, Formulae 9–19–1, 9–19–2

    feet-to-meters, Appendix B, Table B–4

    force, power, pressure, energy or work, Appendix A, Table A–12

    horsepower, Appendix A, Table A–14

    inches-to-centimeters, Appendix B, Table B–3

    international nautical miles and kilometers, Appendix A, Table A–16

    kilometers-to-miles, Appendix C, Table C–5

    km/hr - to - m/s, Appendix C, Table C–1

    length, Appendix A, Table A–8

    linear relationships, Appendix A, Table A–3

    meters-to-feet, Appendix C, Table C–4

    miles-to-kilometers, Appendix B, Table B–5

    momentum, Appendix A, Table A–13

    mph - to - ft/s, Appendix B, Table B–1

    torque, Appendix A, Table A–15

    velocity and speed relationships, Appendix A, Table A–4

    volume, Appendix A, Table A–10

    weight, Appendix A, Table A–9

    weight - mass, Appendix A, Table A–11

Coordinate, defined, 6.071(i)

    methods, 6.072

Coroner-medical examiner, 1.078

Crash. *see also* under investigation and accident

    analysis, 1.003, 1.005, 1.008, 1.009, 1.026, 1.028, codes, 1.027

    analysis using *Series of Events*, 1.026–1.028

    applying principles of perception, dynamics and

    general physics, 1.003

    at-scene investigation, 1.026. *See also* Chapter 7; 7.038, 7.039, and under *Series of Events*

    cause analysis, 1.029

    contacts in collision, 1.018

    definition, 1.001, 1.004

    etiology of, Fig. 2–01, 2.007

    events in, 1.016

    introduction to, *see* under *Series of Events*

    included items and summary of evidence, *see Investigation and Evidence Check List,* 1.030

    objectives, 1.005–1.008

    phases and levels of, 1.036

    process, objectives, 1.005

    role of human reliability, cognition and effect in coping with hazards, Fig. 2.02, 2.012

Critical speed, 9.108

Crush speed analysis, 9.135

Cupping, tire, 7.060

Curves, vehicle motion in, 9.010

Curve skid mark measurements, 9.095(c)(ii)

D

Damage

    air bag, Fig. 8–46

    contact, 8.144, Figs. 8–42, 8–43

    impact and damage sequence, 8.146

    imprints, p. 169, Fig. 8–41

    induced or incidental, 8.129, 8.145, Fig. 8–45

    sequence of glass damage, 8.146

    spider web, glass, 8.144

    superimposed, 8.128

    vehicle, 8.126

    Evidence and Investigation Check List, 8.132

Debris, roadway, 7.044; 7.090, Fig. 7–56

Decimal places, 1.062–1.065

    rounding off, 1.065

Definitions and symbols, 6.062, 9.035

Digital photographs, *see* Chapter 6

Dentists, orthodontists, 1.080

Depth perception, 3.034

Design flaws, defective products, 2.022

Detached utility trailer skid marks, 7.095, Fig. 7–61

Devices, traffic-control, 7.001

Digits, 1.062

Disclaimer, manual, p. xvii

Distance and time relationships, 9.032

Distractions, 3.055, 8.078

general, 3.055

horn, siren, 8.077

noise within vehicle, 8.078

smoking, 3.054

Evidence and Investigation Check Lists, 8.077, 8.078

DNA, 1.091

collection, 5.030

Documentation

exhibits, 1.122

reports, 1.121

Door locks and malfunctions, 8.079

Evidence and Investigation Check List, 8.079

Drag factor, 9.041–9.043. Figs. 9–11 to 9–13. *See also* Coefficient of friction

accelerometer-electronic devices, 9.057, Fig. 9–18

calibration, 9.058

accuracy, 1.054, 1.055

averaging skid marks, 9.054, Fig. 9–17

adjustments (± grades, braking efficiencies,) and examples, 9.075–9.083. *See* Formulae 9–30, 9–30A, B, C, D, E, pp. 208–213

braking efficiency and capability, 9.053, 9.081, Table 9–01

brakeless trailer, 9.099

calculation, 9.066; Formula 9–27

Caution in testing, 9.048

clothing slide drag factors, 10.040

derivation, Formula 9–27, 9.066, *Example* Formula 9–28

defined, 9.041, 9.043

drag sleds, 9.067

calibration, 9.072–9.074; *Example*, 9.074,Formula 9–29

operation, 9.069–9.071, 9.118(2); 9.069, pp. 205, 206, Figs. 9–20, 9–21, 9–22

protocols, 9.071

types, 9.067, 9.068, Fig. 9–19

yaw procedures, 9.071(6), Fig. 9–22

Examples, Figs. 9–11, 9–12, 9–13

Formulae 9–23 (*see* 9.045); 9–30 (*see* 9.078); Formulae 9–30A, 9–30B (*see* 9.080).

influences on braking distance, 9.084

lead-in skid mark, Figs. 9–16, 7–52

longest skid mark, 9.056, Fig. 9–17

methods of determining, 9.048

motorcycle slide drag factors, 10.040

rounding off, 9.055

shot marker, 9.050, Fig. 9–15

slopes, 9.076, 9.080

special problems, 9.100

speedometer accuracy test, 9.052, Formula 9–26

test skids, 9.049

averaging, 9.054

longest skid mark, 9.054, 9.056, 9.095(d); Fig. 9–17, p. 200

measurements, 9.055

procedures, 9.052, 9.054, Figs. 9–16, 9–17

rounding off measurements, 9.055

tolerances, 1.054, 1.055

trailers, brakeless, 9.099

when slope involved, 9.076, Figs. 9–23, Formula 9–30

Drag Factor and Coefficient of Friction Guide, Table 9–02, 9.090. *See also* 9.053, 9.081 and Table 9–01

Drag sleds, 9.067

calibration, 9.072

operation, 9.053, 9.069, 9.071(6), Figs. 9–20, 9–21, 9–22

types, 9.067, 9.068

yaw procedures, 9.071(6), Fig. 9–22

Drive trains, 8.004

FWD, 8.004(2), Fig. 8–04

RWD, 8.004(1). *See* Figs. 8–02, p. 133; 8–08, p. 140

4WD, 8.005

Driver's compartment

Evidence and Investigation Check Lists, 8.069, 8.132

seating positions, 4.024–4.029, 8.132, 8.153

Driver, factors, 1.017

distractions, 8.078

Evidence and Investigation Check List, 8.078

injuries, front and rear, 4.027, 4.028

Drop-off, trafficway, edge, 7.040, Fig. 7–12

Duties of investigator, 1.042

Dynamic friction, 9.025

E

Edge, trafficway, drop-off, 7.040, Fig. 7–12

Education and training, 1.040

Education professionals, 1.094

Engineering, highway, basic principles of, *see* Chapter 7, Part 1

local engineers plans, 7.028

photography, importance and use of, 6.026

traffic-control devices, 7.003

Environmental factors, 1.017, 1.018, 3.056

clothing, 3.057

highways, 3.058

lighting, 3.056

lights, 3.056

Errors in the investigation process, 1.051–1.061, 2.005, 2.022

error possibilities, 1.061

human error, *see* Chapter 2

mistake, defined, 2.017(2)

points to be covered, 2.022

tolerances, 1.051–1.061

Ethics, 1.126

definitions, 1.128

Events in a crash, *see Series of Events*, 1.016

defined, 1.010

factors, 1.017

Evasive actions, 1.018

Evidence

definitions, 1.001, 1.104

expert, defined, 1.103

fixing liability, 1.002

opinion, 1.105

physical, 1.002

recognition, significance, preservation of, 1.002

safeguarding of, 1.046

technicians, 1.092

Exhaust system, 8.065, Fig. 8–26

air-conditioning, 8.066

carbon-monoxide, 8.066

muffler, 8.065, Fig. 8–26

See: *Evidence and Investigation Check Lists*, 8.065, 8.067, 8.069

Exhibits, 1.122, 1.125

External forces, 9.007

Eyesight. *See* Chapter 3

adaption, 3.037

day and night vision, 3.024

eye function, 3.009

rods and cones, 3.012

visual field, 3.016, 3.033

Expert, 1.103. *See also* under Duties and Responsibilities, 1.042–1.044

business, trade, industrial, 1.093

definitions, 1.104

documentation, 1.121

educational, 1.094

evaluator, 1.114

opinion, 2.022

qualifications, 1.105–1.110

responsibilities, 1.108

witness, 1.110

F

Formulae Summary *

Acceleration, Formulae 9–08, p. 190; 9–18, p. 192 (*see also* under 9.030, 9.033)

Acceleration factor, Formulae 9–20–14, p. 195; 10–04, p. 237; 10–09, p. 238 (*see* under 9.035, 10.015, 10.026)

Acceleration from a known speed, Formula 9–20–16, p. 195 (*see* under 9.035)

Acceleration rate, Formulae 9–20–13, 9–20–18, p. 195; 10–05, p. 237 (*see* under 9.035, 10.015)

Aquaplaning (hydroplaning), Formula 9–30E, p. 213 (*see* 9.087)

Average speed and velocity, Formula 9–20–2, pp. 193, 194 (*see* under 9.035)

Coefficient of friction, Formula 9–23, p. 198 (*see* under 9.045)

Combined speed, Formula 9–39, p. 228 (*see* under 9.134)

Converting speed (mph or km/h) to Velocity (ft/s or m/s), Formula 9–19–2, p. 193; Table 10–01, p. 236 (*see* under 9.035, 10–011)

Converting velocity (ft/sec or m/s) to speed (mph or km/h), Formula 9–19–1, p. 193; Table 10–1, p. 236 (*see* under 9.035, 10–011)

Deceleration rate and drag factor, Formula 9–20–18, p. 195 (*see* under 9.035)

Distance covered during acceleration/deceleration from a known velocity, Formula 9–20–8, p. 194 (*see* under 9.035)

Distance covered during acceleration from a stop, Formula 9–20–9, p. 194 (*see* under 9.035)

Distance covered when acceleration rate and time are known, Formula 10–06, p. 237 (*see* under 10.017). *See also* Formula 9–20–9, p. 194 under 9.035

Distance and time, Formulae 9–11, 9–15, pp. 191, 192

---

* Velocity and speed change formulae are explained in Paras. 9.034 and 9.035. (*See also* Chapter 10, containing formulae specific to motorcycles which are also indexed above.)

(*see also* under 9.031, 9.032, 9.033)

Distance traveled during constant acceleration, Formula 9–20–3, p. 194 (*see* under 9.035)

Distance traveled each consecutive second during deceleration when skid distance and drag factor are known, Formula 9–20–22, p. 196 (*see* under 9.035)

Distance required to stop when initial speed and drag factor are known, Formula 9–20–22, p. 196 (*see* under 9.035)

Distance required to pass, Formula 10–10, p. 238 (*see* under 10.027)

Distance traveled when speed or velocity is constant, Formula 9–20–1, p. 193 (*see* under 9.034)

Drag factor adjustments, Formulae 9–30, 9–30A, B, C, D, pp. 210, 211 (*see* under 9.078, 9.080, 9.082)

Drag Factor and Coefficient of Friction Guide, 9.090, Table 9–02, pp. 213, 214

Drag Factor, Formulae 9–24, p. 198; 9–27, p. 203; ± grade 9–30, p. 208; (*see* under 9.045, 9.066)

Drag factor calibration, Formula 9–29, p. 207 (*see* under 9.074)

Force, Formulae 9–01, p. 185: 9–29, p. 207 (*see* under 9.006, 9.074)

Falls, Formulae 9–35, p. 225; 9–36, p. 226 (*see* under 9.129, 9.130)

Flip and vault, level takeoff and landing, Formula 9–37, p. 226 (*see* under 9.132)

Flip and vault, non-level takeoff and landing, Formula 9–38, p. 228 (*see* under 9.132)

    Vault speed, Formula 10–14, p. 243 (*see* under 10.049)

Grade, slope, superelevation, Formula 9–25, p. 199 (*see* under 9.047)

Hydroplaning, Formula 9–30E, p. 213 (*see* under 9.087)

Kinetic energy, Formula 9–04, p. 187 (*see* under 9.016)

Mass, Formula 9–02, p. 186 (*see* under 9.011)

Motion, Formula 9–11 to 9–13, p. 191 (*see* 9.031)

Motorcycle Formulae, Chapter 10

    acceleration factor, Formula 10–04, p. 237 (*see* under 10.015)

    acceleration factor during acceleration, Formula 10–09, p. 238 (*see* under 10.026)

    acceleration rate, Formula 10–05, p. 237 (*see* under 10.016)

    distance when acceleration rate and time are known, Formula 10–06, p. 237 (*see* under 10.017)

    initial speed calculation, Formula 10–11, p. 239 (*see* under 10.028)

    lean angle, Formula 10–01, p. 235 (*see* under 10.010)

    passing distance, Formula 10–10, p. 238 (*see* under 10.027)

    passing potential, Formula 10–08, p. 238 (*see* under 10.019)

    radius of curve and lean angle, Formula 10–02, p. 236 (*see* under 10.011)

    slide-to-stop speeds, Formulae 10–7, p. 238 (10.018); 10–12, p. 241 (10.039)

    speed based engine revolutions, Formula 10–13, p. 242 (*see* under 10.044)

    speed based on vault of operator or motorcycle, Formula 10–14, p. 243 (*see* under 10.045)

Passing potential, Formula 10–08, p. 238 (*see* under 10.019)

Pythagorean Theorem, Formula 9–05, p. 188 (*see* under 9.023)

Radius, Formulae 9–33, p. 223; 10–02, p. 236 (*see* under 9.118, 10–011)

Skid distance required to stop when initial speed and drag factor are known, Formula 9–20–22, p. 196 (*see* under 9.035)

Speed and velocity when distance and time are known, Formula 9–20–4, p. 194 (*see* under 9.035)

Speed after uniform acceleration and time, Formula 10–08, p. 238 (*see* under 10.019)

Speed, initial, when distance and acceleration factor known, Formula 10–11, p. 238 (*see* under 10.028)

Speed at any time during known acceleration rate from a stop, Formula 9–20–10, p. 194 (*see* under 9.035)

Speed at any point during deceleration, Formula 9–20–19, p. 195 (*see* under 9.035)

Speed when acceleration factor is known, Formula 9–20–15, p. 195 (*see* under 9.035)

Speed from skid marks, Formulae 9–28, p. 210; 9–31, p. 217; 10–07, p. 238; 10–12, p. 241 (*see* under 9.082, 9.096, 10.018, 10.039). Derivation of the formulae, *see* p. 204

Speed from MC engine revolutions, Formula 10–13, p. 242 (*see* under 10.044)

Speed from skid marks on different type of surfaces, Formula 9–32, p. 218 (*see* under 9.098)

Speedometer accuracy test, Formula 9–26, p. 201 (*see* under 9.052)

Speed and velocity after certain period of time, Formula 10–08, p. 238 (*see* under 10.019)

Tangent of Lean Angle, Formula 10–01, p. 235 (*see* under 10.010)

Time, Formulae 9–07, 9–12, pp. 190, 191 (*see also* under 9.030, 9.032)

Time to accelerate from stop to a given velocity when acceleration rate is known, Formula 9–20–12A, p. 194 (*see* under 9.035)

Time to decelerate to a stop when initial velocity and deceleration rate are known, Formula 9–20–12B, p. 194 (*see* under 9.035)

Time for acceleration from a known speed, Formula 9–20–17, p. 195 (*see* under 9.035)

Time required to slide (skid) to a given point when slide distance and drag factor are known, Formula 9–20–20, p. 196 (*see* under 9.035)

Time required to slide (skid) to a stop when slide distance and drag factor are known, Formula 9–20–21, p. 196 (*see* under 9.035)

Time to travel a distance at a constant velocity, Formula 9–20–7, p. 194 (*see* under 9.035)

Vault speed (general), Formula 10–14, p. 243 (*see* under 10.045)

Velocity at any point during deceleration, Formula 9–20–19, p. 195 (*see* under 9.035)

Velocity, acceleration, time and distance formulae, various, pp. 189–192 (*see* explanations under 9.030, 9.031, 9.033)

Velocity, average, Formulae 9–09, 9–10, 9–13, 9–14 (*see* under 9.030, 9.031)

Velocity after acceleration from stop at known acceleration rate and distance, Formula 9–20–11, p. 194 (*see* under 9.035)

Velocity after acceleration from a known velocity, distance, and rate, Formula 9–20–16, p. 195 (*see* under 9.035)

Velocity or speed at any point during deceleration when skid distance and drag factor are known, Formula 9–20–19, p. 195 (*see* under 9.035)

Velocity when radius and lateral acceleration are known, Formula 10–02, p. 236 (*see* under 10–012).

Velocity (initial), Formula 10–11, p. 239 (*see* under 10.028)

Weight, Formula 9–03, p. 186 (*see* under 9.011)

Yaw speed, Formula 9–34, p. 223 (*see* under 9.118)

Fail to remain at scene. *See* and apply specific elements of an investigation under index headings, with emphasis on driver identification.

Fall, flip and vault speeds, 9.126, 10.047

fall, 9.127, Fig. 9–33

defined, 9.127

level takeoff area, Formula 9–35 (*see* under 9.129)

non-level takeoff area, Formula 9–36 (*see* under 9.130)

flip and vault, 9.131

defined, 9.131, Fig. 9–34

level takeoff and landing, Formula 9–37

non-level takeoff and landing, Formula 9–38

See also MC speed calculations under Chapter 10.

Fatal injury, 1.018(y)

Fault

entire system, 2.022

product design, 2.022

Field measurements. *See* under *Scene Measurements and Plan Drawing*, Chapter 6, Part. 2

Field sketch, 6.056

Field of vision, 3.033

Final position, 1.018(v)

Fire victims. *See* under Pathology and 4.056

Fires, 8.150, Figs. 8–47 to 8–49

Caution to investigators: 8.152

causes, 8.151

Evidence and Investigation Guides and Check Lists, 8.151, 8.152

fraud, *see* 8.151

objectives of investigation, 8.150

Flip, fall and vault speeds, 9.126, 10.047. *See also* under fall, flip and vault speeds, in Chapter 10.

Forensics

laboratories, 1.090

specialists, 1.075

Force, 9.006. *See also* Appendix A, Table A–12

centrifugal and centripetal, 9.008, 9.009

defined, 9.006

external, 9.007

Formula 9–01, p. 185, under 9.006

principal direction of, 8.127, Figs. 8–39, 8–40

Forensic specialist services

business, 1.093

chemistry, 1.075

definitions, 1.075

engineers, 1.075

industrial, 1.093

mechanics, 1.075

medical professionals, 1.075
    trade, 1.093
Forward-reverse acceleration marks, 7.072, Fig. 7–42
Fraud, 1.117–1.119
Fraudulent reports
    ingredients for investigation, 1.117
    suicide, 1.117
Friction, 9.024
    defined, 9.025
    dynamic, 9.025(2)
    kinetic, 9.025(2)
    static, 9.025(1)
Furrows, ruts, 7.073, Fig. 7–43

G

Gap skid marks, 9.095(g)
Gear shift position and speed, 8.088, 10.034
Glare, 3.054; 7.024(d), (e); 7.031, 7.032, 7.043, 8.147; Fig.
    7–15, p. 107
Glass damage and condition, 8.141
    causes, 8.143
        direct/indirect causes, 8.143
    contact, 8.144, Figs. 8–42 to 8–44
    Evidence and Investigation Check List, 8.069
    fragments, 8.142
    impact and damage sequence, 8.146
    induced, 8.145, Fig. 8–45
    occupant, air bag cover impact, 8.143, Fig. 8–46
    sequence of glass damage, 8.146
    smoke film, 3.054
    spider web damage, 8.144
    types, 8.141
        laminated, 8.141
        tempered, 8.141
    windshield and windows, 8.068, 8.069, 8.147
        obstructions to visibility, 8.068, 8.069, 8.147
        positions (open/shut), 8.068, 8.069, 8.147
Gouge, 7.047, Fig. 7–18
Grade, slope, superelevation, 9.046, Fig. 9–14B, Formula
    9–25
Gravity, center of (C/M), 9.018
Grinding, pavement, 7.064
Groove, 7.046, Fig. 7–17

H

Hemastix®, use of in blood stains, 5.023

Hit and run. *See* and apply specific elements of an inves-
    tigation under index headings, with emphasis on
    driver identification.
Hole, 7.048, Fig. 7–19
Horn, siren, 8.077
    noise and distractions within vehicle, 8.078
    Evidence and Investigation Check List, 8.077
Horsepower, Appendix A, Table A–14
Highway–*see* Trafficway, Chapter 7
Highway engineering, principles of, *see* Chapter 7, Part 1
Highway marks, tire marks, skid marks,
    damages, etc., *see* Chapter 7, Part 2, Trafficway
Human error. *See* Chapter 2
    as a systems failure, 2.001
    in investigations, Chapter 2, 2.005
Human factors. *See* Chapter 2 and *Series of Events*
    defined, 1.016, Chapter 2
    inferiority complex, 1.030
Human reliability and error, 2.006. *See* Chapter 2
    error and risk-taking, 2.017, Fig. 2–03
    investigating role of, 2.002
Hydroplaning, 9.085, Formula 9–30E

I

Identification and interpretation of trafficway obstruc-
    tions, defects, marks and damage evidence,
    7.037–7.039. *See* Example, Fig. 7–11, p. 104.
    See also under Tire marks.
    acceleration marks, 7.071, Figs. 7–41A, B, C, D
    chip or gouge, 7.047, Fig. 7–18
    cross-over tire marks, 7.068, Fig. 7–38
    debris 7.044, 7.045, 7.090, Figs. 7–11, 7–16
        tire deposit, 7.090, Figs. 7–56A, 7–56B, 7–56C
    flat tire marks, 7.059, Fig. 7–29
    forward-reverse acceleration mark, 7.072, Fig. 7–42
    furrows and ruts, 7.078, Figs. 7–43A, B
    glare, 7.043, Fig. 7–15
    gouge or chip, 7.047, Fig. 7–18
    groove, defined, 7.046, Fig. 7–17
    hole, defined, 7.048, Fig. 7–19
    matching undercarriage parts, 7.050, Fig. 7–21
    matching vehicle damage to roadside objects, 7.049,
        Figs. 7–20A, B
    overloaded or underinflated (overdeflected) tire mark,
        7.060, Fig. 7–30
    pavement-edge drop-off, 7.040, Fig. 7–12
    pavement grinding, 7.064, Fig. 7–34

roadway alignment, 7.041, Fig. 7–14

roadway damage, 7.041, Fig. 7–13

scrapes and scratches, 7.045, Fig. 7–16

scuff mark, 7.070, Fig. 7–40

shadow evidence, 7.061, Fig. 7–31

spinning tire, 7.063, Fig. 7–33

striation marks, 7.065, Fig. 7–35

studded tire striation marks, 7.067, Fig. 7–37

tire deposit, 7.090, Figs. 7–56A, 7–56B, 7–56C

tire prints, 7.069, Fig. 7–39

tire shapes and contours, 7.056, 7.058, Fig. 7–27, Figs. 7–28A, B

tire sideslipping and tread groove debris, 7.062, Fig. 7–32

undercarriage evidence, 7.051, Fig. 7–22

yaw mark striations, 7.066, Fig. 7–36

Impending skid marks, 7.086, 9.091; Fig. 7–52, p. 123. *See also* Fig. 9–12C, p. 197

    calculating a minimum speed, 9.093. *See also* Fig. 9–12C, p. 197

Industrial forensic specialists, 1.093

Inferiority complex, 1.130

Information sources, 1.116

Injuries. *See also* under Pathology

    burns, 4.018

    classification and description of, 4.014

    driver, 4.026

    fatal, 1.018(y)

    location of person, determinations from injuries sustained, 4.025–4.030; motorcyclists and cyclists, 4.034

    passengers, 4.027, 4.028

    patterns, 4.024. *See* Chapter 4, Part 1

    pedestrian, 4.030

    personal, 1.018(x)

    primary and secondary impact determinations, 4.024, 4.051

    safety restraints, 4.022

Inspections, vehicle. *See* Chapter 8

Investigation, *see also* under accident and crash introduction. *See Series of Events*

    item summary and *Evidence Check List, see* 1.030

    objectives, 1.006

    process, objectives, 1.005

Intermittent skid marks, 7.091, Fig. 7–57; 9.095(g)

Incipient skid marks, 9.091

Incident, defined, 1.004

Inertia, defined, 9.004, 9.007, 9.009

Instruments, measuring

accuracy, errors, tolerances, 1.051–1.061

    integer values, 1.063

    significant digits, 1.062

Investigator's

    conclusions, 1.115

    duties, 1.042

    responsibilities, 7.002

K

Kinetic energy, 9.016, Formula 9–04

    defined, 9.016, 9.017

Kinetic or dynamic friction, 9.025(2)

L

Laboratory services, 1.071

    forensic, 1.090, 1.075

    medical, 1.088

    names of, 1.074

Lamps and reflectors, 8.007

    commercial vehicles, 8.012

    disclaimer, 8.044, p. 150

    failure to dim, 8.007

    filament examination, 8.010, 8.011

        hi-beam indicator, 8.007

        forcing vehicle off road, 8.007

        pedestrian collisions, 8.007

    overdriving, 8.007

    switch, 8.008, 8.009

        push-pull type in crash, 8.008

        Caution: do not turn on or off, 8.009

    Evidence and Investigation Check List, 8.012

Laws of motion, 9.003

    examples, 9.005

Legal assistance, 1.101

Levels

    investigation, 1.036

    training, 1.036

Liabilities, 1.002

Lighting, 3.056

    environmental, 3.056

    lamps, 3.056

Limitations of comments and interpretations in this manual, 1.073

Loads, 8.076

    falling off, 8.076

    vehicle control, etc., 8.076

    view obstructions, 8.076

Evidence and Investigation Check List, 8.076
Longest skid mark
    rounding off, 9.055
    use of, procedure, 9.054, 9.056, 9.095(d)
Looming
    defined, 2.012
    model, 2.013, Fig. 2–02
    role of human reliability, Fig. 2–02
    vulnerability, 2.012
Luminol, use of in blood stains, 5.023

M

Marks and highway damages, Fig. 7–11. *See* Chapter 7
    matching marks and damage with vehicle, 7.038; Fig.
        7–11, p. 104
Markings, roadway, 7.003, 7.023, 7.024
Mark, tire, 7.056
Mass, 9.011
    center of, 9.019
    defined, 9.001
    example, 9.012
    Formula 9–02
    weight, 9.011
Matching collision damages, Fig. 7–11. *See* Trafficway
        Evidence, Chapter 7
    roadside, 7.049; Fig. 7–20, p. 110
    undercarriage parts, 7.050, 7.051; Figs. 7–21, 7–22,
        pp. 111, 112
Measurement (*see* Chapter 6, Part 2). *See also* under *Scene
        Investigation and Evidence*
    accuracy, to within 6 in or 15 cm, 9.095(b)
    devices, 1.055, Table 1–02
    error possibilities, 1.061
    format, 9.095(b)
    markers, use in, 9.095(b)
    methods and devices, 1.055, Table 1–02
    procedures, 9.095 (c)
    straight-line method, 6.077
    tire, skid marks, 9.095(c)
Mechanical inspections, *see* Chapter 8
Medical. *See also* under Pathology
    examiner, *see* Chapter 4, Part 2
    professionals, 1.076
Meters
    accuracy in readings, 1.062, 1.063, 1.064
    integer values, 1.063
    significant digits, 1.062
Minimum speed, 9.093

Mirrors, 8.070
    Evidence and Investigation Check List, 8.070
Mistake, defined, 2.017(2)
Momentum. *See* Appendix A, Table A–13
    defined, 9.014
    discussed, 9.097
Motion. *See* Formula 9–11 and Para. 9.031
    defined, 9.013, 9.031
Motorcycles
    ABS investigation, 10.037
    acceleration, 10.013, 10.015
        factor, 10.015
            defined, 10.015
            during acceleration, 10.026, Formula 10–09
            Formula 10–04, p. 237
        rate, 10.016
            conversion to acceleration factor, 10.018
            Formula 10–05, p. 237
    basics, 10.005
    brake systems, 10.035–10.037
    braking, 10.029
    chopper, 1.008
    clothing slide drag factors, 10.040
    controls, 10.004, Fig. 10–06
    dynamics, 10.006
    gear shift lever position during passing, 10.034, 10.043
    high-siding, 10.030
    introduction, 10.001
    mechanical considerations, 10.034
    motorcycle slide drag factors, 10.040
    passing potential, 10.019, Formula 10–08, p. 238
    rake, 10.008, Fig. 10–10
    reaction time, 10.033
    skid-marks, 9.095(j)
    slide-out, 10.037
    slide-to-stop speeds, Formulae 10–7, p. 238 (10.018);
        10–12, p. 241 (10.039)
        clothing slide drag factors, 10.040
        motorcycle slide drag factors, 10.040
    speed from gear shift position, 10.043
    speed based on engine revolutions, 10.041, 10.044,
        Formula 10–13
    speed based on vault of operator or motorcycle,
        10.045, Formula 10–14
    speed, initial, calculation, Formula 10–11
    tachometer, 10.004
    trail, 10–009
    types, 10.002, Figs. 10–01 to 10–8
    turning, 10.010

lean angle, Formula 10–01
radius of curve, Formula 10–02

N

Nautical miles and kilometers, Appendix A, Table A–16
Newton's Laws of Motion, 9.003
Noise and distractions within vehicle, 8.078
    horn, siren, 8.077

O

Objectives of investigation, 1.006
Obstructions, marks, damages, 7.037. *See* Chapter 7
Occupational specialists, 1.042, 1.044, 1.071
Offset skid marks, 7.088, Fig. 5–54
    measurements, 9.095(i)
Operator error, 2.005
Opinion evidence, 1.105
Orthodontists, 1.080
Overlapping skid marks, 7.087, Fig. 7–53

P

Paint chips and transfers, 8.133–8.135
Parking brake, 8.052, Fig. 8–23
Pass-over tire marks, 7.068, Fig. 7–38
Passenger injuries
    driver, 4.052
    front-seat, 4.027
    infants and children, 4.029
    rear-seat, 4.028
Pavement edge, drop off, 7.040
Pedestrian
    injuries, 4.030
    walking rate, 9.035
Perception, depth, 3.034
Physics, 9.002
    center of gravity, 9.019. *See also* Figs. 9.01A, 9–01B,
        p. 188
    center of mass, 9.019, Figs. 9.01A, 9–01B, p. 188
    centrifugal force defined, 9.009
    centripetal and centrifugal forces, 9.008
    curves, 9.010
    external forces, 9.007
    force defined, 9.006
    gravity, 9.018
    inertia, 9.004, 9.007(b), 9.009
    kinetic energy, 9.016

mass and weight, 9.011, 9.012
    mass defined, 9.011
    weight defined, 9.011
momentum, 9.014
motion, 9.013
Newton's three laws of motion, 9.003
vectors, 9.022, Fig. 9–02
work, 9.015
Pathologist, 1.077, 1.079
    Evidence and Investigation Guide/Check List, 4.036,
        4.037
Pathology. *See* Chapter 4, Part 1
    at-scene investigations, 4.024
    burns, 4.018, 4.056
    classification of injuries, 4.014
    cyclists, 4.034
    driver injuries, 4.026, 4.052
    dynamics of crash injury, 4.002
    fire victims, 4.056
    fractures, 4.020
    front-seat passenger injuries, 4.026
    information for the pathologist, 4.039
    infants, small children injuries, 4.029
    injuries
        classification, 4.014
        infants, small children, 4.029
        interpretation, 4.013
        rear-seat passengers, 4.028, 8.154
        related to impact areas, 4.024, 8.154
        restraints, safety, 4.022
        rear-seat passenger injuries, 4.028, 8.154
        types of, 4.015
    introduction to pathology and accident reconstruction,
        4.001
    location of victims at scene, 4.003
    medical condition following crash, 4.005
    motorcyclists, cyclists, 4.034, 4.055
    pedestrians, 4.030, 4.049
    post-mortem examination, 4.035
    prior medical history, 4,008
    rear-seat passenger injuries, 4.028, 8.054
    relating injuries to impact areas, 4.024
    restraint injuries, 4.022
    seating positions, 4.035, 8.054
    victims, 4.021, 4.024, 4.052
        location at scene, 4.003
Pathology and the Medical Examiner, *see* Chapter 4,
    Part 2
    driver, passenger victims, 4.052

expectations of the medical examiner, 4.046
fire victims, 4.056
motorcycle victims, 4.055
pedestrian victims, 4.049
safety restraint evidence and procedures, 4.022, 4.052
Pedestrian
bloodstain analysis, 5.022
clothing, 3.057
injuries, 4.030, 4.049
traffic signal, Fig. 7–03(B)
walking rates, 9.035
Perception, 1.016, 1.018, 3.042. *See Series of Events*
blind spot, defined, 3.015
definition, 1.018
four-step process, 3.042
time, defined, 3.007
Perception-reaction time (2.5 + 3.5 seconds explained),
    3.042, 3.044
Photography. *See* Chapter 6, Part 1
application, 6.001
bloodstains, at-scene, 5.026
introduction, 6.001
personal injury documentation, 6.032
policies, directions, limitations, 6.021
series of events and photography, 6.026
techniques, 6.016
testimony, 6.002
timelines, 6.030
traffic engineering and photography, 6.026
upon arrival at scene, 7.031
what a photograph should show, 6.027
Physics, defined, 9.002
Plan drawing, 6.051
Point of no escape, 1.018(m)
Polarized sunglasses, 9.091
Pool, definition, 7.044, Fig. 7–11
Post-mortem examination, 4.035
Points of contact, 8.154
Pre-trial
consultations, 1.129
responsibilities, 1.113
testimony, 1.129
Principal direction of force, 8.127, Figs. 8–39, 8–40
Prints, tire, 7.068, Fig. 7–39
Product, design flaws, 2.022
Professionals
business, trade and industrial, 1.093
Proximate cause, 2.002, 2.003

Psychiatrist, 1.087
Psychologist, 2.004
Puddle, definition, 7.044, Fig. 7–11
Pumping brakes, skid marks, 7.091, Fig. 7–57

Q

Qualifications, expert, 1.105

R

Rage, possible, driver, 2.022(7)
Reaction. *See also Series of Events*
complex, 1.018(e)(ii)
defined, 1.018(e)
distance, 1.018(h)
road sight design, 3.042
time, 1.018(f),(g)
Reconstruction
elements of, 2.022
responsibilities, 1.042, 1.044, 2.001
Reflectors and lamps, 8.007
Responsibilities of the investigator, 1.042
Restraints. *See* under Air bags and Safety restraints
Rills, defined, 7.004, Fig. 7–11
Rims and wheels, 8.026, 8.027
Evidence and Investigation Check List, 8.027
Road rage, 2.022(7)
Roadway. *See also Trafficway Evidence,* Chapter 7, Part 1
alignment, 7.042, Fig. 7–14
damage, 7.041, Fig. 7–13
matching, 7.049
roadside objects, 7.049
debris, 7.044, 7.090, Figs. 7–11, 7–16, 7–56
edge, drop-off, 7.040, Fig. 7–12
engineering investigation, 7.026–7.031
glare, 7.043; Fig. 7–15, p. 107
investigation of, 7.027
markings, 7.003, 7.023
investigation, 7.024
surfaces, skid distance, 9.084
Role of human reliability, cognition and effect in coping
    with hazards, 2.012, Fig. 2.02
Rounding off, 1.062, 1.065, 9.055, 9.095(b)
coefficient of friction, 9.055
distance, 9.055
drag factor, 9.055
Ruts and furrows, 7.073, Fig. 7–43

S

Safe (true) area, 1.018(l). *See also Series of Events*
Safety restraints, 4.022, 8.096. *See also* under
   air bags, 8.113
      air bag cover impact, 8.143, Fig. 8–46
      Caution to investigators, 8.118
      how air bags work, 8.114–8.118, Figs. 8–36 to 8–38
      investigation procedures, see also Chapter 4
      occupant, air bag cover impact, 8.143(e), Fig. 8–46
      on-off switch, 8.119
      tell-tale light, 8.120
      Evidence and Investigation Check List, following
         8.120
   child restraints, 8.111
      Evidence and Investigation Check List, following
         8.112
   seat belts, 4.022, 8.096, 8.097, 8.099
      cuts, 8.103
      functions, 8.100–8.102
         path, 8.100
         retractors, 8.101, 8.102
      injuries, 4.022–4.029, 4.052, 8.104
      parts, 8.098, Figs. 8–32, 8–33, 8–34, 8–35
      types, Figs. 8–30, 8–31
      use or non-use evidence, 4.022–4.029, 4, 8.104,
         8.105, 8.110, 8.154, 8.155
      Evidence and Investigation Check Lists, 8.110
Scene investigation and evidence
   baselines, 6.067
   conventions for recording measurements, 6.063
   coordinates, 6.071
   evidence, 6.054
      long-term, 6.054(2)
      short-lived, 6.054(1)
   field sketch, 6.056
   instruments, 6.059
   introduction, 6.051
   investigation, general, 7.024–7.031
   measurement
      markers, paint, 6.055
      methods, 6.071
         coordinate, defined, 6.071(1), 6.072
         triangulation, defined, 6.071(2), 6.073
      measurements and plan drawing. *See* Chapter 6,
         Part 2
      Examples, Figs. 6–11 to 6–17, pp. 89–93
      Table 6–02
   photographs and measurements, 6.055

recording conventions, 6.053
reference points, 6.068
   intangible, 6.068(2)
   tangible, 6.068(1)
   Examples, Figs. 6–11, 6–12, 6–13, pp. 80–91
scale diagrams, 6.058
spots, 6.069
symbols, Fig. 6–10, p. 88
template, 6.061, Figs. 6–06, 6–07, 6–08
triangulation, defined, 6.071(2), 6.073
Scrapes, scratches, 7.045; Figs. 7–11, 7–16, pp. 104, 108
Scrub mark, defined, 7.084
Scuff marks, 7.070
Seating positions, 4.024, 4.025, 5.001, 8.132, 8.153, 9.020;
   Fig. 8–53, p. 180
   driver identification from shoe prints, 8.155; Fig. 8–53,
      p. 180
   occupant contact points during collision, 8.154, 8.155;
      Figs. 8–50 to 8–53, pp. 179, 180
   predicable occupant movements during collision, Fig.
      8–50, p. 179
Series of Events, 1.016–1.028
   acceleration related to, 9.028
   action point, 1.018(I)
   actual perception, point of, 1.018(b). *See also* 3.042
      analyzing series of events, 1.026–1.029
   at-rest position, 1.018(w)
   at-scene, 1.016(b), 1.018
   definitions, 1.016
   disengagement, 1.018(s)
   distance, evasive action, 1.018(j)
   evasive action, 1.018(j)
      distance, 1.018(k)
   events and factors, 1.017
   fatal injury, 1.018(y)
   final position, 1.018(v)
   maximum engagement, 1.018()r)
   perception, a 4-step process, 3.042
   perception delay, 1.018(c)
   perception explained, *see* 3.042
      depth perception, 3.034
   perception-reaction time, *see* 3.044
   perception distance, 1.018(d)
   personal injury, 1.018(x)
   point of actual perception, 1.018(b). *See also* 3.042
   point of impact, 1.018(o),
   point of no escape, 1.018(m)
   point of possible perception, 1.018(a)
   post-secondary contact, 1.018(u)

pre-scene, 1.016(a), 1.017
pre-trip events, 1.017(1)
primary contact, 1.018(p)
reaction, 1.018(e)
    complex, 1.018(e)(ii)
    distance, 1.018(h)
    time, 1.018(f),(g)
safe (true) area, 1.018(l)
Series of Events Evidence and Investigation Check List, 1.030
Series of events and human factors, 1.016
    definitions, 1.016
    described, 1.019
Series of events, importance of photographs, 6.028
Shock absorbers, 8.021
Shot marker, 9.050, Fig. 9–15
Sideslipping, tire, 7.062
    devices, 7.001
    investigation, 7.023, 7.024
    obstruction, 7.024(b), Fig. 6–02
Signal examination, 8.010
Signal, phases and investigation, 7.021, 8.010
Signals, traffic, 7.008
    devices, 7.001
Significant digits, 1.062
Signs, markings, traffic, 7.004, 7.007, 7.015, 7.016, 7.017, 7.024
Siren, effect on cause, 8.077
    Evidence and Investigation Check List, 8.077
Sketch, field, 6.056
Skid distances, factors affecting, 9.084
    braking, 9.084
    hydroplaning, 9.085
    tires, 9.084
        air pressure, 9.084
        chains, 9.084
        studded, 9.084
        tread, 9.084
        type, 9.084
    vehicle weight, 9.084
    wind direction and velocity, 9.084
Skid mark
    definition, 7.084
Skid mark measurement methods, 9.095
    accuracy, 1.054, 8.053, 9.095(b)
    averaging, 9.095(c)
    Caution, 8.053
    commercial vehicle, 9.095(f)
    different type of surfaces, 9.098, Formula 9–3
    gap or intermittent, 9.095(g)

longest in straight skid, 9.095(d)
markers, 9.095(a)
minimum speed, 9.093
motorcycle, 9.095(j)
motorcycle slide-to-stop speeds,10.039, Formulae 10–6, 10–12
    offset, 9.095(I)
positive, 9.091
procedures, 9.095(c)
rounding off, 9.055
skid-to-stop defined, 9.094
skip, 9.095(h)
slide-to-stop, defined, 9.094
traversing various-type surfaces, 9.095(k)
varied lengths, 9.095(e)
various types of skid marks, 9.095(c)
    straight, curved, spin, 9.095(c)
Skid mark types, 7.085, 9.091, 9.095, Fig. 7–51. *See also* under Tire marks
    bounce, 7–093, Figs. 7–59A, 7–59B
    braked-wheel tire evidence, 7.089, Fig. 7.55
    commercial vehicle, 7.092, Fig. 7–58
    definition, 7.084
    detached utility trailer, 7.095, Fig. 7–61
    format, 9.095
    impending, 7.086, 9.091, Figs. 7–52, 9–16
    incipient, 7.086, 9.091, Figs. 7–52, 9–16
    influences on, 9.084
    intermittent, 7.091, Fig. 7–57
    measurements of, 9.095
    offset, 7.088, Fig. 7–54
    overlapping, 7.087, Fig. 7–53
    positive, 9.091
    scrub, 7.094, Figs. 7–60A, 7–60B
    shadow, mistaken, 7.061, Fig. 7–31
    skip, 7.092, Fig. 7–58
        measurements, 9.095(h)
    tire debris deposit, 7.090, Fig's 7–56A, 7–56B, 7–56C
    towed vehicle skid marks, 7.096, Fig. 7–62
    trailer, detached, 7.095, Fig. 7–61
    various types, 9.095
    weight shift, 7.085, Fig. 7–51
Skid tests, 9.049, Figs. 9–15, 9–16, 9–17
    average skid distance, use of, 9.054(2)
    longest skid mark, use of, 9.054(1), 9.056
    procedures, 9.052, 9.056
    rounding off skid distances and drag factors, 9.055
    speedometer accuracy, 9.052
Skid-to-stop defined, 9.094

Skip, 9.095(h)

Slide-to-stop, defined, 9.094

Slip, defined, 2.017(1)

Slug, explained, 9.012

SEM examinations, 1.071

SM examinations, 1.071

Sources, information, 1.116

Spatter, defined, 7.044, Fig. 7–11

Speed analysis. *See also* Chapter 9, Part 2, and Chapter 10, Motorcycle

    acceleration, 9.026

        defined, 9.027

        rate, 9.035

    calculation, a minimum speed, 9.093, 9.096. *See also* Fig. 9–12C

        tolerances, 1.054

    combined speeds, 9.133

        explained, 9.133

        Formula 9–39 (*see* under 9.134)

    crush analysis, discussed, 9.135

    deceleration, 9.027

        defined, 9.027

        rate, 9.035

    definitions, 9.001

    different types of roadway, 9.098

    Drag Factor and Coefficient of Friction Guide, 9.090, Table 9–02

    falls, flips, and vaults, 9.126

    fall, 9.127, Fig. 9–33

        defined, 9.127

        level takeoff area, Formula 9–35 (*see* under 9.129)

        non-level takeoff area, Formula 9–36 (*see* under 9.130)

    flip and vault, 9.131

        defined, 9.131, Fig. 9–34

        level takeoff and landing, Formula 9–37

        non-level takeoff and landing, Formula 9–38

        speed based on vault of operator or motorcycle, 10.045, Formula 10–14

    from skid marks, 9.091, Example 9.096, Formula 9-31

        assumption when there are no skid marks, 8.053

    various surfaces, measurements, 9.095(k)

    motorcycle, Chapter 10

        slide-to-stop speeds, 10.031, 10.039, Formulae 10–6, 10–12

            clothing slide drag factors, 10.040

            motorcycle slide drag factors, 10.040

        speed based on engine revolutions, 10.041, 10.044, Formula 10–13

        speed based on vault of operator or motorcycle, 10.045, Formula 10–14

        speed from gear shift position, 10.043

        speed, initial, calculation, Formula 10–11

        speed when substantial object is struck, 9.097

    skid marks, 8.053, 9.083, Example 1, 9.091, 9.096, Formulae 9–31, 9–28

        calculations, 9.096, Formula 9–31

        Caution, 1.054, 8.053

        factors required, 9.094

        polarized sunglasses, 9.091

        slide-to-stop speeds, 9.096, MC 10.039

        terms and definitions, 9.001

        tolerances, 1.059 (±%)

        velocity defined, 9.001

    yaw, 9.106–9.123

        speed, 9.117

        Caution, 9.121

Slide-to-stop speed calculations, 9.096; MC 10.039, Formula 10–12, p. 241

    clothing, metal, MC 10.040

Spatter, defined, 7.044

Speed and velocity

    defined, 9.001

    formulae, 9.034

Speed of light, Appendix A, Table A–18

Speed of sound in air, Appendix A, Table A–17

Speedometer, recording devices and methods, 1.057, 1.058, Table 1–03, 8.080

    accuracy check, 9.052, Formula 9–26

    Calibration Check List, see Appendix D

    black boxes, 8.081, 8.082

    calibration, importance of, 1.057. *See also* Appendix D

    errors, 1.057, Table 1–03

    gear-shift position, 8.088, 10.034

    on-board computers, 8.083

    readability, 1.058

    speedometer, 8.080, Fig. 8–27

    tolerances, 1.059

    Evidence and Investigation Check Lists, 8.080, 8.082

    stuck needle, 8.080, Fig. 8–27

    Tachographs, 8.084–8.087

        charts, 8.086, 8.087, Fig. 8–28

        investigation, 8.084

        Evidence and Investigation Check List, 8.085

Special speed problems, 9.135

Speed and velocity defined, 9.001

Speeds combined, 9.133

Speedometer accuracy check list, Appendix D

Spin skid mark measurements, 9.095(c)(iii)

Spinning tire, 7.063

Spots, 6.069

Static friction, 9.025

Steering systems, 8.022, Fig. 8–09
    examination methods, 8.023
    Evidence and Investigation Check List, 8.023, 8.024
    free-play, 8.022
    power-assisted, 8.024
    Evidence and Investigation Check List, 8.024
    Evidence and Investigation Check List (steering problems), Table 8–03 following 8.024

Stippling, 9.092

Straight skid marks, 9.095(c)(i)

Striations, 7.065, 7.066, Figs. 7–35, 7–36, 7–37

Stuck speedometer needle, 8.080, Fig. 8–27

Studded tires
    effect on skid distance, 9.084
    marks, 7.067, Fig. 7–37

Substantial object, speed analysis, 9.097

Suicide, fraud, 1.118
    notes, 4.047

Suspension systems, 8.016
    air type, 8.020
    independent front, Fig. 8–07
    instability, causes, 8.018
    modifications, to, 8.019
    parts, 8.017
    solid axle, rear, Fig. 8–08
    shock absorbers, 8.021
    shock and strut combination, Fig. 8–09
    types, 8.017
    wheel alignment, 8.025
    Evidence and Investigation Check Lists, 8.019, 8.025, 8.027

Symbols, 6.062, 9.035; Fig. 6–10. p. 88; Appendix E

System (crash) failure, 2.001

T

Tachograph, 8.084, 10.004
    charts, 8.086, Fig. 8–28
    motorcycle, 10.004
    Evidence and Investigation Check Lists, 8.085, 8.087

Tests
    contrast sensitivity, 3.041
    skid. *See* under Skid tests
    visual acuity, 3.038
    visual performance, 3.038

Testimony, 1.129

Time, acceleration and velocity relationships, explained, 9.029

Time and distance relationships, 9.032

Tire marks
    acceleration, 7.071, Fig. 7–41
    blow-out, 8.041, Fig. 7–29
    braked wheel, 7.089, Fig. 7–55
    breakaway trailer, 7.095, Fig. 7–61; 8.089, Fig. 8–29
    bounce, 7.093, Fig. 7–59
    Caution: overhead wire shadow, 7.061, Fig. 7–31
    commercial vehicle, 7.092, Fig. 7–58
    cupping, 7.057, Fig. 7–27(B), 7.060, Fig. 7–30
    flat-tire, 7.059, Fig. 7–29
    forward-reverse, 7.072, Fig. 7–42
    furrows and ruts, 7.073, Fig. 7–43
    grinding, 7.064, Fig. 7–34
    impending, 7.086, 9.091
    intermittent, 7.091, Fig. 7–57
    overlapping skid, 7.087, Fig. 7–53
    overloaded, 7.060, Fig. 7–30
    pass-over, 7.068, Fig. 7–38
    positive skid, 9.091
    prints, 7.069, Fig. 7–39
    pumping brake, 7.091, Fig. 7–57
    ruts and furrows, 7.073, Fig. 7–43
    scrub, 7.094, Fig. 7–60
    scuff, 7.070, Fig. 7–40
    sideslipping, 7.062, Fig. 7–32
    spinning, 7.063, Fig. 7–33
    striations, 7.064, Fig. 7–34; 7.065, Fig. 7–35; 7.066; 7.067, Fig. 7–37
    studded, 7.067, Fig. 7–37
    towed vehicle, 7.096, Fig. 7–62
    underinflated, 7.060, Fig. 7–30
    weight shift, 7.085, Fig. 7–51
    yaw, 7.066, Fig. 7–36

Tires
    air pressure, effect on skid distance, 9.084
    chains, effect on skid distance, 9.084
    damage to, prior or during collision, 8.040, 8.041
        examination, 8.042
    debris, pre-crash, 8.039, Fig. 8–17. *See also* 8.040
    descriptions, 8.029
    DOT/MOT numbers and designations, 8.031
    evidence mark prior to removal, Fig. 8–18
    failure analysis, 8.044
    Evidence and Investigation Check List, 8.044

inflation and failures, 8.036, Figs. 8–14, 8–15

load index, 8.034

loading ratings, 8.033

    indices chart, Chart 8–05, following 8.044

marking standard, 8.035

markings, 8.029, 8.030, 8.051, Fig. 8–13

    Evidence and Investigation Check List, 8.030

matching roadway marks, 7.058

    polarized glasses, 9.091

numbers and designations, 8.031

recaps, 8.039

removal from rim, 8.042

    Caution: 8.043

service description, 8.034

shapes and contours, 7.056, Figs. 7–27, 7–28

speed ratings, 8.032

    chart, Table 8–04, following 8.032

tread, 8.036, Figs. 8–14, 8–15, 8–16

    bars, Fig. 8–16

    grooves, 8.038, Fig. 8–16

types, 8.028, 8.030, Fig. 8–12

    Warning: De-mounting dangers, 8.043

Tolerances and errors, 1.051–1.061

Torque, Appendix A, Table A–15

Towed vehicle, skid marks, 7.096, Fig. 7–62

Tracking, normal, 9.107, Fig. 9–28

Trade, forensic specialists, 1.093

Traffic crash

    analysis, 1.009

    defined, 1.004, 1.009

    investigation

        levels of, 1.036

        objectives, 1.006

Traffic unit, defined, 1.020

Trafficway engineering, principles of, 6.026. *See also* Chapter 7, Part 1

Trafficway evidence. *See* Chapter 7, Part 1. *See also* under Highway.

    analysis, 7.027, 7.037; 7.025–7.032

    basic engineering and design, 7.001. *See* Chapter 7, Part 1

    damages, *see* Chapter 7

    detectors, 7.010, Figs. 7–04A, B, C

    Identification, Interpretation, Defects and Damage. *See* Chapter 7, Part 2

    marks, *see* Chapter 7

    pedestrian signal, Fig. 7–03B

    signal unit, 7.009, Fig. 7–03A

        traffic-control devices, 7.003

signs, 7.002, Figs. 7–01, 7–02

    descriptions, 7.005

    environmental factors, 7.007(a)

    placement, 7.006

skid marks, *see* Chapter 7

tire marks, *see* Chapter 7

traffic-control unit, Fig. 7–03(A)

    pedestrian traffic signal, Fig. 7–03(B)

Traffic-control devices, 6.027, 7.001, 7.003. *See also* Chapter 7, Part 1

    traffic-control unit, Fig. 7–03

Traffic-control signals, 7.008

    contact local engineer, importance of, 7.009, Fig. 7–04C

    controller, 7.013

    cycles, 7.009

    detectors, 7.010, Figs. 7–04A, 7–04B, 7.014, 7.015

    pedestrian traffic signal, Fig. 7–03(B)

    phases, 7.009

    signal unit, 7.009

        descriptions, 7.009

    timing, 7.021

    zones, 7.012

Traffic engineering issues, 7.023

Traffic signs, 7.004

    defined, 7.004

    descriptions, 7.005

    environmental factors, 7.007(a)

    placement, 7.006

Traffic unit, defined, 1.020

Trail, defined, 7.044, Fig. 7–11; MC 10.009

Trailer breakaway, 7.095, 8.089

    skid marks, 7.095, Fig. 7–61

    Evidence and Investigation Check List, 8.090

Trailer connections, 8.089–8.090, Fig. 8–29

Trailers, utility, brakeless

    drag factor, 9.099

    speed, 9.099

Training

    education, 1.040

    levels, 1.036

Trial

    pre-trial responsibilities, 1.113

Triangulation

    defined, 6.071

    method, 6.073

True (safe) area, 1.018(l). *See also Series of Events*

U

Unit, traffic, defined, 1.020
Utility trailer
  breakaway, 8.089
  detached, 7.095, Fig 7–61
  drag factor, 9.099
  skid marks, 7.095, Fig. 7–61
  speed, 9.099
  tire marks, 7.095, Fig. 7–61
  Evidence and Investigation Check List, 8.090

V

Vault, fall and flip speeds, 9.126, 10.047
Vectors, 9.022, 9.023: Fig. 9–02, p. 189
Vehicle acceleration rates, 9.035
Vehicle damage, 8.126. *See also* under Damage
  factors, 1.017
  imprints, 8.130, Fig. 8–41
  induced, 8.129
  measurements, 8.131
  principle direction of force, 8.127, Figs. 8–39, 8–40
  superimposed, 8.128
  types and causes, 8.126
  Evidence and Investigation Check List, 8.132
Vehicle inspections. *See* Chapter 8
  components, Figs. 8–02, 8–03, pp. 133–136; Table 8–01, p. 132
    Evidence and Investigation Check List (components), Table 8–01, p. 132; Table 8–02, p. 137
  component failures, evidence of, 8.006, Figs. 8–05, 8–06
    bolts, Fig. 8–05
    common indicators, Table 8–02
    drive shaft, pipes, lines, Fig. 8–06
  drive train, 8.004
  importance of, 8.001
  items, 8.003, Table 8–01
    Evidence and Investigation Check List, Table 8–01, p. 132
  lamps and reflectors, 9.007
  paint chips and transfers, 8.133–8.135
  weld deficiency, failure, 8.002
Vehicle weight, effect on skid distance, 9.084
Velocity, acceleration and time relationships explained, 9.029
Velocity and speed
  defined, 9.001
  formulae, 9.034
  relationships, Appendix A, Table A–4

V.I.N. (Vehicle Identification Number), 8.003; Format, Figure 8–01
Drive trains, 8.004
  FWD, Fig. 8–04, 8.004(2)
  RWD, 8.004(1). See Figs. 8–02, 8–08
  4WD, 8.005
Violation, defined, 2.017(3)
Visible, defined, 3.003
Visibility. *See* Chapter 3. *Evidence and Investigation Check List*, 3.059
  acuity, 3.032, 3.038
  brain and vision, 3.019
  color blindness, 3.049
  components of, 3.031
  contrast sensitivity, 3.035
  day and night, 3.024
  depth perception, 3.034
  discernability, 3.003
  factors affecting, 3.047
    color blindness, 3.049
    environmental, 3.056
    external, 3.054
    psychological, 3.0048
  field of vision, 3.033
  glare, effects of, 7.043
  photopic, the day eye, 3.027
  scotopic, the night eye, 3.028
  Summary, 3.059
Vision, defined, 3.003; *see also* 3.048, 3.050. *See* Chapter 3
  20/20 explained, 3.038
  blind spot, defined, 3.015
  field of, 3.033
  parts and functions of the eye, 3.009
  Summary, 3.059
Visual
  20/20 explained, 3.038
  acuity, 3.038
  static, 3.038

W

Walking rates, pedestrian, 9.035
Weather conditions, 1.016. *See also* under Environmental factors, 1.017, 1.018
Weight, 9.011, Formula 9–03. Appendix A, Tables A–9 and A–11. *See also example* under 9.012
  defined, 9.011
  effect on skid distance, 9.084
  shift, 7.085, Fig. 7–51, MC 10.029

shift mark in yaw, 9.111, Figs. 7–36(D), 9–29

Wheel alignment, 8.025, Fig. 8–11

Evidence and Investigation Check List, 8.025

Wheels and rims, 8.026

Evidence and Investigation Check List, 8.027

failure evidence, 8.027

causes, 8.027

Wind direction and velocity, effect on skid distance, 9.084

Windshield and windows, 3.054, 8.068, 8.069, 8.147

glass damage and condition, 8.141

causes, 8.143

contact, 8.144, Figs. 8–42 to 8–44, pp. 171, 172

direct/indirect causes, 8.143

fragments, 8.142

impact and damage sequence, 8.146

induced, 8.145, Fig. 8-45, p. 173

laminated, 8.141

outward bulge, 8.143, 8.144

seat belt, non-use, Fig. 8–42, p. 171

sequence of damages, 8.146

tempered, 8.141

types, 8.141

obstructions to visibility, 3.054, 8.068, 8.069, 8.147

occupant, air bag cover impact, 8.143, Fig. 8–46

positions (open/shut), 8.068, 8.069, 8.147

Evidence and Investigation Check List, 8.069

Windshield

defrosters, 8.068

wipers, 8.068

Evidence and Investigation Check List, 8.069

Witness

expert, 1.110

fact, 1.112

lay, 1.111

Work, defined, 9.015, 9.017

Y

Yaw , 9.106

beginning of yaw mark, 9.114; Figs. 7–36, 9–29, pp. 117, 220. *See also* 9.122

Caution: 9.122, *see also* Fig. 9–29, p. 220

center-of-mass path, 9.116; Fig. 9–30, p. 221

centrifugal and centripetal forces, 9.109, 9.112; 9.008, 9.009

critical speed, 9.108

defined, 7.066, 9.106

definite, 9.107, 9.114, Fig. 7–36. *See also* 9.111 and 9.122

drag sled, use of, 9.071(6); Fig. 9–22, p. 206

marks, described, 7.066, Fig. 7–36A, B, C, p. 117

MC curve mark, braking, 10.030

phases of yaw, Fig. 9–29, p. 220

plotting radius and center-of-mass path, 9.116; Figs. 9–31, 9–32, pp. 221, 222

radius calculation, 9.115

speed calculations, 9.106

speed from yaw, 9.106, 9.117

critical curve speed, 9.117(2), 9.118

defined, 9.117(2), 9.118

critical vehicle curve speed, 9.117(1), 9.118

defined, 9.117(1)

radius, Formula 9–33, *example* 9.118

speed, Formula 9–34, *example* 9.118

confirming validity of speed calculation, 9.120

Evidence and Investigation Guide, 9.121, 9.122

tire tracking dynamics, Fig. 9–28, p. 219

use of three radius measurements, 9.114

vehicle dynamics in yaw, Fig. 9–29

weight shift mark, 9.111–9.114, 9.122